TRAFFIC
IN ASIAN
WOMEN

NEXT WAVE: New Directions in Women's Studies
Caren Kaplan, Inderpal Grewal, Robyn Wiegman, Series Editors

LAURA HYUN YI KANG

TRAFFIC IN ASIAN WOMEN

Duke University Press *Durham and London* 2020

© 2020 Duke University Press. All rights reserved
Printed in the United States of America on acid-free paper ∞
Designed by Courtney Leigh Baker
Typeset in Portrait, Sang Bleu, and Futura by Westchester Publishing Services

Library of Congress Cataloging-in-Publication Data
Names: Kang, Hyun Yi, [date] author.
Title: Traffic in Asian women / Laura Hyun Yi Kang.
Other titles: Next wave (Duke University Press)
Description: Durham : Duke University Press, 2020. | Series: Next wave | Includes bibliographical references and index.
Identifiers: LCCN 2019054644 (print) | LCCN 2019054645 (ebook)
ISBN 9781478008804 (hardcover)
ISBN 9781478009665 (paperback)
ISBN 9781478012283 (ebook)
Subjects: LCSH: Women—Asia—Social conditions—20th century. | Women—Violence against—Asia. | Women's rights—Asia—History—20th century. | Comfort women. | Women and war—Asia—20th century.
Classification: LCC HQ1726 .K36 2020 (print) | LCC HQ1726 (ebook) | DDC 305.42095/0904—dc23
LC record available at https://lccn.loc.gov/2019054644
LC ebook record available at https://lccn.loc.gov/2019054645

Duke University Press gratefully acknowledges the support of the University of California, Irvine, UCI Humanities Commons, which provided funds toward the publication of this book.

Cover art: Map of "The Itinerary of the Commission *of* Enquiry" (detail), *Enquiry into Traffic in Women and Children in the East*, 1932.

for my mother & for Junsu and Minsu

CONTENTS

Acknowledgments — ix

Introduction. Traffic in Asian Women — 1

1 Asian Women as Method? — 19
2 Traffic in Women — 51
3 Sexual Slavery — 83
4 Violence against Women — 117
5 Truth Disclosure — 153
6 Just Compensation — 189
7 Enduring Memorials — 221

Notes — 261
Bibliography — 311
Index — 331

ACKNOWLEDGMENTS

This book began many years ago when Lisa Yoneyama invited me to consider the issue of "comfort women" for a session that she organized for the annual meeting of the American Studies Association. I had been very ambivalent and even a little skeptical about the passionate investment in the issue and the consequent will to represent this history on the part of Korean/American artists, writers, and scholars, myself included. That session pushed me to unpack and articulate the contours of my unease and, more consequentially, brought me together with Lisa and Kandice Chuh for what has turned out to be a most generative, sustaining friendship and intellectual exchange in the many years since. This book would not exist without their steadfast support and much-needed interventions. Their scholarly brilliance and critical grace continue to inspire me to try harder. From my first book to this book, Lisa Lowe has provided me with a singular model of broad intellectual engagement and deep thinking.

I would like to thank the friends who have sustained me by sharing the joys of good food, wine, music, and laughter in SoCal: Brian Albert, Eve Oishi, Sheri Ozeki, Cindy Cheng, Rachel Park, Jenny Terry, Surina Khan, Catherine Sameh, Lucy Burns, Anjali Arondekar, Christine Balance, Patty Ahn, Arlene Keizer, Alex Juhasz, Rachel Lee, Gabe Spera, David Wong Louie, Jackie Louie, Juliet Williams, Ali Behdad, Kathleen McHugh, Yong Soon Min, David Lloyd, Sarita See, and Karen Tongson. Brian, Eve, Cindy, and Lucy took very good care of me when I needed it most. Across a wider geography, these friends and colleagues have steadfastly provided the gift of intellectual community: Kandice Chuh, Karen Shimakawa, Gayatri Gopinath, Rod Ferguson, Siobhan Somerville, Alex Vazquez, Leslie Bow, Elena Creef, Minoo Moallem, Caren Kaplan, Cynthia Young, Gabrielle Foreman, Fred Moten, and Myung Mi Kim.

At the University of California, Irvine, I have been very fortunate to work with some wonderful colleagues in the Department of Gender & Sexuality Studies: Jenny Terry, Heidi Tinsman, Catherine Sameh, Jeanne Scheper, Michele Goodwin, Emily Thuma, Inderpal Grewal, Elora Shehabuddin, Bob Moeller, Vicki Ruiz, Mary Underwood, Bindya Baliga, Kasey Ning, Rina Carvalho, Jasmine Robledo, Robert Escalante and Jennifer Choy. The publication of this book was supported by a subvention from the UCI Humanities Commons.

I would like to thank the following people and institutions for inviting me to share early iterations of the ideas and arguments presented in this book: Rosemary George and the Program in Critical Gender Studies and Yen Le Espiritu and the Department of Ethnic Studies at UC San Diego; Clare Yu and the Center for Korean Studies at UC Berkeley; Kandice Chuh and the Department of English and Seung-kyung Kim and the Department of Women's Studies at the University of Maryland, College Park; Eileen Boris and the Center for Research on Women and Social Justice at UC Santa Barbara; Kim Eun-Shil and Chang Pilwha and the Korean Women's Institute at Ewha University; Elora Shehabuddin and Rosemary Hennessy at the Center for the Study of Women, Gender, and Sexuality at Rice University; Anjali Arondekar, the Department of Feminist Studies, and the Institute for Advanced Feminist Research at UC Santa Cruz; Min-Jung Kim and the Institute of the Humanities at Ewha University; Stella Oh and the Bellarmine Forum at Loyola Marymount University; Inderpal Grewal and the Department of Women, Gender and Sexuality Studies at Yale University; Gayatri Gopinath, Karen Shimakawa, and the Asian/Pacific/American Studies Program in the Department of Social & Cultural Analysis at New York University; Eve Oishi and the Cultural Studies Department at the Claremont Graduate University; Kara Keeling, Viet Nguyen, and the graduate students in the American Studies & Ethnicity Department at the University of Southern California; Laura Nelson, Stephanie Kim, and the Institute for East Asian Studies at UC Berkeley; Gracen Brilmyer, Maria Montenegro, and the graduate students in the Department of Information Studies at UCLA; and Minoo Moallem and the Department of Women & Gender Studies at UC Berkeley.

At Duke University Press, I am very grateful to Ken Wissoker for his abiding commitment to this book project and support through its extended revision. As the project editor, Susan Albury expertly and promptly moved the manuscript through the production process. Donald Pharr's corrections and suggestions as copy editor effectively smoothed over my writing quirks. I would like to thank Inderpal Grewal, Caren Kaplan, and Robyn Wiegman for inviting this book into the *Next Wave: New Directions in Women's Studies* series.

Parts of chapter 6 were published earlier in "The Uses of Asianization: Figuring Crises, 1997-1998 and 2007-?," *American Quarterly* 64, no. 3 (September 2012): 411-36. This special issue on "Race, Empire and the Crisis of the Subprime" was edited by Paula Chakravartty and Denise Ferreira da Silva. Portions of chapter 2 were published in "Surveillance and the World of Antitrafficking: From Compulsory Examination to International Coordination," in *Feminist Surveillance Studies*, edited by Rachel E. Dubrofsky and Shoshana Magnet (Durham, NC: Duke University Press, 2015): 39-57. Much thanks to Denise, Paula, Rachel, and Shoshana for the collegiality and editorial commitment.

I thank the many wonderful undergraduate and graduate students whom I have had the pleasure to teach and think with at UC Irvine for the past twenty years. As an immigrant, first-generation college graduate myself, I appreciate and admire how many of our students work so earnestly and diligently to learn and grow as critical thinkers and ethical subjects. Every day, they remind me of the need for and the promise of a truly accessible and equitable public university. The longer I teach, the more I appreciate the teachers from whom I learned so much. So thank you always to Donna Haraway, Angela Davis, Jim Clifford, Judy Yung, Stephen Heath, Hayden White, and Barbara Epstein at UC Santa Cruz and to Elaine Kim, Barbara Christian, Paula Gunn Allen, Carla Trujillo, Laura Nader, David Lloyd, Michael Omi, Ling-chi Wang, Loni Ding, Carlos Muñoz, Ron Takaki, and Barry Stroud at UC Berkeley.

This book is dedicated to Junsu and Minsu. They arrived in my life shortly after the completion of my first book and have filled it up in ways that provided a sweet release from feeling compelled to write because life was full enough and I was now bound only to living it fully with them. Whenever I was nearing the point of accepting that I had just one book in me and that was enough, they would pose an impossible question or make a freshly urgent observation, which moved me to tussle with my own bewilderments and to play with new curiosities. I have tried to trace out some of them in the pages that follow.

Thank you each and all.

INTRODUCTION

TRAFFIC IN ASIAN WOMEN

This book offers several ways of making critical sense of the transnational circulation of "Asian women" as distinguished figures of female injury and women's empowerment in the 1990s. One of the most well-known and sustained campaigns was organized around documenting and adjudicating the Japanese military "comfort system," which forcibly conscripted two hundred thousand women for systematic rape by soldiers and officers of the Imperial Army across a broad swath of East and Southeast Asia before and during World War II. The issue first captured international news headlines on December 6, 1991, when Kim Hak-sun and two other Korean women survivors joined a thirty-five-person lawsuit filed in Tokyo against the Japanese government for violations perpetrated during the colonial occupation of Korea (1910–45). In addition to requesting 20 million yen in compensation for each plaintiff, the lawsuit demanded a thorough investigation and proper memorialization of this history of Japanese colonial violence and exploitation.

Although it was widely heralded as a shocking revelation of Japanese wartime atrocities, the memories of these military "comfort stations" had never been forgotten or fully suppressed. How the issue was able to garner so much international publicity in the early 1990s must be understood within the context of several overlapping economic, political, and discursive shifts that crisscross national and regional demarcations. After nearly three decades of U.S.-backed military dictatorship in South Korea, massive popular protests in the 1980s led to the restoration of civil rights and direct presidential elections in 1987. The country's rapid economic growth was showcased in its hosting of the 1988 Summer Olympics in Seoul. With its earlier economic ascendance and expanding reserves, Japan became an influential source of bilateral aid and direct investment in South Korea, Taiwan, and throughout East and Southeast Asia. Although the U.S. played a key role in supporting the economic growth of Japan and South Korea as part of its Cold War strategy of containment, the end of the Cold War in 1989 combined with greater intra-Asian diplomatic rapprochement and regional economic integration to engender new spatiotemporal imaginaries such as "the rise of Asia" and "the Asian century." Japan also began to play an increasingly prominent role in global governance through increased financial contributions to the United Nations and the World Bank and also through a sustained campaign to gain a permanent seat on the UN Security Council. The death of Japanese Emperor Hirohito in 1989 rekindled bitter memories of Japan's brutal colonial rule in South Korea and its expansionist drive throughout Asia and the Pacific. That same year, Japan sent observers to UN peacekeeping forces, provoking renewed concerns and protests over its remilitarization and refocusing attention on the past atrocities of the Japanese Imperial Army. In 1992, the passage of the International Cooperation Law authorized Japan to send military personnel to UN peacekeeping operations.

The multisited recall, revelation, and problematization of the history of Japanese military "comfort system" unfurled within these shifting configurations of sovereignty, cooperation, and ambition. In February 1988, three members of Korean Church Women United (KCWU), Yun Chung-ok, Kim Hye-won, and Kim Sin-sil, conducted a research trip to investigate former "comfort stations" in Okinawa and Fukuoka. In April 1988, Yun gave a presentation about their findings on the Japanese military "comfort system" at an international conference on "Women and Tourism" on Korea's Cheju Island, a popular destination for "sex tours" by Japanese men taking easy advantage of the strength of the Japanese yen against the Korean won. These tours had become the target of public protests by Korean women's groups in the early 1970s, which later expanded into an allied regional network that connected activists in South Korea, Japan, Taiwan, Thailand, and the Philippines working on the conjoined problems of sex tourism and U.S. military prostitution in Asia. Following the "Women and Tourism" conference, the KCWU organized the *Chongshindae* Research Association in July 1988. *Chongshindae*, commonly translated as "voluntary labor corps," was the Korean term used to designate the Japanese colonial state's conscription of Korean girls and women to work often far from home and homeland in support of its imperialist expansion, which included the military "comfort stations."

On January 7, 1989, a broad coalition of women's groups, including the KCWU, the YWCA of Korea, and the Federation of Korean Women's Associations, composed an open letter protesting the South Korean government's plan to send a representative to the funeral of the Japanese Emperor Hirohito. They pointed to the coercive and violent expropriation of Korean women as laborers and "comfort women" for Japanese soldiers and demanded an apology. In May 1990 the occasion of a state visit to Japan by President Roh Tae-woo set off impassioned protests in South Korea and new debates in Japan but also internationally over whether Japan should apologize for its forced annexation and colonial exploitation of Koreans.[1] South Korean women's groups seized this opening to issue a joint statement about the *Chongshindae*. Following Roh's visit, Motooka Shoji, a Social Democrat member of the Japanese Diet, requested clarification from Shimizu Tadao, then Director-General of the Employment Security Office, about whether military "comfort women" (*jugun ianfu*) were included in the forced labor mobilizations of Koreans during the colonial period. Shimizu's facile denial of official involvement and forced recruitment roused more anger. On October 17, 1990, a coalition of thirty-seven South Korean women's groups drafted an open letter of protest to the Japanese Diet and later formed the Korean Council for Women Drafted for Sexual Slavery by Japan (hereafter referred to as the Korean Council) on November 16, 1990. Through mass media appeals, the Korean Council set about to locate survivors. On August 14, 1991, the Korean Council held a press conference in which Kim Hak-sun became the first survivor to testify publicly about her experiences in the Japanese military "comfort stations," which moved other survivors to come forward. In November 1991 two allied *zainichi* (Korean residents in Japan) organizations were formed, the Uli Yosong Network on Comfort Women (Yosong Net) in Tokyo and the Group Considering the Korean Military Comfort Women Issue in Osaka.[2] In February 1992 the Korean Council first raised the issue at the United Nations.

This recharged attention to Japanese military "comfort stations" coincided with an unprecedented proliferation of new communication technologies, media platforms, and institutional forums through which atrocities and grievances could be publicized and debated. The United Nations became more hospitable to nongovernmental organizations (NGOs) working on a broader range of issues and representing new, previously ignored, or marginalized constituencies. As Jutta Joachim matter-of-factly characterized this interregnum, the "thaw" of the Cold War "freed up agenda space." There was a closely staggered convergence of multiple discursive and organizational shifts: "In the absence of the East-West conflict, issues that UN policymakers had once considered important began to appear meaningless. Looking for new issues to fill the vacuum, UN policymakers decided to hold a series of specialized conferences in the early 1990s, starting with the UN Conference on Environment and Development in Rio de Janeiro in 1992, followed by the World Human Rights Conference in Vienna in 1993 and the International Conference on Population and Development in Cairo in 1994."[3] An incitement to documentation and a consequent will to declaration, which motor the work of global governance, accrued new urgency and created new openings. There was a groundswell of new social movements and knowledge formations that assiduously catalogued multiple violations of human rights, including several concerted efforts to publicize, codify, and redress specific abuses of women. The organized mass rapes of women in the former Yugoslavia in the spring and summer of 1992 spurred the UN Security Council to establish a Commission of Experts to call for an investigation. In December 1992 the Security Council declared that "massive, organized and systematic detention and rape of women, in particular Muslim women, in Bosnia and Herzegovina" constituted an international crime. The Statute of the International Criminal Tribunal for the former Yugoslavia (ICTY), first adopted in May 1993, would consequently include rape as one of the "crimes against humanity" in Article 4 alongside enslavement, deportation, imprisonment, and torture. Even as it was upheld for its singular and unfathomable brutality, the Japanese military "comfort system" strikingly instantiated multiple modes of gendered violence, degradation, and exploitation. As Indai Lourdes Sajor, a prominent activist, enumerated this expansive relevance, "Based on the testimonies given by the Asian comfort women, it is evident that more than one crime has been committed against every woman. Evidence points to crimes of rape, murder, abduction, forced labour, kidnapping, sexual slavery, torture, racial discrimination, forced sterilization, massacre and genocide."[4]

Although it was widely held up as exemplifying these varied offenses, the belated—and still very contested—recognition of the Japanese military "comfort system" incriminates a longer, more jagged history of international maneuvers to categorize, document, and regulate female vulnerability and their often dubious, ex-centric delineation of Asian women. The Japanese military "comfort system" presented a compelling instance of the traffic in women, which had long been a persistent fixation and flash point for domestic and international regimes of surveillance and control over female migration, labor, and sexuality. The title of this book, *Traffic in Asian Women*, partially echoes this notorious career of the traffic in women but also notates the distinguished place of Asian women in anti-trafficking discourses and policies, which reach back into the nineteenth-century crusades against "white slavery" and Asian female migration. Later, in the interwar period, the League of Nations undertook a "worldwide" study that was published in two parts: *Report of the Special Body of Experts on Traffic in Women and Children* (1927) and *Enquiry into Traffic in Women and Children in the East* (1932). The 1932 enquiry report drew a clear line between what were separately designated as "Traffic in Occidental Women in Asia" and "Traffic in Asian Women." In the aftermath of World War II, the newly established United Nations resumed the League of Nations' anti-trafficking work and inherited these demarcations. The UN General Assembly passed a "Convention for the Suppression of the Traffic in Persons and of the Exploitation of the Prostitution of Others" in 1949 and sponsored the publication of a "Study on Traffic in Persons and Prostitution" in 1959. This 1959 report reinforced a demarcation between "Asia and the Far East" and "North America and certain European countries."[5]

The "traffic in women" reemerged as a problem for concerted international investigation and action with the designation of the UN Decade for Women (1975–85). Its many associated international conferences and preparatory activities fueled a new drive to document both old and new forms of gendered abuse. The First World Conference of the International Women's Year, convened in Mexico City in 1975, yielded Resolution 7, on the "Prevention of the exploitation of women and girls," which began by characterizing prostitution as "one of the most grievous offences against the dignity of women" and then noted concern with "the injustice and suffering imposed especially on women who are forced into prostitution." This resolution concluded by urging governments "to take energetic action to put an end to forced prostitution and the traffic in women, both of which are forms of exploitation" and invoked the recently passed UN General Assembly Resolution 3218 (XXIX), on "Torture and other cruel, inhuman or degrading treatment or punishment in relation to detention and imprisonment," to request the Secretary-General to explore "the possibility of undertaking a worldwide survey of houses of prostitution where torture is practiced." The traffic in women was thus narrowed and subordinated to forced prostitution, which was, in turn, amplified as a form of torture in its resurgence as a feminist issue in the 1970s.

In 1979 Kathleen Barry published her influential book *Female Sexual Slavery*, where she offered this bracing definition: "Female sexual slavery is present in all situations in which women or girls cannot change the immediate conditions of their existence; where regardless of how they got into those conditions they cannot get out; and where they are subject to sexual violence and exploitation." Arguing that "virtually the only distinction that can be made between traffic in women and prostitution is that the former involves crossing international borders," Barry concluded that "the practices used to force women into prostitution are the same whether they are trafficked across international boundaries or from one part of a city to another." In addition to more accurately describing their coercive conditions, "female sexual slavery" was more all-encompassing because it "refers to international traffic in women *and* forced street prostitution taken together."[6] Both geographical distinctions of scale and political-juridical demarcations of sovereignty were rendered insignificant.

Barry would go on in the 1980s to lead a concerted international campaign to install the more visceral and emotively powerful category of "sexual slavery" in the lexicon of feminist organizing, scholarship, and global governance. At the 1980 Mid-Decade World Conference on Women in Copenhagen, Barry helped U.S. Congresswoman Barbara Mikulski draft Resolution 43—"Exploitation of the Prostitution of Others and Traffic in Persons"—which was included in the World Plan of Action. The emphasis on force in the 1975 Mexico resolution was amplified by declaring now that "women and children (boys and girls) are still all too often victims of physical abuse and sexual exploitation constituting virtual slavery."[7] In addition to helping draft Resolution 43, Barry also led workshops on "female sexual slavery" at the parallel NGO Forum in Copenhagen.

In 1982, at the request of the UN Commission on the Status of Women (CSW), the Economic and Social Council (ECOSOC) appointed Jean Fernand-Laurent as a Special Rapporteur charged with producing a new UN report on the traffic in women, which he completed and submitted in March 1983. The report declared that in taking a "human rights approach" to the issue, "we, like the Commission on Human Rights, consider prostitution to be a form of slavery."[8] Then, in April 1983, Kathleen Barry, Charlotte Bunch, and Shirley Castley co-organized the ten-day Global Feminist Workshop to Organize Against Traffic in Women in Rotterdam. In the introduction to the published proceedings, *International Feminism: Networking against Female Sexual Slavery*, Bunch and Castley pressed for the adoption of "female sexual slavery" as a more accurate term: "Traditionally, forced prostitution has been somewhat euphemistically referred to as 'traffic in women,' thus often masking the actual condition of involuntary servitude and violence against women that this practice entails."[9] Note the emergence of this new category of "violence against women" as one aspect of the older category of traffic in women. In her opening paper at the Rotterdam workshop, Barry recalled that she had been "motivated to understand the relationship of force, coercion and violence in prostitution to the violence in all women's lives around the world, in wife battery, rape, incest, bride burning, excision and pornography." She continued: "In these meetings we realized that as we defined female sexual slavery, it applied to women who are the victims of sex tourism, who are the victims of gangs that traffic in women from South America to Europe, women who are sexually tortured and enslaved as political prisoners in totalitarian dictatorships and women enslaved in their own homes." Thus, sexual abuse, physical violence, and spousal rape could now be placed under the rubric of female sexual slavery. Barry went on to explain a key difference between the prevailing United Nations definition of traffic in women and a feminist definition of female sexual slavery: "We include in our concerns *any* situation a woman is in, in which she cannot get away, and in that situation is physically abused and sexually exploited."[10] The ambiguous situation of "women enslaved in their own homes" could also be extended to any form of compulsory and uncompensated domestic labor, thus suggesting a very broad compass of female slavery, but this was circumscribed by emphasis upon its sexual forms, which was further reduced to and conflated with prostitution. By May 1983, the ECOSOC passed Resolution 1983/30, which declared that "the enslavement of women and children subjected to prostitution is incompatible with the dignity and fundamental rights of the human person." The nondistinction between trafficking and prostitution and between prostitution and slavery became merged and codified as a distinctive human rights position considerate of women.

A parallel and sometimes overlapping effort to identify violence against women (VAW) as a distinctive phenomenon necessitating focused attention and documentation also created new activist linkages, institutional openings, and knowledge formations. Although international organizing around the issue can be traced back to the formation of the Women's International Information and Communication Service (ISIS) in 1974, "violence against women" was not included in the agenda for the first UN Decade for Women (1975–85), which had the focus of "Equality, Development, and Peace."[11] Neither the phrase "violence against women" nor the word "violence," for that matter, appears in the 1979 Convention on the Elimination of All Forms of Discrimination against Women (CEDAW). It was not until the 3rd World Conference on Women in Nairobi in 1985 that the problem was explicitly addressed and included in the resulting *Nairobi Forward-Looking Strategies for the Advancement of Women:* "Violence against women exists in various forms in everyday life in all societies. Women are beaten, mutilated, burned, sexually abused and raped. Such violence is a major obstacle to the achievement of peace and the other objectives of the Decade and should be given special attention."[12] Perhaps the easy opposition of violence versus peace created a special discursive opening in 1985, but this suturing of obstacle and goal was muddled by their incommensurable scales. Violence against women was still largely confined to the domestic sphere and not fathomable as a matter of interstate relations and negotiations.

In the aftermath of the Cold War, violence against women was able to command greater attention and gained much traction with the intertwined growth of human rights and feminist activism. The Center for Women's Global Leadership (CWGL), which was established in 1989 at Rutgers University under the leadership of Charlotte Bunch, organized a three-year program on the theme of "women, violence, and human rights," which included the convening of a two-week-long Women's Leadership Institute and the publication of pamphlets and reports. In 1990 Bunch published in the *Human Rights Quarterly* an influential essay titled "Women's Rights as Human Rights." Versions of this essay were also reprinted and circulated as part of the CWGL's publications. The essay outlines several examples of how "sexism kills" and how "being female is life-threatening": "Sex discrimination kills women daily. When combined with race, class, and other forms of oppression, it constitutes a deadly denial of women's right to life and liberty on a large scale throughout the world. The most pervasive violation of females is violence against women in all its manifestations, from wife battery, incest, and rape, to dowry deaths, genital mutilation, and female sexual slavery."[13] Female sexual slavery was now configured as one specific manifestation of a much broader and "most pervasive" rubric of violence against women.

The CWGL launched several linked initiatives to raise international awareness around violence against women (VAW). According to the 1992–93 report of the CWGL, "The Center has focused on violence against women as the issue that clearly and urgently highlights the importance of expanding human rights to include women."[14] In June 1991 the first Women's Leadership Institute brought together twenty-three women from twenty countries to share information and strategize collectively. In anticipation of the June 1993 UN World Conference on Human Rights in Vienna, the CWGL organized the still-active campaign titled "16 Days of Activism against Gender Violence," which begins November 25, designated as the International Day against Violence against Women, and ends December 10, on Human Rights Day.[15] The 16 Days Campaign included a worldwide petition drive coordinated with the International Women's Tribune Centre (IWTC), which called on the Preparatory Committee of the Vienna Conference to recognize violence against women as "a violation of human rights requiring immediate action." The center also coordinated the Global Campaign for Women's Human Rights, a network of ninety NGOs that held local and regional hearings and rallied together to make violence against women a "special theme" of the 1993 conference. Finally, it organized the Global Tribunal on Violations of Women's Human Rights, which was to be convened parallel to the intergovernmental UN conference in Vienna.

These coordinated efforts proved effective. According to paragraph 18 of the Vienna Declaration and Program of Action, "Gender-based violence and all forms of sexual harassment and exploitation, including those resulting from cultural prejudice and international trafficking are incompatible with the dignity and worth of the human person, and must be eliminated." By December 1993, the UN General Assembly adopted without a vote the Declaration on the Elimination of Violence against Women (DEVAW), which called for the appointment of a Special Rapporteur on violence against women. Radhika Coomaraswamy, a Sri Lankan lawyer educated in the U.S. who had served on the Steering Committee of the Asia Pacific Forum on Women, Law and Development (APWLD), was appointed to the position and would serve until 2013. Violence against women soon came to be decried and was codified in several other sectors of the United Nations and global governance. The Programme of Action emerging from the 1994 International Conference on Population and Development in Cairo declared that "the elimination of all kinds of violence against women and ensuring women's ability to control their own fertility are cornerstones of population and development-related programmes." Also in 1994, the World Bank sponsored the publication of a study titled *Violence against Women: The Hidden Health Burden*. These moves to recognize and codify the problem were hailed as the successful fruition of international feminist organizing. As Margaret E. Keck and Kathryn Sikkink pointed out in *Activists beyond Borders: Advocacy Networks in International Politics*, "By the mid-1990s, it had become the most important international women's issue, and the most dynamic new international human rights concern."[16] As violence against women was defined and deployed as an all-encompassing category but more stirring than discrimination against women, the transnational movement against VAW generated and proliferated a growing catalogue of variously particular modes of injury, proper ways of knowing and systematically recording their occurrence, and their corresponding remedy, punishment, and prevention.

These multiple power/knowledge streams on traffic in women, female sexual slavery, and violence against women merged with and amplified one another in the 1990s. The distinctively and viscerally imperiled groupings of "trafficking victims" and "sex slaves" were thus crucial to the early arguments for "women's rights as human rights." But the newly activated categories of abuse also delineated smaller demographics for documentation, analysis, and redress, and thereby effected the neutralization of "women" (unmodified). The inclusion of Asian women as "Asian women" but also under its many subcategories was also necessary to qualify for the global and international banners of these efforts.

A new discourse joining trafficking and "Asian women" gained much traction through the overlapping proliferation of activist forums, social services, philanthropic projects, and global governance maneuvers specifically attentive to the traffic in Asian women. In addition to academic studies, a sizable number of surveys, reports, and recommendations were produced by several different divisions of the United Nations, including the UN Development Program, UNICEF, and the International Organization of Migration. Many NGOs and INGOs convened conferences, published their proceedings, and commissioned their own reports focusing on different countries and specific border regions.[17] For example, Women's Rights Project and Asia Watch, two divisions of Human Rights Watch, conducted and published several investigations into the trafficking of Asian women throughout the 1990s, including the widely cited *A Modern Form of Slavery: Trafficking of Burmese Women and Girls into Brothels in Thailand* in 1993.[18] Throughout the 1990s, several commercial and academic publications focused specifically on the traffic in Asian women.[19] Although it bears a generic title, *The Traffic in Women: Human Realities of the International Sex Trade* (1997) is focused specifically on the trafficking of women into and out of Thailand. Additionally, some version of "traffic" or "trafficking" has been used in titles and subtitles by authors writing about "Asian women" more generally.[20] These earlier efforts fed into the production and dissemination of ever more articles, monographs, and edited collections into the twenty-first century, such as Louise Brown's *Sex Slaves: The Trafficking of Women in Asia* (2000).

A specific cohort of Asian women played an active role in this process of making "Asian women" visible, sometimes alongside activists and researchers from other regions in broad international settings but also through the organization of several regionally focused events and nongovernmental entities. Although there had been regionally focused intra-Asian feminist meetings and collaborations since the 1970s, there was a new wave of workshops, conferences, and tribunals focused on "Asian women" and often spearheaded by Asian women. The recharged attention to the history of Japanese military "comfort stations" proved to be a dynamic rallying point for intra-Asian feminist affinity and networking. In December 1991, four months after Kim Hak-sun first spoke out in a press conference, the Asian Women's Human Rights Council (AWHRC) sponsored the Regional Meeting and Conference on Traffic in Women in Seoul. Many attendees first learned of the Japanese military "comfort stations" at this gathering, which spurred on new investigative and political projects. On February 20, 1992, the Taipei Women's Rescue Foundation began to collect reports from Taiwanese victims, and shortly thereafter, on March 12, the government organized the Taiwan Comfort Women Project Task Force. In July 1992 the AWHRC, GABRIELA (General Assembly Binding Women for Reforms, Integrity, Equality, Leadership, and Action), and the BAYAN Women's Desk established the Task Force on Filipino "Comfort Women" (TFFCW), made up of thirteen groups, which worked to locate Filipina survivors. Then on August 10–11, 1992, the first Asian Conference for Solidarity for Women Drafted for Sexual Services by Japan was convened in Seoul and included over one hundred participants from South Korea, Japan, Taiwan, the Philippines, Hong Kong, and Thailand.

At the United Nations, the issue of the Japanese "comfort system" was first raised by the Korean Council at the Commission on Human Rights in a February 1992 memorandum that requested an investigation. In short order the issue was addressed and debated in May at the Working Group on Contemporary Forms of Slavery and then at the Sub-Commission on Prevention of Discrimination and Protection of Minorities in August 1992.[21] In her oral presentation to the Sub-Commission in August 1992, Shin Heisoo, speaking on behalf of the Korean Council, categorized the "comfort system" as sexual slavery. The issue would be debated at the Working Group on Contemporary Forms of Slavery throughout the 1990s.

The United Nations World Conference on Human Rights, which was convened in Vienna in June 1993, was an especially important turning point. At the parallel NGO forum, Korean civil rights lawyer Park Won Soon delivered a paper titled "'Comfort Women,' Justice and International Law." The Global Tribunal on Violations of Women's Human Rights, which was also convened parallel to the Vienna Conference, prominently featured the issue. A panel on "War Crimes Against Women" was moderated by Nelia Sancho of the Asian Women's Human Rights Council and featured presentations by Chung Chin Sung of the Korean Council and Kim Bok-dong, who was identified as "a survivor of sexual slavery in Japan."[22] These concerted efforts led to the inclusion of the issue in Article 38 of the Vienna Declaration and Programme of Action, which explicitly states that "violations of the human rights of women in situations of armed conflict are violations of the fundamental principles of international human rights and humanitarian law. All violations of this kind, including in particular murder, systematic rape, sexual slavery, and forced pregnancy, require a particularly effective response." According to Donna J. Sullivan, "The draft version of this provision included the term 'current' before the reference to violations; its elimination from the final text brought the abuses by Japanese forces against Asian women during World War II, particularly Korean and Filipina 'comfort women' who were forced into prostitution in military brothels, clearly within the scope of the text."[23]

This inclusion would later prove to be crucial to the decision by the Sub-Commission on Prevention of Discrimination and Protection of Minorities to appoint Linda Chavez as a Special Rapporteur to undertake "an in-depth study of systematic rape, sexual slavery and similar practices during wartime, including internal armed conflict." The Japanese military "comfort system" was prominently featured in a "preparatory document" that Chavez submitted in September 1993. After noting that "forced prostitution during wartime has also been practiced on a large scale, notably during the Second World War" and that "rape has been widely and systematically used in the former Yugoslavia, especially in Bosnia and Herzegovina, as a method of ethnic cleansing," the report continues: "While the immediate harm and anguish to victims caused by rape is readily apparent, we are only now coming to understand better the long-term emotional and/or physical consequences for victims. Recent publicity concerning the continued deleterious effects suffered by Chinese, Dutch, Filipino, Indonesian and Korean women forced into sexual slavery during the Second World War confirms that systematic rape can have a devastating impact on its victims, which lasts years beyond the immediate horror of the act itself."[24] By imbuing historical depth and geographical breadth to contemporary atrocities in Bosnia and Rwanda, the "comfort women" redress movement thus fortified the campaign to codify rape, forced prostitution, and sexual slavery as war crimes and crimes against humanity.

The "comfort women" issue also featured prominently in the earliest UN-sponsored investigations of violence against women in the 1990s. The *Preliminary Report on Violence against Women*, which was published in November 1994 by Radhika Coomaraswamy, the newly appointed Special Rapporteur on violence against women, included a detailed account critical of the Japanese military "comfort system" as an instance of "violence against women in situations of armed conflict," which was delineated as a newly recognized subcategory of "violence perpetrated or condoned by the state."[25] At the invitation of both the governments of Japan and South Korea, Coomaraswamy later undertook an investigative mission to the two countries in July 1995 and then drafted a report with an addendum that also included information about North Korea.[26] Noting the Japanese government's objection to the use of the term *military sexual slavery* as inaccurate, Coomaraswamy firmly articulated "the opinion that the practice of 'comfort women' should be considered a clear case of sexual slavery and a slavery-like practice."[27]

The setting of the 1995 4th World Conference on Women in Beijing would prove especially opportune for large numbers of Asian women to attend and participate in the parallel NGO forum. Activists working on the "comfort women" issue organized the Asian Tribunal on Japanese Military Sexual Slavery. In her presentation, Shin Heisoo framed the issue as "an example of an extreme form of violence against women in wartime."[28] Their successful effort to seek recognition was reflected in the final Platform of Action, which identified "rape in the conduct of armed conflict" as a "war crime" (section E, paragraph 147 [e]) and called on the United Nations to "undertake a full investigation of all acts of violence against women committed during war, including rape, in particular systematic rape, forced prostitution and other forms of indecent assault and sexual slavery, prosecute all criminals responsible for war crimes against women and provide full redress to women victims" (section E, paragraph 147 [f]). In 1998 the Rome Statute of the International Criminal Court explicitly recognized "sexual slavery" as a war crime and a crime against humanity. It is difficult, if not impossible, to ascertain who or what came first and authorized the other.

I have laboriously recited this only partial but crowded genealogy to emphasize from the outset of this book that the category of "Asian women" and specifically the "comfort women" case importantly shaped the negotiated categorization and recalibration of injuries and violations in need of proper certification and adjudication by the United Nations and newer entities such as the International Commission of Jurists and the International Criminal Court in the 1990s.[29] The resurgent and avowedly feminist anti-trafficking movement could hold the Japanese "comfort system" up as a clear and documentable instance of direct state involvement in the traffic in women. With the growing legibility of violence against women, activists and scholars would strategically cast the "comfort system" as a definite and especially egregious instantiation of VAW.[30] The "comfort system" case also offered a clear demonstration of how such crimes against women had gone unpunished, were suppressed, and were made illegible in the intervening decades. For example, although the examples of "violence against women in situations of armed conflict" in Coomaraswamy's *Preliminary Report* included several contemporary instances in Rwanda, Haiti, and the Kashmir as well as the mass rapes in Bangladesh in 1971, she drew special attention to the "comfort women" case following a discussion of the problem of "impunity" or "official failure to condemn and punish rape." She continued to point out that although an apology had been made by Japan in July 1992, the matter of compensation and related recognition of the "comfort system" as a crime under international humanitarian law were still unresolved: "It is a crucial question that would set a legal precedent at the international level for the prosecution of perpetrators of systematic rape and sexual slavery in times of armed conflict. A symbolic gesture of compensation would introduce a remedy of 'compensation' for victims of violence perpetrated during times of armed conflict."[31] The tenacious demands for apology, admission, and reparations by the survivors of the Japanese military "comfort system" challenged the emerging "women's rights as human rights" platform and the global governance entities charged with their protection and promotion to grapple with the proper calculation and distribution of monetary compensation alongside other rights violations.

By the end of the 1990s, both the past atrocity and the contemporary redress movement came to be heralded for their extraordinary transnational visibility. The authors of *The Traffic in Women* (1997) characterized the "comfort system" as "one of the most notorious episodes in the 20th century," and Louise Brown distinguished it as "the most well-publicized antecedent of modern-day sexual slavery in the region."[32] This extraordinary visibility was hailed by some as confirmation of a democratizing transnational public sphere that was especially attuned to women's rights as human rights. As Katharine H. S. Moon noted in 1999, "South Korean survivors of Japanese military sexual slavery ('comfort system' or *chongshindae*) and activists on their behalf have been noted as some of the most persuasive and omnipresent advocates of women's human rights at international meetings and conferences."[33] Reflecting on the success of the redress movement, Chih-Chieh Chou emphasized in 2003 that "the comfort women issue is promoting a new claim for human rights, in particular, women's rights in Asia. East Asian women have been extremely effective in networking—creating NGOs with transnational links which have been able to raise this issue, mobilize people and victim survivors for political action, gain support of the United Nations and international media, and put pressure on the target Japanese government."[34]

This super-visibility has incurred cautious skepticism and increasingly frank criticism. In that 1999 essay, Moon pointedly questioned the reasons for this international prominence in contrast to the effacement of the older movement against the abuses of U.S. military–related prostitution in South Korea.[35] Noting how "the wartime and postwar experiences of these mostly poor and uneducated old ladies has sparked enormous scholarly and popular interest in Asia, Europe, Oceania, and North America," Laura Hein went so far as to frame "that suddenly augmented imaginative power" in the 1990s not as enlightened justice but a "savage irony." Asking readers to consider "Why them? Why now?" Hein pointed out that this history had been "public knowledge in Japan for decades" and declared even more unsentimentally that "many—Japanese and non-Japanese alike—who knew about the military comfort women at the end of the war thought of them as the unfortunate losers in a normal social and legal relationship rather than as victims of human rights violations or war crimes."[36]

I propose to recast this double-edged exemplarity—of both atrocious violation and impressive publicity—as a broader problematic about the collision and co-constitution of global governance, capital flows, transnational politics, feminist knowledges, and new communication technologies in the 1990s, which were importantly shaped by earlier deployments of U.S. economic, military, political, and epistemological power in Asia in the twentieth century. The claim of "breaking the silence" justified—and continues to underwrite—the production of a plethora of impassioned political, scholarly, and artistic endeavors about the "comfort system." But we must keep in mind the partiality of any narration of these events and be especially skeptical about any account that claims a linear, positive unfolding—a displacement of silence with voice, a filling of absence and ignorance with knowledge, a welcoming by those in power after convincing entreaties for recognition by the victimized—through a series of rational exchanges between distinct yet univocal parties. Both the supposed silence around Japanese military sexual slavery and the much-heralded breaking of that silence in the 1990s were forged by older racist and imperialist power/knowledge regimes that disqualified, segregated, and demoted "Asian women" from both humanity and women. These persistent taxonomic habits and their attendant methods of knowing and nonknowing these distinguished collectivities predisposed the compositional methods of these late twentieth-century projects to document female vulnerability, including a persistent delineation of an Asian difference and unknowability. Then too, the tapered attention to physical and especially sexual violence against women displaced the concern with female labor exploitation, which had been the focus of much important feminist scholarship on the global assembly line and the new international division of labor in the 1980s. The acclaimed induction and circulation of Asian women as newly empowered and mobile subjects of women's rights and human rights propped up the vision of a world made borderless for both capital accumulation and pursuing justice.[37]

Given that all of these problems afflicting Asian women continue to exist and fuel ever-more projects of representation and redress, this book asks: How and why did "Asian women" become intelligible through particular modes of documenting their violation and violability? Put differently, how and why did "Asian women" function as an especially demonstrative and portable embodiment of both the taxonomic singularities and the compounded intensity of female oppression? But also, how did the privileging of spectacularly and especially sexually violated Asian female bodies foreclose other terms and conditions for making "Asian women" intelligible? Each chapter traces how "Asian women" might be reframed not as a bounded and knowable population but as a critical prompt for mapping varying configurations of power, knowledge, and justice. In the wishful trajectory of gradual accretion and orderly conversion from silence to voice to recognition to justice, there's an illusory isomorphism that would say that at the end of so much effort and contestation, "Asian women" end up right where and what they have always been or where they should be like other already protected and empowered subjects. I have rehearsed a chronicle of just such a positive and progressive becoming-into-being earlier in this introduction, which would effectively contain the disparate figurations of Asian women. In contrast, the rest of this book will attempt to trace out multiple generic, speculative tangents and to pinpoint their significant but occluded overlaps, adjacencies, and divergences. In each chapter I examine how "Asian women" were made visible but also incoherent and inconsequential through specific methods of documentation, categorization, calculation, and compilation across multiple nodes of national archiving, global governance, nongovernmental advocacy, media coverage, and academic scholarship. Simply put, my aim is to have "Asian women" mean less intensely and matter more broadly, a knotty proposition that I will elaborate upon in chapter 1, "Asian Women as Method?"

The next three chapters will trace how "Asian women" have figured in the composition and permutation of three categories of female vulnerability and harm: traffic in women, sexual slavery, and violence against women. The early twentieth-century efforts to construct a regime of international governance entailed the production of new modes and networks of data gathering, beginning with the League of Nations between the two world wars and continuing to the postwar period of decolonization and the expansion of the United Nations in the 1960s, and to the ongoing efforts focalized through the developing United Nations bodies and protocols in the 1980s and especially the 1990s. The final three chapters will explore three different modes of justice and redress—monetary compensation, disclosure of truth, and proper memorialization—that partially constitute the list of six demands first articulated by the Korean Council in October 1990:

1. the Japanese government acknowledge the fact that (the military) forced Korean women to accompany troops as comfort women;
2. the Japanese government issue an official apology for these practices;
3. the Japanese government disclose all acts of brutality (committed by the government or military);
4. a memorial to the people victimized be erected;
5. survivors or their families be compensated; and
6. in order to prevent the recurrence of these wrongs, the facts be taught as a part of history education.[38]

As many different subjects and stakeholders became involved in investigating and adjudicating the Japanese military "comfort system," they have generated new questions and odd permutations which demand that we rethink those specific forms of remedy but also the categorical enclosures of female injury and vulnerability. Each chapter considers specific responses and attempts to resituate them in terms of both their heterogeneous effects and implications and to speculate upon alternative, not-taken paths of inquiry and analysis.

I have deliberately excised the definite article in the odd title of this book, *Traffic in Asian Women*, so that we might bear in mind that there is no single phenomenon or discourse that could contain the multiple figurations, textualizations, calculations, archives, itineraries, and detours that are examined in the chapters that follow.[39] Cast as a stirring appeal, *Traffic in Asian Women* calls us out to recognize and account for the violated and dispossessed, which we cannot refuse and turn away from. But, framed as a command, it can mean a forceful summons, a compulsion to render "Asian women" as recognizable and worthy subjects in ways that are preset, limited, and obfuscating. What compels and what is so compelling about these multiple claims for truth and justice? How does each petition stake out its own urgency and singularity, especially its unique significance and potential consequences for the Asian women that are conjured up? Why and how is it that in the aftermath of so much effort and often celebrated success in securing international visibility for battered, exploited, and aggrieved Asian women, so much of the social, political, economic, and psychic conditions of violence, inequality, and injustice has not been transformed? Why do so many Asian women continue to suffer in the same coeval space of so much publicity, knowledge production, and activism? Then too, how do certain spectacular but habituated modes of their visibility obscure other bodies in pain and other modes of subjectivization and politicization? These are indeed impossible questions that I can only approach from acute, peculiar angles. Perhaps Asian women might be impressed not to know and represent what we can readily name but to open up and out to alternate modalities of thinking together about the hows and whys of what we do not know but cannot not want.

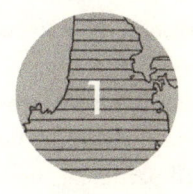

ASIAN WOMEN
AS METHOD?

The question animating this chapter—"Asian women as method?"—echoes and mutates the title of Kuan-Hsing Chen's 2010 book, *Asia as Method: Toward Deimperialization*.[1] Chen diagnoses an epistemological impasse in *thinking Asia* within and across several specific fissures that have been shaped by multiple, overlapping imperialisms. First, Japanese imperialist expansion, specifically its colonization of Taiwan and Korea and later invasion of Manchuria as part of the Greater East Asian Co-Prosperity Sphere, was framed as resistance to European imperialisms. Then, the U.S. Cold War military empire habilitated Japan's post–World War II economic recovery and regional domination while also crucially shaping and sustaining divisions between North Korea/South Korea and Taiwan/China. Third, when South Korea and Taiwan achieved their own economic growth in the 1970s, they became extractive and exploitative of other Asian nations. Chen claims that, as early as the 1980s, "Korean scholars began describing South Korea as sub-imperialist, in terms of its reproduction of imperialist expansion." Pointing to Taiwanese investment in export-processing zones (EPZs) in Vietnam, Indonesia, and the Philippines as fueled by a "sub-imperial desire" articulated as a discourse of "southward advance," Chen writes, "Constricted economically by a mega-empire, it joined the game of imperialist competition by investing downward in order to seize markets, resources, and labor in less developed countries."[2]

Chen outlines several important epistemological ramifications of these multiple, imbricated imperialisms. The very founding of Asian studies as "area studies" in the U.S. authorized particular methods of knowing and delineations of expertise; this primacy has demoted knowledges produced *in* Asia as always belated to the body of knowledge produced *about* Asia in the West. This epistemological ordering has been further cemented by the hierarchical division of theory and data: "We serve as the native informant to the theoretically minded researcher. The agony implied by this relation is caused by a serious problem of our own: the worship of theory. Indeed, theory has been narrowly understood as a set of superior knowledge, and it is associated with the name of specific authors." Chen notes how those scholars in Asia who have followed the theoretical and methodological lead of the West, specifically the U.S., suffer from "anxiety over the West,"[3] and this has restrained the sharing and comparing of knowledges within and across Asia. Third, and most relevant to my proposition of Asian women as method, the Cold War and specifically U.S. hegemony in relation to Japan, Korea, and Taiwan functioned to stunt and distort the reckoning with intra-Asian violence, which should inform any intra-Asian epistemological exchange.

Against this nexus of epistemological anxieties and agonies, "Asia as method" is first and foremost a "method of engagement." As Chen explains, "Using the idea of Asia as an imaginary anchoring point, societies in Asia can become each other's points of reference ... the diverse historical experiences and rich social practices of Asia may be mobilized to provide alternative horizons and perspectives."[4] My reservation about this move is that it starts off from *a* society *in* Asia as a bounded unit of knowledge, which is untenable in the convoluted aftermath of multiple imperialisms, diasporas, and transnational capitalisms. Thus, instead of *intra*-Asian, I prefer the designation of *inter*-Asian, which was introduced earlier in 2007 by Kuan-Hsing Chen and Chua Beng Huat, and other scholars associated with the journal *Inter-Asia Cultural Studies* to name a critical consciousness that "there is no unity to the imaginary entity called 'Asia.'"[5] I would add that attending to the discrepant yet linked histories of intra-Asian sexual violence and gendered labor exploitation—in short, *thinking* Asian women as method—both compels and instructs us to probe the contours of that nonunity. Then, too, as I hope to demonstrate in the rest of the book, the narrow interests and large blind spots of many different U.S. actors and agencies in the investigation, documentation, categorization, archiving, and circulation of "Asian women" might clarify the terms and conditions of nonknowing and thereby pierce any aura of epistemological primacy and superiority.

Chen makes repeated, conscientious acknowledgments of the significance of women and gender, but he does not take them up in any sustained and substantive manner. So it is notable that the issue of "comfort women" is invoked in two key places in the book's introduction. He first includes it within a list of postcolonial reckonings by South Korea, which "started to work out its colonial relations with Japan (on such issues as the 'comfort women,' history textbooks, and popular television dramas jointly produced by Japanese and Koreans) and with the United States (on issues like the removal of military bases)." Then, on the following page, Chen emphasizes the significance of the issue in Japan's own reckoning with its history as the perpetrator of intra-Asian violence: "The moment of 'decolonialization' (this is how the activist thinker Muto Ichiyo refers to what I have described as deimperialization), when Japanese intellectuals finally took up Japan's imperialist relations with its former colonies, only came into being in the 1990s. This moment first concerned itself with the issue of the comfort women, but in the late 1990s, it expanded into a series of heated debates on a variety of issues."[6] Chen does not explore this formative moment any further, but the fact that the "comfort women" problematic is called forth in both instances attests to its power to prod and disturb multiple epistemes regarding their customary presumptions, categories, and methods.

This epistemological challenge was powerfully registered in a 1997 special issue—"The Comfort Women: Colonialism, War, and Sex"—of the journal *positions: east asia cultures critique*, edited by Chungmoo Choi. In her illuminating introduction, Choi pointed to the determining force of U.S. geopolitical interests in obviating both postcolonial and deimperialist reckonings: "During the cold war, not only was debate on Japan's colonialism suppressed under U.S. hegemony, but so was discussion of such heinous crimes as the experiments on live human subjects for the development of biological warfare by Japanese Army Unit 731. Evidently the perpetrators of these crimes were swiftly exonerated on the condition that they share this military technology with the United States, which, it is suspected, in turn used it in the Korean War five years later." The inhumane tactics of intra-Asian violence were thus acquired and redeployed by the U.S. military against Koreans. Choi went even further to argue that the concerted inattention to the Japanese military's sexual enslavement of *Asian* women in the postwar tribunals exposes "the fallacy of Western humanism":

> While European tribunals focused on crimes against humanity, such a category was not relevant at the Asian tribunals, which were conducted by the Western allies, led by the United States. The Allies were well aware of the magnitude of the Japanese use of comfort women throughout Asia, and in 1948, thirteen Japanese soldiers were punished (three were executed) by the Batavia Court for mobilizing Dutch women in Indonesia for sexual service. However, no charge was ever brought to the Tokyo War Crimes Trials for the sexual enslavement of Asian women. In other words, under the assumptions of Western humanism, which was the philosophical basis of the Nuremberg and Batavia Trials, Asians did not belong to the category of humanity and women were all the more excluded therefrom. In this light, the comfort women issue is not simply a wartime use of women or an event of the past, nor is it a matter just between Japan and other Asian countries. The politics surrounding the silent history of the comfort women threatens the fundamentals of humanity.[7]

Thus, the initial postwar immunity and durable illegibility of the "comfort system" focalize the disqualification and detachment of Asian women from the enclosures of humanity, which undergird a longer history of U.S.-led governing and knowing structures.

In her incisive contribution to the special issue, Hyunah Yang alerted readers to the belated and overdetermined terms of the induction of this group of Asian women as noteworthy subjects, given the significant temporal lag between the atrocity and its recognition and investigation as a violation of human rights in the early 1990s: "The possible danger in this move is that it may freeze the identity of the former comfort women as international victims, 'existential' comfort women. It should be kept in mind that one of the indispensable ingredients in characterizing the category of 'Third World women' is their status as the victims of male violence—a monolithic, powerless group prior to any analysis. As such, military comfort women would fit neatly into the stereotyping image of Third World women prevalent in mainstream Western academia and media." Here Yang cited Chandra Mohanty's influential 1988 essay, "Under Western Eyes: Feminist Scholarship and Colonial Discourse." Thus, the marked visibility of the "comfort women" in both international news and global governance in the early 1990s crossed in troubling ways with a feminist decolonial watchfulness and even skepticism toward such fixations upon abused and violated "Third World women." As Yang also pointed out, grappling with the history of the "comfort system" held out the possibility for understanding differences *among* Asian women, which have been occluded by persistent divisions of West/East, First World/Third World: "But the comfort women issue has the potential to reveal to the international community Western-dominated world history's ('the' world history's) neglect of crimes committed by Japanese imperialism in *Asia*. Seen from the West-centered positionality/ies, imperial Japan has signified only as the country that was nuclear-bombed and defeated by the United States and its allies, rather than as the country that invaded other Asian countries."[8] The Japanese military "comfort system" foregrounded the matter of *intra*-Asian racisms and their gendered, sexualized violence. Pointing to the Korean Council's characterization of the "comfort system" as "the genocide of the Korean people," Yang emphasized its racial and ethnic dimensions: "I conceive of the crime as a case of genocide not only in terms of uprooting the reproductive capability of young women, but also as an attempt to deplete the Korean ethnic identity."[9] Later, she stated even more strongly, "The Japanese categorization of 'Korean' as a valueless race was a significant dimension in building the project."[10] The nonrecognition of the "comfort system" as a technology of genocidal racism was ordained by the insufficient qualification of Koreans and Japanese as possible victims and perpetrators of crimes against humanity.

Although many have upheld the "comfort women" case as exemplary of both the past violation and the contemporary empowerment of Asian women, I would argue that it has profoundly destabilized the imaginary unity and conceptual demarcation of the category. When understood as a method of racist, colonial genocide against Koreans, the "comfort system" brings to the fore the underexplored matter of racial, ethnic, and national differences and hierarchies *among* Asian women. The Japanese military established "comfort stations" throughout the vast territory that it invaded and occupied, extending west to Burma and Indonesia and across many Pacific Islands from Guam south to Papua New Guinea, where it forcibly conscripted, confined, and brutalized native women, women belonging to European colonial settler communities, and Korean, Taiwanese, Japanese, and Chinese women brought there on Imperial Army ships. Although some of these women were repatriated at the end of World War II, a countless number died abroad in the battlefields or remained abroad. An attempt to map the "comfort system" troubles any certain emplacement of "Asian women" and further elucidates the noncorrespondence of "Asian women" and "women in Asia."

Asian Women as Method?   23

The "comfort women" problematic demands that we start off from the recognition of "Asian women" as a category borne of the material violence and attendant epistemological limits of what Lisa Yoneyama effectively sums up as "the simultaneity and entanglement of the Japanese empire and the U.S. empire."[11] As I will demonstrate in later chapters, the U.S. state, military, and capital were particularly invested and also liable agents in the management and forgetting of Japan's violent conscription, uprooting, and relocation of women throughout its Asia-Pacific empire. Several scholars have attributed the lack of will to recognize, prosecute, and problematize the Japanese military "comfort system" to its similarities and connections to the wartime rapes and institutionalized coordination of prostitution by the U.S. military in its successive interventions in and occupation of Japan, Okinawa, Korea, Vietnam, Laos, Cambodia, and the Philippines.[12] Framing the "comfort women" redress movement from the 1990s and beyond as part of what she alternately calls "transborder redress culture," "Asia-Pacific redress culture," and "post-1990s redress culture centering on the discourse of Japanese imperial violence," Yoneyama elucidates how it "contains profound critiques of the way the transpacific arrangement of Cold War justice has set the parameters of what can be known as violence and whose violence, on which bodies, can be addressed and redressed."[13]

This book attempts to trace out this complex of power/knowledge/violence and belated address/redress in an expanded historical and geographical grid, moving further back in time to the early twentieth century and scanning both transpacific and transatlantic routes by which "Asian women" have been configured and transacted in war, law, culture, economics, and politics. To clarify, I will not be locating and analyzing every instantiation of "Asian women." I have not set out to address what some would deem the most prominent and consequential cases. Some chapters will hew more closely to "Asian women," but more often than not, my investigation will appear to stray far and even, at times, lose sight altogether of "Asian women." Lisa Lowe compellingly models in *The Intimacies of Four Continents* how her "interest in Chinese emigrant labor is not to pursue a single, particularist identity, not to fill in a gap or add on another transoceanic group, but to explain *the politics of our lack of knowledge*, and to be more specific about what I would term the economy of affirmation and forgetting that characterizes the liberal humanist understanding."[14] This book will be more focused on the composition and effacement of "Asian women" within a geohistorical arc of the emergence, decline, and permutation of the United States—and its variously enfranchised subjects of power and knowledge—in and against a broader, shifting architecture of global governance and transnational capital in the twentieth century.

To take one node that is of great personal interest and curiosity, we can turn to how a particularly distorted "transpacific arrangement" of power/knowledge partially but importantly shaped the terms and conditions by which "Asian women" came to figure in "second-wave" U.S. feminist scholarship and theory in the 1970s and 1980s. One very specific and enduring puzzle for me surrounds the transpacific relay and occlusion of inter-Asian feminist knowledges about the Japanese military "comfort system," which were enunciated earlier in the 1970s as part of the coordinated protests against Japanese sex tourism in Asia. In July 1973 the Women's League of the South Korean Christian Church raised the problem at a joint international conference of the Japan-Korea National Council of Christian Churches: "We wish to call your attention to the shameful fact that many Japanese tourists, whose numbers have been ceaselessly swelling, are making Korean women into 'sexual slaves.'"[15] Then, on October 23, 1973, a group of students at Ewha University released a statement in protest of the martial law, which had been declared the previous year on October 7, 1972, by General Park Chung-hee. Decrying the "maximum suppression of the people's inner voices and daily life" and the violent repression of "democratic students," the statement also pointedly condemned how the Park regime's program of economic growth relied upon and indeed necessitated Korean women's sexual exploitation by Japanese men: "Our mother country must not become a colony of Japan once again. Because of an astronomical debt of five billion five hundred million dollars, numerous women are presently sold as toys to foreign economic animals under a masquerade elegantly called 'promotion of tourism.' In the place of military boots the clatter of Japanese wooden clogs (*geta*) increases."[16] The statement went on to link Japanese sex tourism to Park's brutal regime of surveillance, crackdown of antigovernment protests, and harsh labor discipline: "Under the whip of our government's intelligence-gathering system, none of us can speak or see; we are just coerced into work." Taken together, the Korean churchwomen's and the Ewha students' statements drew attention to the enduring centrality of the sexual violation and exploitation of Korean women under colonization, military dictatorship, and economic development. Their nomination of "sex slaves" and "sexual slavery" emphasized the unfree labor conditions that continued from the colonial era to long after formal liberation and attested to what Chungmoo Choi has characterized as South Korea's "deferred decolonization."[17]

On December 23, 1973, several Ewha students along with other Korean women's groups began staging protests against Japanese male tourists arriving at Kimpo International Airport and at hotels catering to these Japanese group tours. These protests were televised in Japan by news media, alerting many Japanese women to the problem. The Korean women's decolonial provocations inspired Japanese feminists to apprehend Japanese sex tourism as an impetus to their own critical reckoning with the gendered and sexual contours of Japan's imperialist history in Asia and neocolonial economic domination of Korea and other countries in the region. Two days later, on December 25, 1973, a group of Japanese feminists formed an allied Women's Group Opposing *Kisaeng* Tourism in Tokyo and staged a protest of Japanese male tourists departing from Haneda Airport. The protestors passed out a pamphlet titled "Kisaeng Tours: A Denunciation of Sexual Exploitation" (*"Kisen Kankō: Sei Sinryaku o Kokohatsu Suru"*), which declared, "Previously Japan colonized and pillaged Korea, raping many of her daughters as army prostitutes. Now they go back to the same land and disgrace her women again, this time with money. The Japanese government, under the name of economic assistance, is actively cooperating with the institution of brothel tours. We must not permit our husbands, lovers, brothers, and associates to go to South Korea to buy women."[18] The reference to rape and "army prostitutes" illustrates that there was already some clear awareness of the Japanese military "comfort system" as an antecedent to contemporary Japanese sex tourism.

Matsui Yayori, the renowned Japanese feminist activist and journalist, participated in these protests. She would elaborate further upon this link between Japanese sex tourism and the military "comfort system" in an essay titled "Why I Oppose *Kisaeng* Tours: Exposing Economic and Sexual Aggression against Korean Women," which was first published in 1974 in the Japanese feminist quarterly *Onna Eros* and later translated into English and circulated transnationally as a mimeographed pamphlet in 1975 (see figure 1.1). Matsui recalled how she first learned of the problem of sex tourism when reading a small article covering the July 1973 conference where the Korean women made their "accusation," which was published in the Japanese Christian periodical *Kirisuto Shimbun* (*Christian Newspaper*):

> My whole body shook with the shock of realization of this "shameful fact." . . . I could see that nothing had really changed from the prewar period when Japan had forced Korea to bow to its colonial and military rule. The Japanese fascist government, up until 1945, had even gone so far as to outlaw the use of Korean language in public and had forced all Koreans to change their names to Japanese ones in an effort to destroy every vestige of Korean national culture. Because of this imperialist

FIGURE 1.1. Cover page of the translated 1975 mimeograph essay by Matsui Yayori, "Why I Oppose *Kisaeng* Tours."

legacy I felt that there was something fundamentally different between Japanese *kisaeng* tours and the usual type of relationship established between Japanese men and the prostitutes they buy when they go to Rome or New York, or when they buy the bodies of bath girls or bar hostesses in their own country.

After thus recalling the significance of the cultural genocide of Japan's colonization of Korea and its continuing power to shape Japanese perceptions of Korean people and especially Korean women, the essay moves on to a lucid explication of other key political and economic continuities from the colonial era. In addition to identifying Park Chung-hee as "a former collaborator who betrayed his country and specialized in hunting out and killing nationalist resistance leaders" who later shifted his allegiances to the United States, Matsui interjected, "but he never forgot his old Japanese military training."[19] The essay then articulates this concise, critical summary of the 1965 Treaty on Basic

Relations between Japan and the Republic of Korea, which had been signed against popular protests in both countries:

> Japanese businessmen had been seeking to reenter Korea ever since they were expelled in 1945, but it was only after the military coup that brought [Park] to power that they could start the capital flowing. Because of the Japanese "economic miracle," which was sparked by Japanese servicing of the U.S. military in the Korean War, and the almost total devastation of the Korean country itself, this treaty represented an attempt by Japanese business to find a new unindustrialized area for investment and for cheap labor, and in this they were eagerly assisted by the Korean ruling group. Thus this treaty allowed a huge invasion of Japanese capital mostly in terms of loans with high interest rates and an influx of Japanese businessmen. . . . This was all made possible by the existence of the U.S. Armed Forces in both countries and by the wish of President Johnson that because of military difficulties in Vietnam "peace" should be maintained at all costs between other East Asian allies.[20]

It is impressive and somewhat startling to see how lucid, wide-ranging, and multifaceted Matsui's analysis was so early on. On this point, I want to note that the essay was later translated and published in English in 1975, the same year as two groundbreaking U.S. feminist texts: Susan Brownmiller's book *Against Our Will* and Gayle Rubin's essay "The Traffic in Women," which I will discuss a little later. Matsui pointed to the layering of "sexual imperialism" and "economic imperialism" through this pithy summary: "With the profits reaped by paying miniscule wages to workers, foreign businessmen buy the bodies of South Korean women."[21] At the end of the mimeograph, Matsui also appended a translated summary of the Ewha students' October 1972 statement, thereby acknowledging the original Korean incitement to and the inter-Asian dialogic frame of her essay but also translating and further relaying the students' impassioned analysis to an English-language, international readership.

The most remarkable detail of Matsui's mimeographed essay appears in a section subtitled "Forced Prostitution for the Japanese Army," where she further elaborated upon the connection between contemporary sex tourism and Japan's wartime "comfort system": "Japanese men, who now treat South Korean women as commodities to be bought and thrown away, carry the criminal record of having in the thirties and forties hunted down Korean women and forced them at gunpoint to become 'Women's Volunteer Corps.' These women were sent off as army prostitutes to 'comfort' Japanese soldiers on the World War II warfronts in China and Southeast Asia. Japanese men are now repeating this infamous history."[22] Matsui's genealogy of Japanese sex tourism reached back even further to the rape of Russian women by Japanese soldiers during the "Siberian invasion" (1918–22) and the consequent widespread infections of venereal diseases: "Having learned from this experience, the Japanese brought along their very own army prostitutes when they invaded China. The number of women forced to become prostitutes for the Japanese Imperial Army between 1938 and the end of the war in 1945 is somewhere between 80,000 and 100,000—and 80% of them were Korean."[23] This is one of the earliest feminist analyses of the Japanese military "comfort system" to be published in English. As such, it commands a critical revision of the still-common narrative of the decades-long silence around the issue and the breaking of that silence in the 1990s.

Matsui's essay was also a resolutely anti-nationalist and anti-racist transnational feminist manifesto. A concluding section, titled "Solidarity of Women Transcends National Boundaries," pointedly declares that "both Japanese and Korean women share the condition being held in contempt by Japanese men." Noting how that "fact" was obscured for many Japanese women who were interpellated by powerful patriarchal and ethnocentric discourses to disdain and resent Korean women sex workers under the compensatory "illusion" of being a "lawful wedded wife," Matsui exhorted: "Therefore, in order to put a halt to the *kisaeng* tours, Japanese women must continue to expose Japanese male chauvinism in all its forms. It is not enough simply to denounce the rotting political and economic connections that distort Korean-Japanese relations. We must also squarely face the problems of the scorn for Koreans festering in the minds of so many Japanese. And we must radically—in the true sense of that word—alter the consciousness of Japanese men: for only through a revolution in human awareness can the shameful system of *kisaeng* tours be ended."[24] To that end, Matsui and some of the Japanese feminists involved in the protests against sex tourism would go on to establish a group calling itself the Asian Women's Association (*Aija no Onnatachi no kai*) in March 1977 and publish a journal titled *Asian Women's Liberation*, which was translated into English. The inaugural May 1977 issue contained a "Declaration of the Asian Women's Liberation Committee in Japan" signed by a group of seven Japanese women, including Matsui. This deimperialist feminist manifesto announced the formation of a new Asian women's liberation movement on March 1, 1977, to commemorate the "day (in 1919) when Korean women risked their lives for national independence from Japanese colonial rule" and ended by declaring that "we want to express our sincere apologies to our Asian sisters. We want to learn from and join in their struggles."[25] The following piece, titled "Who Are We?," additionally stated the group's determination to be "entirely independent from any (male-dominated) organization or Western-oriented women's liberation movement."[26] Considering Matsui's mimeographed essay and the "Declaration of the Asian Women's Liberation Committee in Japan" as cotemporaneous texts of feminist knowledge production alongside and against Brownmiller's book and Rubin's essay also commands a critical revision of the archive and historiography of feminist theory. Instead of belated recognition and benevolent inclusion, I would press for minding these inter-Asian feminist texts and their attenuated routes of transmission to the U.S. as the traces of a stubborn nonknowing about Asian women.

There is a clear thread connecting these earlier Asian feminist decolonial *and* deimperial efforts in the 1970s to the later remembering and problematization of the Japanese military "comfort system" in the 1990s. In an important 1993 essay, Alice Yun Chai traced this genealogy as a formation that she named as "Asian-Pacific Feminist Coalition Politics." According to Chai, "Korean and Japanese women have been writing and demonstrating both in Japan and Korea against sex tourism since the 1970s. As early as 1977, the Asian Women's Association was formed to protest the Japanese sex tours to South Korea. It holds monthly study meetings, engages in protest actions, and maintains links with other women's groups in Japan and abroad."[27] Throughout the 1970s and into the 1980s, there was a cross-national coordination of actions against sexual exploitation in Asia, which strategically negotiated specific local conditions of repression.[28] These inter-Asian feminist actions crossed with and fortified several streams of international feminist scholarship and nongovernmental organizing about gender violence and inequality. Chai pointed to the "Solidarity among Migrant Women" workshop at the NGO Forum at the 1985 UN conference in Nairobi as another important connective node of this "Asian-Pacific Feminist Coalition Politics." Within this frame, I would also connect the July 1973 statement by the Women's League of the South Korean Christian Church to the February 1988 "investigative exposure trip" to Fukuoka, Okinawa, and Tokyo by Yun Chung-ok, Kim Hye-won and Kim Sin-sil as members of Korean Church Women United (KCWU). Several accounts of the "comfort women" redress movement trace the beginnings of its broader international visibility to the presentation of the research findings by Yun Chung-ok in April 1988 at the International Seminar on "Women and Tourism" in Cheju Island, South Korea, which was organized by KCWU.[29] Yun's presentation, in turn, "enabled participants from Korea and Japan to make the historical connection between the *Chongshindae/Jungunianfu* and sex tourism."[30] In November 1991 two *zainichi* (Korean residents in Japan) organizations were formed, the Uli Yosong Network on Comfort Women (Yosong Net) in Tokyo and the Group Considering the Korean Military Comfort Women Issue in Osaka. According to *zainichi* activist and scholar Kim Puja, she and other members were moved to form Yosong Net by a presentation that Yun Chung-ok had given in Japan in 1990.[31] It is this longer history and broader analytical frame that Lisa Yoneyama foregrounds through her nomination of "inter-Asian 'comfort women' redress activism": "This genealogy shows that the 'comfort women' redress discourse is not only concerned to critique violence against women, but has addressed the problem of sexual and gendered violence as a constitutive part of postwar transpacific capitalist relations . . . the transnational feminist anti-sex tour activism censured the sexualized and classed conditions of uneven inter-Asia economic development under the Cold War."[32]

TRANSPACIFIC DIVERGENCE

Given these earlier lines of transmission and networking, we must ask how and why the Japanese military "comfort system" did *not* register more prominently and consequentially in the U.S. before the 1990s. I would point to two distinct but related arcs of transpacific and transnational relay of feminist knowledge of the Japanese military "comfort system." First, Matsui's 1975 essay—and the Korean women's earlier provocations that it referenced and responded to—would circulate internationally on several occasions but with some alterations and noteworthy erasures. A slightly modified version would be reprinted under a different title, "Women's Predicament: Why I Oppose *Kisaeng* Tourism. Unearthing a Structure of Economic and Sexual Aggression," in a 1975 magazine-format collection titled *Japanese Women Speak Out*, which was compiled in anticipation of the United Nations Decade for Women Conference in Mexico City in June. Then, in March 1976, a portion of the essay was read out loud as a "Witness Testimonial" at the International Tribunal on Crimes against Women in Brussels and later included in the published proceedings. In 1977 another version with the shortened title "Sexual Slavery in Korea" was published in *Frontiers: A Journal of Women's Studies* in a special section on the Brussels Tribunal. Yet another modified version with the differently shortened title "Why I Oppose *Kisaeng* Tours" would be included in the published proceedings of the 1983 Global Feminist Workshop to Organize against Traffic in Women in Rotterdam, *International Feminism: Networking against Female Sexual Slavery*.

Second, and more significantly, there was a peculiar effacement of the Japanese military "comfort system" in several wide-ranging, influential feminist texts in the 1970s and early 1980s where one would reasonably expect to find it included. Susan Brownmiller's *Against Our Will* (1975) addresses rape and prostitution during the Vietnam War in some detail but makes only glancing references to the Japanese military "comfort system" in the context of her coverage of World War II. As the first brief allusion reads, "Concentration-camp rape and institutionalized camp brothels in which women were held against their will for the pleasure of the soldiery were a most sinister aspect of the abuse of women in World War II."[33] The term *institutionalized camp brothels* gets closest to referencing the Japanese military "comfort system," but this matter-of-fact alignment with "concentration-camp rape" (presumably a reference to Nazi atrocities in Europe) blurs their marked differences from each other. On the following page there is a quotation from an unnamed source describing conditions in Kweilin, China, during the Japanese occupation, which was entered into evidence at the Tokyo tribunal: "They recruited women labor on the pretext of establishing factories; they forced the women into prostitution with the Japanese troops."[34] There is no further information or explication, but this brief mention indicates awareness of the "comfort system" and its documentation. The third reference in *Against Our Will* appears on page 76: "German and Japanese military brothels, into which conquered women were forcibly placed, were considered examples of Axis war crimes at the Nuremberg and Tokyo tribunals, but the American military never rounded up women for the purposes of prostitution during World War II, as far as I know. The lure of the dollar to starving women in war-torn, liberated countries was coercion enough." Given the repeated references to the Tokyo tribunal, I would venture that the nonconsideration of Asian women as noteworthy subjects of violation, exploitation, and subsequent redress in post–World War II transitional justice cast a long epistemic shadow over U.S. feminist knowledge production in the 1970s and into the 1980s. The odd reach for U.S. exception is also repeated later, when Brownmiller proceeds to describe at length how "institutionalized prostitution" became "routine practice" with the growing U.S. military presence in Vietnam, which was established upon "the unspoken theory of women's bodies as not only a reward of war but as a necessary provision like soda pop and ice cream, to keep our boys healthy and happy." She then points to the French Army's use of "the mobile field brothel, or *Bordel Mobile de Campagne*, stocked with girls imported from Algeria" to illustrate her point: "The tradition of military brothels had been established in Vietnam long before the American presence." Later, Brownmiller glosses over the Korean War with a brief discussion of the U.S. Army court-martial convictions for rape and "assault with intent to commit rape" during a two-year period from 1951 to 1953, which she rather blithely characterizes as "a stopover in Korea during this long march through the history of rape in war."[35] This last passage suggests that the minimal mention of the Japanese military "comfort system" was not so much an oversight but rather an unremarkable-ness produced through the determined historical sweep and supposedly global reach of the book. Put differently, we might understand this inattention as a symptomatic enactment of a geopolitically empowered yet culturally specific U.S. episteme that aspires to document and analyze rape and sexual violence on such a large spatiotemporal scale. The differences among Japan, China, Korea, and Vietnam as well as among French colonial rule, Japanese colonization, Japanese occupation, the Korean War, and the Vietnam War are also rendered unremarkable by this long march.

The omission of the "comfort system" is more striking in Kathleen Barry's *Female Sexual Slavery* (1979), where Asian women are featured prominently in chapter 4: "The Traffic in Sexual Slaves." A section of the chapter on "The Market for Sexual Slaves" is further divided into subsections on "The Military Market," "The Businessmen's and Sailor's Market," and "The Immigrant Laborer's Market." "The Military Market" begins with a reference to a recently prosecuted case of a "military bordello" set up in Corsica for the French Foreign Legion, which Barry connects to the establishment of "official military brothels" around U.S. military encampments during the Vietnam War as described by Brownmiller in *Against Our Will*. Then the chapter proceeds to a brief account of "the booming sex industry created for and by American G.I.s in Thailand" during the Vietnam War. From there, the subsection ends with Barry declaring: "The colonization of women's bodies in war begins with massive raping. It culminates in sexual slavery, as the description of postwar Japan reveals."[36] This is followed immediately by a lengthy passage taken from Matsui's 1975 mimeographed essay, "Why I Oppose *Kisaeng* Tours," which describes the establishment of "army brothels" for U.S. occupation forces by the "Recreation and Amusement Association" (R.A.A.) of the Japanese government. As the passage begins, "After its defeat in World War II, the Japanese government presented Japanese women as 'comfort girls' to the United States Occupation Forces." It ends with "At its height, R.A.A. is said to have employed 70,000 'comfort girls.'"[37] Notably, given the fact that Matsui's essay was being cited here, the Japanese military "comfort system" before and during World War II is *not* addressed in this subsection on the "military market." Indeed, Barry never mentions the earlier forced recruitment of Korean and other Asian "comfort women." Instead, Korean women appear as the primary example in the next section, "The Businessmen's and Sailor's Market," where Barry vaguely plots this unbroken line of continuity between wartime and postwar prostitution:

"The women that men no longer need after a war are often recycled from the military market to major cities where businessmen congregate and sailors dock. *Kisaeng* tourism from Japan to South Korea is the practice that resulted from military markets at the close of World War II."[38] Marshaling the sexual exploitation of Asian women as evidence of the transhistorical and global phenomenon of "female sexual slavery" precluded attention to the substantive differences and distance *between* Korean women and Japanese women, which were foregrounded by the Korean churchwomen, the Ewha students, and Matsui.[39]

A third notable instance of this transpacific effacement of the "comfort system" can be seen in Cynthia Enloe's 1983 book, *Does Khaki Become You?* In the second chapter ("The Militarisation of Prostitution"), Enloe discusses the *Karayukisan*, Japanese women who were "sold into debt bondage to brothel keepers throughout Southeast Asia and North Asia during the period 1890–1945."[40] She then describes how "the Japanese military government in the 1930s and early 1940s continued to *use* prostitution, now of Korean women, as an integral tool of military expansionism." Enloe then quotes this remarkable passage from Michiko Hane's 1982 book, *Peasants, Rebels and Outcastes: The Underside of Modern Japan:* "In every area Japanese conquered during World War II, prostitution was restored. In fact, in 1941, the Japanese authorities actually conscripted Korean women into a corps of 'entertainers' to 'comfort' the Japanese troops in Manchuria. With the beginning of the Pacific War, from 50,000 to 70,000 Korean girls and women were drafted and sent to the front to 'entertain' the Japanese troops." Enloe does not comment on the significance of the specific *intra*-Asian contours of this violence but instead frames it as one of several instances of the sexual violation and exploitation of Asian women as an aggregate. Following a section on Vietnam, Enloe proceeds to discuss how "Asian women are being sexually exploited by a powerful alliance of militarism and tourism.... Most affected are women in the Philippines, Thailand and South Korea, countries in which the militarism/tourism syndrome is especially potent." Later, Enloe points to the protests against Japanese sex tourism, but largely credits the movement to one group in particular: "Japanese feminists have led the way in exposing the role of Japan's government-owned airlines and private tourist bureaus in promoting the prostitution industry—under the guise of tourism—in the Philippines and South Korea. They interpret the Japanese government's encouragement of the overseas sex tours as part of its more general policy of reestablishing Japanese influence in Southeast and North Asia."[41] Enloe here cites a 1980 issue of *Asian Women's Liberation* on "Prostitution tourism." The decolonial analyses and actions of feminists in the Philippines, Thailand, and South Korea in the inter-Asian feminist movement fade out between the homogenization of "Asian women" and the foregrounding of "Japanese feminists."

In pointing to these textual effacements, generic framings, and partial relays of the Japanese "comfort system" into the U.S.-anglophone registers of feminist scholarship in the 1970s and 1980s, my aim is not to correct an error and to supplement the archive with proper notice of Asian women. Rather than grasping "comfort women" as exemplary of both the violation and the belated empowerment of Asian women, I propose to recast it as a multivalent problematic activated and foreclosed by certain modes of expertise, contestation, and nonknowing within a particularly "American" power/knowledge architecture. To clarify, my recasting of Chen's proposal in this chapter title transposes some of the epistemological anxieties and agonies that he diagnoses regarding Asian studies to bear upon the epistemological tendencies and blind spots of U.S. power/knowledge formations. If we start off from "Asian women" as an imperial effect and a multivalent discourse of intra-Asian contestation and transpacific nonknowing, we (those practitioners of U.S. women's, gender, and sexuality studies, American studies, and Asian American studies in the aftermath of their much-touted transnational turns in the 1990s) could and would have to think and think again through "Asian women" as bodies of knowledge and ways of knowing rather than resort to benevolent, nominal inclusion or empathetic identification with *those* bodies in pain. Far from proposing a new subfield of specialization and expertise, "Asian women as method?" is an open-ended question posed from my own distinctively enabled and constrained position as a U.S.-based scholar and teacher of women's, gender, and sexuality studies; American studies; and Asian American studies in an attempt to deimperialize and rework these overlapping interdisciplinary knowledge formations.

THE TRAFFIC IN WOMEN

Here I would frame another epistemological impediment to approaching Asian women as method in how the "traffic in women" has functioned as a persistent, enabling metaphor for sex and gender inequalities in U.S. feminist theorizing. In her influential 1975 essay, "The Traffic in Women: Notes on the 'Political Economy' of Sex," Gayle Rubin surveys an extensive archive of what she alternately refers to as "the ethnographic record" and "the ethnographic literature" to formulate a starkly gendered binary between "exchange partners" and "objects of exchange" in *the* traffic in women. Conceding that some men are also trafficked but as "slaves, and not as men," Rubin argues that "women are transacted . . . simply as women."[42] This stark sex/gender binary presupposes a bounded conceptualization of the local. Indeed, the firm boundaries around distinct cultures make it possible for Rubin to argue for gender identity as *socially* constructed and to map a strict demarcation of masculinity and femininity through a *locally* defined and enforced suppression of certain "personality" traits.[43] The invocation of a dazzling array of ethnographic cases as illustrative evidence tends to obfuscate their synchronic-diachronic divergences, rendering all of them into one flat coextensive grid. When the essay turns to psychoanalysis—is it record or literature?—in order to supplement the disciplinary limits of anthropological knowledges, it makes a sharp move of casting all of the ethnographic archive that Rubin had been working off of into the "dim human past," distinguished from "the more recent data on which Freud bases his theories."[44] This epistemological splitting and hierarchy between description and theory, which is also a temporally staggered demarcation, also implicates feminist theory and U.S. women's and gender studies in the epistemological agonies and anxieties of area studies discussed by Chen.

In a 1994 published conversation with Judith Butler, Rubin notes that "at the time I wrote 'Traffic,' there was still a kind of naive tendency to make general statements about the human condition that most people, including me, would now try to avoid."[45] I would argue for historicizing both the sweeping reach and the blind spots of Rubin's 1975 essay as well as Brownmiller's and Barry's monographs as indicative of how U.S.-anglophone feminist research and theory in the 1970s seized upon new possibilities and expansive horizons of feminist knowledge production in ways that were propelled by a broader but culturally particular epistemological disposition ("a kind of naive tendency to make general statements about the human condition"). Conditioned partly by an older, persistent imperialist cosmology, the universal (and naive) claims to speak about and on behalf of *women* under the rubrics of "traffic in women" and "female sexual slavery" were enabled by the still formidable and not-yet-fully-diminished political, economic, and military power of the U.S. But this feminist will to global authority was enacted amid a changing political economy of globalization and the new international division of labor, which revealed and magnified stark gaps and inequalities between women and even among Asian women. We might also understand the self-reflexive, self-critical epistemological reckonings within U.S. feminist theory in the late 1980s and early 1990s as compelled by Third World and postcolonial feminist interventions but also by the then more evidently diminished political, economic, and military power of the U.S. Placed within these broader shifts of power/knowledge, how might we make different critical sense of the acclaimed and suspect super-visibility of the "comfort women" problematic in the 1990s?

In that regard I would recall Emma Goldman's 1917 essay, "The Traffic in Women," as offering another method. As she makes plain from the beginning, her aim is not to uncover the announced subject in the title but to contest its scandalous visibility and draw attention to what this might be eclipsing. Goldman's angry skepticism is worth reciting at length:

> Our reformers have suddenly made a great discovery—the white slave traffic. The papers are full of these "unheard of conditions" and lawmakers are already planning a new set of laws to check the horror. It is significant that whenever the public mind is to be diverted from a great social wrong, a crusade is inaugurated against indecency, gambling, saloons, etc. . . .
>
> To assume that the recent investigation of the white slave traffic (and, by the way, a very superficial investigation) has discovered anything new, is, to say the least, very foolish. Prostitution has been, and is a widespread evil, yet mankind goes on its business, perfectly indifferent to the sufferings and distress of the victims of prostitution. As indifferent, indeed, as mankind has remained to our industrial system, or to economic prostitution.[46]

Goldman goes on to outline a number of causes for "the trade in women," beginning with "Exploitation, of course; the merciless Moloch of capitalism that fattens on underpaid labor, thus driving thousands of women and girls into prostitution." In addition to the mystification of this "economic factor," Goldman points to the simultaneous suppression of "the sex question": "It is a conceded fact that woman is being reared as a sex commodity, and yet she is kept in absolute ignorance of the meaning and importance of sex. Everything dealing with that subject is suppressed, and persons who attempt to bring light into this terrible darkness are persecuted and thrown into prison." Goldman also cites religion and "the better-than-thou woman" who moralistically disavows the prostitute. Most presciently, she points to the abuses of policing and the courts: "She is not only preyed upon by those who use her, but she is also absolutely at the mercy of every policeman and miserable detective on the beat, the officials at the station house, the authorities in every prison."[47] Earlier in the essay, Goldman predicts that even as the outcry over the "white slave traffic" functions as a distraction from capitalist exploitation, "it will help to create a few more fat political jobs—parasites who stalk about the world as inspectors, investigators, detectives, and so forth." Goldman's essay thus orients critical attention to how the outraged spectacle of female injury and vulnerability does the double work of activating new power/knowledge regimes of investigators, experts, and adjudicators while occluding a much broader analysis of gendered violence, racial inequality, knowledge suppression, and labor exploitation.

In contrast to Goldman's and Rubin's deliberations on the "traffic in women" as ruse and metaphor, there was a concerted feminist attempt to investigate, document, and codify trafficking as an empirical phenomenon in the 1980s and into the 1990s. A new discourse conjoining trafficking and the specified category of "Asian women" gained much traction through the overlapping proliferation of activist forums, social service and philanthropic projects, and global governance maneuvers. A fairly small group of institutionally well-situated U.S.-American feminists wielded remarkable power in shaping the distinct contours of this institutional legibility, but the published record also evinces how a specific cohort of Asian women played active roles in this process. At the NGO Forum of the 1980 Mid-Decade Conference in Copenhagen, Kondo Uri of the Asian Women's Association, along with Kathleen Barry, led sessions on "female sexual slavery, trafficking in women and sex tourism."[48] This was followed up by a flurry of smaller meetings and international conferences, including a Philippines consultation and later an Asian meeting in 1982.[49] As a member of the Asian Women's Association (AWA), Matsui Yayori helped organize the 1983 Global Feminist Workshop to Organize Against Traffic in Women in Rotterdam. The twenty-four invited participants included Sister Mary Soledad Perpiñan of the Manila-based NGO Third World Movement against the Exploitation of Women (TWMAE); Takazato Suzuyo, a former member of AWA and there representing a group identified as "80's Okinawa Association"; Siriporn Skobanek of the Friends of Women (Thailand); and Lin Lap (later Chew), originally from Singapore and then working as the organizer of a Dutch group called Asian Women United, which was seeking "to provide links between European feminists and Asian women in the Netherlands."[50] After attending the Rotterdam workshop, Sister Perpiñan would go on to launch STOP (Stop Trafficking of Filipinas) on November 25, 1983, designated as International Day against the Exploitation of Women. Specific attention to the sexual exploitation of Asian women in military prostitution and sex tourism in Korea, Thailand, and the Philippines appears throughout the published proceedings of the Rotterdam workshop.

This prominent inclusion of Asian women was certainly shaped by and responsive to the inter-Asian feminist network against sexual exploitation, which had already been active for a decade. Elaine Kim's 1984 essay "Sex Tourism in

Asia" cites the published work of Japanese and Filipina scholars and journalists on the subject, demonstrating that a significant body of critical analysis was in circulation in and across Asia and internationally through such journals as *Asian Women's Liberation* and *ISIS International*. The 1983 United Nations report on trafficking explicitly credits the AWA, the TWMAE, and the Asian Confederation of Women's Organisations for effecting "a perceptible reduction in organized sex tourism in that region."[51] In her revised introduction to the 1984 reprint of *Female Sexual Slavery*, Barry similarly exhorts: "Over the past decade, the singularly most effective work against sex tourism and mail-order bride traffic has been launched by Asian feminists, particularly the Asian Women's Association in Japan and the Third World Movement against the Exploitation of Women in the Philippines. Asian and European feminists have begun to act in solidarity to confront these tours."[52] In October 1984 the recently formed International Feminist Network against Female Sexual Slavery organized a consultation on "Female Sexual Slavery and Economic Exploitation: Making Local and Global Connections" in San Francisco, where it was represented by Charlotte Bunch. According to the published report of this consultation, "Over 75 women organizers from nearly as many nongovernmental organizations gathered together at the invitation of the UN Non-Governmental Liaison Service in San Francisco on October 25, 1984, to examine the effects of industrialization and militarism in relation to sex gender exploitation. Since the consultation took place in San Francisco, the Pacific Rim was chosen to be the geographic focus as the economy and cultural life of the West Coast USA is closely tied to this region of the world."[53] This strategic orientation toward the Asia-Pacific makes it all the more baffling that the Japanese military "comfort system" was not taken up as a noteworthy issue in U.S. feminist activism and analysis in the 1980s.

This cannot be attributed to deliberate exclusion or simple omission. As Asian women came to matter as victims of sexual coercion and violence, a specific generational and occupational cluster of Asian women became authorized as especially knowledgeable and empowered agents of research, amelioration, and governance. Although the invention of expertise on specific problems in and through international governance has a longer genealogy reaching back to the League of Nations, it became an especially malleable and useful imprimatur as an international cohort of feminists, led by those from the U.S. in many cases, seized upon new power/knowledge openings. An interweaving account of specific NGO strategies and actions, unfolding world events, academic publications, expert investigations, and general declarations provides a good sense of these mutually generative and sustaining dynamics. In some instances, there would be a direct call and response, but more often the authorizations and reinforcements would be citational, selectively acknowledging the other's work and significant accomplishments while also legitimating one's own work as part of that broader power/knowledge nexus through such citations.

To trace one illustrative instance, on March 18–21, 1986, the UN Division of Human Rights and Peace convened the International Meeting of Experts on the Social and Cultural Causes of Prostitution and Strategies for the Struggle against Procuring and Sexual Exploitation of Women in Madrid. According to the final report of this meeting, there were thirteen "participants from different parts of the world, who had been selected for their competence in the field," including Barry (USA), Takazato (Japan), and Sister Perpiñan (Philippines).[54] In later recounting the significance of the 1986 meeting, Barry would give this account of the effectiveness and pliability of expertise for declaring and legitimating very particular framings of a problem: "It was not until 1986 in a UNESCO meeting in Madrid, I proposed, and the group of experts adopted, the position that we should call for the criminalization of customers.... The sex they are buying is an act of aggression, a violation of women—whether or not they consent. As in the case of all other human rights violations, it is understood that one cannot legitimately consent to the violation of one's human rights."[55] Note how this expert group, made up largely of women, worked to effect the nullification of women's consent. As evident in this passage, there was a differential hierarchy of power/knowledge among this international group of experts. We can see this in the bibliographies that "took stock of research in the social and human sciences," which were commissioned by the Secretariat and compiled in preparation for the meeting.[56] Barry prepared an *Annotated Bibliography on Social and Cultural Causes of Prostitution in the United States and the United Kingdom*, and Sister Perpiñan prepared an *Annotated Bibliography on Prostitution in East and Southeast Asia*. These regional designations, which are already uneven in their geographical and multinational breadth, did not signify an equally accorded distribution of expertise and analytical labor. The bibliography compiled by Barry is much longer, with significant, evaluative summaries of many of the texts through which she could authorize other writers and activists as experts on the topic. We can see this unidirectional authority to authorize others in the introduction to Barry's 1996 book, *The Prostitution of Sexuality*, where she acknowledges how "in the Asian region in particular women have mounted massive campaigns against sex industries and their consumers" and specifically credits Aurora Javate De Dios (Philippines), Yayori Matsui (Japan), Jean D'Cunha (India), and Sigma Huda (Bangladesh), "who have brought deeply felt and powerful analysis to the issue of sexual exploitation of Asian women."[57]

Asian women came to be prominently featured, but they could only stand as particularized yet generalized—"Asian"—cases. This Asianization of female oppression and gendered injury echoed earlier Orientalist tropes, but it was now part of a broader formalization and professionalization of knowledge production within the university and academic publishing and also through the proliferation of NGOs, as well as the working groups, commissions, and special rapporteurs in the United Nations and other international and supranational agencies such as the World Bank. The epistemological and methodological boundaries of these differently enabled *and* constrained modes of knowledge production were effaced through a generic yet highly programmatic invocation of "expertise" across the fields of activist, governmental, and academic discourses. Several early feminist activists would go on to take positions of consultation and authority within various agencies of the United Nations or accredited NGOs whereby they became duly accredited but also invested in the specific protocols and discourses of that authority. Some became experts on "women and ___"; others were relegated to particular regions, single countries, and constituencies. The efforts to make Asian women visible were bound to demonstrate a distinctive *Asian*-ness of a particular generic category or problem, thus instantiating the homogenizing rubrics of "Asia" and "Asian women." Even when these categories were disaggregated into most often national but also regional, ethnic, and religious subcategories, they repeated this double move of distinction and homogenization. The critiques of *intra*-Asian racism and imperialism, deferred decolonization, and uneven capitalist development, which formed the crux of the earlier inter-Asian feminist protests in the 1970s, receded in this discursive transaction.

This may partially explain how the "comfort women" problematic became submerged and then seemingly emerged with such force in the early 1990s. I suggest that the issue captured so much attention and energy in the 1990s for several understudied reasons. First, we should bear in mind what, at first glance, appears to be the distinctively and narrowly *Asian* contours of the "comfort women" case. As one participant/observer has noted, "Never before in Asian history have so many crimes been systematically perpetrated against individual women on such a massive scale and with impunity."[58] Although Dutch women had also been subject to Japanese military rapes and sexual enslavement, most victims were local and indigenous women in Korea, Okinawa, China, Taiwan, the Philippines, Malaysia, Burma, Guam, Papua New Guinea, and Indonesia. Several scholars have pointed to the complicity of the U.S. in the system of Japanese military sexual slavery, the postwar immunity granted to the perpetrators and planners of the system, and the effective silencing of this history, but the "comfort women" presented a case of *nonwhite* and *non-U.S.* abuse and exploitation of Asian women. Therefore, it did not initially trouble the U.S.-centric focalization of human rights and women's rights as human rights. Though not minimizing the scale of Japanese state responsibility, the guilt of Japanese military officers, soldiers, and civilians in the establishment and operation of the "comfort stations," and the knowing complicity of many others both during and after the war, it is important to be critical of the racism that subtended a certain strain of shock and outrage about the "comfort system" as the expression of a uniquely Japanese barbarism.[59] To that would be added the culturalist explanation of Korean Confucianism and its low valuation of girls and women and overattachment to female chastity and marital reproduction. In short, it was a distinctly *Asian* problem.

Second, I would argue that the predominant focus on sexual violation in a distant past deflected critical attention from contemporary casualties of political economic power and inequality across Asia and globally as well as the ongoing problem of gendered labor exploitation. In her excellent overview of the representation of sexual violence against women by mainstream human rights groups in the 1990s, Alice M. Miller underscores how "the difficulty of bringing attention to interrelated rights (health-oriented protections, enabling conditions of labor, political equality for women, and so on) while telling stories of sexual harm is painfully clear." As an illustrative example, Miller points to how "the more simplified version of 'sexual slavery' told in early Women's Rights/Human Rights Watch (HRW) reports on trafficking in Asia have garnered and retained more public attention than the far-more-nuanced 2000 HRW report addressing labor rights, racism, violence, and immigration law in the 'traffic' of Thai women to Japan." Noting how anti-trafficking projects have oscillated between "a labor/slavery model" and "a VAW paradigm," Miller concludes that "today, the VAW model dominates and, interestingly, includes the language of sexual exploitation at the same time."[60] I would further add that *exploitation* was dislodged from labor in its sexual amplification.

A third reason for the super-visibility of the issue was the coincidence of its revelation with significant demographic and discursive shifts in U.S. universities and culture industries. The early 1990s was a key transitional moment in the admission and training of Asian American and Korean American students, and the related growth of Asian American studies. From the outset of its international publicity in 1991, the issue was energetically taken up by scholars across several academic disciplines as well as newer interdisciplinary fields, which were undergoing expansion, formalization, and professionalization: women's and gender studies, American studies, Asian studies, Asian

American studies, and postcolonial studies. There was also a cohort of Asian American students who benefited from limited openings in MFA programs of creative writing, visual arts, and film production, and who would produce novels, artworks, videos, and films to be analyzed and written about by a cohort comprised largely of Asian American scholars. Asian American and specifically Korean American *women* were especially empathetic and impassioned agents in remembering and representing the "comfort women" issue in the United States. In September 30–October 2, 1996, an international conference titled, "The 'Comfort Women' of World War II: Legacy and Lessons," was convened at Georgetown University, which later resulted in the publication of a book, *Legacies of the Comfort Women of World War II*, edited by Margaret Stetz and Bonnie B. C. Oh. Pointing to the prominent participation of Asian American women at this gathering, Pamela Thoma asserted in a 2000 essay that "the conference offers an opportunity to recognize and analyze Asian American transnational feminist cultural activism" and went so far as to characterize it as an "autobiographical text of Asian American transnational feminism."[61]

The proliferation of knowledge production around "comfort women" in the United States could thus be marshaled to confirm and affirm a range of other "American" identity categories. By 2002, the remarkable academic productivity led Stetz to note that "the body of material . . . around 'comfort women' issues has grown so rapidly, over just the last decade, that we can now speak of there being a 'comfort women's literature,' in the same way that we refer to a 'Holocaust literature.'" She continues: "Its size and scope suggest that the day is not far off when we may also be able to talk of 'Comfort Women' Studies as an academic subject. This would institute a formal means to acknowledge the continuing importance of the women themselves and the significance of their experiences; it would also mirror the development of Holocaust Studies programs at many universities." Such prognosis presumes that formalization as "an academic subject" is both a desired goal and reparative process. But for whom? Stetz ends the essay by emphasizing the importance of feminism and "feminist perspectives" in this emerging "'Comfort Women' Studies": "The majority of these activist-artists so far have been Asian or Asian-American, including a number of Japanese women, giving lie to the myth of feminism as a white Western phenomenon, interested only in middle-class concerns."[62] Thus, the very fact of Asian and Asian American women's active and extensive participation could function to redeem *feminism* from the charges of racism, imperialism, and class bias, which had been powerfully and persistently put forth in the 1980s and into the 1990s. By rendering the U.S. academy as the expansive repository of knowledge *about* and also *by* multiply disenfranchised subjects, the activation and institutionalization of "comfort women" studies also pitched the United States as the enabling locus of such committed remembering and representation by variously marginalized *American* subjects.

TROUBLING EMPATHY AND AUTHORITY

Against the wishful telescoping of knowledge to justice and justice to even better knowledge, I would underscore the contingency and indeed the fragility of so much that was so assiduously exposed, researched, documented, and circulated in the 1990s and into the 2000s. Let me point to two especially troubling later developments. In a press conference on March 2, 2007, recently elected Japanese Prime Minister Shinzo Abe declared that "there is no evidence to prove there was coercion, nothing to support it."[63] His statement was part of a concerted effort by Japanese conservatives to retract and revise what is known as the 1993 Kono Statement, which had admitted direct Japanese military involvement in the establishment of the comfort stations. Since 1997, Abe had worked actively in the Japan Society for Textbook Reform, which has contested the inclusion of the "comfort system" in Japanese textbooks and education. As Abe added, "So, in respect to this declaration, you have to keep in mind that things have changed greatly." This immediately provoked renewed protests and widespread international criticism, including a *New York Times* editorial titled "No Comfort." Nevertheless, on March 16, 2007, Abe's position was "put into a written statement and endorsed by the cabinet as the government's official position."[64]

Then again in 2015, in an interview with the *Washington Post*, which was to serve as a preview of his impending visit to the U.S. capital and his historic address to the full Congress in April, Abe ventured a more muted and coy denial through a generic resignification and universalization: "On the question of comfort women, when my thought goes to these people, who have been victimized by human trafficking and gone through immeasurable pain and suffering beyond description, my heart aches." As the article then explained, "An aide said this was the first time he had publicly referred to 'trafficking' in connection with the women."[65] It is not a stretch to infer that the gender-neutral locutions of "human trafficking" and "these people" were meant to align the "comfort women" case as just one of many instances of a widely touted global problem. If recognition as and inclusion under the "human" was a belated and hard-earned achievement for Asian women, it could also be deployed as a generic, equivocal cover. Abe's denials and obfuscations demonstrate the impermanence and insubstantiality of "official" admissions and apologies.

The second disconcerting development for me was the 2008 publication of *The Comfort Women: Sexual Violence and Postcolonial Memory in Korea and Japan* by C. Sarah Soh, who had previously published twenty-two (!) articles and essays on the subject between 1996 and 2008. Soh asserts her singular authority on the subject in two troubling ways. First, she invokes her disciplinary training to offer what she characterizes as "a critical anthropological perspective on the comfort women phenomenon." Citing the "felicitous" inspiration of James Peacock's explanation of anthropology's method of casting a "harsh light" with a "soft focus" on its objects of study, Soh summarizes this "anthropological worldview as having two complementary elements: a concern with the basic reality of the human condition and a methodological holism that would enable a comprehensive understanding of that condition." Soh applies this disciplinary method to "examine critically the dominant understanding of the comfort women as 'sex slaves' and a war crimes issue, which I refer to in this work as a 'paradigmatic story.'" She goes on later to refer to this alternately as the "activists' paradigmatic story," "the master narrative, or the feminist humanitarian paradigmatic story," and "the transnationally dominant humanitarian paradigmatic story of the comfort women." Finally, in an appendix titled "Doing 'Expatriate' Ethnography," Soh further distinguishes her "methodological stance" from this constricted activist narrative: "I have situated myself as a concerned observer rather than an active participant in the comfort women redress movement in order that I may maintain a reasonably objective scholarly position."[66]

Such disciplinarily standard aspirations to realism, holism, and objectivity are brought into marked confrontation with a repeated will to epistemological distinction. Noting that she "will not dwell on the horrid degradation of the women's lives as comfort women per se," Soh explains that "this approach is in stark contrast to the existing English-language literature, which defines the Japanese comfort system as sexual slavery and refers to the personal ordeals suffered by individual women as evidence of Japan's war crimes."[67] This was a marked departure from many of Soh's own earlier publications, which characterized the "comfort system" as sexual slavery.[68] Soh further distinguishes her book from the many books already published on the subject by 2008 as "the first book-length treatment in any language to provide an anthropological interpretation" and then offers this as her unique analytical contribution: "Korea's comfort women embody what I call 'gendered structural violence' in the context of patriarchal colonialism."[69] This transfiguration of "Korea's comfort women" demonstrates the odd scholarly compulsion to label the most unfathomable singularities of history as one's own invented category even as that very bid toward methodological and analytical self-distinction can call up only a string of worn-out words and generic phrases. Such proprietary marking must also beckon the performative authority of disciplined knowledge production, but, in doing so, the knowing subject betrays the epistemological constraints of those methods and their distance from the object of knowledge.

How might we make critical sense of the Japanese leader's belatedly aching heart regarding the "immeasurable pain and suffering beyond description" alongside and against the Korean American expatriate scholar's late refusal to "dwell on the horrid degradation of the women's lives" in a reach for anthropological objectivity? If the first posits the inadequacy of language and the impossibility of accessing the truth, the second steers away from the problem of over- and underrepresentation through a reconsolidation of disciplinary expertise. Against such reach for political, economic, and epistemological enclosure, I propose that the drawn-out negotiations, multiple remediations, surprising devolutions, bold reversals, and new realignments around the "comfort women" problematic constitute an instructive and unruly archive for *thinking* Asian women as method. How might the overlaying and the mismatch between "Asian women" and "comfort women" be reframed in terms of broader vexing questions of nomination, knowledge production, and justice?

Both the historical atrocity and contemporary redress movements clarify the nonunity of the category of "Asian women" and its noncorrespondence to "women in Asia." The predominantly used English terms *comfort woman* and *comfort women* are translations of the Japanese *ianfu* and the Korean *wianbu*. In addition to the patently misleading implications of comfort-*giving* in *ian-*, the character-*fu* also carries the charge of bride or wife. The longer term, "military comfort women" (*jugun ianfu*), specifies this as a militarist formation, but it has been criticized because it "has the connotation of 'following' (*ju* in Japanese, *chong* in Korean) the military (*gun*) due to the nature of one's occupation—such as nurse, journalist, or photographer—and thus gives the mistaken impression of the 'comfort women' as *voluntary* camp followers."[70] Interestingly, Soh points out that "Japanese ultranationalists are also opposed to the use of [*jugun*] . . . due to its connotation of *official* affiliation with the military."[71] The term is often attributed to Senda Kako's 1973 book *Jugun Ianfu*, but Soh points out that Korean *zainichi* scholar Kim Il-myon deployed it in an earlier 1971 article and later in his 1976 book, *Tenno no Guntai to Chosenjin Ianfu* (*The Emperor's Forces and the Korean Comfort Women*). Kim's moniker of *chosenjin ianfu* emphasizes the women's Korean ethnicity. Another noteworthy modification of *ianfu/wianbu* appeared in a July 1992 South Korean "government interim report," which used the term *ilchae kunde wianbu* (military comfort women under Japanese colonial rule). Pointing out that *kundae* "simply refers to the military without the connotation of following," Soh further explains that the periodizing modifier of *ilche* ("under Japanese colonialism") was intended to distinguish these women from the Korean women sex workers for the U.S. military who were and are also referred to in Korean as *wianbu*.[72]

The most common Korean term, *Chongshindae* ("corps volunteering their bodies" or "volunteer corps"), which is also transliterated into English as *Jungshindae*, was used in the longer name of the Korean Council, *Hanguk Chongshindae Munje Taechaek Hyobuihoe*. Characterizing *Chongshindae* as a "wartime fascist term," Soh cites Kang Man-kil (1997), who traced its usage in Korea back to 1941 and specifically the *Yoja Chongshindae* Law (Women's Volunteer Corps Law) of 1944. In a 2000 publication, Soh suggests that the Korean Council chose *Chongshindae* because its two cofounders, Yun Chong-ok and Lee Hyochae, had both lived through the colonial period and remembered being personally affected by these laws. Pointing out that some inductees in the *Chongshindae* "performed only manual labor and no sexual labor," Soh argues that "the Korean usage of the term *Chongshindae* to refer to 'comfort women' thus appears to be a political strategy on the part of activists, used to highlight the deceptive and/or coercive methods that had been used in the recruitment of comfort women in colonial Korea."[73] Secondly, Soh adds, *Chongshindae* "symbolically distinguishes wartime comfort women from contemporary *wianbu* serving the American military in Korea . . . [and] functions as a considerate euphemism born out of cultural sensitivity for the survivors in order to avoid the negative image of prostitutes evoked by the term *wianbu*." This aversion to association with contemporary Korean military sex workers who are denigrated as "willing whores" demonstrates the intractable heterogeneities and ideological fissures even among one specific national node of Asian women.

The challenge of proper naming was further amplified and exacerbated as the issue began to garner international attention in the early 1990s. There has been a wide range of English translations and nominations: "comfort girls" and "comfort women" but also "prostitutes," "sexual services," and "brothels." Many early English-language essays and books duly drew attention to the problem of terminology, and "comfort women" soon became suspect, especially after the transnational coalition of survivors and activists decided in 1994 to use "military sexual slavery" as the accurate and preferred term. In a 1994 law journal article, Karen Parker and Jennifer F. Chew propose several preferred alternatives: "women and girls forced into sexual slavery," "sex slaves," and "war-rape victims," explaining that the last term was also the one used by many claimants.[74] An early and still common practice has been to place "comfort women" in quotation marks. As Kazuko Watanabe notes in her 1994 essay, "the use of the term 'comfort women' is obviously itself a travesty, and it would certainly be more accurate to refer to women who did this work as 'enforced military sex laborers or slaves,'" but she elected to retain the term because "this remains the way they are most commonly referred to."[75] She adds that "I would prefer to at least encase the term in quotes to register my disapproval of it, but I have not done so because that would be cumbersome if it were done throughout the article." Several years later, in a 1998 United Nations report, Special Rapporteur Gay J. McDougall continues to use "comfort women" but explains differently: "The term has obvious derogatory connotations and is used solely in its historical context as the term assigned to this particular atrocity. In many ways, the unfortunate choice of such a euphemistic term to describe the crime suggests the extent to which the international community as a whole, and the Government of Japan, in particular, has sought to minimize the nature of the violations."[76] A most notable retention and reification of the term occurs in the 2000 English edition of Yoshimi Yoshiaki's book, where the Japanese title, *Jugun ianfu*, was shortened to *Comfort Women* and accompanied by the subtitle *Sexual Slavery in the Japanese Military during World War II*. In her "Translator's Introduction," Suzanne O'Brien explains that "I place the terms 'comfort women' and 'comfort station' in quotation marks on first use to emphasize the fact that these terms themselves played a role in concealing and normalizing the violence used against these women." Acknowledging that "many survivors explicitly reject the term 'comfort woman,'" O'Brien continues: "Here I generally use 'survivor' and 'victim' interchangeably to refer to women who were forced to serve as comfort women. I've retained the use of 'comfort women' to describe wartime practices and attitudes that perpetuate wartime views of the women."[77]

This case foregrounds a tension between historical accuracy and political sympathy. In the first instance, it makes sense, as McDougall does, to retain the English translation of the Japanese terms: "comfort women" (*ianfu*) and "comfort stations" (*ianjo*). However, to do so would be to disregard the expressed and persistent demands for its renaming as "military sexual slavery" by survivors and activists from as early as 1993. Their antipathy to the term has been justified and intensified by those seeking to deny or minimize the atrocities of the Japanese military "comfort system," especially on the question of whether the girls and women were forcefully and deceptively recruited, who insistently deploy "comfort women" and use it alternately with *prostitutes*. I would argue that the still hesitant yet most prevalent resort to using "comfort women" implicates the vexed terms and conditions of publicity, propriety, and efficacy in a multiply mediated and ever-mutating transnational public sphere. It marks the problem of nomination and translation across multiple languages but also under the hegemony of English as the language of international news, activism, governance, and knowledge production. As I will show in chapter 3, even "military sexual slavery" bears its own problematic historical baggage and political complications. The repeated compulsion to deploy but to distance oneself from "comfort women" reminds anew that the naming of any particular atrocity or crime, in a transnational frame, risks focalizing certain subjects at the expense of derogating others. The qualified and recursive invocation of "comfort women" indicts the ongoing irresolution of the issue after and perhaps *as a result* of its energetic transnational circulation.

Even as the issue brought together a dynamic activist network both regionally and globally, the redress movement has also foregrounded intractable differences and disagreements among Asian women survivors and activists. In her important 1993 essay on the beginnings of the redress movement, Alice Yun Chai partially attributes the lack of earlier feminist attention to the issue to the "racism" or "the sense of racial or ethnic superiority on the part of Japanese women."[78] In an affectionate yet sober remembrance of Matsui Yayori written in 2003, Yun Chung-ok pointed to Matsui's reluctance to consider the imperial/racist aspects of the "comfort system": "It was her understanding of the Japanese military sexual slavery as the outcome of the patriarchal system only. She could not accept the argument asserted by Korea as the representative of the victimized countries: the Japanese military sexual slavery was not only gender discrimination but also segregation of Asian peoples."[79] The *zainichi* feminist scholar Kim Puja disputes Yun's characterization of Matsui.[80] If the "comfort women" problematic has been a forceful yet contested instance of Japanese "deimperialization" even within the inter-Asian feminist network, it has also brought out the atrocity of South Korean soldiers' rape of Vietnamese women during the Vietnam War and thereby called on Korean women to reckon with South Korea's own history as perpetrators of brutal sexual violence during wartime and sub-imperial sexual exploitation of other Asian women.[81] This Korean "deimperialization" is still unfolding, and also implicates the United States within a much longer historical arc of selective attentiveness to and targeted exploitation of and violence toward Asian women in the twentieth century, which warrants its own distinctive deimperialization. It is my hope that both critical reckonings might proceed differently from the recursive denials and equivocations but also the persistent binaries and vehement judgments that we have endured thus far.

In closing, I want to recall that the word *munje* (problem or dilemma) constitutes the full name of the Korean Council, *Hanguk Chongshindae Munje Taechaek Hyobuihoe*. That this key term has dropped out in the conventional English translation of the organizational name seems particularly inexplicable and inopportune, given that both the past atrocity and the ongoing struggle for justice pose multiple problems: of nomination, of identification, of representation, and of knowledge production. In a 2003 article in a special issue of the *Journal of Asian American Studies*, Kandice Chuh judiciously proposed a critical rethinking of "comfort woman" whereby it would be "dislodged from functioning as an identity or as a description of a person, and reconstituted as a reference to multiple ideological and institutional discursive practices that materialize bodies—that make bodies matter, both literally and figuratively—in various ways."[82] As a recurring and often exemplary but also disparately positioned case across different frames of intelligibility, documentation, and management, the "comfort women" problematic exposes and troubles the political and epistemological enclosures of "Asian women." But I must clarify that the gambit of Asian women as method is not pitched toward rendering "comfort women" or "Asian women" as an especially capacious and portable methodological resource. Rather, it is meant to account for my own geographical, linguistic, and institutional boundedness as an interested reader of a selectively chosen range of *entextualizations* of Asian women. Almost all the texts I draw from and try to make critical sense of are English-language publications and reports that are readily available to U.S.-based researchers. I make no efforts or claims to referencing the vast amount of scholarship, archival documents, laws, policies, and NGO-produced texts that exists and ever proliferates about Asian women in other languages and sites. In committing myself to the partial assembly and reshuffling of a diverse and ever-expanding body of texts and documents that traffic in Asian women, each chapter will run up against this question: how far into the reading of a given area of specialization and expertise does it become possible to make critical sense of a discursive field and to pose questions? An entire monograph could be spun out of each chapter, but I have chosen to highlight the expansive significance of Asian women through multidirectional connections and untried juxtapositions. In lieu of tidy conclusions or righteous pronouncements, we must proceed with this ineffable condition of a responsibility to read, probe, and wonder without the guarantees of the wishful and willful *telos* of identification-knowledge-justice.

TRAFFIC IN WOMEN

There has long been a persistent association of trafficking with Asian women, Asian culture, and the Asian region, even as these three categorizations could never be made to line up neatly with one another. This conjoined gendering-culturalization-regionalization confuses and confounds two adjacent but distinguishable phenomena: "traffic in Asian women" and "traffic in women in Asia." Beginning with the campaign against "white slavery" in the nineteenth century, the work of anti-trafficking has always been scored by a racializing and racist fault line between white and nonwhite women, which has betrayed its internationalist and globalist claims. I would argue that beyond being expressions of the racialist and racist worldview of individual anti-trafficking subjects, these conceptual, methodological, and rhetorical habits enact the paradoxical hyper-visibility *and* unknowability of the "traffic in women." As one of the most hyperbolized and enduring subjects of journalistic exposés, academic scholarship, government investigations, and international relations, the subject bears an immense and prolific archive of documentation and analysis. However, as activists, policy makers, and academic experts have repeatedly pointed out, the clandestine, coercive, dispersed, and mobile aspects of trafficking resist unequivocal verification and clear representation. The Asianization of both trafficking and anti-trafficking circumvents this unknowability through an assured cultural-regional delineation.

There was a notable resurgence of the Asianization of the "traffic in women" in the 1990s across news media, scholarship, and policy documents. A January 11, 1998, article in the *New York Times* titled "Trafficker's New Cargo: Naïve New Slavic Women," begins with this easy, commonsense declaration: "The international bazaar for women is hardly new, of course. Asians have been its basic commodity for decades." In their introduction to the 1997 edited collection *Sites of Desire, Economies of Pleasure: Sexualities in Asia and the Pacific,* Lenore Manderson and Margaret Jolly note, "The traffic in women has been a particular feature of colonial and postcolonial Southeast Asia, and to a much lesser extent, of the ports, commercial and administrative centers of the Pacific."[1] Andrea Marie Bertone reaches even further back in time and declares, "Prostitution has existed for thousands of years in many different societies. However, South and Southeast Asia are one of the original areas of the world where sexualized work and sex trafficking developed."[2] One of the most assured Asianizations appears in Louise Brown's monograph, *Sex Slaves: The Trafficking of Women in Asia,* where she confidently asserts, "In Asia there is plenty of opportunity for the creation and maintenance of systems of sexual slavery because there are such massive differences between the rich and poor and because Asia is the grim home to some of the worst gender discrimination on earth." She adds, "Female sexual slavery is found everywhere. Asia, however, is worthy of special attention because it is here that the industry and trafficking networks are most sophisticated and well-developed."[3]

This Asianization of the traffic in women echoed older Orientalist stereotypes but must also be distinguished in relation to several significant social, economic, and political shifts in the 1990s, including the emergence of a cohort of Asian women as empowered subjects of anti-trafficking within the transnational movement for women's rights as human rights. On April 2–4, 1993, two months before the global UN meeting in Vienna, the Human Rights Conference on the Trafficking of Asian Women brought together more than one hundred participants representing seventeen countries in Quezon City, Philippines. As Aurora Javate de Dios, one of the conference organizers, pro-

52 Chapter 2

claimed, "Trafficking in Asian women has, in the past few years, become a crisis of global dimensions."[4] The proceedings of that conference, published under the title *Women Empowering Women,* include the Keynote Address by Kathleen Barry, an introduction titled "The Global Trafficking in Asian Women" authored by de Dios, and separate country and region reports for the Philippines, Southeast Asia, and South Asia. A section on "Receiving Countries" includes an essay by Matsui Yayori titled "Trafficking in Women and Prostitution in Japan" and another essay titled *"Jugun Ianfu, Karayuki, Japayuki:* A Continuity in Commodification," by Liza Go, which connects the Japanese military "comfort system" in World War II to the contemporary migration of Filipinas and Thai women to Japan, and traces both back to the earlier history of Japanese women who migrated to work in brothels in China and Southeast Asia in the nineteenth century. As Cecelia Hoffman of the Philippine Organizing Team acclaimed in the foreword, this conference marked a new stage in the maturation of Asian women as agents of anti-trafficking: "Women from the Asia Pacific are addressing the issues of trafficking in women and prostitution as a human rights crisis currently affecting millions of women in the region." Noting that the conference was being "recognized as a satellite meeting in Asia" of the upcoming UN World Conference on Human Rights in Vienna, Hoffman proudly noted that the gathering "constitutes a major contribution of the Asia-Pacific region to the international discourse on women's human rights."[5] Hoffman's heralding of Asian women's central, coeval participation in anti-trafficking contrasts markedly with Kathleen Barry's peculiar emplotment of the history of women's sexual exploitation and feminist thinking around the topic in her Keynote Address at the conference:

> In prostitution, men buy not a human being but a body that performs as woman and women are reduced to the most harmful, damaging racist and sexist concepts of women. Western men, particularly more "liberal" ones often require from Western women an enactment that is sexually active and responsive as well as emotionally engaged. By contrast, traditional Western men and Asian men, may require of Asian prostituted women sexual behavior that is enacted with passivity, submissiveness, and slavishness.
>
> Racism, like sexual exploitation, is the foundation of the prostitution industry. Customer demand includes specification of color and cultural characteristics. They are advertised and sold. To Westerners an Asian woman is selling not only a "sexed" body, but a "colored" one as well—and it is from her Asian features and racial characteristics that she must

dissociate as that, too, is part of herself that men buy for sex. And so it goes through different cultures; whatever the cultural context, prostitution in the sex exchange itself invokes and plays out the most reactionary racist and sexist stereotypes while segmenting women into their buyable parts.[6]

Note how color, race, and culture are readily collapsed. Barry's authoritative characterization of the peculiarly named category of "Asian prostituted women," which is deployed interchangeably here with the generic, individual "an Asian woman," demonstrates how the Asianization of the "traffic in women" has long been co-constituted and consolidated through the Asianization of *anti*-trafficking endeavors. Asianization refers to multiple and contradictory discursive moves that range from the projection of a specific bounded territory called "Asia" to the racialization of "Asians" and "Asian women" as distinctively nonwhite or "colored" bodies and non-Western populations to the projection of a monolithic "Asian culture" that wields oppressive force over "Asian women" in and across Asia but also beyond through divergent transnational migrations and diasporas.

Varying constellations of Asian women and their affiliated NGOs played active and even prominent roles in organizing and aiding these anti-trafficking endeavors. Aurora Javate de Dios and some of the other participants in the 1993 Quezon City conference would go on to establish a region-specific satellite of the Coalition against Trafficking in Women (CATW), the NGO that Barry had cofounded in 1988. The mission of this CATW-Asia Pacific network was "to better coordinate information and responses to trafficking of Asian women, and to address the issues with a strong and united voice."[7] As further evidence of this intensive focalization around Asia and Asian women in the 1990s, the Foundation for Women in Bangkok became the host of an alternative anti-trafficking NGO, the Global Alliance against the Traffic in Women (GAATW) in 1994. Both CATW-Asia Pacific and GAATW would go on to conduct and publish several studies focused on the region. In March 1994 the Asian Women's Human Rights Council (AWHRC) organized the Asian Tribunal and International Public Hearing on Traffic in Asian Women and War Crimes against Asian Women, which presented testimony by seventeen women from eleven nations. As these NGO efforts drew increasing attention to the issue, more international funding became available to conduct subregional and nationally focused studies and to publish these findings and recommendations.

By the second half of the 1990s, with the proliferation of more and more studies, many different stakeholders became engaged in the subject of "traffic in Asian women," now approached as a real empirical phenomenon with multiple policy consequences for several overlapping jurisdictions and widely dispersed populations. I have already pointed in the introduction to the multiple reports published by Human Rights Watch in the 1990s. The International Organization of Migration (IOM) also became actively involved in jointly producing or funding several reports. In March 1997 the IOM collaborated with the GAATW and the Cambodian Women's Development Association to produce *Two Reports on the Situation of Women and Children Trafficked from Cambodia and Vietnam to Thailand*. The first report was focused on "Cambodian and Vietnamese sex workers along the Thai-Cambodian border," and the second addressed "Cambodian and Vietnamese women and children in detention for illegal entry into Thailand." One of the three stated purposes of these investigations was "to assess whether, and in what way, IOM's return and reintegration program for trafficked women and children can be applied to assist the women trafficked to the Thai-Cambodian border."[8] Then, in October 1997, the IOM, along with the Center for Advanced Study, published *Trafficking of Cambodian Women and Children to Thailand*.[9] In addition to these studies focused on Cambodia and Thailand, the IOM also sponsored studies in 1997 on the trafficking of women and children in central and southern Vietnam and Philippine women to Japan. These findings would be compiled in a larger 1999 IOM publication titled *Paths of Exploitation: Studies on the Trafficking of Women and Children between Cambodia, Thailand and Vietnam*.

By the end of the twentieth century, "traffic in women" became a widely recognized field of expertise and mutually reinforcing citational archive for a select group of cosmopolitan subjects, including a group of Asian women who became authorized agents of international knowledge production and policy recommendation about the "traffic in Asian women." The proliferation of varying and often contested approaches to documenting its local and regional manifestations foregrounded and compounded the abiding paradox of trafficking's hypervisibility/unknowability. In turn, there was a concerted drive to authorize, standardize, and professionalize particular methods of investigating and documenting the "traffic in women." Is it more effective and even necessary to disaggregate "traffic in *women*" to smaller sub-groups of women and to specific regions and locations? Are some methods of investigation and documentation better than others? Does it matter who does the work of investigation, documentation, and intervention? Are Asian women more liable to produce reliable and actionable knowledges about the "traffic in Asian women"? This chapter will attempt to consider these questions by reaching back to an early twentieth-century inquiry into the "traffic in women" by the League of Nations during the interwar period. This attempt to constitute the "traffic in women" as an actionable field of "international cooperation" and extranational intervention proceeded through introducing what was hailed as an innovative method of multinational, site-specific "on-the-spot" investigations by specially authorized agents who could better discern the objective facts of the problem. This social-scientific mode of investigation and knowledge production was a distinctively U.S.-American formation, which was importantly shaped by economic-philanthropic power and its myopic vision of management, which imposed the racialist preoccupations of an older social hygiene movement in the U.S. onto a newly—and vertically—integrated architecture of global governance. The two published reports of this international inquiry inscribed a clear partitioning and demotion of Asian women from the "traffic in women."

THE LEAGUE OF NATIONS

The work of anti-trafficking in the League of Nations during the interwar period served as an important historical and institutional pivot between the imperial regimes carried over from the nineteenth century and the post–World War II emergence of newly decolonized countries and the global governance regime associated with the United Nations. In the aftermath of World War I, the "traffic in women" occasioned a compelling rationale and platform for the coming together of nations with divergent interests, shifting borders, and unequal resources. From its inception, the League of Nations was engaged with addressing the traffic as an urgent and indisputably *international* problem. Article 23c of its 1919 Covenant thus "entrusted the League with the general supervision over the execution of agreements with regard to the traffic in women and children."[10] On December 15, 1920, the Assembly of the League of Nations adopted several linked resolutions. In addition to urging those governments that had signed the earlier 1904 agreement and the 1910 Convention for the Suppression of White Slave Traffic to put them into operation "immediately," another resolution called on the league council to convene an international conference, which would be charged with the "task of endeavouring to harmonise the opinions of the different Governments in order that common action may be taken."[11] Toward that end, the assembly authorized the Secretariat to issue a questionnaire to all member states, which inquired about domestic laws regarding trafficking, the penalties prescribed for specific cases, and statistics of prosecutions and convictions. From June 30 to July 1, 1921, the league convened an International Conference on the Traffic in Women and Children in Geneva.

Calibrating the surveillance of women's cross-border movements among states and nongovernmental organizations was crucial to the incipient conceptualization and enactment of "international co-operation." In his opening speech at the 1921 Geneva conference, Belgian Foreign Minister Paul Hymans heralded the occasion: "Hitherto treaties of peace have only dealt with questions of frontiers, indemnities and commercial and financial interests. For the first time in the history of humanity other interests are therein included and among them the dignity of human labor and the respect for women and children."[12] In the spirit of this "new internationalism," it was suggested that the term *traffic in women and children* replace *white slavery*, thereby "making it clear that measures adopted should be applied to all races alike."[13] Such universalizing platitudes covered over the imperialist genealogy, with its persistent racial demarcations and national interests, of the discriminating and targeted surveillance of women's bodies, sexuality, work, and migration. In principle, the framing of the "traffic in women" as a global human problem necessitating international cooperation and coordination rendered the member states and their varied laws and policies regarding sex work, labor, age of consent, emigration, and immigration as the objects of a new supranational regime of surveillance, judgment, and proper accreditation. Thus, it held out the potential of clarifying the uneven sexual economies and topographies that had been carved out by racism, patriarchy, and competing empires. In practice, however, even after the move to replace *white slave traffic* with the more neutral and inclusive *traffic in women*, a distinction continued to separate "white women" and their racial others, including Asian women. Such persistent racial obsessions and racist blind spots evinced the limits of the league's attempts to coordinate international policy and action against the "traffic in women" by implementing what were deemed as newly effective modes of undercover surveillance and expert data gathering.

The International Conference on the Traffic in Women and Children concluded with the recommendation that each member nation submit annual reports on the traffic in their territories as well as the nation's domestic anti-trafficking efforts. The League of Nations thus took on the role of an international clearinghouse. It also passed a new, more expansive International Convention for the Suppression of the Traffic in Women and Children in September 1921, which increased the age of consent for women engaged in prostitution from twenty to twenty-one and thereby increased the numbers of women subject to surveillance and data gathering. The league also appointed a permanent Advisory

Committee on the Traffic of Women and Children, comprising nine national "delegates" and five "assessors," each representing an international voluntary organization, which were precursors to contemporary NGOs. Later, the league would sponsor its own official investigation of the traffic, which proceeded in two stages and resulted in two separate publications. The first, titled *Report of the Special Body of Experts on Traffic in Women and Children: Enquiry Into the International Organisation of, and Certain Routes Followed by, the Traffic Between Various Countries of Europe, North Africa, North America, South America and Central America* (hereafter referred to as the 1927 Report), was published in 1927 and comprised 270 pages. The second report, titled *Enquiry into Traffic in Women and Children in the East*, was published five years later and was much longer, at 556 pages.

These reports conferred both expert confirmation and empirical validation of the "traffic in women." Countering Judith Walkowitz's 1980 argument that "'white slavery' and 'child prostitution scandals' in late nineteenth century Britain had all the symptoms of a cultural paranoia," Barbara Metzger asserts that "investigations by the League of Nations later confirmed the existence of trafficking as a long-standing phenomenon."[14] Paul Knepper has distinguished these inquiries as not only "the first worldwide study of human trafficking" but also "the first ever social scientific study of a global social problem."[15] The 1927 Report was notable for inaugurating the use of a traveling commission of specially trained "experts" who visited 112 cities and districts across 28 countries to conduct "on-the-spot" inquiries. In addition to producing first-person observations of local conditions, they interviewed more than 6,500 individuals, including government officials, law enforcement officers, and anti-trafficking voluntary associations in these far-flung locations. The commission also relied on undercover investigations by specially contracted agents and sometimes met directly with members of the "underworld," including procurers, madams, and prostitutes in order to uncover "facts" that might be hidden or misrepresented by official statistics and national reports. The 1927 Report was held up at the time as having "revolutionized League methods in the investigation of social problems."[16] The exemplary method and authority of these reports would be later affirmed when the United Nations took up the subject after World War II.

Three specific aspects of these two reports compromise the claims to both their international coverage and empirical accuracy. First, both reports were unabashedly concerned with the fate of *white* women. The 1932 inquiry is especially striking on this point in its clear demarcation of "Traffic in Occidental Women in Asia" and "Traffic in Asian Women" and its undisguised alarm about the sexual fate of Russian women refugees in China. This demonstrates

58 Chapter 2

how the imperialist, racist, and nationalist foundations of early British state regulation of and voluntary vigilance against prostitution from the nineteenth century preconditioned the later anti-trafficking work of the League of Nations. Second, there was a specifically American genealogy of the 1927 Report's use of "on-the-spot" and "undercover" investigations, which had been deployed earlier as part of the "social hygiene" movement in the United States. Third, I point to substantive differences of methodology and composition between the two reports, which demonstrate the epistemological blind spots imposed by a persistent racialist and racist thinking.

The league's racially motivated and demarcated handling of the "traffic in women" must be framed in relation to a longer history of imperial expansion, labor exploitation, and gendered labor migration in the nineteenth century. Well before the domestic enactment of the Contagious Disease Acts in England in the 1860s, the practices of medical surveillance, forced treatment, and physical isolation of certain women were a crucial component of British colonial administration throughout Asia in the early 1800s. A "lock hospital" was established in Madras Presidency in 1805 and could be found throughout the British empire in Asia, including Penang in the Malay peninsula.[17] In her comprehensive study, *Prostitution, Race, and Politics: Policing Venereal Disease in the British Empire*, Philippa Levine writes that "it is in India, however, that we see the workings of the early system most vividly." Levine continues: "William Burke, inspector general of hospitals for the army in India, outlined his ideal plan in 1827: a register of prostitutes; their compulsory examination fortnightly, with certification for the healthy and hospitalization for the infected; and punitive measures for women failing to appear for examination. These principles would become the core of the empire wide regime enacted three decades later."[18] Thereafter, Hong Kong's Ordinance No. 12 was passed in 1857 and mandated brothel registration and regular medical examination. Because "the ultimate goal of regulated prostitution was to provide 'clean native women' for foreign military personnel," the ordinances in Hong Kong were "effectively limited to Asian women servicing foreigners."[19] British-administered lock hospitals could be found throughout Asia, including treaty ports in Japan.

In addition to the presence of British colonists and soldiers throughout Asia, several significant migrations in the nineteenth century would shape the peculiar contours of the League of Nations reports. A migratory route of women who were "typically already professional sex workers" from Europe and the U.S. to China began with the Opium War (1841–42) and accelerated after the introduction of steamship travel and the opening of the Suez Canal in 1869.[20] The rapid economic development of port cities such as Hong Kong and Singapore was accompanied by the growth of large red-light districts, employing mostly Chinese and Japanese women, which were tolerated by colonial authorities as a "necessary evil" to placate the large population of migrant male laborers.[21] In her account of what she calls a "traffic in sexual labor," Scully includes Chinese women's immigration to the U.S. in the 1840s as an early example of such traffic and further points to the presence of Chinese and Japanese women in Latin America, Southeast Asia, Australia, and South Africa by the late 1800s.[22] Borders, ports, and other transit zones became regarded as especially dangerous and were closely monitored spaces in order to ward off diseases. The increasingly vociferous discourse of venereal diseases as a "racial poison" and a "racial threat" was not validated by the actual numbers of infections, which were declining in the 1860s. Rather, it expressed anxieties about racial-sexual purity in the face of both increased white female emigration and the immigration of nonwhite others. Levine also points out that there was some variation in how infected women were treated, including expulsion and visibly marking them by cutting off their hair: "In other colonies, the means chosen were less dramatic and ritualized, but still focused on women's mobility: the governing assumption was that knowing women's whereabouts and having the ability to register, detain, or expel them bodily was desirable."[23]

The authors of the 1927 Report explicitly acknowledge the earlier strands of anti-trafficking work and its internationalization, which began in England and Western Europe in the nineteenth century. In 1869 Josephine Butler and other reformers founded the Ladies National Association (LNA) for the Repeal of the Contagious Disease Acts. Regarding the compulsory physical examinations as "symbolic rape," the LNA "meticulously kept track of the number of examinations in which no venereal disease was discovered" and considered them to be "the central inequity of the Acts."[24] Butler later established the British, Continental, and General Abolitionist Federation in 1875, which extended the movement to abolish licensed brothels to the Continent because it was believed that the system of state-regulated prostitution in certain countries such as France encouraged and enabled the cross-national trafficking of women and girls. The federation convened an international congress in 1877 and played a crucial role in sponsoring and financially underwriting targeted and on-the-ground investigations of the traffic. The 1927 Report mentions how these efforts led to an official British inquiry into the traffic of women and girls to the Continent, which in turn resulted in the 1885 Criminal Law Amendment, as a model precedent for how concerted investigations could lead to effective regulation.

After the repeal of domestic laws in 1889, the continued use of contagious-diseases ordinances in the British colonies and protectorates shifted the focus of anti-trafficking measures to these overseas territories. The British, Continental, and General Abolitionist Federation was renamed the British Committee for the Abolition of the State Regulated Vice in India and throughout the British Dominions. In addition to interviewing soldiers returning from abroad, the organization employed both paid agents and voluntary supporters who conducted investigations in India in 1891 and 1892, and also in Hong Kong, Shanghai, and the Straits Settlements.[25] According to Antoinette Burton, the work of anti-trafficking enabled Butler and her allies to exploit "Indian women's plight as an incentive for British women to work in the empire and as proof of British women's contributions to the imperial civilizing mission." It also enjoined early Anglo American alliances that provided opportunities for a small group of women reformers to participate actively in incipient forms of transnational knowledge production, which predated and presaged the League of Nations inquiries. In 1882 Butler personally encouraged the American missionaries Elizabeth Wheeler Andrew and Katharine Bushnell of the Women's Christian Temperance Union to undertake an on-site investigation of trafficking and regulated brothels in India, which was later published as *The Queen's Daughters in India* (1899). They reported that "regulation was rampant and that Indian women submitted rather than face expulsion from the cantonments."[26] It is important to note that the women's vigilant gaze was also trained on the imperial state and its "sanctioning of incorrigible soldierly behavior."[27]

Another strand of anti-trafficking work emerged in Britain in the 1890s, which was affiliated with social purity reformers who advocated state oversight and regulation of prostitution. The National Vigilance Association (NVA) began to organize an international campaign against the "white slave traffic" and garnered the support and endorsement of state officials. It also convened the International Congress on the White Slave Traffic in London in June 1899, which the 1927 League of Nations Report hailed as "the starting-point of a complete organization for defensive and active measures against the traffic."[28] The NVA would spearhead a new organization, named the International Bureau (IB) for the Suppression of the Traffic in Women, which would foster "a close and permanent agreement ... among the philanthropic and charitable societies of different countries to communicate to each other information as to the emigration of women under suspicious circumstances, and to undertake to protect the emigrants on their arrival."[29] The various national committees of the IB became actively engaged in the work of monitoring and managing the transnational movements of European women. In addition to being prominently led by men, the NVA and the IB cultivated and enjoyed a closer relationship to the state than the women-led organizations. They received some financial support from their respective governments and also worked with law enforcement and immigration officials in the exclusion and repatriation of foreign women suspected of being prostitutes.³⁰ Such heightened vigilance did not translate into increased protection of women from exploitation. Writing of the period from 1895 to World War I, Scully points out, "Policing and regulatory responses exacerbated the situation, as migratory prostitutes under siege became more reliant on pimps and more vulnerable to corrupt officials."³¹

In 1902 delegates from sixteen nations convened in Paris for a conference where they drafted the first International Agreement for the Suppression of the White Slave Traffic, which was signed on May 18, 1904. The delegates used the French term *traite des blanches*, which marked both an alignment with and a differentiation from *traite des noires*. According to Nora Demleitner, "The delegates to the Madrid Conference of 1910 for the first time discussed the use of the label and challenged the term because it was not sufficiently broad to cover women of all colors. Nevertheless, the conference decided to retain the term because it had become a household word."³² The term was thus deployed in the subsequent 1910 International Convention for the Suppression of the White Slave Traffic. The internationalization of the work of anti-trafficking in the League of Nations necessitated a shift from "white slave traffic" to the more universal rubric of the "traffic in women and children," but as I will show, much of the discourse and subsequent work of the League of Nations maintained a hierarchical racial distinction. Question 8 in the 1921 questionnaire explicitly focused upon protective measures against "White Slave Traffic." Several annual government reports also continued to deploy the term. I would argue that this persistent usage of "white slave traffic" was not residual but indeed crucial to the fashioning of international consensus in an era marked by both inter-imperialist jockeying and uneven nation-state formations. In proposing a new International Convention for the Suppression of the Traffic in Women and Children at the second meeting of the Assembly of the League of Nations in September 1921, the British delegation framed it as "an unprecedented opportunity for the League to demonstrate political will and determination."³³ The 1921 convention bore a notable exception in its Article 14: "Any Member or State signing the present Convention may declare that the signature does not include any or all of its colonies, overseas possessions, protectorates or territories under its sovereignty or authority, and may subsequently adhere separately on behalf of any such colony, overseas possession, protectorate or territory so excluded in its declaration."³⁴ Thus, the very assertion of a new international agreement entailed explicit sanctions of imperialist and racist double standards imposed

62 Chapter 2

onto different women's bodies. Japan ratified the convention in 1925, but with reservations for Korea, Taiwan, and Kwantung, where the age limit was set at eighteen instead of twenty-one. Japan later withdrew this reservation in 1927. This example demonstrates the pliable and strategic intermeshing of imperialist sovereignty and early global governance. How might we make different critical sense of the establishment of the Japan military "comfort system" and specifically its systematic recruitment and massive deployment of Korean girls and women as partially sanctioned by this authorization of colonial powers to represent and to exclude the colonized from emerging global regime of rights and protections?

The League of Nations expanded upon the signatory state's responsibility for monitoring the transnational movement of girls and women, which was adopted from the earlier 1904 agreement and 1910 convention. According to Article 1 of the 1904 agreement, the signatory countries would "establish or name some authority charged with the co-ordination of all information relative to the procuring of women or girls for immoral purposes abroad."[35] Article 2 called for the parties "to have a watch kept, especially in railways stations, ports of embarkation, and *en route*, for persons in charge of women and girls destined for an immoral life." This concerted surveillance over traveling female bodies was later incorporated almost verbatim in the questionnaire that the League of Nations circulated in 1921: "4. Has the government taken any steps to have ports and railway stations watched for the purpose of checking the Traffic in Women and Children? If not undertaking this duty to themselves, have they delegated this responsibility, and if so, to what agency?"[36] Articles 3 and 4 of the 1904 agreement, which addressed the matter of the repatriation of "women and girls of foreign nationality who are prostitutes," became incorporated as question 5: "Has the Government taken steps to ascertain from foreign prostitutes the reasons for which they left their countries? If so, what has been the outcome of this enquiry?"

The significance of monitoring female migration was prominent in the expanded "Questionnaire issued by the special body of experts on the traffic in women and children, April 3, 1924," which was printed as Annex II of the 1927 report. In addition to requesting government statistics on the "number, age, nationality and length of residence of foreign women who are known to be regularly engaged in prostitution, either in licensed houses or elsewhere," the lengthy, multipart question 5 asks for "any available statistics regarding immigration and emigration for the years 1919–1923," including the "total number of male and female immigrants classified according to nationality" and additionally specifies "foreign women who have been admitted in the last five years . . .

classified according to age-group (under 18, 18–21, 21–30, and over 30), and according to occupations."[37]

The exercise of the league's "political will and determination" through surveying the traffic in women was challenged by the unknowable contours of the purported problem. Trafficking is difficult to espy, document, and control. The two reports and the archives of the official *League of Nations Journal* repeatedly demonstrate a fissure between convincing demonstrations of diligent surveillance and acknowledgments of the impossibility of a thorough monitoring and documentation of the phenomenon, especially given the uneven political economy of different sections of the League of Nations. Because the league as a whole, but especially its undervalued Social Section, which included the Advisory Committee, lacked the financial resources to gather information about local and national conditions, it was still largely dependent upon official government communiqués and "field reports" submitted by voluntary associations such as the International Bureau. There was the very likely possibility of underreporting the extent and severity of the traffic in women by state authorities. Pointing to how several of the countries represented on the Advisory Committee, including France, Italy, and Japan, did not move toward abolition in practice, Jessica R. Pliley goes so far as to assert "the fact that many governments wanted to appear [to be] actively addressing the problem of trafficking without having to take any meaningful action."[38] Further complicating questions of accuracy, objectivity, and accountability, Great Britain, France, Portugal, Japan, the Netherlands, and the United States submitted replies and reports on behalf of their colonies, overseas possessions, protectorates, and/or territories.[39] Also, many nations were in the chaotic and fractious midst of state self-constitution in the first decades of the twentieth century, making it difficult to attribute a single, unified agency to such reports. For example, in her study of prostitution in Shanghai in the early twentieth century, Gail Hershatter points out that "no systematic statistics were collected" and further questions the record-keeping practices of the state: "Counting, like classifying and regulating, is not a neutral activity. The creation of statistics, in Shanghai as elsewhere, was part of a state-building process, an intrusive aspect of the project of modernity, often resisted by the people it sought to incorporate. Numbers that give the impression of precision were collected by an inconsistent group for changing reasons from a population that had every reason to lie."[40] There was also some skepticism toward "field reports" by voluntary organizations that could be differently motivated to inflate their numbers and sensationalize their narratives.

It was under this shifting and contested framework that on March 21, 1923, Grace Abbott, a representative of the advisory committee from the United

States, submitted a memorandum recommending a new international inquiry sponsored by the league. Its scope would be ambitiously broad and multidimensional: "Geographically the investigation should include, if possible, the principal cities of the world, but, if this is not possible, typical cities should be selected from which there is reason to believe the traffic is or is not being carried on, those in which regulated houses and those in which abolition is the policy, those situated in countries in which prostitutes and all those who live or benefit by prostitution are excluded from admission, and those whose laws regulating immigration make no or inadequate provisions for immoral persons."[41] Note how three different kinds of cities were delineated according to state regulations regarding prostitution and immigration restriction, suggesting that an assessment of the warrant and efficacy of state regulation was at stake. The rubric of "traffic in women" thus enabled a more far-reaching and probing investigation into a broad range of national laws and enforcement mechanisms. Abbott went on to explicate the need for an on-the-ground investigation to supplement the limits of the information provided by governments and voluntary associations:

> From official sources, the facts as to the administration of laws designed to eliminate the traffic can be learned. To secure the information as to the traffic itself, it will be necessary to send to the cities included in the survey, agents of high standing with special training and experience to make personal and unofficial, investigations. It is recognised that such investigations are difficult, not to say dangerous; but they are absolutely necessary to secure the facts to refute sensational exaggerations or general denials as to the traffic and—what would seem to be for the Committee of supreme importance—an intelligent basis for a sound programme for international co-operation for the suppression of the traffic, if it is found to exist.

Having earned a master's degree in political science from the University of Chicago and having worked with Jane Addams at Hull House, Abbott was a prominent member of a new generation of social workers who "crafted their professional identities and asserted their expertise by embracing scientific practice methods, with an emphasis on investigation, detailed case records, scientific nomenclature, and social diagnosis."[42] After serving as the director of the Immigrant's Protective League from 1908–17, Abbott was appointed in 1921 as the first chief of the Children's Bureau in the U.S. Department of Labor. She also published numerous articles in such venues as the *American Journal of Sociology* on a range of issues, including immigrant labor, social welfare, child labor, and juvenile delinquency.

In addition to Abbott's instigation, the leading position of U.S. actors in overseeing and funding this investigation merits closer scrutiny, especially considering that the United States was not a formal member of the League of Nations.⁴³ In the memorandum, Abbott invoked an earlier U.S. Senate inquiry on the "Importation and Harbouring of Women for Immoral Purposes" in 1908–9, which found that women and girls from Europe and also from Asia were brought to the United States, as proof and as a model of the efficaciousness of such investigation. Abbott stated that "the authorities charged with the enforcement of American law as well as private organisations in the United States interested in the abolition of prostitution will, I am sure, be glad to give all possible assistance." As appreciatively acknowledged in the introduction to the 1927 Report, both multinational League investigations were financially supported by the Bureau of Social Hygiene (BSH), which provided $75,000 and then $125,000 to the two inquiries.

ROCKEFELLER INTERESTS AND THE BUREAU OF SOCIAL HYGIENE

The BSH was established in 1911 by John D. Rockefeller Jr. as a private philanthropic organization devoted to investigating and combating specific social problems, especially prostitution. In a statement released to the public on January 27, 1913, titled "The Origin, Work and Plans of the Bureau of Social Hygiene," Rockefeller opens by tracing the founding of the BSH to the Special Grand Jury "appointed to investigate the white slave traffic in New York," for which he had served as the chair. Subsequently, there were several conferences that gathered "over a hundred leading men and women in the city" to discuss the possibility of a public commission to address the problem:

> These conferences developed the feeling that a public commission would labor under a number of disadvantages, such as the fact that it would be short lived; that its work would be done publicly; that at best it could hardly do more than present recommendations. . . .
>
> So the conviction grew that in order to make a real and lasting improvement in conditions, a permanent organization should be created, the continuation of which would not be dependent upon a temporary wave of reform, nor upon the life of any man or group of men, but which would go on, generation after generation, continuously making warfare against the forces of evil. It also appeared that a private organization would have, among other advantages, a certain freedom from publicity and from political bias, which a publicly appointed commission could not so easily avoid.⁴⁴

In contrast to the moralism and sensationalism of the earlier purity crusades against the "white slave traffic," the BSH sought to achieve "instrumental reform that was efficient, scientific, elitist" by engaging trained experts to study social problems such as prostitution and venereal disease.[45] As Rockefeller pointed out, one of the first funded projects of the BSH was the establishment of the Laboratory of Social Hygiene near the New York State Reformatory for Women in Bedford Hills.[46] The statement ends with "In conclusion, it cannot be too strongly emphasized that the sprit which dominates the work of the Bureau is not sensational or sentimental or hysterical; that it is not a spirit of criticism of public officials; but that it is essentially a spirit of constructive suggestion and of deep scientific as well as humane interest in a great world problem." Before it pledged financial support for the league's inquiries into the traffic in women, the bureau had funded investigations into prostitution in the United States and Europe and published the findings in 1913, 1914, and 1921.[47] These earlier projects laid out much of the groundwork for the league inquiries.

Though bearing a generic name, the BSH was a very small, closed entity made up of Rockefeller and a handful of close associates, and it served as a conduit through which Rockefeller could channel funding for special projects and investigations. It made a negligible sum from royalties of the studies it published, but it was funded almost entirely by periodic contributions from Rockefeller, which amounted to nearly $5.8 million from 1912 to 1935. According to the memos, ledgers, and correspondences housed at the Rockefeller Archive Center, there was often a tacit yet structured protocol whereby face-to-face meetings and internal discussions around the possibility of funding specific projects preceded a formal written request. Even when funding was formally approved and pledged, there was often a maximum figure denoted in the language of "up to $amount as necessary," and certain conditions were attached. Additionally, the total pledged funds would be disbursed in portions rather than all at once, thus requiring periodic written requests for additional funds, which would often be accompanied by an update on the use of the funds.

The BSH also funded the American Social Hygiene Association (ASHA), which merged two older organizations, the American Federation for Sex Hygiene and the American Vigilance Association, and focused on combating venereal disease through sex education. The ASHA received a large majority of BSH disbursements, especially in the early 1920s. The Rockefeller philanthropies also played a key role in the establishment of the Social Science Research Council in 1923. Thus, an emerging power/knowledge regime of the social sciences came to supplement and legitimate rather than to supplant older private modes of surveillance, calculation, and control. The ASHA was led by Dr. William F. Snow, a professor and public health expert, and included Jane Addams, the social reformer and close mentor to Abbott. The ASHA applied what it considered "forward-looking scientific approaches derived from advances in medical knowledge" and private investigators to uncover and document pressing social problems such as prostitution.[48] It was Snow who served as chairman of the League of Nations' Special Body of Experts on the Traffic in Women and Children from 1924 to 1928. Snow, in turn, was responsible for the appointment of Bascom Johnson, who had earlier served as the head of the legal affairs at ASHA, as the director of investigations of the two league inquiries. During World War I both Snow and Johnson had successfully worked with the U.S. Army Commission on Training Camp Activities to control the epidemic of venereal diseases by closing down or moving red-light districts near military encampments.[49] Their efforts were related to a nationwide wave of vice commissions in the 1910s whose investigations led to more repressive laws and policies against women suspected of engaging in prostitution: "Many states established reformatories for women . . . and required medical examinations for venereal diseases prior to marriage."[50]

It is worth noting that Snow had also served as the vice president of the American Eugenics Society. Eugenicist ideologies of "racial preservation" through forced sterilization and immigration restriction were expressed in the ASHA's official *Journal of Social Hygiene,* which also published articles by Bascom Johnson. As a 1919 article published in the journal begins, "For any country at any given stage of advancement of its arts, and of exhaustion of its resources there is an optimum number of inhabitants up to which the country can continue to increase its population without producing an undue pressure upon subsistence. . . . A well-ordered community will strive to reach this adjustment. It may do so by encouraging or discouraging emigration, or by raising or lowering the birth-rate."[51] Another article from 1920, titled "Eugenical Sterilization in the United States," argues, "The relation between the inheritable qualities of our immigrants and the destiny of the American nation is very close. . . . Thus, if the American nation desires to upbuild or even to maintain its standard of natural qualities, it must forbid the addition through immigration to our human breeding-stock of persons of a lower natural hereditary constitution than that which constitutes the desired standard."[52] Rather than attribute these eugenicist positions to Snow and Johnson, I point them out to suggest the broader racist and xenophobic cosmology that likely shaped this preoccupation with the traffic in women.

Raymond Fosdick is another key figure who bridges the work of the BSH, ASHA, and later the Rockefeller Foundation with the U.S. government and military and the League of Nations. Fosdick was hired at the BSH in 1913 but took a leave during World War I after he was appointed as Chairman of Training Camp Activities of the War Department. Upon Fosdick's request, Rockefeller committed $25,000 for this work. Fosdick would go on to serve as the Under-Secretary General of the newly formed League of Nations. When the U.S. ultimately did not join the league, Fosdick resigned his position in January 1920 and resumed employment with the BSH. During his short tenure at the league, there was a cryptic exchange with Rockefeller, where Fosdick expresses approval of Snow's efforts at "revivifying" ASHA after the "impetus that was gained during the war": "Snow is *the* man for the job, and with Johnson as assistant, their organization should be a power in the land...."[53] Both during his brief tenure as the Under-Secretary General and afterward, when he was no longer officially affiliated with the League of Nations, Fosdick would advise Rockefeller to offer financial support for specific league initiatives, and he also advocated directly with league officials to assert a certain degree of control over the implementation and outcome of these projects, including the two inquiries into the traffic in women.

According to the archived correspondences, after Abbott had consulted directly with Fosdick about the possibility of the BSH's funding the league study, Fosdick wrote to Rockefeller on June 12, 1923, about the proposed study. On June 18, in a reply to Fosdick, Rockefeller wrote, "On the basis of the facts presented, the Bureau of Social Hygiene will contribute toward the cost of this survey. I assume that you will arrange the details for carrying out this pledge."[54] In an October 1 letter to Abbott, Charles O. Heydt, then secretary of the BSH, explained this generous outlay:

> The Bureau of Social Hygiene has considered the suggestion which you made some time ago in conversation with Mr. Raymond B. Fosdick in regard to the possibility of our supporting the proposed study of the international traffic in women and girls, which is being projected under the auspices of the Permanent Advisory Committee of the League of Nations. We understand that you yourself, acting as the unofficial representative of the American government, brought to the attention of the international conference at Geneva the desirability of this survey. Because the subject is one in which we have long been interested and because we believe that this proposed step is essential to any solution of the problem, the Bureau of Social Hygiene will contribute toward the

costs of the investigation whatever may be necessary up to Seventy-five thousand dollars ($75,000).[55]

A year later, on September 5, 1924, Snow sent a letter written from the League of Nations in Geneva and addressed to Abbott in which he requested "the transfer of $15,000 additional from the Bureau of Social Hygiene to the League of Nations for use of the Special Commission of Experts to Study the Traffic in Women and Children" in order to cover the "expenses of members and their honoraria."[56] As Snow also later added, "Doubtless you have seen Mr. Johnson and know from him about the conditions he found." Thus, Grace Abbott and Bascom Johnson were evidently in communication during the investigation for the 1927 Report.

Given the clear overlap of personnel in Snow, Johnson, Abbott, and Fosdick, I would venture that having the inquiry conducted under the aegis of the League of Nations worked to legitimate and obscure the specific Rockefeller influence and U.S. interests in the issue. The main target of the inquiries was regulated prostitution (often referred to as "the system of licensed brothels") as motivating and facilitating the cross-border movement of women engaged in prostitution. As such, both reports conclude by recommending the abolition of state regulation and better international coordination toward that end. A concerted mystification of this particularly motivated, privately financed and coordinated agenda was enacted through both press releases and scholarly publications. For instance, in 1926 Snow published an essay titled "The Program of the League of Nations Advisory Committee on the Traffic in Women and the Protection and Welfare of Children and Young People" in the *Proceedings of the Academy of Political Science*. Snow narrates the funding arrangement as a salutary story of coincidence and cooperation: "The need [for the inquiry] being agreed upon, the [League] Council said, 'We will go ahead if there are funds.' As we could not draw, for this commission, on the official funds of the League, we hoped to finance the project by securing voluntary contributions in the United States, and as a matter of fact, the Bureau of Social Hygiene made the generous contribution of a sum necessary to carry on this investigation. Perhaps I should say that this is an interesting and very simple illustration of how the Council and voluntary agencies work together on such *purely non-political* problems." Snow discloses that Abraham Flexner, who had written *Prostitution in Europe* (1914), also funded and published by the Bureau of Social Hygiene, had been the first choice to serve as chairman: "When Mr. Flexner could not serve because of illness they still had certain reasons why they wanted an American to serve as chairman, and it fell to my lot to act as chairman of the commission."[57] Snow does not explicate what these reasons were and why he in particular was chosen for this role. But he does seize the occasion to highlight the important research contributions of his own ASHA to the final report:

> Again referring to the documentation side of the work, we wanted to get all the laws and regulations that related to this subject and interpretations of the regulations so far as practice was concerned. It takes a great deal of time and effort to put such a mass of laws and regulations into any proper shape. Here again the League did not hesitate to call upon volunteer service. For instance, the American Social Hygiene Association was asked whether it would not be able to put into orderly system for filing, with interpretive notes, all of the laws gathered. The Association has done this and turned over to the library in Geneva the completed studies. That is only one instance. There are many illustrations of cooperation of that sort. Every agency desires to work toward the common purpose of getting a factual basis for the reports of such commissions.[58]

The determining influence of a distinctly U.S. preoccupation with prostitution, immigration, and racial purity in shaping the 1927 enquiry was largely eclipsed by highlighting the incontrovertible rigor of direct observation of "facts" by trained experts. The inclusion of professional women such as Dr. Alma Sundquist of Sweden, who served on the three-member Traveling Commission, further provided an aura of neutrality and legitimacy. Even as the authors of the 1927 Report ceremoniously acknowledged "the most cordial response" from all the countries that were investigated, "with the result that the representatives of the Body of Experts were given every facility on carrying out their work and received the active help of officials and other persons concerned," the greater authenticity and reliability of independent expert observations were repeatedly upheld. In addition to acknowledging how Bascom Johnson's "legal training and long experience of social studies proved invaluable," the 1927 Report described how the commission was "assisted by a group of highly qualified investigators."[59] In a 1927 article in the *Journal of the Royal Institute of International Affairs*, Dame Rachel Crowdy, the head of the Social Section of the League of Nations, relayed a detailed account of how the inquiry came into being. She was particularly laudatory about how the expert commission was "lucky enough to get hold of eight or ten very courageous and very resourceful men and women, and for the last three years those people have been working as part of the underworld."[60]

A review of the 1927 Report that was published in the recently founded journal *Social Service Review* also commended it as "an admirable example of methods of securing and publishing information on a subject involving official policies." Noting that the investigators interviewed more than six hundred officials, including "chiefs of police and of migration and of health services," the article described how "a detailed inquiry was also made with regard to emigration, the issuing of passports to prostitutes and their *souteneurs*, and the safeguards adopted in granting passports to women and girls whether traveling to neighboring countries or farther afield and overseas." The following paragraph on method describes "the difficult task of establishing contact with the underworld and of obtaining first-hand information as to its activities. . . . Some five thousand underworld characters were interviewed. The investigators associated with *souteneurs* and prostitutes, frequented their clubs and cafés, and became acquainted with the inmates of the houses of prostitution."[61] As a summary assessment, the *Social Services Review* concludes that "the Report as a whole represents a valiant attempt on the part of the League of Nations to set out the facts regarding one of the most terrible evils in the modern world." The review does not stop there but proceeds to reveal and indeed emphasize the specific national provenance of this international study and its particular methods: "Americans may well be proud of the fact that this Report is, in fact, their work. The investigation was the plan of the American delegate, Grace Abbott, who secured the funds for the inquiry in her own country, and the inquiry was later put in charge of the American Social Hygiene Association, with Dr. William Freeman Snow as chairman of the body of experts. Having got the facts, it remains for America to get her own house thoroughly in order as well as to help the more backward nations of the world to blot out the whole hideous system."[62] Snow had been appointed to chair the multinational group of experts, but this was not the same as having ASHA "in charge" as a specific nongovernmental organization. In Snow's own account, quoted earlier, he made a more modest claim about how ASHA provided the "volunteer service" of organizing the various national laws ("with interpretive notes").

We can better grasp the American heritage of the League of Nations inquiries into the traffic in women by retracing how the use of "on-the-spot" and "underworld" investigations had been deployed earlier as part of the wave of vice commissions in the U.S. in the 1900s. A key figure was George Kneeland, who served as the director of investigation for the Research Committee of the Committee of Fourteen in New York City, the Vice Commission of Chicago, and several other investigative commissions. In recognition of this work, Kneeland was elected to the National Institute for Social Sciences in 1914. In 1912 Rockefeller invited Kneeland to direct a new investigation of New York City for the recently launched Bureau of Social Hygiene, and Kneeland went on to publish his report in 1913 as *Commercialized Prostitution in New York City*. In his introduction to this book, Rockefeller touted how "Mr. Kneeland, with a corps of assistants, has been making a thorough and comprehensive survey of the conditions of vice in New York City." Paul Kinsie was one of these assistants employed by Kneeland. Emphasizing that the investigation was guided by "the spirit of scientific inquiry" and that the "data" were based on "reliable information secured by careful and experienced investigators, whose work was systematically corroborated," Rockefeller promised "a dispassionate and objective account of things as they were ... the whole network of relations which had been elaborated below the surface of society."[63] Rockefeller's introduction also recast his earlier press statement, "The Origin, Work and Plans for the Bureau of Social Hygiene," to make the point once again about the comparative advantages of having a private organization investigate social problems instead of a public commission. These privately financed and controlled investigations served several related public functions: (1) to document the problem in order to shape public opinion, (2) to function as an extralegal source of information on which police and city leaders could act, and (3) to expose the inadequacies of existing laws and the inefficiencies of state agencies. Even earlier, in fact, Rockefeller had hired George Kneeland to author *The Social Evil in New York City: A Study of Law Enforcement*. As illustrated in the second part of the title, this 1910 report was a detailed critical assessment of multiple failures and lapses in both legislation and law enforcement, which would strengthen the case for the particular recommendations and remedies proposed by the studies. Rather than herald their innovation and scientific rigor, I would argue that the League of Nations reports attest to the shared genealogy and porosity among private undercover, state-sanctioned, and "social scientific" modes of knowledge production, and how each served to prop up the factual aura of the others' truth claims.

INQUIRY INTO TRAFFIC IN WOMEN AND CHILDREN IN THE EAST (1932)

The second inquiry into the Far East posed several unforeseen challenges, as documented in a detailed report to the BSH trustees that covered the years 1928–30. In a section titled "League of Nations—Survey of Traffic in Women and Children," the report describes the subtle yet hedged negotiations around implementing the second inquiry: "Through Mr. Fosdick the League was advised that funds for extending this enquiry probably would be made available upon its request, provided support from the countries to be visited was obtained and official assurance given of the co-operation of the governments affected. Before these conditions were fully met, the Bureau was informed that the Secretary-General greatly desired to incorporate in a preliminary report to the Council of the League a statement that funds for the survey would be made available." The BSH trustees resolved to provide $125,000 for the new investigation: "The resolution stipulated that the survey was to be conducted under the auspices of the League of Nations by its Body of Experts. It was presumed that the formal request from the Council of the League would contain assurances that the investigation would be conducted by the same Body of Experts which made the previous survey." Without naming them explicitly, the BSH expected that Snow and Johnson would again oversee the research, investigation, and writing of the new report. Much to their surprise, the league moved to replace Snow as chairman of the Commission of Enquiry into the Traffic in Women and Children in the East with Eugène Regnault of France and also to eliminate Johnson as well as the use of "underworld investigation" for the second inquiry. As the memorandum described, "In this crisis, it was fortunate indeed that Mr. Fosdick had occasion to visit Geneva. He took the position that in this, as in all other organizations, a Rockefeller organization would not attempt to exercise the slightest control over the methods to be pursued, choice of personnel, or conclusions to be reached, but that the fundamental basis on which this appropriation was made was that an honest, intelligent, and energetic attempt would be made to ascertain the facts, and that the facts in this case could only be developed through an underworld investigation."[64] The compromise agreement allowed for the continued use of "underworld investigation under the direction of Mr. Bascom Johnson, assisted by one or more trained investigators, hired by and responsible to him." However, this arrangement was again called into question when the league determined that it could pay Johnson an annual salary of only around $2,000, which was standard for similar services provided to the league, whereas Johnson's annual salary with the ASHA was $12,000. Here too, the BSH Executive Committee (namely Raymond Fosdick and Arthur Woods) intervened by pledging a separate "supplemental grant" of $10,000 to make up the difference and "to assist the American Social Hygiene Association in meeting this deficit." The resolution for appropriation #2856 characterized this as a move to "reimburse the American Social Hygiene Association for salary payments made to Mr. Bascom Johnson during the time he is engaged in the survey."[65]

On October 10, 1930, the three-member Commission of Inquiry embarked on their multicontinental journey by steamer from Marseilles to Bangkok via Singapore (figure 2.1). As this appended map of their itinerary illustrates, they traveled by land through "Indo-China," stopping and enquiring in Phnom-

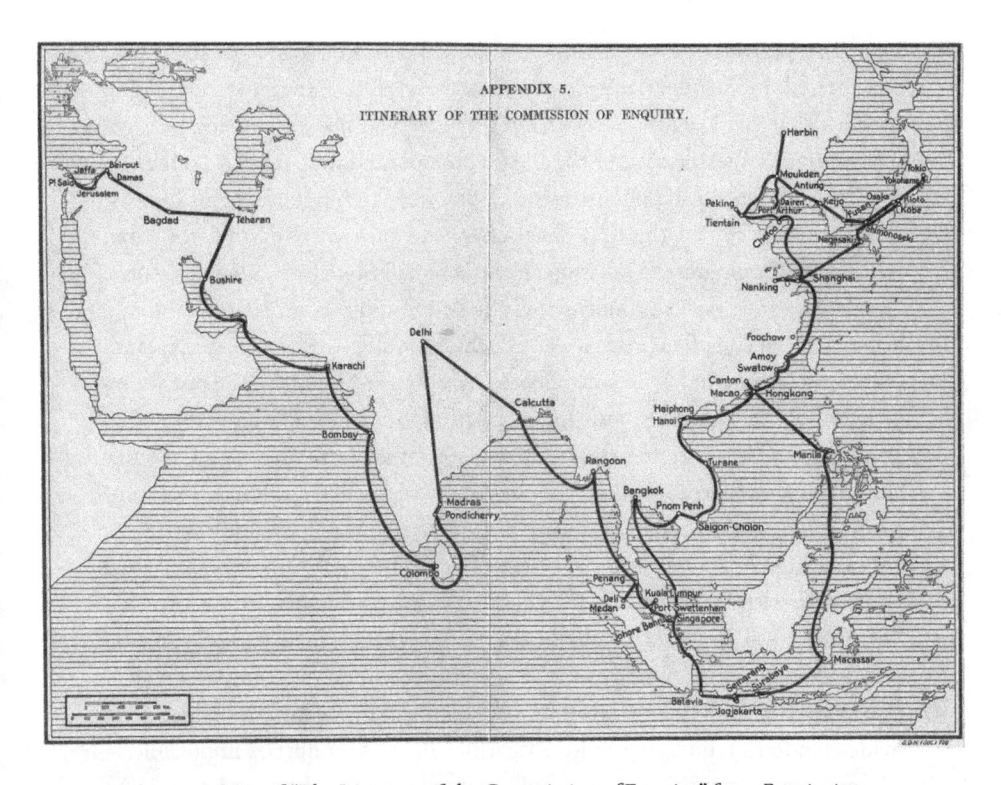

FIGURE 2.1. Map of "The Itinerary of the Commission *of* Enquiry" from *Enquiry into Traffic in Women and Children in the East* (Geneva: League of Nations, 1932).

Penh, Saigon, Cholon, Hanoi, and Haiphong and then on to Hong Kong, arriving in Manila on January 24, 1931. From there, the commission went to Canton and made their way up the eastern coast of China, making stops at Swatow and Amoy and arriving in Shanghai on March 10, 1931. After spending eleven days (May 2 to May 13, 1931) in Peking, the commission went north to Mukden by train and proceeded further to Harbin, where it investigated the local conditions for a week from May 21 to May 28. As the 1932 Report then traces this itinerary: "It then spent three days at Dairen and two days at Keijo (Seoul), arriving at Tokio, via Fusan and Shimonoseki on June 9th. The Commission remained in Japan until July 12th."[66] Departing from Nagasaki, the group headed southwest to the "Netherland Indies," with stops in Batavia, Semarang, Surabaya, and then fourteen days on the "Malay Peninsula"— Singapore, Johore, Kuala Lumpur, Penang, and Medan. In November 1931, the commission conducted enquiries in Rangoon (November 4–November 11) and then Calcutta (November 18–December 1), followed by stays in Delhi (December 3–December 6) and Madras (December 10–December 13).

Traffic in Women 75

Returning back to the U.S. financial underwriters of this expansive transcontinental, multi-imperial itinerary, by the end of 1931, there was increasing concern that the League survey in the Far East was not progressing satisfactorily from the perspective of the BSH. A memorandum dated December 23, 1931, conveys several statements made by Snow regarding the Far East inquiry. First, Snow informed the BSH that ASHA was not receiving updates from, Johnson of his progress "in getting essential facts." More intriguingly, it notes, "Probably, Mr. Johnson cannot write fully and frankly about what he is doing, because of the risk of having it leak out, which would, from the League's standpoint be a fatal error." This was followed by veiled references to the possibility of making direct contact with Johnson through a "qualified go-between" so that "it would be possible to learn the actual status of the survey and to judge whether it should be continued." Finally, Snow expressed that Johnson's recent reports "contain practically nothing that relates to the main question under consideration."[67] A week letter, on December 30, another memorandum, titled "Interview with Dr. Snow and Dr. Clarke, December 29, 1931," confirmed that "Dr. Snow is still in the dark as to the degree of success or failure which Johnson feels is crowning his investigations." But it then clarified: "It is apparently definite from Johnson's letters, however, that conditions in China and Japan have made clandestine underworld investigations in those countries impossible."[68] The enigmatic "conditions" here could be in reference to the Mukden incident of September 1931, which was followed by the Japanese invasion of Manchuria. Or it could be referring to how the "revolutionary" method of employing covert agents and underworld investigations could not be effectively transported to and applied in Asia. As Knepper notes, "Because the traffic in women in Asia involved Asian women, [Johnson] had 'little use for [a] white investigator.'"[69] Instead, the 1932 report had to rely mostly on interviews with government officials and testimonies from local voluntary organizations. Thus, the racially discriminating and geopolitically selective origins of anti-trafficking in the imperial age were reinscribed in the shift to "international co-operation" built upon "expert" and "on-the-spot" investigations. The memorandum still held out some hope that the underworld investigations could be undertaken elsewhere in Syria and Palestine: "These might be used to show how cautiously facts obtained in other countries, without the check of clandestine investigations must be interpreted."[70] Thus, it appears that the "clandestine investigations" were intended to discredit the self-reporting of member states and weaken claims to national sovereignty on the issue of the state regulation of prostitution. "Asian women" were never the intended objects of investigation and concern.

More significant than the method of information acquisition, the two reports differed markedly in their composition and organization. The 1932 report imposed a clear racial demarcation between "Occidental women" and "Asiatic women." Indeed, the authors outline how they considered two different possibilities of the report's organization. The first option, "dividing it into chapters according to the territories visited," would have demonstrated "the problem under enquiry in the light of the social and economic conditions, laws and administrative measures of each territory." However, with such an approach, "the actual stages of international traffic would appear in fragmentary form with no proper link." In addition, the nation-based organization would produce "a considerable amount of duplication." The authors ultimately elected the second approach, of dividing the report into "chapters treating the problem according to racial groups of victims," because "this arrangement, which, like the international traffic itself, disregards political frontiers, would convey to the readers a more living picture of all causes, methods and consequences of traffic, following it through all stages from place of origin to the place of destination."[71]

The first section, "The Findings of the Inquiry," opens with a subsection on "General Remarks" that are divided into two racial distinctions, clearly denoted in paragraph headings titled, "Traffic in Occidental Women in Asia" followed by "Traffic in Asiatic Women." The rubric of "international traffic" is also further distinguished into two categories as "traffic between Asia and other continents" and "traffic between different territories of Asia." After assuredly noting that "the Commission has found that there is a certain movement of occidental prostitutes to the Orient, while hardly any oriental women are known to go for purposes of prostitution to the Occident," there is this telling statement: "Within the group of Occidental victims of traffic in Asiatic countries, the most serious problem and one which is fraught with the danger of further development concerns Russian women of the refugee class in Northern China and Manchuria. It is not in the fully accepted sense of the word a traffic between Occident and Orient, as the victims either are residents of China or come from the Asiatic parts of Russian territory. But even when staged entirely within the borders of China, it clearly bears the stamp of international traffic."[72] Note the slippage among *interracial, inter-regional,* and *international* in the overriding concern with sexual relations between Russian women and Chinese men, which is categorized as a matter of "international traffic." Even as the rubric of the "international" was marshaled to herald a new, racially neutral concern about the traffic in women and to authorize the League of Nations with an unprecedented supranational political will, this passage demonstrates a persistent inability to transcend the racialist and racist worldview of empire. The next paragraph covers "women who actually come from the Occident to the Orient for prostitution" and reports that demand for these women is decreasing, so if "provided efforts to check traffic are maintained, there is no need to fear a revival of the conditions of twenty or thirty years ago, when considerable numbers of Occidental prostitutes, beginning with the countries nearer their homes, went farther and farther afield in the Orient in the various stages of their search for new opportunities to exercise their profession."[73] The assurances about interracial sexual contact are reiterated again on the following page in a section titled "Prostitutes Go Abroad for Own Countrymen." After noting that "traffic in the East is characterized by the fact that prostitutes going to foreign countries do so exclusively in search of clients among their own countrymen abroad," the report adds, "The analogous [sic] tendency is even true of occidental prostitutes who go to the Middle and Far East, for they, too, seek their clients almost solely among occidental men."[74]

Significantly, it is only *after* registering concern about Russian women and Occidental prostitutes that the "General Remarks" section turns to Asian women: "The bulk of the traffic with which this report is concerned is traffic in Asiatic women from one country of Asia to another." This group is then further specified: "The largest group of victims of this kind of traffic is composed of women of Chinese race; the next in numerical importance are women of Japanese nationality—that is Japanese, Koreans and Formosans—followed in very much smaller numbers by Malay, Annamite, Siamese, Filipino, Indian, Iraqi, Persians and Syrians."[75] Note the peculiar mix of *race* and *nationality* as well as the categorization of Koreans and Formosans as Japanese, which are never explained but rather rendered as inconsequential in and through the predominant concern with the separation of the Occidental and the Asiatic. This easy disregard of any meaningful intra-Asian differences and contestations is further expressed in the second substantial subsection of the "Findings," which is titled "Racial Groups of Victims" and divided into these lettered sections:

> "Occidental Women (Excepting Russians of the Far East) as Victims of the Traffic to the Orient"
> "Russian Women in the Far East as Victims of International Traffic"
> "Chinese Victims of International Traffic"
> "Women of Japanese Nationality as Victims of International Traffic"

These four sections are followed by shorter sections on "Filipino Women," "Annamite Women" (in reference to women from what was then identified as the Union of Indochina), "Siamese Women," "Women of Malay Race," "Indian Women," "Persian Women," "Arab and Other Women of the Near East," and "African Victims of International Traffic in Asia." This vast range of geographical location and ethnic diversity belies the report's most urgent concern for the plight of the Russian women refugees as truly "unwilling" victims who were forced to engage in prostitution and interracial sexual relations with Chinese men. The judgment and measure of force or non-consent in prostitution were thus racially cast in this early moment of global governance.

Despite the questionable methods used in these reports, they were widely read and endorsed, fueling further enactments against and surveillance over women's cross-border movements. The anti-trafficking efforts also fed into the calls for greater involvement of women in policing and public patrols, with mixed results. Some women activists publicly objected to how the expanding reach of the protocols and conventions would limit the mobility of *all* women.[76] This was partially borne out in 1933, when, based partly on the persuasive force of these reports, the League of Nations passed a more far-reaching International Convention for the Suppression of the Traffic in Women of Full Age, which declared, "Whoever, in order to gratify the passions of another person, has procured, enticed or led away *even with her consent*, a woman or girl of full age for immoral purposes to be carried out in another country, shall be punished."[77]

There have been divergent assessments of the prominence of the "traffic in women" in the League of Nations' activities. Some scholars see it as an achievement and a vindication of the concerted efforts of women's groups that sent delegates to Geneva to campaign for a range of issues, including an equal rights treaty. To be sure, the multimodal work of anti-trafficking created an opening for a limited number of women professionals and activists in this newly emergent international framework of advocacy and governance. Fröken Forchhammer addressed the topic in the first speech ever given by a woman to the Assembly of the League.[78] The Social Section of the League, which was charged with addressing the "traffic in women and children," was the only section headed by a woman, Dame Rachel Crowdy. In addition to Grace Abbott, the permanent Advisory Committee on the Traffic in Women and Children also included Dr. Paulina Luisi from Uruguay and Princess Bandini of Italy, who also served on its eight-member international committee of experts. In 1922 the secretary-general took special note of how the Committee on the Traffic in Women and Children "contained a larger representation of women than any other Committee of the League, since the question with which it dealt required the fullest co-operation of women."[79] In an article published in 2007, Katarina Leppanen notes the absence of the issue in the first draft of the Covenant for the League from February 1919 and concludes that "it demonstrates the fact that feminist interests were highly visible in the League and shows how successfully women and feminist organisations lobbied the League from the start."[80] Stephanie A. Limoncelli is more measured and ultimately skeptical. Pointing to the initial resistance from the mostly male leadership, she argues that "officials wanted to ensure coordinated policy for overseeing existing international conventions already signed by member states, including the 1904 and 1910 accords dealing with the white slavery traffic." Limoncelli thus concludes: "Bureaucratic logic rather than humanitarian concern seems to have led the League to its anti-trafficking work."[81] I have proposed a third framing of the league's work in anti-trafficking as demonstrating how the coordinated surveillance over women's sexuality, labor, and migration made international cooperation thinkable, even as this very effort testified to the intractability of racial hierarchies and racialized geopolitical imaginaries, which precluded its effective enactment. In February 1937 the League of Nations convened the international Conference of Central Authorities in Eastern Countries on "Traffic in Women and Children" in Bandoeng, Indonesia. The conference attendees adopted a resolution that recommended that the League of Nations establish a special "Far-Eastern Bureau" to coordinate information among different countries and colonial territories in the region. One scholar has characterized this pivotal moment as a "shift toward Asia" in the history of international anti-trafficking efforts.[82] Yet the outbreak of the Second Sino-Japanese War in July 1937 scuttled this specific initiative, and the work of the League of Nations itself came to an end in 1939 with the onset of World War II. The next year, the Bureau of Social Hygiene would be formally dissolved as well.

The League of Nations reports would cast a long shadow over post–World War II efforts to name and manage the "traffic in women" in global governance. On March 29, 1947, the United Nations Economic and Social Council passed Resolution 43 (IV), which called for resuming the work of anti-trafficking and updating the 1921 and 1933 conventions and ultimately led to the General Assembly's adoption of the Convention for the Suppression of the Traffic in Persons and the Exploitation of the Prostitution of Others on December 2, 1949. Recall that the 1933 convention had nullified the consent of an adult woman to cross international borders to engage in prostitution, but it had not decreed that she was not allowed to do so *within* national boundaries. Despite its long, unwieldy name, the 1949 convention foregrounded prostitution from the outset in its preamble: "Whereas prostitution and the accompanying evil of the traffic in persons for the purpose of prostitution are incompatible with the dignity and worth of the human person and endanger the welfare of the individual, the family and the community." Article 1 bound signatories "to punish any person who, to gratify the passions of another: (1) Procures, entices or leads away, for purposes of prostitution, another person, even with the consent of that person; (2) Exploits the prostitution of another person, even with the consent of that person." Article 2 further extended the compass to punish "any person who: (1) Keeps or manages, or knowingly finances or takes part in the financing of a brothel; (2) Knowingly lets or rents a building or other place or any part thereof for the purpose of the prostitution of others."

This contraction of the gradually expanded and race-, gender-, and age-neutral rubric of the "traffic in persons" and its subordination to the "exploitation of prostitution" might explain how both would be taken up sporadically and unevenly across several different bodies of the emerging United Nations bureaucracy in the next two decades. Article 21 of the 1949 convention called for signatory states to provide an annual report to the UN Secretary-General on relevant laws and regulations, but no specific body was charged with the review of these reports. The Commission on the Status of Women (CSW), which was established originally in 1946 as a subcommission of the Commission on Human Rights and later granted full commission status, identified the elimination of the traffic in women as necessary to achieving social and economic equality for women. However, it devoted much of its initial efforts to securing equal political rights, including the establishment of independent nationality for women, consent to marriage, and minimum-age-of-marriage laws.

Certain forms of the traffic in women and prostitution were most consequentially brought within the purview of UN deliberations on slavery and slavery-like practices, but as I will show in the next chapter, this too would be a contested and jagged process. The scuttled initiative to establish a "Far-Eastern Bureau" of the League of Nations was partially revived by the UN under a broader initiative on crime prevention. Following the first Asia and the Far East Seminar on the Prevention of Crime and the Treatment of Offenders, which was held on October 25–November 6, 1954, in Rangoon, a second Asia and the Far East Seminar was convened in Tokyo from November 25 to December 7, 1957. Among the conclusions of this meeting was a call for the establishment of a regional bureau for Asia and the Far East, which would provide "technical assistance . . . for the prevention and suppression of the traffic in persons, the prevention of prostitution and the rehabilitation of prostitutes."[83]

Then, in 1959, the UN Department of Economic and Social Affairs commissioned a new expert investigation that would evaluate the effectiveness of the 1949 convention, which resulted in the publication of *Study on Traffic in Persons and Prostitution (Suppression of the Traffic in Persons and the Exploitation of the Prostitution of Others)*. This report begins by crediting the 1904 agreement, the 1910 convention, and the two conventions passed by the League of Nations in

1921 and 1933 but distinguishes the broader and more forceful authority of the 1949 convention: "This Convention (hereafter referred to as the Consolidated Convention) consolidates earlier instruments and embodies the abolitionist policy upon which should be based any programme of action against the traffic in persons and the exploitation of the prostitution of others. The policy comprises the abolition of any form of the regulation of prostitution (thus making unnecessary a definition of prostitution), the repression of the third party profiteers, the prevention of prostitution and the rehabilitation of its victims." In addition to the repeated emphasis on the abolition of regulation, the 1959 study affirmed the League of Nations reports by highlighting their supranational acquisition of direct, objective knowledge. The more reliable, "on-the-spot" findings of large-scale trafficking in the 1927 and 1932 reports were invoked to contrast with and cast doubt upon more recent reports submitted by member states in reply to the UN Secretariat's questionnaire, which tended to deny or downplay the existence of trafficking in their territories. After a prompt reminding readers that "the Council of the League of Nations appointed in 1927 a special body of experts to conduct an inquiry on the spot," the introduction to the 1959 study explained the extension and modification of this method to "Asia and the Far East": "A new body of experts was appointed for this purpose and its report, issued in 1932, largely supported the conclusions arrived at by the earlier body of experts and noted that 'the principal factor in the promotion of international traffic in the East is the brothel.'" The problem of the regulation of prostitution in the past was now attributed specifically to "the East." The 1959 study later reintroduced this Asian difference when describing *contemporary* conditions: "The social factors conducive to prostitution do not act in every country with equal potency. Economic hardships, for example, which constitute important predisposing factors to prostitution in Asia and the Far East, do not appear to play a major role in North America and certain European countries."[84] The Second Asia and the Far East Seminar on the Prevention of Crime and the Treatment of Offenders is cited in several points throughout the 1959 UN trafficking study, which also included the full text of the seminar conclusions in an appendix. Here we see the intertwined Asianization and criminalization of prostitution, which gained its authority from a misreading of the uneven methods and equivocal conclusions of the League of Nations reports. The UN would not issue a new study on the traffic in women until 1983, but a resurgent interest in the problem of slavery and slavery-like practices in the decolonizing milieu of the 1960s would create new openings for the recognition of prostitution as a form of *sexual slavery* and the delineation of Asian women as distinct subjects of sexual slavery.

SEXUAL SLAVERY

Before being identified as forms of *discrimination* against women under the 1979 Convention for the Elimination of Discrimination against Women (CEDAW) and *violence* against women through the Declaration on the Elimination of Violence against Women (DEVAW) in 1994, the traffic in women and forced prostitution were brought within the purview of slavery in the newly formed United Nations. The League of Nations had adopted the 1926 Convention to Suppress Slavery and the Slave Trade (hereafter the 1926 Slavery Convention), which defined *slavery* as "the status or condition of a person over whom any or all of the powers attaching to the right of ownership are exercised" (Article 1). Article 4 of the Universal Declaration of Human Rights (1948) declares that "no one shall be held in slavery or servitude: slavery and the slave trade shall be prohibited in all their forms." In 1949 the UN Economic and Social Council

(ECOSOC) called for the establishment of an *Ad Hoc* Committee on Slavery, comprising five members, "appointed in their individual capacity as experts" to produce a new study.[1] The committee drafted a "Questionnaire on Slavery and Servitude," which was circulated to member states. After asking about slavery and slave trade as defined in the 1926 convention, the questionnaire inquired about the existence of "any practices . . . which are restrictive of the liberty of the person and which tend to subject that person to a state of servitude." In addition to serfdom, debt bondage, and the "exploitation of children under the form of adoption," the questionnaire added the "forms of prostitution of women and children involving the exercise of ownership over them" to a list of such practices.[2]

In 1953 the UN General Assembly adopted the 1926 Slavery Convention through a protocol amendment, and the ECOSOC appointed Hans Engen, a Norwegian journalist and ambassador to the UN, to prepare a new report on slavery. Engen's report, completed in 1955, was divided into six sections, which included slavery, serfdom, debt bondage, exploitation of children, and the purchase of wives, which had all been listed in the questionnaire drafted earlier by the ad hoc committee. Engen decided to omit prostitution in his report and supplied the rationale that "although the available materials contain numerous statements on the evils of the traffic in women and children for the purposes of prostitution, these statements for the most part do not relate to 'forms of prostitution . . . involving exercise of ownership.'"[3] Thus, the matter of ownership was a defining qualification for "slavery and other institutions and customs resembling slavery." Engen added that the UN had "already dealt with prostitution 'in all its forms'" in the 1949 Convention for the Suppression of the Traffic in Persons and of the Exploitation of the Prostitution of Others. However, as I have already noted, there was no specific body or committee appointed to investigate the problem and monitor the member states' adherence to the 1949 convention.

This wavering inclusion/exclusion of certain forms of traffic in women—e.g., the "purchase of wives" but not prostitution—under the rubric of slavery would shift yet again in 1956, when the UN passed a Supplementary Convention on the Abolition of Slavery, the Slave Trade, and Institutions and Practices Similar to Slavery (hereafter the 1956 Supplementary Convention). In spite of Engen's deflection and exclusion of prostitution from his report, Article 1 of the Supplementary Convention enlarged the list of "institutions and practices similar to slavery" from the 1926 convention to also include specific instances of "abusive forms of treatment of women" such as when "a woman is sold by her family for the purpose of entering into a marriage and has no right to refuse, a family has the right to transfer a wife to another person, and a woman may be inherited by another person when her husband dies." Article 1 also added a fourth subcategory, identified as the practice of delivering "a child or young person under the age of 18 years . . . with a view to the exploitation of the child or young person or of his labor." Although prostitution was not explicitly included, some instances could qualify as a practice "similar to slavery" when they involved the labor exploitation of a person under the age of eighteen. In addition, some cases of *forced* prostitution could be covered under a new rubric in Article 5, which bound signatories to "take all necessary measures to prevent compulsory or forced labor from developing into conditions analogous to slavery." However, as with the 1949 convention, there was no specific mechanism for monitoring the implementation of these antislavery measures, and most member states denied the existence of slavery in their territories.[4]

The Sub-Commission on the Protection of Minorities and the Prevention of Discrimination was established in 1947 under the Commission on Human Rights. The long and virtuous name of the Sub-Commission belies its genesis as a compromised result of Cold War rivalries at the United Nations. The United States first made a motion in the Economic and Social Council for the establishment of a Sub-Commission on Freedom of Information and of the Press. The Soviet Union's response to this veiled criticism was to argue that there should be a subcommission on the prevention of discrimination and the protection of minorities. The Soviet representative pointed out that "even in the most highly developed countries, the rights of minorities are not respected."[5] Although the Economic and Social Council authorized the creation of separate subcommissions for each problem, the Commission on Human Rights later moved to merge them into one designated as the Sub-Commission on the Prevention of Discrimination and the Protection of Minorities. According to John P. Humphrey, "It thus made it more difficult for the Sub-Commission to get started on what was to become its most important contribution, the prevention of discrimination; and it also made it easier for the United Nations to dodge responsibility for the protection of minorities, something to which the League of Nations had attached very great importance indeed."[6]

Beginning in 1959, a group of NGOs, including the Women's League of Peace and Freedom and the UK-based Anti-Slavery Society, came together to call for the establishment of a committee to monitor the implementation of the 1926 and 1956 antislavery conventions. The British government led an effort to block this initiative until 1963, when, according to Suzanne Miers, it "fended them off with a new suggestion—the appointment of a UN Special Rapporteur to collect information on slavery."[7] As Miers explains, "This was less threatening than a committee, which might become permanent and even acquire powers of supervision."[8] The ECOSOC appointed Dr. Mohamed Awad, an Egyptian geographer and a member of the Sub-Commission, as the Special Rapporteur on Slavery and charged him with collecting information about the existence of slavery and any eradication measures from member states, various UN agencies, and NGOs. To that end, a new fifteen-part questionnaire was circulated to member states in 1964 and again in 1965.

Awad first submitted a 260-page report in May 1965, which collated the responses. A revised and expanded *Report on Slavery* was published in 1966. As a courtesy perhaps to Hans Engen's earlier decision to exclude prostitution, Awad was careful to clarify that the questionnaire, which had been formulated by the Secretary-General, was "limited to matters relating to slavery, the slave trade, and institutions and practices similar to slavery" and further added that "in so far as possible, [this report] avoids dealing with matters covered by the Convention for the Suppression of Traffic in Persons and the Exploitation of Prostitution of Others of 1949, the Convention on Consent to Marriage, Minimum Age for Marriage and Registration of Marriages of 1962, or the conventions and recommendations on forced labor of the International Labour Organization."[9] But Awad also chose to consider "other relevant texts," including, most significantly, responses to the Questionnaire on Slavery and Servitude, which had been composed earlier by the 1949 ad hoc committee and included "prostitution of women and children" as an example of servitude. Contrary to his stated claim to avoid the matter, the Awad report reinstated both the traffic in women and prostitution under the rubric of slavery.

The Awad report activated a new discourse of prostitution as *sexual slavery* within the United Nations, which also circulated beyond the UN through pseudo-investigative popular publications in the 1960s and 1970s. The term was later adopted and legitimated by a feminist project to install it as a distinct category in global governance in the 1980s. We need to understand the activists' decision to rename the Japanese "comfort system" as "military sexual slavery" in the 1990s as partially but importantly shaped by this older, variegated archive of sexual slavery. Taking Awad's 1966 *Report on Slavery* as a historical and institutional fulcrum, this chapter attempts a genealogy of Asian women as subjects of sexual slavery in several retrospective, deconstructive layers and across several political, economic, discursive, and bureaucratic frames. The first section analyzes three linked developments in the Awad report: (1) a proposal for greater United Nations action on slavery, (2) the recognition and inclusion of prostitution as a form of slavery, and (3) the acknowledgment of the important contribution of nongovernmental organizations. I trace how the Awad report led to the question of slavery being taken up by the Commission on Human Rights, specifically through its Sub-Commission on the Protection of Minorities and the Prevention of Discrimination, and the Commission on the Status of Women (CSW). Even as the Sub-Commission was being tasked with addressing "*apartheid* and colonialism" as forms of slavery in the decolonizing milieu of the late 1960s, the parallel but differentially motivated recognition of *women* as especially vulnerable victims of slavery and slavery-like practices worked to feminize and hyperbolize "sexual slavery" as a universal form of female subordination. The second section traces how feminist activists worked from several angles to install "sexual slavery" and "female sexual slavery" in the United Nations through a series of publications, workshops, offshore consultations, and fortuitous UN certification procedures in the 1980s. Although the category is often attributed to the 1979 publication of Kathleen Barry's *Female Sexual Slavery*, the Awad report importantly shaped and helped authorize Barry's claims, especially the contention that all forms of prostitution—forced or consensual, international or domestic—qualified as sexual slavery. The considerate inclusion of Asian women as both objects and subjects of knowledge production was crucial to this international antiprostitution feminism. But the intra-Asian inequalities and fissures that had been foregrounded through the earlier decolonial *and* deimperial reckonings became unintelligible as Asian feminist contributions were reduced to minor knowledges and particularized instantiations of female sexual slavery. The third section traces how these hierarchical terms and conditions were preconditioned by earlier inter-imperial maneuvers around naming and adjudicating slavery and forced labor, which took place alongside the equivocal moves to document and control the traffic in women in the League of Nations. The following section recounts how this struggle continued into the United Nations and culminated in the creation of the Working Group on Slavery in 1975, which became charged with reviewing the 1926 Slavery Convention, the 1949 Trafficking Convention, and the 1956 Supplementary Convention. Finally, the fifth section reframes how these earlier histories molded the early activists' decision to rename the Japanese "comfort system" as "military sexual slavery" and to focus their efforts on the Working Group on Contemporary Forms of Slavery and the Sub-Commission on the Protection of Minorities and the Prevention of Discrimination in the United Nations. The "comfort women" case, in turn, played an important role in spurring several actions—declarations and special investigations—to recognize "sexual slavery" as a distinct category of human rights violation. The itinerary of the issue through the various commissions, subcommissions, and conferences of the United Nations in the 1990s offers one situated narrative about the expansion of the UN and the refinement of its human rights architecture in that decade.

THE AWAD REPORT ON SLAVERY (1966)

The 1966 *Report on Slavery* brought the traffic in women and prostitution back under the rubric of slavery and slavery-like practices, which had been excluded in the 1955 Hans Engen slavery report. Notably, this was done through referring specifically to the response from Laos to the questionnaire that was circulated to the member states. In its response to Question I asking about existing measures to prevent and eliminate "slavery and institutions or practices similar to slavery," Laos had responded plainly and unequivocally: "There is no slavery or any institution or practice similar to slavery as defined in Question I, in Laos." This was reiterated in the country's full response to Question IV, which asked, "What legislative, administrative or other measures have been, or are being taken, and what other methods have been applied to prevent or eliminate slave trade?" The full response from Laos, as it appeared in the 1966 *Report on Slavery*, reads, "There is no slave trade, as defined in the questionnaire, in Laos. Certain methods of recruiting women for prostitution may, however, be considered to be forms of traffic in women punishable under articles 166/3 and 166/4 of the Laotian Penal Code. Procuring is spreading from South Viet-Nam and Thailand to Laos. This new social evil is favoured by the destitution suffered in particular by the poor, whose living conditions call for a reform of the Labour Code." It is fascinating but perplexing to see how these responses become reframed and appropriated in the summary discussion and concluding recommendations of Awad's final report. Part III of the report, titled "Suggestions for Possible Action by the United Nations in the Field of Slavery," collates and relays the member states' replies to three related questions about possible measures to be taken through international and regional cooperation (XII), by the United Nations and its specialized agencies (XIII), and by non-governmental organizations (XIV). Here the report draws special attention to the response from Laos: "Laos does not receive any external assistance for the prevention of procuring, which is a form of traffic in women for the purpose of prostitution. It would be helpful if regional meetings could be held to consider methods likely to solve the problems connected with this new form of slavery of our times, which is rife in the south-east of Indo-China." Awad then adds, "In this statement, we have clearly a case of a Member State complaining of an existing evil, and asking the United Nations for help in combating it."[10] The slight rewordings effect two substantive transfigurations. The "new social evil" of procuring and "this new form of slavery" in the Laos response becomes both "this new form of slavery" and "an existing evil." Moreover, the Laos response is recast from a denial of having received external assistance into a request for UN intervention.

The Awad *Report on Slavery* spurred several key actions and changes within the United Nations. The established practice of circulating a questionnaire to member states took on a special charge in the decolonizing milieu of the 1960s; the report makes note of the significance of "the recent increase in the membership of the United Nations, which now includes many newly independent States, which are in a position to write their own replies to the questionnaire and send them directly to the Secretary-General."[11] In its reply Mali pointed to colonialism as "a new system of general slavery."[12] As a direct criticism of Britain, South Africa, and the U.S., Russia also pointed in its response to "colonialism, *apartheid* and racism" as slavery-like institutions. In 1966 representatives of Tanzania, Gabon, Algeria, and Iraq sponsored a resolution to add "the slavery like-practices of *apartheid* and colonialism" under the definition of slavery.[13] On July 26, 1966, the ECOSOC passed Resolution 1126 (XLI), which referred to "the question of slavery and the slave trade in all their practices and manifestations including the slavery-like practices of apartheid and colonialism." Awad would reproduce the phrase in the section on possible actions to be taken, which appears at the end of the 1966 report.[14]

In 1967 the Commission on Human Rights directed that the subject of slavery and related institutions be taken up by its Sub-Commission on the Prevention of Discrimination and the Protection of Minorities. Soon thereafter, the membership numbers and composition of the Sub-Commission would change significantly:

> The world was divided into five geographic areas: Africa, Asia, Latin America, "Western Europe and others," and Eastern Europe.... Before 1969, the number of members from each area was not fixed and the eight Western powers were the largest group. In that year, at the request of the African and Asian delegates to the Commission on Human Rights, the membership was increased to twenty-six to give a fairer representation to the new members of the UN. Thereafter, the Afro-Asian members formed the largest bloc, with seven African and five Asian seats, against six for the Western powers, five for Latin Americans, and three for Eastern Europe.[15]

Thus, it is important to understand the heightened and expanded import of slavery under the still incipient human rights framework as the result of this broader geopolitical, discursive, and institutional contestation over colonialism. An updated report, which Awad completed in 1971, defined *colonialism* as "the status of a country and its inhabitants when they are subjected to foreign rule" and then explained: "The extent to which the dominant Power's social, cultural, economic and even political interests are imposed may be regarded as the yardstick for the evaluation of colonialism and its effects in certain areas. As regards the analogy of colonialism with slavery and servitude, the acquisition of colonies by imperialist Powers had significant parallels to the acquisition of slaves to be exploited by their master."[16] It is worth probing the insightfulness and the limits of this analogy, but for my present task of tracing the genealogy of *sexual slavery*, I will attend to how the problem of colonialism—reframed now as any case in which "the dominant Power's social, cultural, economic and even political interests are imposed"—drops out when slavery becomes differently routed through the category of *women*.

The 1966 *Report on Slavery* was also pivotal to the question of slavery being taken up by the Commission on the Status of Women (CSW). On June 6, 1967, the ECOSOC passed Resolution 1232 (XLII), which recommended that the Commission on Human Rights request the CSW to study the report and "to formulate specific proposals for immediate and effective measures which the United Nations could adopt to eradicate all forms and practices of slavery and the slave-trade affecting the status of women." The CSW took up this task at its twenty-first session, which was convened from January 29 to February 19, 1968. According to the report of this session, this was the first time that the CSW deliberated on "the question of slavery" (para. 62), and those present took special notice of how slavery was included in the provisional agenda of the upcoming International Conference on Human Rights to be held at Teheran in April 1968 (para. 64). Although the CSW members were "unanimous in condemning slavery in all its manifestations" (para. 66), there was some debate over whether slavery fell within the purview of the CSW. Some suggested that this was duplicating work already being undertaken in other UN bodies, whereas others "considered it appropriate . . . , particularly because women especially were among the victims of slavery in its various forms" (para. 67). The CSW repeated this assertion of gender difference in drafting Resolution 1331 (XLIV), which the ECOSOC passed in May 1968 and begins, "*Concerned* that the *Report on Slavery* . . . indicates that slavery and the slave-trade and similar institutions and practices still exists in many parts of the world and that women especially are among the victims of such institutions and practices." It then goes on to "condemn" specific instances, including "marriages without consent, traffic in persons for purposes of prostitution, transference and inheritance of women and other similar degrading practices." The inclusion of traffic in women and prostitution under the broadened rubric of slavery and "similar institutions and practices" was thus affirmed and fortified as a gesture mindful of the unequal status of women.

Outside the United Nations, the Awad report added to and legitimated a revived popular discourse of "white slavery" in a cluster of mass-market books. Somewhat reminiscent of earlier campaigns against "white slavery," there was a mutually reinforcing cross-citation among pseudo-investigative reporting through popular publications, reports by nongovernmental organizations, and studies sanctioned by intergovernmental bodies. In 1965 Sean O'Callaghan published *The White Slave Trade* and followed up in 1968 with *The Yellow Slave Trade: A Survey of the Traffic in Women and Children in the East* (figure 3.1). The subtitle of *The Yellow Slave Trade* clearly hearkens back to the 1932 League of Nations study, which O'Callaghan references at several points. Significantly, *The Yellow Slave Trade* also includes several brief references to the Japanese military "comfort system." Following the confident declaration that "the traffic in women and children in China is of ancient origin," O'Callaghan proceeds to frame the "comfort system" within an old lineage in Asia: "During the reign of Emperor Han Wu, at about the time of Christ, prostitutes were first sent as camp followers to the armies of the great warlords. This was a practice which continued right down to the army of Kuomintang, and which was copied by the Japanese who had special brothels set up for their troops in all the major towns and cities they captured during the Second World War."[17]

Also in 1968, Stephen Barlay published *Sex Slavery: A Documentary Report on the International Scene Today*, which became a paperback best seller. The threading together of the popular, the nongovernmental, and the intergovernmental was more explicit in this book, with Barlay gratefully acknowledging research assistance from the Anti-Slavery Society and citing the then recently published United Nations *Report on Slavery*. In later editions of his book, Barlay would claim credit for coining the term *sex slavery*, which he "devised to cover modern forms, and sometimes more sophisticated but no less cruel, crude and brutal methods than those associated with the so-called 'white slavery.'" Explaining that "any girl, or for that matter man or boy, who is enslaved and sold for the purpose of sexual exploitation, becomes a 'white slave' whether his or her skin is black, yellow or white," Barlay makes a clear distinction between *sex slaves*

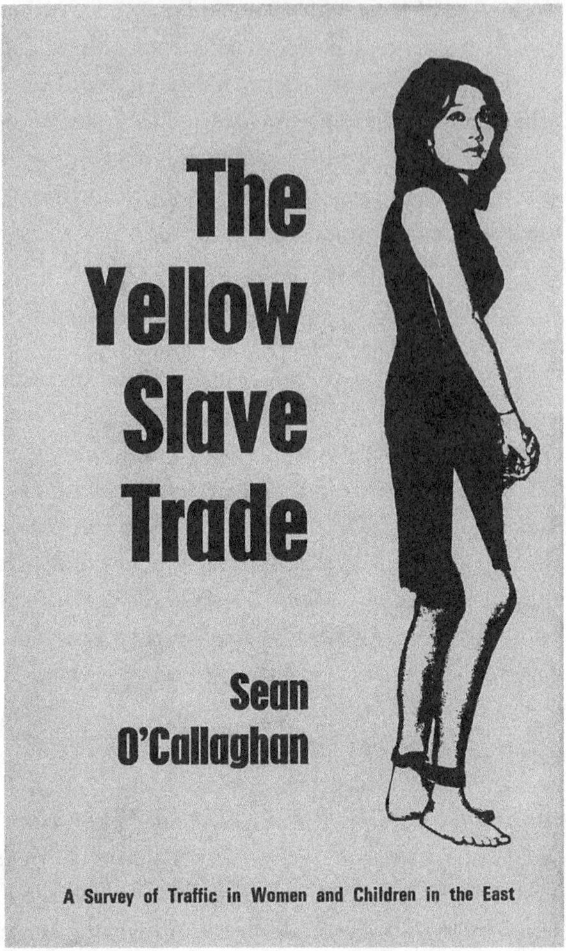

FIGURE 3.1. Front book jacket cover of Sean O'Callaghan, *The Yellow Slave Trade: A Survey of the Traffic in Women and Children in the East* (London: Blond, 1968). Photograph by Dunstan Pereira.

and *prostitutes:* "The prostitute who has a pimp or 'business manager' is often forced to bring in more and more money, but unlike a slave, she can retain her favours if she is determined to, she herself gets a varying share of her earnings, she has the freedom to travel and can change her 'lover' or 'manager' . . . and usually becomes a prostitute first and is accepted, employed or taken over by a protector only afterwards."[18] In addition to the denial of payment and nonchoice in physical mobility and pimp/manager, what distinguishes the sex slave, according to the last detail, is that she or he was *not* "a prostitute first" before the sexual enslavement. A claim to the status of sex slave necessitates a disavowal—the never having been—of the prostitute.

FEMALE SEXUAL SLAVERY (1979)

Barlay's book would later be referenced by the inexplicably altered title, *Sexual Slavery*, in Kathleen Barry's influential 1979 book, *Female Sexual Slavery*. As Barlay had done in his book, Barry also gratefully acknowledges the assistance of the Anti-Slavery Society and specifically its leader, Colonel Montgomery, in her research. But there were important differences between the two books. In contrast to Barlay, who argued that there were no distinctions of sex, age, or race in "sex slavery," Barry reinserted sex difference through her nomination of "female sexual slavery." From the outset of the book, Barry resolutely contests Barlay's cleaving of "sex slave" and "prostitute." Barry narrates how, prior to embarking upon her research for the book, she had assumed that there was a difference between cross-border trafficking and domestic prostitution. However, she soon came to recognize that "virtually the only distinction that can be made between traffic in women and prostitution is that the former involves crossing international borders." Consequently, Barry argues, "The practices used to force women into prostitution are the same whether they are trafficked across international boundaries or from one part of a city to another." We can see in this repudiation of the distinction between domestic and international trafficking the late twentieth-century feminist fulfillment of the earlier effort to disallow that distinction in the League of Nations inquiries. Barry further extends the nullification of women's consent in the 1933 anti-trafficking convention to domestic prostitution. In addition to more accurately describing coercive conditions, she offers "female sexual slavery" as more encompassing because it "refers to international traffic in women *and* forced street prostitution taken together."[19] Both geographical distinctions of scale and political-juridical demarcations of sovereignty are rendered insignificant under "female sexual slavery." In that light, Barry's marked demarcation of the *sexual* exploitation of Asian women, which I already pointed to in chapter 1, is crucial to providing evidence of the global relevance and enduring manifestation of "female sexual slavery." But precisely in order to fulfill that evidentiary function, none of the specific instances that Barry marshals can be thought of and re-presented as (1) instances of *intra*-Asian violence and inequalities, and, relatedly, (2) texts of *inter*-Asian feminist communication and knowledge production.

To that, I would also point to another peculiar deviation of Asian women as subjects of sexual slavery in their transnational relay into *Female Sexual Slavery*. Citing the Awad report as an authoritative source, Barry too highlights the response from Laos to the questionnaire. In "The Military Market" section of chapter 4, "The Traffic in Sexual Slaves," Barry writes: "Procuring for military

Sexual Slavery   93

prostitution in South Vietnam had by 1965 become a major problem in Southeast Asia. Laos, in its response to the 1965 UN slavery survey by Dr. Awad, noted a sizable increase in the traffic in women and stated that 'procuring is spreading from South Vietnam and Thailand to Laos.'"[20] Thus, Barry selectively extracted a small portion of the Laos response and interjected "military prostitution" to the more generic statement about procuring to magnify and regionalize it as "a major problem in Southeast Asia." But this mischaracterization and amplification blotted out the initial denial of the existence of a slave trade in the Laos response as well as the concluding explanation of poverty as the cause and the proposal of labor code reform as a remedy.

Following the publication of her book, Barry would lead a concerted feminist effort to recast prostitution as sexual slavery. At the 1980 Mid-Decade World Conference on Women in Copenhagen, she helped draft Resolution 43 of the World Plan of Action, which identified "forced prostitution" as "virtual slavery." After strongly "deplor[ing] the scant interest shown by Governments and international organizations," the resolution continues: "it would be desirable to improve the procedures and expand the activities of organs in the United Nations system, the Commission on the Status of Women, the Committee on Crime Prevention and Control and the Working Group on Slavery of the Sub-Commission on Prevention of Discrimination and Protection of Minorities of the Commission on Human Rights, which could help to prevent forced prostitution, suppress its exploitation and facilitate the rehabilitation of its victims." Barry would later assess the significance of this accomplishment in a 1981 essay:

> This is no mere rhetorical victory—it provides official, international recognition of a practice which nations and pimps alike have kept invisible and thus proliferating. Potentially this resolution will help empower the UN Status of Women Commission to receive complaints on female sexual slavery that until now have been under the exclusive jurisdiction of the heavily backlogged and male-dominated Human Rights Commission. In addition, official UN recognition of sexual slavery as an international violation of women's human rights is a necessary although insufficient condition leading toward provoking national action. As such it can be used by feminists as a tool for organizing.[21]

Although this passage refers to "sexual slavery" as an established, knowable, and thus chargeable violation in 1980, it is important to note that the term was *not* included as such in the text of the World Plan of Action. Barry prematurely claimed "UN recognition" for "sexual slavery," which was only later categorized as a distinctive violation of women's human rights through a new UN trafficking study in 1983.

Barry's stated hope that this would empower the Commission on the Status of Women (CSW) relative to the male-dominated Commission on Human Rights (CHR) suggests that the turn to "female sexual slavery" was shaped in part by a pragmatic reading of the unequal distribution of power/knowledge within the United Nations. Both UN bodies had been established in June 1946, but the Commission on Human Rights had long commanded greater resources and authority. The authority of the Commission on the Status of Women was further diffused in 1979 when the Committee on the Elimination of Discrimination against Women was created to monitor progress made in the implementation of CEDAW. According to Toepfer and Wells, "This bifurcation of the people and the resources that are devoted to promoting women's rights effectively diminished the power of both the Committee on the Elimination of Discrimination against Women and the Commission on the Status of Women."[22] The 1980 Copenhagen World Plan of Action had requested a new "report on prostitution throughout the world," but it was another two years later that, at the request of the Commission on the Status of Women, the Economic and Social Council passed a resolution (1982/20) calling for the appointment of a special rapporteur to produce "a synthesis of the surveys and studies on the traffic in persons and the exploitation of the prostitution of others" and to propose "appropriate measures to prevent and suppress those practices that are contrary to the fundamental human rights of human beings." Jean Fernand-Laurent was appointed in October 1982 and submitted a report in January 1983.

In chapter III the report outlines a detailed account of how the problem had been addressed within the United Nations system, paying attention to the work done in the following specific branches:

- The United Nations Centre for Human Rights
- The Working Group on Slavery
- The Commission on Human Rights
- The Centre for Social Development and Humanitarian Affairs (which had prepared the 1959 Study on Traffic in Persons and Prostitution)
- The Advancement of Women Branch
- The Commission on the Status of Women
- The Division of Narcotic Drugs
- Regional commissions for Africa, Latin America, Western Asia, and Asia and the Pacific

- The United Nations Children's Fund
- The Office of the United Nations High Commissioner for Refugees
- The International Labour Organisation
- UNESCO Division of Human Rights and Peace
- The World Health Organization
- The World Tourism Organization (linked to the United Nations Development Programme)
- The Economic and Social Council

Although this long list attests to broad, preexisting institutional concern, it also suggests the diffuse attention to the matter or, perhaps more accurately, to the epistemological and effective gaps produced by the expansive yet compartmentalized and overlapping jumble of the United Nations. In order to buttress the categorization of prostitution as slavery, Fernand-Laurent specially highlights the Working Group on Slavery: "From the outset this Group considered traffic in women and children to be a form of slavery; at its annual sessions, it heard many submissions from non-governmental organizations and made various recommendations which were ratified by the Commission." The report also notes that the 1982 update of the 1966 Awad *Report of Slavery*, composed by Special Rapporteur Benjamin Whitaker, included "extensive information on the exploitation of the prostitution of others."[23]

A fascinating detail of the Fernand-Laurent report appears in chapter 1, titled "A Universal and Interdisciplinary Question." Fernand-Laurent explains the "many angles" of possible analysis of the subject matter: "One can approach it from the angle of ethnology, sociology, or cultural history, for example; or again from the point of view of political economy, one can see the world of prostitution as a closed economic system; or from the point of view of criminology, as a branch of the criminal world because of the procuring involved. Prostitution can also be judged by the standards of public health, religion or morality." Even as this list attests to the greater academic legibility of prostitution and the availability of multiple disciplinary frames for producing knowledge, the epistemological and material implications of such multiplicity are swiftly bypassed in favor of a differently compelling diagnostic: "We ourselves, without overlooking any of these approaches, shall take the *human rights approach*, as does the Economic and Social Council; and from that point of view we, like the Commission on Human Rights, consider prostitution to be a form of slavery."[24] On the following page, Fernand-Laurent justifies and bolsters this classification of prostitution as slavery by asserting that "the alienation of the person is here more far-reaching than in slavery in its usual sense, where what is alienated is working strength, not intimacy."[25] The classification of prostitution as slavery proceeds in the mode of emphatic, affectively charged declaration, which precludes further explication and critical analysis. How is this alienation of intimacy (not "working strength") related to but also different from the defining criteria of ownership in slavery?

When Benjamin Whitaker, the Special Rapporteur of the Sub-Commission on Prevention of Discrimination and Protection of Minorities, updated his 1982 slavery report in 1984, he too would echo and reinforce this categorization of prostitution as slavery. A section on "Slavery-like practices involving women" cites Barry's *Female Sexual Slavery* under the specific subcategory of "traffic in women." Here Whitaker also replicates Barry's quotation of the 1974 Interpol report, including the detail about a distinctive "East Asian market." A third numbered section, titled "Exploitation of prostitution," begins by acknowledging that "participation in voluntary prostitution can be considered a matter of personal moral choice" but then goes on to argue that "its exploitation (involving coercion of children, for example) falls fully within the terms of the present report." Note how the complexities of individual volition and consent have been whittled down to "a personal *moral* choice." Whitaker continues to explain that "the exploitation of prostitution can be termed sexual slavery when a woman or child is owned, unable to change her residence, or forced to do acts she does not wish to perform." The "or" here suggests that any one of the three conditions, but especially the last vague and potentially very broad category, would qualify as sexual slavery. At the same time we can see the contraction of adult victims from Barlay's "any girl, of for that matter man or boy" back to "a woman or a child." In addition to citing Barlay's often salacious 1968 book, *Bondage: The Slave Traffic in Women Today*, the re-gendering and sexualization of slavery are legitimated and fortified through Whitaker's quoting of Janet Cockcroft, a representative of the Commission on the Status of Women, who stated at the thirty-first session of the Sub-Commission in 1978 that the CSW "considered enforced prostitution to be a form of slavery."[26] A year later in 1985, the Forward-Looking Strategies that were drafted at the 3rd International Women's Year Conference in Nairobi characterized prostitution as "a form of slavery imposed on women by procurers."[27]

This multisited recognition of prostitution as slavery was an affirmative institutional response to the Decade for Women and international feminist efforts to decry women's subordination and exploitation. In addition to making reference to Barry's *Female Sexual Slavery*, Fernand-Laurent duly acknowledged the recommendations for action at both the 1975 Mexico and 1980 Copenhagen conferences in his report. The UN recognition, in turn, emboldened the concerted feminist moves to recast trafficking and prostitution as sexual slavery. The proceedings of the April 1983 Global Feminist Workshop to Organize against Traffic in Women in Rotterdam would be published in 1984 under the title *International Feminism: Networking against Female Sexual Slavery*. As Barry summarizes the workshop in her contribution to the volume, "Forms of female sexual slavery which were considered for political action included sex tourism, international traffic in women and children, pimp controlled prostitution, forced and arranged marriages, and sexual mutilation."[28]

Sex tourism was now included as one of many forms of sexual slavery, but the critiques of intra-Asian racism and imperialism, deferred decolonization, and uneven capitalist development, which formed the crux of the earlier inter-Asian feminist articulations of "sex slaves" and "sexual slavery," became largely effaced in this induction of Asian women under international feminism and global governance. Then too, the specific political actions and analytical contributions of Asian women to that process would become subordinated to an individual authorship and vitae. In his 1983 report, Fernand-Laurent explicitly credited the Asian Women's Association (AWA), the Third World Movement against the Exploitation of Women (TW-MAE), and the Asian Confederation of Women's Organisations for effecting "a perceptible reduction in organized sex tourism in that region."[29] But a June 1985 feature article on Kathleen Barry in the *New York Times* titled, "A Personal Crusade against Prostitution," reported that her book *Female Sexual Slavery* served as "the basis for a 1983 United Nations report that said 'prostitution is slavery' and a grave cause for international concern."[30]

The official UN recognition of prostitution as sexual slavery fell short of fulfilling Barry's stated goal of empowering the Commission on the Status of Women. Instead, the ECOSOC Resolution 1983/30 recommended that the UN Secretary-General designate the Working Group on Slavery as the "focal point" of UN efforts and suggested "the possibility of inviting the Commission on the Status of Women to designate a representative to participate in all sessions of the Working Group." But the official recognition of "sexual slavery" did have the salutary effect of activating more national and international work in studying, documenting, and addressing this pressing problem. In addition to calling on member states to sign, ratify, and implement the 1949 Convention, Resolution 1983/30 recommended more policies geared toward the prevention of prostitution through "moral education and civics training" and also the employment of more women "having direct contact with the populations concerned." It also invited "the regional commissions to help Member States and the United Nations bodies wishing to organize regional expert meetings, seminars or symposia on the traffic in persons."

If "sexual slavery" afforded a greater affective and political charge than the "traffic in persons" or prostitution, the challenge of attempting to understand both the scope and the complexity of the problem was bypassed in favor of decrees of condemnation and intertextual citation through a familiar but delimited rhetoric of intensity and urgency. For example, Fernand-Laurent acknowledges but easily sidetracks the problem of how "precise statistics are unattainable" by arguing that "in any case, the important point is not the scale of the phenomenon but its degree of seriousness as a violation of the fundamental rights of the human person." He then adds, "In the terms of General Assembly resolution 32/130 of 16 December 1977, that violation is 'mass and flagrant'; it therefore requires, in the words of the same resolution, 'priority' attention from the international community."[31] As the repeated quotation marks demonstrate, intertextual, intra-institutional citation stands in for and even partially obviates investigation and documentation of the specific phenomenon. In March 1988 the Commission on Human Rights passed Resolution 1988/42, which stated that, in consideration of the "excellent report of Mr. J. Fernand-Laurent," the Commission was inviting the Sub-Commission and its Working Group to draw up "a plan of action in its future work regarding the elimination of contemporary forms of slavery, including traffic in persons and the exploitation of the prostitution of others." The resolution also conveyed to the member states "the recommendation by the Sub-Commission that freedom of attendance and freedom of speech before the Working Group be solemnly reaffirmed, and that any step taken by any authority designed to interfere with those freedoms or to punish their exercise be strongly condemned."[32] This exceptional provision for nongovernmental participation explains why so many different NGOs working on a wide range of problems subsequently focused their efforts on the Working Group.

The categorization of prostitution as sexual slavery also revivified the earlier racialization of the traffic in women as "white slavery" and the associated move of tethering the work of anti-trafficking to earlier antislavery campaigns and conventions. Here, we should keep in mind that the term *white slave* has a multipronged, contested genealogy. According to Nora Demleitner, "The term 'white slave' had originally been used to apply to factory workers in England but fell into disuse after the passage of the ten-hour factory law. Addressing the struggle against the Contagious Diseases Act, Victor Hugo breathed new life into the term in an 1870 letter to Josephine Butler, the British social reformer: 'The slavery of black women is abolished in America; but the slavery of white women continues in Europe.'"[33] Thus, the focused concern for "white women" was not just racially exclusionary of nonwhite women, but the naming of "white slavery" in early anti-trafficking was predicated upon a wishful and even willful misreading of the effective end of black enslavement in the U.S. This faith in the efficacy of the categorization of prostitution as slavery mistakenly presumed that official recognition and prohibition would change the material realities that were nominally decried. In the next section, I will retrace how this wager was premised upon a limited understanding of the longer and constitutively equivocal history of attending to the problem of slavery and forced labor in global governance, which reaches back to the League of Nations and even earlier to the abolition of the slave traffic in the nineteenth century.

INTER-IMPERIAL BEGINNINGS AND ENDS

As Suzanne Miers points out, slavery was *not* initially a priority issue for the League of Nations.[34] But the League Covenant notably included Article 23, which bound members to "secure fair and human conditions of labor" both domestically as well as in the nations with which they traded. As with the case of the traffic in women, these principled international commitments posed a conflict with both national sovereignty and inter-imperial rivalries in the aftermath of World War I. Indeed, the dubious blending of colonial ambitions and antislavery rhetoric has a longer history, going back to the 1890 Brussels Act (General Act for the Suppression of African Slave Trade), which, according to Claude E. Welch Jr., was "based on the belief that expanded, more effective colonial administration provided the best protection against slavery in Africa."[35] Moreover, although the signatories agreed to end the slave *trade*, "Forced labor was justified as necessary for infrastructure development."[36] As Miers cogently frames the disingenuous drafting of the Brussels Act, "By stating that the best means of attacking the traffic was to establish colonial administrations in the interior of Africa . . . it put an anti-slavery guise on the colonial occupation and exploitation of Africa."[37] After World War I the Peace Treaty of Versailles transferred authority over the former colonial territories of Germany to the victorious Allied states, which also included Japan, under the auspices of a League of Nations Permanent Mandates system. The treaty also called for the establishment of the International Labor Organization (ILO) as a specialized agency affiliated with the league. Many leading league members, most notably Britain, France, Belgium, Italy, and Portugal, were colonial powers that benefited from a range of coercive and exploitative labor practices in their overseas territorial possessions.

In 1920, shortly after the establishment of the League of Nations, the Anti-Slavery Society waged a persistent campaign of lobbying for the league to deal with slavery, which was deflected by the colonial powers: Great Britain, Netherlands, France, and Japan. These colonial powers "insisted that only evidence from governments could be circulated" and further opposed proposals by the Anti-Slavery Society for "a permanent office established in Geneva to deal with slavery, like one recently formed to combat trafficking in women and children," because they "were afraid that it might monitor their policies."[38] A League Assembly resolution on September 21, 1922, placed slavery on the agenda for 1923 and called on the League Council to compose a report. According to Jean Allain, this resolution had started out as a move to target Ethiopia: "In 1922, the British Member of the Permanent Mandates Commission, Frederick Lugard, circulated a memorandum which proposed that Ethiopia be placed under a Mandate shared by France, Italy and the United Kingdom, or administered directly by the League of Nations, because of that State's inability to suppress the slave trade." Pointing out that "it was in this context of the suppression of slavery as a standard of civilization that the 1926 Slavery Convention and the definition of slavery emerged," Allain explains: "While slavery was deemed to be unacceptable to 'civilised nations,' it should be noted that forced labour was not; in fact, it was deemed essential to the civilizing mission."[39] Thus, the charge of slavery could be marshaled strategically to sustain the racist and ethnocentric hierarchies of the imperial age into the new era of international amity.

But two rounds of requests in 1922 and again in 1923 for information from member states did not generate many responses. In a memorandum on May 31, 1923, the League's Secretary-General instructed the Council to prepare a report on slavery and noted that it "may base its report on information of two kinds: it may rely solely on the data officially forwarded to the Governments of the States Members, or it may resort to other sources." Noting that the government replies "are not in themselves sufficient to form the basis of an adequate report," the Secretary-General added that "the sifting of information drawn from the many and various other accessible sources is a task of extreme difficulty, and the Council might hesitate, for obvious reasons, to represent to the fourth Assembly a report based on such material, unless it had been compiled under the authority of a recognized body of experts."[40] The memo then ended by suggesting that the council entrust the preparation of the report to the already formed Permanent Mandates Commission, "an independent body of experts chosen by the Council for their personal competence and thus peculiarly well qualified to undertake the necessary work of somewhat specialized research." The League of Nations circulated another questionnaire in December 1923, and in the following spring it appointed the Temporary Slave Commission (TSC—first called the "Temporary Committee on Slavery") of "independent experts," which would be made up of seven members appointed by or in consultation with their respective governments along with one additional member who was a representative of the International Labor Organization.

Their initial deliberations on the proper scope of the TSC contained distinctive echoes of the League's actions on the traffic in women, but with more overt considerations of inter-imperial competition. Those member states which were worried that the TSC would uncover incriminating information about abuses perpetrated in their colonial territories sought to circumscribe its scope of activity. But the members of the TSC also made some independent decisions that would later prove to be quite consequential. After deliberating on the definition of slavery to be used to guide their inquiry, they "decided not to attempt a watertight definition but to list in their report all practices restricting personal liberty, including slave raiding, trading, and dealing, as well as slavery, serfdom, and all forms of debt bondage."[41] The TSC members also decided to consider forced or compulsory labor, but after objection from Portugal and other colonial powers, they agreed to allow for cases involving "essential public works and services and in return for adequate remuneration."[42] An important procedural innovation of the TSC was to consider nongovernmental sources of information in their inquiry. Miers's account of this complex negotiation merits full citation:

> The TSC was only too aware that all the colonial powers were uneasy about admitting evidence from unofficial sources for fear the Commission might be turned into a tribunal bringing accusations against particular states. To calm these fears, they stated that they would only take account of information from sources "whose competence and reliability" were recognized by their own governments. This was the forerunner of the system of "accrediting" certain NGOs to the United Nations. However, although it enabled a government to rule out information from individuals or organizations based in its own territories, it did not protect them from evidence from foreign NGOs or individuals whose governments certified them as reliable. To meet this difficulty, the TSC proposed that unofficial information would be sent to the government

concerned, and would only be used in the report after its comments had been received. This enabled governments to refute charges or to avoid reference to them in the report by delaying their answers until after the TSC had finished its work.[43]

Thus, even as new openings were created for "unofficial" or nongovernmental participation, these opportunities were constrained by new tactics of governmental denial and evasion. The TSC submitted its final report in June 1925, which later served as the basis of the 1926 Convention to Suppress the Slave Trade and Slavery.

The definition of *slavery* that was enshrined in Article 1 of the 1926 Slavery Convention as "the status or condition of a person over whom any or all of the powers attaching to the right of ownership are exercised" had been proposed in 1925 by Robert Cecil (the Viscount Cecil of Chelwood), a British delegate to the league. At the objection of the colonial powers, forced labor and the other practices considered by the TSC were not included in the final convention.[44] Article 5 bound the signatories to "take all necessary measures to prevent compulsory or forced labor from developing into conditions analogous to slavery," but the narrow focus on "ownership" in Article 1 made it possible for forced and compulsory labor to continue to be used and tolerated without violating the Slavery Convention. The vestiges of the earlier exception allowing for the use of forced labor for "public purposes" remained as well as the affirmation that "the responsibility for any recourse to compulsory or forced labor shall rest with the competent central authorities of the territory concerned." Thus, the categorical separation of forced labor from slavery and the prohibition of *only* slavery defined narrowly as ownership continued to serve colonial and capitalist interests. One could argue that the mandatory conscription of Korean girls and women by the Japanese colonial authorities into the Imperial Army's military "comfort system" and also the civilian labor corps for its various war industries in the 1930s and 1940s could proceed, not in violation of the 1926 Slavery Convention, but partly through its constitutive exceptions and loopholes.

In 1949 the UN ECOSOC passed Resolution 238 (IX) calling for the appointment of an Ad Hoc Committee on Slavery to "consider the possibility and desirability of proposing a new convention on slavery."[45] Although the committee stated in its first report in 1950 that "it might prove desirable to draft a new convention broader in scope," the second report in 1951 recommended that the definition of *slavery* in the 1926 convention, which foregrounded ownership, "should continue to be accepted as an accurate and adequate definition."[46]

The Committee decided that it would "restrict its factual survey to the period following the adoption of the International Slavery Convention of 1926, and would pay particular attention to the period following the Second World War."[47] Considered alongside Engen's move to exclude prostitution from his 1955 report on slavery, this decision to focus on the *post*-1945 period may partially explain how the Japanese military "comfort system" (1932–45) had fallen through yet another of many cracks in the shifting international edifice of investigation and monitoring.

THE UN WORKING GROUP ON SLAVERY

Beyond shaping the discourse of sexual slavery, the Awad report would prove to be especially consequential in expanding the possibilities of nongovernmental participation and expert consultation in the UN Commission on Human Rights. In addition to the questionnaire addressed to member states, Awad attempted to confer with nine NGOs with consultative status, including the International Council of Women (ICW) and the Women's International League for Peace and Freedom (WILPF). The 1966 report registers disappointment about the "scanty materials" received from the NGOs, with the notable exception of the Anti-Slavery Society of London, which "prepared an extensive memorandum, dealing with a number of areas of the world," and Awad gratefully acknowledged his "indebtedness to this great Society for the services which it has rendered to him in the course of his assignment." Later, in a summary of recommendations from the nongovernmental organizations, Awad conveyed the suggestion made by the Anti-Slavery Society for "the establishment of a permanent committee to concern itself with all the aspects of combating slavery in accordance with the wish expressed in 1933 by the Statutory Advisory Committee of the League of Nations." Noting that several other NGOs, including the ICW and WILPF, had also made similar suggestions, Awad prepared and attached a draft resolution to the end of the 1966 report, which authorizes the establishment of "a committee of experts on slavery, the slave trade and institutions and practices similar to slavery."[48]

It was not until May 1974 that the Economic and Social Council approved the recommendation of the Sub-Commission on the Prevention of Discrimination and the Protection of Minorities to establish the Working Group on Slavery, which was charged with reviewing "developments in the field of the slave trade and the slavery-like practices of *apartheid* and colonialism, the traffic in persons and the exploitation of others" as defined in the 1926 Slavery

Convention, the Supplementary Convention of 1956, and the 1949 Convention for the Suppression of the Traffic in Persons and of the Exploitation of the Prostitution of Others. The first Working Group comprised five lawyers, one from each of the five main UN regions (Britain, India, Yugoslavia, Sierra Leone, and Colombia). During its first meeting in 1975, the five expert members agreed that the three conventions did not "cover the concept of slavery under all its present aspects" and charged itself to investigate "all institutions and practices which, by restricting the freedom of the individual, are susceptible of causing severe hardship and serious deprivation of liberty." This was a marked departure from the narrow focus on ownership. In order to carry out this considerable task, they recommended that the Working Group be made a permanent body with broad powers and open procedures: "Its most controversial recommendations were that it should be allowed to seek and receive communications, visit countries where slavery existed, and invite governments, NGOs, and individuals to attend its meetings and 'assist' in its work."[49]

Although it operated under the Sub-Commission and the Commission on Human Rights, the Working Group turned out to be an exceptionally accessible forum for nongovernmental participation on a wide range of issues. Because it allowed for any NGO with consultative status to address the body and submit documentation for its consideration in advance of the annual meetings, this opening combined with "the absence of observers from member states in the early years" to enable NGOs to wield greater influence in both agenda setting and document preparation than other branches of the United Nations.[50] In 1978 the Sub-Commission recommended that the 1966 Awad report be updated and named Benjamin Whitaker, a member of the Working Group, as a Special Rapporteur. After revising and circulating a new questionnaire to member states, Whitaker submitted an updated slavery report in 1982; his recommendations included strengthening the Working Group. In 1980 the Sub-Commission agreed to consider annual reports from the Working Group. By the 1980s, NGOs could comment on drafts of the meeting reports before they were finalized.

Given the broad scope of issues that could be raised, its procedural flexibility, and the extraordinary reach of a very particular kind of nongovernmental influence, the Working Group on Slavery came to serve as an important forum for drawing attention to and deliberating on many various violations of human rights, including women's human rights. In 1979 the Minority Rights Group, which had been established in 1969 by David Astor, the editor of the UK newspaper *Observer*, with the assistance of a major grant from the Ford Foundation, drew the attention of the Working Group to the dowry system in India as an instance of "the traffic in persons and exploitation of the prostitution of others." The Working Group would go on to examine "violence against women, including murder, for reasons of 'family honour' (e.g., in the Middle East)" in 1980 and "female circumcision and the sexual exploitation of children" in 1981. This focused attention was certainly calibrated to the designation of the United Nations Decade for Women (1975–85), but this list also attests to Zoglin's skeptical observation of a clear division of labor in the Working Group and, more importantly, the *direction* of its concerted attention: "The significant impetus provided by the NGOs has come from largely western organizations. In contrast, the majority of topics under consideration have focused on slavery-like practices in the Third World."[51]

In March 1988, partly in response to the breadth of issues raised and the unwieldy volume of requests for its attention and intervention, the Commission on Human Rights passed Resolution 1988/42, which renamed the body more narrowly as the Working Group on Contemporary Forms of Slavery. The Sub-Commission also approved a proposal by the Working Group to undertake a more focused program to address three specific themes in successive years from 1989 to 1991. The first year would focus on the sale and prostitution of children and child pornography followed by attention to child labor and debt bondage in 1990. The "prevention of traffic in persons and exploitation of the prostitution of others" was designated as the theme for 1991. Although the 1989 and 1990 meetings of the Working Group were nominally focused on children, the durable category of "women and children" allowed some NGOs to include adult women in their presentations. This provided an opening for NGOs focused on women's rights, including the Coalition against Trafficking in Women (CATW), which had only recently been established in 1988 by Kathleen Barry and Dorchen Leidholdt. As Barry would later recall, several feminists, including notably Robin Morgan, had suggested early on that Barry "begin a new wave of NGOs, nongovernmental organizations in consultative status with the United Nations." Recognizing that "the international networking I had been developing on the issue of traffic in women would qualify our coalition for human rights (Category II) status with the United Nations," Barry initiated the application process.[52] By 1989, CATW would gain Consultative Status II with the UN Economic and Social Council and participate in meetings of the Working Group.

The Working Group would serve as an important site for framing prostitution and the traffic in women as "sexual slavery." At the 1989 meeting a representative of the International Abolitionist Federation asserted that "the number of women and children living in sexual slavery and becoming victims of traffic had increased at an alarming rate in the past 15 years" since the Mexico City conference and further emphasized that prostitution was "a form of sexual slavery" that was "interlinked" with a range of crimes and problems that included "battering of women, broken home, incest, physical and emotional neglect, cruelty and abuse during childhood." An unnamed representative of CATW asserted that "all instances of prostitution violated women's human rights" and contested the distinction between free and forced prostitution in the 1949 convention: "As long as prostitution itself was ignored as a violation of the human rights of women, and men could buy sex and women's bodies with impunity, other more degrading human practices would flourish, placing the human rights of women, both prostitutes and non-prostitutes, increasingly at risk."[53]

Both Barry and Leidholdt attended the 1991 meetings of the Working Group as representatives of CATW along with five other members of the group. In addition, Jyoti Sanghera attended as a representative of the International Federation Terre des Hommes, and she spoke about trafficking and exploitation of Nepalese women and children. Marking ten years since CEDAW came into force in 1981, this 1991 meeting also considered the problem of the extraordinary number of reservations that member states had made in ratifying the convention and called for the Working Group to request the International Court of Justice to review the validity of these reservations. This move was in response to the CSW Resolution 35/30, passed earlier in the year at its thirty-fifth session in February-March 1991. The representative of Anti-Slavery International pointed to cases of slavery in India, Turkey, and Burmese women in Thailand. A representative of the International Commission of Jurists described specific cases in Asia, including "organized sex tourism," commercial marriage arrangements, and "the trafficking of workers and prostitutes from third world countries to industrialized ones," and pointed to Japan as responsible for all three forms. According to the proceedings, several unnamed NGOs alleged that there was an "increasing number of prostitutes particularly women and children, working in connection with 'sex tourism' enterprises and military bases" and proposed that the Working Group "consider all types of prostitution as a violation of human rights, and thereby to making invalid any distinction between forced and voluntary prostitution." The resulting draft program of action of the 1991 Working Group meeting took a far-reaching antiprostitution and antipornography position. In addition to declaring that "using the enticement of sex with women and children to market tourism should be penalized on the same level as procurement," it recommended that "legislation should be adopted to prevent new forms of technology from being used for promoting and encouraging prostitution" and urged member states to "enact legislation making it a crime to produce and distribute pornographic material involving women and children."[54]

Although the Working Group provided an important opening for such feminist declarations and recommendations, it had no power to effectively implement them. Thus, Zoglin identifies the Working Group's important political and institutional function as a *forum* that "enables aggrieved individuals and groups to address the United Nations fairly and directly."[55] She adds: "Despite the fact that the process sometimes ends there, a sounding board alone may satisfy the group since some official body has listened and taken note of its grievances. Second, the aggrieved group may attract publicity from home and abroad as to its plight." These speculations about the minimal consolations of testimony and publicity were ventured in 1989, before the technological advances in distant communication and the proliferation of events, forums, and "sounding boards" for the airing of grievances in the 1990s and beyond.

MILITARY SEXUAL SLAVERY

This was the discursive and bureaucratic terrain wherein Lee Hyo-chae, representing the Korean Council, first made a written request for an investigation of the Japanese military "comfort system" to the UN Secretary-General in New York in February 1992. Here we should bear in mind that South Korea gained its UN membership only in 1991. In a somewhat vague formulation, Chin Sung Chung notes that "Lee also met with the person in charge of women's and human rights issues and was advised to share her concerns with the UN's Human Rights Commission."[56] The 1992 report on *Contemporary Forms of Slavery* by the Working Group refers to Lee's memo as "the appeal initiated by the Korean Council for Women Drafted for Sexual Service by Japan, and its requests to the Commission on Human Rights to investigate the Japanese atrocities committed against Korean women during the Second World War and to the Sub-Commission on Prevention of Discrimination and Protection of Minorities to help press the Government of Japan to pay damages to individual women who had filed suit in Japan."[57] Note this initial English mis-translation of *Chongshindae* as "sexual *service*." Six months later, on August 10, 1992, when Shin Heisoo made an oral presentation at the forty-fourth session of the Sub-Commission on Prevention of Discrimination and Protection of Minorities in Geneva, she was similarly identified as a representative of the Korean Council for Women Drafted for Sexual Service by Japan.[58] According to the *Summary*

Record of this eighth meeting of the 1992 session of the Sub-Commission, Shin raised "the question of the 200,000 Korean girls and women who had been forced to act as prostitutes for the Japanese army between 1932 and 1945" and argued that "they were in fact sexual slaves, servicing as many as 100 soldiers per day, and risking torture and even death if they attempted to escape."[59] In addition to the research done by the Korean Council, Shin referred to a recent South Korean government report in which "some 390 women—comfort women and victims of forced labour—had given evidence." Adding that "women from other Asian countries were also concerned: Chinese, Taiwanese, Filipinas and Indonesians," Shin's presentation made note of a multinational conference that was being convened concurrently on August 10-11, 1992, in Seoul, which brought together more than sixty participants from Korea, Japan, Taiwan, Hong Kong, Thailand, and the Philippines. The *Summary Record* refers to this regional meeting as the "Asian Conference on Prostitution."[60] Shin relayed the request of the Korean Council that the Sub-Commission adopt "a resolution against the sexual slavery imposed on Koreans and other Asian women."[61] At this threshold of the introduction and induction of the "comfort women" problem into late twentieth-century global governance, we see the beginnings of the determined shift from *prostitutes* to *sexual slaves* and *sexual slavery* even as these terms were still deployed alongside both *sexual service* and *prostitution*.

At the second Asian conference on the issue, which was convened the following year in October 1993, the participants agreed to use the English term *Japanese military sexual slavery* going forward. These meetings would thereafter be referred to as the Asian Solidarity Conference on Japanese Military Sexual Slavery. The full English name of the Korean Council would be changed to the Korean Council for the Women Drafted for Japanese Military Sexual Slavery. Other organizational names also changed accordingly. For example, in the Philippines the Task Force on Filipino "Comfort Women" (TFFCW), which was established in July 1992 by thirteen women's groups, including the Asian Women's Human Rights Council (AWHRC), GABRIELA, and the BAYAN Women's Desk, changed its name to the Task Force on Filipina Victims of Military Sexual Slavery by Japan. At the NGO forum convened alongside the 1995 4th World Conference on Women in Beijing, the Korean Council organized an Asian Tribunal on Military Sexual Slavery by Japan.

Recall that the full Korean name of Korean Council, *Hanguk Chongshindae Munje Taechaek Hyobuihoe*, uses the term *Chongshindae* ("volunteer labor corps"). In a 2004 article in the journal, *Critical Asian Studies*, C. Sarah Soh explained that the translation and trans-coding of the term as "military sexual slavery" was a strategic disavowal of the implications of choice and foreknowledge in the Korean term. Pointing out that some former members of the *Chongshindae* "performed only manual labor and no sexual labor," Soh argued that "the Korean usage of the term *Chongshindae* to refer to 'comfort women' thus appears to be a political strategy on the part of activists, used to highlight the deceptive and/or coercive methods that had been used in the recruitment of comfort women in colonial Korea." Secondly, Soh added, *Chongshindae* "symbolically distinguishes wartime comfort women from contemporary *wianbu* serving the American military in Korea ... [and] functions as a considerate euphemism born out of cultural sensitivity for the survivors in order to avoid the negative image of prostitutes evoked by the term *wianbu*."[62] Thus, we need to keep in mind that *Chongshindae* was a measured dissociation of the survivors from contemporary Korean women sex workers for the U.S. military.[63] If *Chongshindae* was deployed partially to desexualize and destigmatize its surviving subjects, it is worth exploring how and why activists and allies later reinserted the *sexual* in settling upon "Japanese military sexual slavery" as the preferred English term and how this redress movement further propelled the installation of "sexual slavery" within global governance as a distinctive form of female injury. According to Kern and Nam, the Korean Council settled on the term *military sexual slavery* in accordance with "the counsel of international legal specialists."[64] They frame the turn to "military sexual slavery" as a tactical move to augment the legibility of the issue under the expanding activist and legal frameworks of "women's rights as human rights" in the early 1990s. In contrast, Soh suggests a later, differently motivated terminological shift: "As the internationalization of the redress movement has progressed, some South Korean survivors and their advocates have felt compelled to declare that they were not 'comfort women,' especially after [Jan] Ruff-O'Herne's forceful criticism. Strongly condemning the widespread usage of 'comfort women' as itself 'an insult' to herself and other survivors, she insisted that they were 'war-rape victims, enslaved and conscripted by the Japanese Imperial Army.'"[65] Several accounts have pointed to the crucial role of Ruff-O'Herne's participation in the redress movement, especially given that, as Margaret Stetz puts it, she is "white, educated, from a privileged background, and an English speaker."[66] But Ruff-O'Herne's specific reformulation appears in her 1994 memoir *Fifty Years of Silence*, and there was already a concerted activist rejection of "comfort women" in favor of "sexual slavery" by this time. In her 2007 monograph, Soh cites Kim Il-myon's designation of *sekkusu no dorei* ("sex slave") in his 1976 book as one possible early precursor, but she more confidently asserts that "the categorical representation of comfort women as sex slaves could emerge only in the 1990s, owing to the post–Cold War world politics of human rights."⁶⁷ In an earlier article published in 2000, Soh characterized "sex slaves" even more narrowly as a "1990s feminist label."⁶⁸ But, as I have discussed in chapter 1, the inter-Asian feminist movement against sex tourism and military prostitution in the 1970s had used the term *sex slaves* to contest the persistent centrality of sexual violence and female labor exploitation under colonial rule and neocolonial domination. Rather than authenticate a single origin, I would press for contextualizing "sexual slavery" in terms of a longer, broader, multisited discursive history, which I have tried to outline throughout this chapter.

The reformulation of "comfort women" and "comfort stations" into "sex slaves" and "military sexual slavery" proceeded along many different axes and by many actors in and outside of the UN in the 1990s. Although this stated preference for "military sexual slavery" was usually framed as a gesture of political sympathy and a reach for empirical accuracy, different subjects had different rhetorical aims, ideological leanings, and institutional motivations. There were select openings and fortuitous opportunities along several dispersed and sometimes convergent channels of advocacy, documentation, and adjudication. The written request by Lee Hyo-chae coincided with an oral presentation to the Commission on Human Rights on February 17, 1992, by Totsuka Etsuro, a Japanese human rights advocate and then representative of International Educational Development, an international NGO with consultative status. Totsuka drew attention to "the situation of Korean girls and women abducted by Japanese forces during the Second World War for use as sex slaves" and the fact that "the victims had received no remedy." He then suggested: "The international community could usefully participate in seeking solutions to such violations. The Commission might establish a mediation panel to suggest remedies, including compensation for victims." Finally, Totsuka also suggested that the Special Rapporteur on the Rights to Restitution, Compensation and Rehabilitation for Victims of Gross Violations of Human Rights and Fundamental Freedoms "might also be requested to study the situation and recommend remedies."⁶⁹ In 1989 the Sub-Commission had appointed Theo van Boven to the position and entrusted him to prepare a study that might lead to developing some basic principles and guidelines. The lawsuits filed against Japan in December 1991 coincided with and further fueled this initiative on restitution and compensation for gross violations of human rights at the United Nations.

The special theme of the sixteenth session of the Working Group on Contemporary Forms of Slavery in 1991 on "prevention of traffic in persons and exploitation of the prostitution of others" emboldened NGOs to raise a range of problems affecting women, and it also paved the way for the introduction of the Japanese military "comfort system" for deliberation at its seventeenth session on May 4–13, 1992. Three months following his first presentation to the Commission on Human Rights in February, Totsuka again "raised the issue of Korean girls and women abducted or compulsorily displaced by the Japanese imperial forces during the Second World War for use as sex slaves. They number as many as some 200,000." In addition, he pointed out, "Some 1.5 million Korean men had been abducted or compulsorily displaced to Japan and enslaved there for the hardest works by the Japanese Government during the war." Against Japan's claim that the 1965 normalization treaty with South Korea had resolved all claims, Totsuka argued that that "neither Government had any legal capacity to nullify the human rights of any individuals because the Governments and the individual victims were different entities," and added: "Human rights are inalienable. Claims for restitution, compensation and rehabilitation were part of the human rights of the victims."[70]

This seventeenth session of the Working Group on May 4–13, 1992 was an especially important early setting that brought many different stakeholders and supporters together at the UN. A representative of the International Abolitionist Federation presented a fairly detailed account of the Japanese military "comfort system." The report of the meeting notes that the Coalition against Trafficking in Women (CATW) also spoke up in support of the requests by the Korean Council "to the Commission on Human Rights to investigate the Japanese atrocities committed against Korean women during the Second World War and to the Sub-Commission . . . to help press the Government of Japan to pay damages to individual women who had filed suit in Japan."[71] An "observer" from North Korea attended the seventeenth session and also spoke in support of these motions. In its subsequent report to the Sub-Commission, the Working Group requested the Secretary-General to transmit information regarding "the situation of women forced to engage in prostitution during wartime" under section IV on "Prevention of Traffic in Persons and Exploitation of the Prostitution of Others" rather than the next numbered section on "Machinery for Monitoring the International Convention on Slavery.[72] The Sub-Commission later endorsed this request, but it is notable that neither body would use the terms *sex slaves* or *sexual slavery*.

The call for compensation for survivors, which was prominent in the earliest interjections of the issue at the UN, may also have shaped the turn to military sexual slavery. At the end of her August 10, 1992, presentation to the Sub-Commission, Shin relayed the request of the Korean Council that "the Special Rapporteur . . . draft a recommendation concerning the compensation of the victims and recommend that the Commission should form a 'mediation committee' on the issue of reparation." Beyond its exceptional openness to NGO participation and influence, the specific demand for compensation might have also dictated the focus on the Working Group as the site of publicity and mechanism for redress, which aligned the "comfort women" redress campaign with other efforts to obtain compensation from Japan for its use of POW labor during World War II. The demand for compensation through the rubric of slavery connected the "comfort women" redress movement to an older decolonial struggle around forced and unpaid labor conscription of Koreans under Japanese rule. On August 25, 1992, following the earlier presentation by Shin, the NGO Liberation submitted a written statement on behalf of Korean and Taiwanese soldiers who had been conscripted for the Japanese Imperial Army. Pointing out that a Japanese government representative had alluded to the possibility of a redress measure for "the so-called comfort women of Japan," the note went on to request the Sub-Commission "as regards the gross violation of the human rights of Korean comfort women, Korean men and women victims of forced labour and ex-Japanese soldiers in Taiwan and Korea" to "urge" Japan to "pay full compensation to each of the victims."[73] But it is still unclear to me *what* the different victims were to be compensated for.

It is also unclear but worth asking whether and how the demand for compensation was informed in part by the fact that the Sub-Commission had already authorized and initiated the van Boven study by the time that the issue was introduced to the UN in 1992. Even before Special Rapporteur van Boven submitted his final report in June 1993, which included the Japanese military "comfort system" as an illustrative case and strongly endorsed the victims' claims for compensation, he would play a key supportive role in the nascent redress movement. In December 1992 an International Public Hearing Concerning Postwar Compensation by Japan was convened in Tokyo; Totsuka was one of the organizers of the hearing, and van Boven attended as an unofficial observer. Indai Sajour attended with the Filipina survivor and author, Maria Rosa Luna Henson, who also testified at the hearing. Following the international public hearing and ahead of the eighteenth session of the Working Group, which was to be convened in May 1993, van Boven sent a letter to its members stating that "he is ready to undertake a study on the situation of women forced to engage in prostitution during wartime on the basis of the documentation received by him and in the light of the basic principles and guidelines which will be included in his final report on the Sub-Commission."[74]

The *Final Report* that van Boven submitted on July 2, 1993, includes a lengthy consideration of the rubric of "gross violations of human rights and fundamental freedoms." Van Boven produces this list: "genocide; slavery and slavery-like practices; summary or arbitrary executions; torture and cruel, inhuman or degrading treatment or punishment; enforced disappearance; arbitrary and prolonged detention; deportation or forcible transfer of population; and systematic discrimination, in particular based on race or gender."[75] The Japanese military "comfort system" could qualify under many of these categories, which are not fully captured by the term *military sexual slavery*. Under the heading of "special issues of interest and attention," the van Boven report delineates a wide-ranging array of "serious damages and grave injuries to human dignity": the territorial dispossession and forced relocation of indigenous peoples, environmental damage, medical experimentation in Nazi concentration camps, the planting of land mines, and the Iraqi invasion of Kuwait. The report also highlights "violence against women" as "a matter of urgent and widespread concern," and lists the various "remedial and reparational measures" that are outlined in the draft of the Declaration on Elimination of Violence against Women. Pointing to the Working Group's May 1993 request for information about "the situation of women forced to engage in prostitution during wartime," which had been endorsed by the Sub-Commission, van Boven again states his willingness to conduct such a study.

In August 1993 the Sub-Commission adopted a resolution calling for the appointment of a Special Rapporteur to undertake "an in-depth study on systematic rape, sexual slavery and slavery-like practices during wartime." The Sub-Commission appointed Linda Chavez, a member of the Working Group, as the Special Rapporteur. The "comfort women" case was prominently featured in the "preparatory document" that Chavez submitted on September 7, 1993, and the preliminary "Working Paper" that Chavez submitted in 1995. When Chavez was unable to continue in the position, Gay J. McDougall was appointed as the Special Rapporteur and submitted a final report in 1998. All three reports strongly endorse the categorization of the Japanese military "comfort system" as a case of "sexual slavery" and support the victims' demand for compensation. Following up from these significant developments at the UN and the Vienna conference on human rights in June 1993, the participants of the 2nd Asian Solidarity Conference, which was convened in October 1993, resolved to move forward with the term *military sexual slavery*.

The newly appointed Special Rapporteur on Violence against Women also played a key role in affirming the renaming as "military sexual slavery." In the 1994 *Preliminary Report*, Coomaraswamy notes: "It is a crucial question that would set a legal precedent at the international level for the prosecution of perpetrators of systematic rape and sexual slavery in times of armed conflict.

A symbolic gesture of compensation would introduce a remedy of 'compensation' for women victims of violence perpetrated during times of armed conflict."[76] The repetition and double equivocation of compensation here are intriguing. On January 4, 1996, Coomaraswamy submitted an addendum to the *Preliminary Report*, which was titled *Report on the Mission to the Democratic People's Republic of Korea, the Republic of Korea and Japan on the Issue of Military Sexual Slavery in Wartime*. This 1996 report emphasizes from the outset that the Special Rapporteur "considers the case of women forced to render sexual services in wartime by and/or for the use of armed forces a practice of military sexual slavery."[77] The installation of "sexual slavery" into the lexicon of global governance culminated in its formal codification as a war crime and crime against humanity in the Rome Statute of the International Criminal Court in 1998.

If the activist strategy to rename the "comfort system" as "military sexual slavery" and the related demand for compensation were partially shaped by and contributed to this twisted history of the recognition and adjudication of slavery and uncompensated, compulsory labor in global governance, it is worth considering how the question of labor became subordinated to the more spectacular, emotional focus on sexual violence. As early as Totsuka's May 1992 presentation of the issue to the Working Group, he pointed out that the "violation of the human rights protected by the Forced Labour Convention (ILO Convention No. 29) of 1930, ratified by Japan in 1932 and which took effect for Japan in 1933, was another ground for compensation."[78] But, as I have pointed out earlier in the chapter, the installation of "military sexual slavery" was partly yet crucially hinged upon a disavowal and distancing from prostitution conceived as both volitional labor and, as such, the sign of a crucial moral, sexual aberration. A 1994 report by the International Commission of Jurists characterized the forcible conscription of both male and female Korean labor as "tantamount to slavery," but it also distinguished the "sexual slavery" of the "comfort system" as follows: "What distinguished the situation of the women taken for the sexual gratification of the Japanese military from those men and women who were forcibly conscripted or mobilized to work in war industries was the inability to fit into Korean society upon their return. The shame and degradation brought upon them ensured that they would live lives of isolation and would consider themselves to be misfits within their own society."[79] The survivors of the "comfort system" were set apart from other victims of forced labor through a particular shame about their presumed moral, sexual degradation.

There was a concurrent attempt to raise the issue for discussion and adjudication at the International Labour Organization. In her fascinating account of this campaign, Chung Chin Sung specifically identifies a seminar convened by Japanese NGOs in Tokyo on September 23-24, 1994, as a pivotal yet under-addressed moment in the history of the international redress movement. The organizers invited P. N. Bhagwati, a member of the ILO Committee of Experts. Bhagwati "stated that forced prostitution as a part of military sexual slavery was a form of forced labor, and referring to diverse legal evidence, confirmed it as a violation of the ILO Convention."[80] Encouraged by this development, a transnational coalition of Korean and Japanese unions, including the Federation of Korean Trade Unions (FTKU) and the Osaka Fu Special English Teachers' Union (OFSET), initiated a joint effort to have the ILO investigate and recognize the Japanese military "comfort system" as a violation of the 1930 Forced Labour Convention: "In November 1995, the Committee of Experts judged that the military sexual slavery had to be specified as a form of sexual slavery. In this view, it was a violation of the Forced Labour Convention, and they expressed its hope that the Japanese government would prepare a suitable policy for compensation."[81] In 2002, after many years of persistent campaigning and frustrating delays, the ILO Committee of Experts on the Application of Conventions and Recommendations (CEACR) arrived at its "final conclusions" on both "victims of wartime sexual slavery" and "wartime industrial forced labor," which was that "it has no mandate to rule on the legal effect of bilateral and multilateral international treaties."[82] Although the Working Group managed briefly to serve as "sounding board," it never had the warrant to push for substantive resolution or action. In June 1994 the Working Group recommended that the "comfort women" problem be taken up and resolved through the Permanent Court of Arbitration in The Hague. The Working Group on Contemporary Forms of Slavery would itself be dissolved after it held its last session in August 2006.

VIOLENCE AGAINST WOMEN

As a more recent category that came into international visibility in the 1980s, the case of "violence against women" (VAW) and the place of Asian women in its installation and permutations offer an interesting point of comparison to both "traffic in women" and "sexual slavery." The UN General Assembly adopted, without a vote, the Declaration on the Elimination of Violence against Women (DEVAW) in December 1993 and consequently appointed Radhika Coomaraswamy as the Special Rapporteur on Violence against Women, Its Causes and Consequences. By the end of the decade, Coomaraswamy could sketch out this impressively broad and inclusive enumeration:

> Common throughout the world, violence against women became a rallying point in this struggle [to name women's rights as human rights],

bringing together a diverse group of women from all regions of the world. Among this group were: those working with victims of the armed conflict in the former Yugoslavia, Rwanda, and with victims of military sexual slavery during World War II; women from the dynamic movement against domestic violence, rape, and sexual harassment; those struggling against trafficking in women, forced prostitution, and forced labor; women working against female genital mutilation, dowry deaths, Sati, and other traditional practices harmful to the health of women; and Women Living Under Muslim Laws who drew the link between religious extremism and violence against women.[1]

It is noteworthy that "military sexual slavery during World War II" appears under the first subcategory along with "victims of the armed conflict" in Rwanda and the former Yugoslavia. This definitional priority attests to the international prominence of the "comfort women" issue in the early 1990s as the initial redress efforts coincided with the systematic rapes in Bosnia and Rwanda and called attention to *sexual* violence against women in wartime. But it is notable that it is now separated from both rape and trafficking in women, forced prostitution, and forced labor. Finally, the identification of "victims" is only used for the first subcategory, whereas the other subcategories point not just generically to "women" but to a specific cohort of activist women working against those specific forms of violence.

As with traffic in women and sexual slavery, Asian women featured prominently in staking the globalist claims of violence against women as an urgent problem and actionable phenomenon. The journal *Violence against Women* has published numerous articles and devoted a special issue to China in 1999 and to East and Southeast Asia in 2003. In a 2002 article titled "Violence against Women: Global Scope and Magnitude," which was published in *The Lancet*, the authors claim under the subheading of "Trafficking, forced prostitution, exploitation of labour, and debt bondage" that "the greatest number of victims are thought to come from Asia (about 250,000 per year)."[2] This article also refers to the Japanese military "comfort system" under the subheading of "Rape in war." Throughout the 1990s, there were several region-specific initiatives on violence against women in Asia by NGOs and various branches of the United Nations.[3] These meetings, workshops, and conferences often yielded publications, which added to a growing body of expert knowledge and academic scholarship. Two collections of essays were also published: *Breaking the Silence: Violence against Women in Asia* (1999), edited by Fanny M. Cheung and Malavika Karlekar, and *Violence against Women in Asian Societies* (2003), edited by

Linda Rae Bennet and Lenore Manderson. In a published review of *Breaking the Silence*, I observed how the heterogeneous range of forms of violence, practices of reporting and documentation, and the methods of research featured in the collection militates against the very premise of delineating VAW in "Asia" or "Asian societies." I raised a series of categorical questions, which bear repeating: What is the difference between "violence against women in Asia" and "violence against Asian women"? What makes violence against women *in Asia* similar to and different from violence against women in other regions? Then too, are women *throughout* Asia subject to particular forms of gender-related violence, which are manifest across subregional, national, religious, ethnic, and class differences? What about non-Asian women in Asia? What about Asian women who are *not in* Asia? As evident in the title to the 1999 collection, these questions have been effectively foreclosed by the Asianization of *silence* about violence against women in Asia.[4]

With that in mind, this chapter takes a marked detour from Asian women to trace the installation of "violence against women" more generically in the power/knowledge mesh of global governance in the 1990s. In this different approach to enacting Asian women as method, I aim to further demonstrate how the discursive traffic in Asian women comprises a range of differential visibilities. Even when Asian women seem to disappear or appear unrecognizable as such in a certain register, there are broader lessons to be gleaned about the peculiar protocols and methods of knowledge and valuation in that register, which might allow us, in turn, to think against the compulsion to represent and include Asian women under *women*.

In the early 1990s *violence against women* shifted from one of many instances of *discrimination* against women to the most expansive and tactical rubric for registering gender inequality and making *women* visible as a constituency burdened with and conjoined by its own distinctive vulnerabilities. That "gender-based violence" was—and continues to be—deployed interchangeably with "violence against women" could be read as the successful achievement of concerted feminist efforts to displace biological *sex* with socially constructed *gender*, but this also demonstrates a still impracticable, if not unthinkable, disentangling of *women* from (only) gender as well as gender from (mostly) women. Second, VAW viscerally enlisted women under *human* rights not through their universal, disembodied abstraction but as an injured corporeality that was distinguished most intensely through *sexual* violation and violability. These effective modes of institutional attention and inclusion would thus condition the grammar and morphology of future, unforeseeable claims for recognition, relief, and justice. Third, *violence* against women and its acronymic, transnational portability as VAW would come to cast a slow but certain eclipse of multiple other *violations* of women's rights and human rights. None of these are new observations, but they demand repeating and remembering before I move on to discuss how "Asian women" came to figure in these discursive transactions and their later refractions.

The chapter will proceed in four parts that trace the staggered emergence and shifting definition of *violence against women* as a distinctive problem and field of intervention for global governance, from the frames of *discrimination* and *development* in the 1970s to *human development* and *health* in the early 1990s. The first section will trace the how the United Nations initially attempted to address violence against women, first through amendments to the 1979 Convention for the Elimination of Discrimination against Women (CEDAW) and later, in December 1993, through the adoption of the separate Declaration on the Elimination of Violence against Women (DEVAW). The next section shows how this passage of DEVAW was the successful culmination of a concerted campaign, organized out of the Center for Women's Global Leadership (CWGL) at Rutgers University and led by Charlotte Bunch, who had earlier played an active role in international feminist organizing around traffic in women and sexual slavery, to prioritize "violence against women" as the most inclusive but also institutionally pragmatic rubric for the recognition of "women's rights as human rights" within the UN. I point to how this strategy relied partly on a problematic analogizing of violence against women to slavery, which was itself based on two misreadings of the effective power of the declarations and conventions of global governance. The third section focuses on the efforts to recognize VAW as an "barrier" and "obstacle" to *economic development*, which spanned the CWGL and the United Nations Development Fund for Women (UNIFEM). The induction and codification of violence against women in the architecture of global governance was crucially advanced by framing the phenomenon as physically and psychologically harmful toward women but also as an impediment to their economic productivity and potential contributions to national economic growth and international competitiveness. This emphasis on the economic costs of violence against women scored a second significant routing of the category from feminist activism to global governance through framing VAW as a *public health* problem. As such, violence against women became the object of interest and documentation by the World Bank in 1993–94 under a new global project to calculate the economic burdens of both lost labor productivity and health care expenditures of all diseases, illnesses, and injuries.

Although my discussion of these event-texts are divided into four parts, there was some simultaneity and considerable overlap in the leading feminist activist-experts working across and moving upward in a particular U.S.-powered *university-NGO-UN complex*. Two feminist researchers—Roxanna Carrillo and Lori Heise—associated with the CWGL played key roles in defining violence against women as a key barrier to economic development. Across several reports and publications in the 1990s, both Carillo and Heise made repeated calls for the United Nations to collect more and better data on VAW. But there was scant explication of what this "data" should be comprised of, how these numbers and records were and could be collected especially given substantive inter-national differences and resource inequalities, and how they could be collated and compared on a global scale. These feminist recommendations for data converged with the introduction of two new metrics in global governance: the Human Development Index in 1990 and a nascent project spearheaded within the World Bank to assess, quantify, and compare the health of a given population through a new quantifiable rubric dubbed the *global burden of disease* (GBD) and a method for its calculation through *disability-adjusted life years* (DALY). The final section of this chapter will analyze how the 1994 World Bank study, which was helmed by Heise, inherited two significant analytical and epistemological habits from earlier development schemas and the GBD project in order to make VAW *count* in and for global governance. First, the world was divided into demarcated *regions*, which were not just geographically delineated but also mapped onto a temporal-historical path of capitalist growth and maturity. Second, gender-based violence was calculated as negatively affecting the economic productivity of women in the "less developed countries," which were disaggregated even further to focus upon women aged 15–44. I show that, unlike the Asianizations of trafficking and sexual slavery examined in the previous two chapters, the category of "Asian women" as such became meaningless and unfathomable under these computations of life and violence.

INSTALLING VIOLENCE AGAINST WOMEN

Violence against women was *not* included in the agenda for the first UN Decade for Women (1975–85), which had the focus of "Equality, Development, and Peace."[5] Neither the phrase *violence against women* nor the word *violence*, for that matter, appear in the 1979 Convention on the Elimination of All Forms of Discrimination against Women (CEDAW). This initial absence and marginalization are often attributed to Cold War bloc politics. As Joachim neatly summarizes it, the three main geographical-ideological factions in the UN highlighted different priorities: "Women's equality, particularly in terms of their legal rights, was being pushed by the West; women in development, calling for more resources and greater access to development programs, was added by the South; and, maintaining the position that women had already achieved equality under socialism, the East sought greater participation by women in the promotion of peace and disarmament."[6] The Decade for Women nevertheless provided the necessary funding and institutional warrant to begin to undertake studies and generate reports, which would condition the later emergence of "violence against women" into the lexicon of global governance: "For the first time, international money and support became available to support women-focused non-governmental organizations (NGOs). Pre-existing women's organizations, as well as new ones, were able to use the 'legitimacy' conferred by the Decade, to deepen their analysis of the social context of their lives."[7]

The 1980 Mid-Decade of Women Conference in Copenhagen adopted a resolution on "battered women and violence in the family." More consequentially, the parallel NGO forum sparked the initial idea for organizing internationally under the explicit banner of "violence against women." As Charlotte Bunch recalled in an interview, "We observed in that two weeks of the forum that the workshops on issues of violence against women were the most successful . . . that they were workshops where women did not divide along north-south lines, that women felt a sense of commonality and energy in the room." Bunch continued:

> It was so visible to me that this issue had the potential to bring women together in a different way, and that it had the potential to do that without erasing difference. Because the specifics of what forms violence took really were different. . . . So you get a chance to deal with difference, and see culture, and race, and class, but in a framework where there was a sense that women were subordinated and subjected to this violence everywhere, and that nobody has the answers. So northern women couldn't dominate and say that we know how to do this, because the northern women were saying: "our country is a mess; we have a very violent society."[8]

Thus, violence against women could be marshaled not only to unify a heterogeneous and uneven collectivity—"women"—but also to upend the geoeconomic stratification of knowledge. According to Keck and Sikkink, this realization led Bunch to later co-organize, along with Kathleen Barry and Shirley Castley, the Global Feminist Workshop to Organize Against Traffic in Women in Rotterdam in 1983. But, as the title of the workshop demonstrates, *traffic in women* was still the more legible and practicable rubric in the early 1980s. Interestingly, Keck and Sikkink judge that the workshop was *not* successful in generating a "real network" for two reasons: "First, the issue of traffic in women provoked debate between those who argued that all prostitution should be abolished and those who advocated less drastic positions. Second, third world women did not want the network to be based in the north, but no organizations in the south could shoulder the financial and infrastructural burden of coordinating it."[9] Inequalities and mistrust between women disabused the dream of a common issue.

In 1986 the UN Division for the Advancement of Women convened an Expert Group meeting on "Violence in the Family with special emphasis on its effects on women," which resulted in a 1989 publication, *Violence against Women in the Family*, authored by Jane Frances Connors and jointly credited to the Centre for Social Development and Humanitarian Affairs.[10] Jutta Joachim highlights a key difference in the composition of participants at this 1986 meeting, which largely comprised lawyers and academics, and the earlier International Tribunal on Crimes against Women in Brussels, where "the experts had been the victims of male violence." According to Joachim, this constriction of expertise demonstrated that "the inclusion of violence against women on the institutional agenda had its price: Women activists lost control over how their issue was defined."[11] I would argue for a more circuitous framing. Recall that the Division of Human Rights and Peace convened the International Meeting of Experts on the Social and Cultural Causes of Prostitution and Strategies for the Struggle against Procuring and Sexual Exploitation of Women in Madrid on March 18–21, 1986, which had been led by Kathleen Barry and included Takazato Suzuyo and Sister Mary Perpiñan. The appointment and convening of experts in "traffic in women" and "violence against women," which proceeded simultaneously under different units of the United Nations, authorized a specific cohort of women activists and scholars as distinctly knowledgeable experts on these global problems, but there was very little, if any, critical feminist interrogation of the methodological and epistemological grounds for expertise, which "women activists" seized or were granted some authority even as others "lost control"?

There were two significant attempts to address violence against women as a form of discrimination through amendments to CEDAW in 1989 and again in 1992. At its eighth session, in 1989, the Committee on the Elimination of Discrimination against Women passed General Recommendation 12 on "violence against women," which declared that "articles 2, 5, 11, 12 and 16 of the Convention require the States parties to act to protect women against violence of any kind occurring within the family, at the work place or in any other area of social life." Although the sphere of violence was expanded beyond home and family to the fuzzy "any other area of social life," the state was still envisioned as a *protector* of women, and the role of the UN would be to hold states accountable to that role. General Recommendation 12 also called for states to submit periodic reports on their domestic legislation "to protect women against the incidence of all kinds of violence in everyday life" and to provide services for women victims. Finally, it called for gathering "statistical data on the incidence of violence of all kinds against women and on women who are the victims of violence." This would consequently spur some states to install programs and agencies to record and gather such data. Thus, "violence against women" and "women who are victims of violence" became additional categories of documentation, calculation, disclosure, and international auditing alongside "traffic in women." But would "violence against women" be more amenable to empirical and statistical capture than the older and persistently unknowable "traffic in women"?

Later, at its eleventh session in January 1992, the Committee for the Elimination of Discrimination against Women passed a much more detailed and emphatic General Recommendation 19 to CEDAW, which began: "Gender-based violence is a form of discrimination that seriously inhibits women's ability to enjoy rights and freedoms on a basis of equality with men."[12] Recalling that it had earlier decided to devote a part of this eleventh session to the issue in anticipation of the upcoming 1993 Vienna World Conference on Human Rights, the committee was now more skeptical about the veracity of the state reports that it had called for in the 1989 amendment: "Not all the reports of States parties adequately reflected the close connection between discrimination against women, gender-based violence, and violations of human rights and fundamental freedoms" (para. 4). Declaring that "the full implementation of the Convention requires States to take positive measures to eliminate all forms of violence against women," General Recommendation 19 went on to explain that the scope of discrimination in Article 1 of CEDAW "includes gender-based violence, that is, violence that is directed against a woman because she is a woman or that affects women disproportionately" and added that "gender-based violence may breach specific provisions of the Convention, regardless of whether those provisions expressly mention violence." Rather than a notable absence or a deliberate omission, *violence against women* was always already accounted for in and by the rubric of discrimination. I want to take note of the sweeping and somewhat murky reach of that last sentence, and its implication that CEDAW (or any convention) was and is applicable to a specific phenomenon without it having to be expressly named. Was violence against women one of many forms of discrimination or a distinctive, separable, and graver phenomenon? Then too, if the reporting of some states is not credible, who or what should be the authoritative source and assessor of this information? But what exactly constitutes violence against women?

Alongside these enlargements of the scope of CEDAW, there was a campaign to develop a new international instrument to explicitly address violence against women. Following a recommendation by the Commission on the Status of Women (CSW) to the Economic and Social Council in March 1991, an Expert Group Meeting on Violence against Women was convened in Vienna on November 11–15, 1991. Then in September 1992, a special Working Group on Violence against Women was convened under the aegis of the CSW; its members composed a "Draft Declaration on the Elimination of Violence against Women," which put forth a much magnified and multiplied definition in Article 1: "For the purposes of this Declaration, the term 'violence against women' means any act of gender-based violence that results in, or is likely to result in physical, sexual or psychological harm or suffering to women, including threats of such acts, coercion or arbitrary deprivation of liberty, whether occurring in public or private life." Article 2 further elaborated upon three distinct spheres of violence:

> Violence against women shall be understood to encompass, but not be limited to, the following:
>
> Physical, sexual and psychological violence occurring in the family, including battering, sexual abuse of female children in the household, dowry-related violence, marital rape, female genital mutilation and other traditional practices harmful to women, non-spousal violence and violence related to exploitation;
>
> Physical, sexual and psychological violence occurring within the general community, including rape, sexual abuse, sexual harassment and intimidation at work, in educational institutions and elsewhere, trafficking in women and forced prostitution;
>
> Physical, sexual and psychological violence perpetrated or condoned by the State, wherever it occurs.[13]

In the cosmology of these expanding circles of family, community, and state, the state is not only to be held accountable for protecting women from violence in the other two realms but is now pointedly named as a possible *perpetrator* of violence against women. We need to historicize the greater salience and power of "military sexual slavery," which insistently names the Japanese military leaders—and related state officials—as perpetrators of sexual violence against women, as a distinctively *post*-Cold War concept/term that was nestled within these discursive shifts in feminist activism, human rights, and global governance. On December 20, 1993, the UN General Assembly adopted the Declaration on the Elimination of Violence against Women (DEVAW).[14]

Following the passage of DEVAW, violence against women soon came to be named, decried, and managed in several other sectors of the United Nations and global governance. There was a productive interweaving of scholarly publications and global governance maneuvers, each citing and fortifying the other to produce a newly knowable and actionable phenomenon. In 1994 the Program of Action emerging from the Cairo Conference declared that "the elimination of all kinds of violence against women and ensuring women's ability to control their own fertility are cornerstones of population and development-related programmes." Then too, a 1994 article titled "Violence against Women: A Neglected Public Health Issue in Less Developed Countries" could open by declaring, "Violence against women has recently been recognized by the United Nations as a fundamental abuse of women's human rights (UN Resolution 48/104)."[15] Also in 1994, the World Bank sponsored the publication of a study titled *Violence against Women: The Hidden Health Burden*.

PRIORITIZING VIOLENCE AGAINST WOMEN

In this section I trace how a specific cohort of feminist scholars and activists associated with the Center for Women's Global Leadership (CWGL) at Rutgers University prioritized violence against women. In June 1991 the CWGL convened its first Women's Leadership Institute (WLI), a two-week residential program that brought together twenty-three women from twenty countries to discuss and strategize around the theme of "women, violence, and human rights." Sex tourism, transnational migration of domestic workers, and the "mail-order" bride phenomenon were all discussed under the major subtheme of "violence under development."[16] Shin Heisoo, then a PhD student in sociology at Rutgers, reported on Korea. Siriporn Skrobanek, who had participated in the 1983 Global Feminist Workshop to Organize Against Traffic in Women, described Southeast Asian women's organizing on the problem.[17]

The organizers had several tactical reasons for choosing this theme. As evident in the names of both the center and the institute, the coordinators explained, "We see this topic as a critical area where women's leadership is essential but not yet well-organized internationally. No government determines its policies toward other countries on the basis of their treatment of women, and the human rights community has generally ignored the massive violations of gender violence." They then added that "we also chose this focus on Gender

Violence and Human Rights because it crosses national, class, racial, age, ethnic lines." Note how the presumed universality of violence against women was secondary to a concern with women's leadership, intergovernmental relations, and the "human rights community." They could also point to the recently passed 1989 amendment to CEDAW as an illustrative and affirmative example of how "the international community is slowly recognizing the systemic nature of the issue."[18]

The participants of the Women's Leadership Institute were interested and skeptical *readers* of contemporary measurements and documents in global governance. They analyzed and discussed the recently introduced 1990 UN *Human Development Report*: "Participants liked the emphasis on choice, but were wary of any definition that did not explicitly guarantee such choices for women as well as men. It is useful to note that the 1991 report was more explicit about the issue of gender—in response to such a critique from women both outside and within the UN." Informed and inspired by the insights of Marilyn Waring's book *If Women Counted* and her characterization of the United Nations System of National Accounts (UNSNA) as the "major tool of male economics," the participants also deliberated about having women's unpaid productive and reproductive labor counted by the UNSNA.[19] I want to underscore how the prioritization of violence against women was motivated by variously partial and interested *readings* of the conceptual, material, and bureaucratic architecture of global governance as much as by the direness of the actual phenomenon.

The emphasis on women's human rights was also in anticipation of the World Conference on Human Rights in Vienna in June 1993. The CWGL went on to coordinate the Global Campaign for Women's Human Rights, a network of ninety NGOs that held local and regional hearings and rallied together to make violence against women a "special theme" of the 1993 conference. Violence against women was tactical in its clear legibility under established, operative UN categories: "Different forms of violence against women clearly parallel other types of human rights violations that the international community has already condemned, such as torture, enslavement, and terrorism, so they were a useful starting point for formulating and demonstrating a gender perspective on human rights." As the organizers of the Global Campaign would later recall triumphantly, they had "made a strategic decision to emphasize issues of gender-based violence since they illustrate best how traditional human rights concepts and practice are gender-biased and exclude a large spectrum of women's human rights abuse."[20] In terms of process, the Global Campaign was able to seize upon the willingness of the United Nations "to recognize the work of 'satellite meetings' officially, by holding several international gatherings that issued statements and reports included in the official documentation of the conference."[21] The Global Campaign for Women's Human Rights also organized the Global Tribunal on Violations of Women's Human Rights, which was convened parallel to the intergovernmental conference in Vienna.

The focus on violence against women was partially shaped by the different funding sources available. The CWGL and the Global Campaign benefited from the financial support of national and international development agencies but also U.S. philanthropic organizations. In 1994 the CWGL and UNIFEM jointly published *Demanding Accountability: The Global Campaign and Vienna Tribunal for Women's Human Rights*, which was coauthored by Charlotte Bunch and Niamh Reilly of the CWGL. The list of donors included the Asia Foundation, OXFAM/UK and Ireland, and a handful of development organizations: CIDA (Canadian International Development Agency), the Netherlands Ministry of Development Cooperation, and SIDA (Swedish International Development Authority). In addition, there were the familiar names of three U.S. philanthropies: the Ford Foundation, the MacArthur Foundation, and the Rockefeller Family Fund. The emphasis on human rights was also calculated according to the unequal distribution power and resources among different bodies *within* the United Nations. As Bunch explained, "Human rights are still considered to be more important than women's rights. . . . In the United Nations, the Human Rights Commission has more power to hear and investigate cases than the Commission on the Status of Women, more staff and budget, and better mechanisms for implementing its findings."[22] What would it mean to reconsider the tactical shift to human rights not as an expansive inclusion of women under the generic rubric of the *human* but as a partial detour from *women*?

As a multiply calculated rubric that was preordained by disparate discourses, conventions, interests, and resource streams, violence against women was also constrained by particular protocols and blind spots. I want to revisit two feminist strategies in particular: (1) the claim of state responsibility and (2) the analogy of violence against women to slavery. The concerted strategy to reframe violence against women as a *public* matter called for greater interstate vigilance, coordination, and action. Even before the passage of DEVAW, the 1992 amendment to CEDAW (General Recommendation 19) included an emphatic clarification of states as direct perpetrators of and often complicit parties to violence against women: "Under general international law and specific human rights covenants, States may also be responsible for private acts if they fail to act with due diligence to prevent violations of rights or to investigate and punish acts of violence, and for providing compensation."[23] Alice M.

Miller effectively summarizes this co-constitution of the problem of violence against women and the doctrine of state accountability (and the reviewing standard of due diligence) in an expanding human rights regime: "Here, an emerging doctrine in mainstream human rights work (on state accountability) was *simultaneously strengthened in its codification and also gendered* in the work of making violence against women a human rights claim. Thus, the political willingness to build a new doctrine in human rights was already present, but the claim of VAW *added an engine* to this doctrine even as women's rights was challenging rights frameworks to respond."[24] I would point out that the Japanese military "comfort women" system, which emerged into international publicity at this very moment, presented a striking, demonstrable instance of systematic *state* coordination of sexual violation and exploitation and thus fortified this co-constitution. But framed as an especially egregious but distinctively and geographically bounded *Asian* case of active state involvement in violence against women, the claim of the Japanese government's responsibility to prevent and investigate the "comfort system," punish the various perpetrators and abettors, and provide compensation to survivors was not readily universalized and extended to many other past and ongoing instances of state-sponsored violence and abuse.

Then too, this strategy of highlighting state responsibility was spurred by an assumption that a proper, official recognition of the problem would lead to its effective enforcement and prevention, which is itself premised on a faith in the efficacy and precision of state interventions. Janet Halley, Prabha Kotiswaran, Hila Shamir, and Chantal Thomas have critically labeled this feminist strategy and its institutional effects "governance feminism." Against the passionate drive to criminalize and punish rape, prostitution, and sex trafficking on the part of feminist activists and scholars working in international law, they register two important disagreements about the effectiveness and precision of these newly codified prohibitions. First, "punishing conduct as a crime does not 'stop' or 'end' it, as governance feminists sometimes seem to imagine. Rather it enables a wide range of specific institutional actors to do a wide range of things." Second, they point to how governance feminists "all imagine their favored criminal law reforms to operate simply by actually eliminating precisely and only the conduct it outlaws. . . . In our view, however, all of these regimes can be given enhanced/intensified enforcement, on the one hand, or weakened/partial enforcement on the other."[25] The older, circuitous genealogies of the "traffic in women" and "sexual slavery" in international and global governance, which I tracked in the preceding chapters, present an object lesson against any such consequential linearity.

A second, related misreading can be seen in the analogy of violence against women with "slavery or racial discrimination and segregation" in arguing for "the state's responsibility for protecting women's human rights," as outlined in Bunch's 1990 essay: "Governments regulate many matters in the family and individual spheres. For example, human rights activists pressure states to prevent slavery or racial discrimination and segregation even when these are conducted by nongovernmental forces in private or proclaimed as cultural traditions as they have been in both the southern United States and in South Africa."[26] In addition to the dubious grammar of "slavery or racial discrimination and segregation," the two specific examples cited at the end wrongly suggest that violence against women has not been and cannot be *racially* organized and implemented, as indeed it was in the Japanese military "comfort system." Bunch would elaborate further upon this analogy in a 1995 essay:

> This duty [of the state] may be analogized to the treatment of slavery as a human rights issue. It is generally understood that the state bears responsibility for preventing slavery, even though the state does not actually practice it. The practice of slavery may properly be classified as a "private" activity whereby individual citizens deprive others of their freedom. The severity of the situation, however, forces governments to acknowledge their obligation to interfere with that "private" relationship and to declare slavery an unacceptable practice that violates human rights.
>
> Much of our discussion on violence against women bears a resemblance to the condition of slavery. Both practices may be deemed "private," yet individual citizens, as well as the state, have a measure of control over what occurs in the private sphere. This is not a novel idea, but simply a question of who decides what type of behavior is acceptable. Understanding this notion contributes to building the political will that denounces this kind of violence in our lives and in our communities, both at the local and state levels.[27]

As with the earlier problematic attempts to align traffic in women with slavery, this late twentieth-century analogy of violence against women and slavery misapprehended the efficacy of *existing* international laws and human rights instruments prohibiting slavery. But a second close reading of these two paragraphs suggests that rather than systematic or material transformation of the broader social, political, and economic conditions that engender violence against women, what is being sought is a "political will" that declares and denounces a specific kind of violence. Once again, there was unquestioned faith in categorical denunciation and targeted prohibition as effective modes of amelioration of a given problem. The analogy to slavery also begs the question of why it was necessary and efficacious to introduce and rally around a new category rather than persist with the earlier and obviously more proximate category of *sexual slavery*.

This analogy to slavery was not a simple repetition of the old imperialist or missionary rescue mission of some "white women saving brown women from brown men." Quite paradoxically, a late twentieth-century misunderstanding of the effective de facto end of slavery through its "treatment as a human rights issue" propelled a belief that the official recognition of and prohibition against violence against women could enable a *domestic* critique of human rights violations *in* and *by* the U.S. Explaining that this was "a scheme for bringing human rights issues home and applying them within the United States," Bunch outlined two "tiers" of U.S. human rights: "The first tier deals with the ways in which people within this country are violated, such as how women, racial minorities, indigenous people, gays and lesbians, and immigrants are subjected to abuse on a daily basis. The second tier addresses how the United States government plays a role in human rights abuses occurring in other parts of the world."[28] This appears to be a noteworthy reversal of the U.S.-centric understanding of the diffusion of rights and democratic principles as always moving outwards from a starting point in the more enlightened West. But given that the hegemonic mapping of human rights in global governance largely retained the West-centric developmentalist teleology and cosmology, we might consider how the strategy of prioritizing violence against women might have stunted this double critique of the U.S. as the locus and perpetrator of human rights violations here at home and elsewhere.

In a less sanguine appraisal of the strategy of the Global Campaign and the Vienna Global Tribunal spearheaded by Bunch, Alice M. Miller notes a troubling "hyper-visibility of sexual harm" as "the worst abuse that can happen to a woman." As Miller describes the strategy, "To build a political force that could not be resisted, advocates had to emphasize and make visible what was different about the experiences of women; they had to make these experiences too horrendous to ignore. Women from diverse settings told stories of horrific abuse and thereby brought attention to a previously naturalized harm reframed as a global (hence universal) rights problem." Thus, we might consider how the much-heralded inclusion and recognition of the "comfort women" in Vienna was also conditioned by this strategic fixation upon "the horror of brutal rapes" as "a maneuver that forced human rights organizations to develop ways to respond to these stories as rights violations, often through the frame of torture in armed conflict."[29] In fact, a concern that this focus on violence and especially sexual violence against women would occlude and marginalize a range of other violations and inequities was registered early on but sidestepped, as in this account:

> The Vienna Tribunal did feature testimonies on violations of women's socio-economic and cultural human rights, and on gender-based political persecution, but these were largely overlooked by the media. Some women were concerned that the focus on gender-based violence in Vienna detracted attention from other types of human rights issues, especially abuses associated with the actions of non-state actors like international financial institutions and transnational corporations, and in such policy areas as women's health. Since Vienna, the Global Campaign has sought to underscore the indivisibility of women's human rights and to emphasize the interconnectedness of the civil, political, social, economic, and cultural dimensions of all human rights.[30]

Both indivisibility and interconnectedness are easier to proclaim than to analyze, explicate, and unravel.

SLOTTING VIOLENCE AGAINST WOMEN UNDER DEVELOPMENT

The UN Development Fund for Women (UNIFEM) had initially argued that violence against women was *not* a development issue. According to Joachim, "UNIFEM's board of directors changed its position in response to a paper written by Roxanna Carrillo, then a staff member of CWGL, titled 'Violence against Women: An Obstacle to Development.'"[31] Carrillo's paper was first published as a booklet in 1991 by the CWGL under the title *Gender Violence: A Development and Human Rights Issue*, along with a reprint of Bunch's 1990 *Human Rights Quarterly* essay, "Women's Rights as Human Rights." This booklet inaugurated the center's series of working papers on "women and human rights." Contrary to Joachim's characterization of the singular force of Carrillo's essay to shift the discursive terrain, Carrillo gratefully acknowledges in the endnotes both Charlotte Bunch and Susan Holcombe (of UNIFEM), as well as a broader network of feminist activists and scholars and funding sources:

> Not only did they come up with the idea of giving me this assignment but they also were thinking partners, and I benefitted enormously from their suggestions and recommendations. I also want to thank my col-

leagues at Rutgers, Niamh Reilly and Susana Fried, as well as the staff from UNIFEM, particularly Thelma Awori, Irene Santiago, Joyce Yu, and Claudia Correia who brainstormed with me about the ideas that helped me to develop the arguments. Thanks also to Elizabeth Reid from the Women in Development Unit at the United Nations Development Program (UNDP) and to the staff of the International Women's Tribune Centre in New York. The basic research for this paper was done under the sponsorship of the United Nations Development Fund for Women (UNIFEM).[32]

Note that Joyce Yu was the co-convener (along with Bunch) of the 1984 international Consultation on "Female Sexual Slavery and Economic Exploitation" in San Francisco in her capacity as Programme Consultant to the UN Non-Governmental Liaison Service (NGLS). Niamh Reilly managed the international campaigns of the CWGL and coordinated the 1993 Global Tribunal for Women's Human Rights in Vienna. Therefore, there was already a larger group of feminists exploring the question as well as a channel of communication and support between the CWGL and UNIFEM. The latter would go on to publish Carrillo's essay in 1992 under the revised title *Battered Dreams: Violence against Women as an Obstacle to Development*. In some subsequent citations this essay would be attributed to UNIFEM rather than Carrillo, simultaneously claiming the neutral, institutional aura of UN authorship and eliding its activist, nongovernmental origins in the CWGL.

There were several important precursors to *Battered Dreams*. In 1990 Christine Bradley, an anthropologist who had led a national program on domestic violence as a Principal Project Officer for the Papua New Guinea Law Commission from 1986 to 1990, drafted a discussion paper at the request of UNIFEM titled "Why Male Violence against Women Is a Development Issue: Lessons from Papua New Guinea."[33] This study has been frequently cited as an illustrative example of both a *non*-Western incidence of VAW and an exemplary precedent for rigorous *expert* investigation of the problem. Opening with the assertion that "in the industrialized countries of the West, male violence against women has been recognized as a serious social problem for some time," Bradley argued that it "should be recognized and addressed by governments and nongovernmental bodies in developing countries, and also by the international organizations working in them."[34] The assertion of a temporal lag in the proper recognition of gendered injury between *industrialized* and *developing* countries is later exaggerated and turned into a warning about possible regression: "Violence against women denies women basic human dignity by reducing interaction to the level of animals. It is a return to the law of the jungle, where might is right and the weak do the bidding of the strong. It is the antithesis of all that women's development programmes are trying to achieve." Citing the skeptical responses of certain Members of Parliament to the commission's findings of widespread wife beating in Papua New Guinea, Bradley quoted one MP as saying that "we are wasting our time instead of discussing the development of the country." Drafted partially as a rejoinder to this dismissal, Bradley's essay proceeded to disaggregate and enumerate the multiple effects of "wife-abuse" (*physical, psychological, social*) on particular subjects: "the wife," "the children," "the husband," "the family," "the community," and "society." Under the heading of "Effects on society," Bradley lists these specific costs:

- can result in high economic costs, in the many work hours (both garden work and paid employment) lost when victims are not well enough to work;
- also results in costs to the services to the victims, such as medical treatment, assistance from the police, the courts, welfare services and so on;
- deprives the country of women's full potential for taking part in development[35]

Bradley also pointed to how some development schemes and activities could spur violence against some women *by* empowering them and thereby provoking resentments and anxieties in some men. On this point, VAW was framed in a different zero-sum equation: "Giving women more *power* over themselves means taking that power away from men. Eliminating all forms of discrimination against women means eliminating all forms of discrimination in favor of men."[36]

The UN *Human Development Report* (1990) was a second important precursor. Indeed, Carrillo's 1991 essay for the CWGL begins with an epigraph from the report: "Human development is a process of enlarging people's choices." The UN Development Programme (UNDP) first began to publish the annual reports in 1990 under the guidance of Dr. Mahbub Ul Haq, a Pakistani economist and development expert, and introduced the *human development index* (HDI) as both a more capacious alternative method of calculation and cross-national comparison to the World Bank's annual *World Development Report*. The foreword by William H. Draper III of the UNDP opened by marking an epochal post–Cold War shift: "An irresistible wave of human freedom is sweeping across many lands. Not only political systems but economic structures are beginning to change in countries where democratic forces had long been suppressed. People are beginning to take charge of their own destiny in these countries. Unnecessary state interventions are on the wane. These are all reminders of the triumph of the human spirit."[37] Inspired largely by the work on capabilities by Indian economist Amartya Sen, the *human development* frame attempted to push beyond the generic yet narrow economistic measures of the World Bank and the IMF such as annual gross national product (GNP) growth and national average incomes. Instead, the *human development index* (HDI) focused upon three other measures of life expectancy, literacy, and "command over the resources to enjoy a decent standard of living."[38] Noting that "a quantitative measure of human freedom has yet to be designed," the authors held up the possibility of quantifiable measures of "more aspects of human choice and development" and further laid out "a concrete priority for better data collection." As Draper's foreword more confidently framed it, the report's *human development indicators* "assemble all available social and human data for each country in a comparable form" with the ultimate goal that they might "come to be used over time as a standard reference for country and global analysis."[39] As standardized and comparable data was embraced as a better alternative and successor to waning state interventions, human freedom became whittled down as human choice. How would *women*, at this transitional moment of emergence as bearers of human rights, fare in these shifts?

Since 1990, the *Human Development Report* has been published annually with some modifications and attention to special "themes" in specific years such as people's participation (1993) and gender (1995). Although the 1995 *Human Development Report* would most clearly highlight gender, "women" were already delineated as a distinctive, if overlooked, population throughout the inaugural 1990 report. For example, literacy was disaggregated by gender into "adult literacy" and "female literacy." In box 2.3, titled "Women count—but are not counted," the report noted that "unpaid household work by women, if properly evaluated, would add a third to global production."[40] It went on to point out that "women have shouldered a large part of the adjustment burden of developing countries in the 1980s" by working more and consuming less and concluded by calling for "much better gender-specific data on development." Here, we can see a UN-sponsored and UN-sanctioned report explicitly, albeit fleetingly, acknowledging how the Structural Adjustment Programs (SAPs), which had been imposed upon poor, developing countries by the World Bank and the International Monetary Fund, had particularly detrimental consequences on women in those countries. In the foreword to the 1995 *Human Development Report*, James G. Speth of the UNDP observed that "the pace of development—robust as it was in the past five

Violence against Women 135

decades—has been accompanied by rising disparities *within* nations and *between* nations."⁴¹ He added that "the most persistent of these has been gender disparity, despite a relentless struggle to equalize opportunities between women and men." Noting the underrepresentation of women in positions of economic and political leadership as well as continuing legal inequalities, Speth wrote, "They often work longer hours than men, but much of their work remains unvalued, unrecognized and unappreciated. And the threat of violence stalks their lives from cradle to grave." The 1995 *Human Development Report* introduced two new measures to supplement the HDI, the GDI (*gender-related development index*) and the GEM (*gender empowerment measure*). The GDI "concentrates on the same variables as the HDI but focuses on inequality between women and men," but the GEM was introduced as "an index that focuses three variables that reflect women's participation in political decision-making, their access to professional opportunities and their earning power."⁴²

From 1995 to 2004, the compilation of the *Human Development Report* was led by Sakiko Fukuda-Parr, a Japan-born development economist who worked for the World Bank from 1974 to 1979 and went on to work in the UNDP. Contrary to Draper's sweeping humanist claim, the HDI was a calculated and compromised measure from its inception. In a very candid account of the "human development paradigm" published in 2003 in *Feminist Economics*, Fukuda-Parr attributes the development of the HDI to Haq's initiative: "Haq was convinced that a simple combined measure of human development was essential for convincing the public, academics, and policy-makers that they should evaluate development by advances in human well-being and not only by advances in the economy." Recalling that Sen "initially opposed this idea," Fukuda-Parr explains that "Sen was concerned by the difficulties of capturing the full complexity of human capabilities in a single index. But he was persuaded by Haq's insistence that *only a single number* could shift the attention of policy-makers from material output to human well-being as a real measure of progress."⁴³ In the notes, Fukuda-Parr also draws brief but noteworthy attention to a very specific trans-coding that happened in the *Human Development Report* (HDR). Sen's approach defined human development as "functionings and capabilities to function, the range of things a person could do and be in her life," but the published report deployed the word *choices* instead. As Fukuda-Parr politely and rather cryptically discloses in the notes, "It is unclear why the term 'choices' replaced 'capabilities' in the HDRs. This replacement can cause confusion, since 'choice' is a common term that means different things to different people."⁴⁴ I would argue that "choices" more effectively contrasts and counters the alleged problem of "unnecessary state interventions" in Draper's foreword. Thus even well-intentioned efforts to *human*-ize the UN development cosmology were deflected and reframed through the preferred lexicon of neoliberalism.

Several other details from the 1990 *Human Development Report* are noteworthy. The overview section listed fifteen major observations and their theses. No. 12 extolled "the movement of nongovernmental organisations (NGOs) and other self-help organisations." No. 13 called for a "significant reduction in population growth" and declared that "there is an urgent need to strengthen programmes of family planning, female literacy, fertility reduction and maternal and child health care." Pointing to the shifting "demographic balance," wherein the share of the world's population in "developing" countries was projected to increase to 84 percent by 2025, the report also warned about the ramifications for migration to the "industrial" countries: "If the developing world's new generations cannot improve their conditions through liberal access to international assistance, capital markets and the opportunities for trade, the *compulsion to migrate* in search of better economic opportunities will be overwhelming—a sobering thought for the 1990s, one that spotlights the urgent need for a better global distribution of development opportunities."[45] It is worth asking, How and why is this scenario of mass compelled migration overwhelming and for whom? The enlarging of "choices" *over there* is the necessary antidote to the perceived threat of uncontrolled immigration.

The invention and gradual installation of *human development* created an opening to install VAW under the "human" in its two, and only two, subcategories of "women" and "men." As Carrillo explains in the 1991 essay published by the Center for Women's Global Leadership, "The human development approach expands the use of indicators by looking at how they impact on the lives of women and men." She also refers to prior UN-sponsored documents such as the 1989 Connors study of violence in the family to illustrate that violence against women had already begun to be taken up by the UN. In Part II of the essay, subtitled "Putting Gender Violence on the Development Agenda," Carrillo points to the lack of documentation, empirical studies, and statistics, a problem that was even more exacerbated for the "developing world" with the notable exception of the Papua New Guinea study. Nevertheless, she points out that "when statistics are available, they document powerfully and make visible the pervasiveness and extent of violence against women."[46] The following subsection, titled "What the Numbers Reveal," begins, "Substantial official statistics and survey data in the United States make vivid the burden of violence against women." Thus, even as Carrillo points to a disparity in available data on violence against women, there was an implicit presumption of the geographical and transnational portability of such statistics generated out of the U.S. as reliable evidence of a global phenomenon.

But then too, this early framing of VAW as a *burden* begs the question of the subject of encumbrance. Arguing that "examining the extent of violence against women globally yields an appreciation of the magnitude of what it costs to the development process," Carrillo enumerates a dizzying catalogue of troubling percentages and averages from Mexico, Papua New Guinea, Korea, Nicaragua, Thailand, Bolivia, India, Pakistan, Bangladesh, Colombia, Kenya, Kuwait, Nigeria, Vanuatu, and Uganda. She then forcefully concludes, "Where domestic violence keeps a woman from participating in a development project, force is used to deprive her of earnings, or fear of sexual assault prevents her from taking a job or attending a public function, development does not occur." Since violence against women had distinctive ramifications for *economic* development, it was necessary to measure and tabulate these costs, which could also enable projections of the benefits of specific interventions. Carrillo deploys the familiar feminist rhetorical strategy of lamenting "women's socio-economic and psychological dependency" on men, which results from patriarchal control and sexual violence, but focalizes it as part of a broader pathological dependency that inhibits national economic development: "Violence against women is often a direct obstacle to women's participation in development projects."[47] Thus, the very call for measures to mitigate violence against women could be rationalized as *contributing to* economic development. However, it is important to distinguish between specific NGO-, UN-, and state-sponsored development *projects* and development as a generic, wholesale economic process and hegemonic cosmology. Interestingly, Carrillo also points to two examples of how development projects could also exacerbate gender inequalities and generate new interpersonal and social tensions that *lead to* violence against some women. She refers to two women, one in Madras, India, and the other in Lima, Peru, who were subject to domestic violence and abandonment by male partners as a consequence of their participation in development-related projects.

In a reoriented echo of the warning about the unfettered "compulsion to migrate" from the 1990 *Human Development Report*, Carrillo delineates its gender-specific manifestations by pointing to how VAW "denies developing countries the full talents of their women" by compelling women's out-migration: "Control and violence by male relatives can lead some of the best educated women to leave their countries, contributing to the brain drain in the Third World, and the loss of highly skilled women in the development process." The eradication of violence against women was necessary and good for women, but it was also useful to improving a nation's economic standing and international competitiveness by discouraging and reducing the out-migration of certain "highly skilled" women. Under the subheading of "Directions for Programmes and Policy," Carrillo calls on development agencies to contribute to the eradication-through-documentation of VAW by "highlighting the obstacles which gender violence places in the path of development, and identifying means of countering this in all phases of the project cycle" and "integrating statistics on gender violence into data collection."[48] This call for research and resource investment in violence against women as part of the UN development program in the late twentieth century offered a different rationale for documenting and controlling international female migration than the earlier international co-operation around the traffic in women, which had been narrowed to *forced prostitution* and *sexual slavery* by the 1980s.

How might we trace this itinerary from "women in development" to "human development" and from "discrimination against women" to "violence against women" and "gender-based violence"? If *discrimination* against women (largely framed as a problem of culture and tradition) became legible and noteworthy as an obstacle to development, the prioritization of economic development made it difficult, if not impossible, to account for *violence* against women. Even as development provided the discursive opening and infrastructural scaffolding to render VAW into something that must be addressed and documented by the United Nations, it also bound that very effort to the prevailing spatio-temporal hierarchies of the development cosmology and episteme. In order to make violence against women legible and noteworthy, it was necessary to show again and again that it was an important obstacle to economic development and later human development. But in doing so, violence against women would be subject to the preferred enumerations, simple combinations, and comparable standardizations of those regimes of global governance. Here, I want to underscore that I am less invested in arguing that violence against women was ultimately diluted and made illegible through its absorption into global governance. Instead, I would ask how did and does the spectacle of the beaten, violated female body in pain complement and enliven the simultaneously proliferating ledgers of numbers, indices, percentages, and rankings?

CALCULATING VIOLENCE AGAINST WOMEN AS PUBLIC HEALTH COST

The calculation of violence against women would spin off from development to converge with a different stream of data collection and calculation around global health. Lori Heise, another feminist scholar affiliated with the Center for Women's Global Leadership, played a key role in framing violence against women specifically as a *public health* issue through a series of slightly modified publications throughout the 1980s and into the early 1990s.[49] According to Keck and Sikkink, Heise had worked on domestic violence in the United States in the 1980s but came to recognize "violence against women as an international concern while doing research on women's environmental movements in India."[50] As Heise recalled in a September 1995 interview, "The big 'ah-hah' for me came around 1985 in northern Garwhal, where I was interviewing women connected to the Chipko movement, a well-known women's movement. So I asked the women, 'If something could change in your life to make it better, what would it be.' I was fishing for 'not having to walk five miles for firewood,' but over and over they would raise issues of alcohol abuse and domestic abuse."[51]

Heise's publications on violence against women in the early 1990s often repeated specific rhetorical strategies. First, there was a strongly worded assertion of the gravity of the problem. For example, an essay titled "Violence against Women: The Missing Agenda" and included in the edited collection *The Health of Women: A Global Perspective* (1993) opened with this forceful declaration: "Violence against women is perhaps the *most pervasive yet least recognized* human rights abuse in the world. It is also a profound health problem sapping women's physical and emotional vitality and undermining their confidence—both vital to achieving widely held goals for human progress, *especially in the developing world*."[52] Second, as demonstrated in the preceding passage, Heise would point to the global scope of the problem while also emphasizing that violence against women was a graver problem in and for developing countries. But then too, statistics culled from different countries and often *across* the First World/Third World, East/West, or industrialized/developing divides would be cited alongside one another as evidence of the global scope of VAW. However, at times, such adjacent positioning could raise questions and even implicit contradistinctions, which would go unremarked upon: "In the United States, one out of every seven married women have been raped by their husbands (Russel 1982). In Seoul, South Korea, the figure is two out of every three (Shim Young 1991)."[53] Third, Heise, like Carrillo, ritually acknowledged the vibrant record of "over two decades of organizing by women's groups around the world to combat gender-based abuse."[54] A telling statistic on the expanding scale and scope of this grassroots organizing was repeated again and again: "A recent directory published by the Santiago-based Isis International lists 379 separate organizations working against gender violence in Latin America alone."[55] Here too, there was a marked geographical distinction as Heise highlighted "a vast amount of energy Third World women are investing to mobilize against abuse."[56]

The early essays often began by tracing recent United Nations actions and reporting on ongoing efforts to install violence against women as a distinctive category of global governance. Heise's cross-citation and mutual legitimation of Carrillo's writings are especially illuminating. For example, the first paragraph of a 1993 article ends with a direct quotation from the 1992 UNIFEM report authored by Carrillo: "As the United Nations Fund for Women (UNIFEM) recently observed, 'women cannot lend their labor or creative ideas fully if they are burdened with the physical and psychological scars of abuse.'"[57] Note how the subject of observation and declaration has shifted to the more anonymous yet authoritative title of UNIFEM. Very much in line with the broader women's rights as human rights campaign, in making the case that VAW was "an issue worthy of international action and concern," Heise would relate it to "issues already high on the international health agenda." To that end, Heise discussed three particular initiatives: "Safe Motherhood," "Child Survival," and "Family Planning and AIDS Prevention." Citing several studies from Colombia, Costa Rica, Indonesia, Cameroon, and India that illustrate how "more self-confident mothers have better-nourished children," Heise argued, "Where women's confidence and status is critical to achieving a development goal—such as improving child survival—violence will remain a powerful obstacle to progress."[58] As Carrillo did, Heise's writings on VAW in the early 1990s also emphasize the need for more and better data, but as I will show later, aligning violence against women with the priorities of the international health agenda would entail the contracted enumeration of VAW according to prevailing categories and measurements in global health as it concurrently became a field of targeted intervention for the World Bank.

The Carrillo/UNIFEM quotation appears again in *Violence against Women: The Hidden Health Burden* (hereafter referred to as *The Hidden Health Burden*), a seventy-four-page report that Heise coauthored with Jaqueline Pitanguy and Adrienne Germain in 1994 as part of the World Bank discussion papers. At the time, all three were consultants to the World Bank's Population, Health and Nutrition Department. The framing of VAW as a "hidden health burden" is summarized in the Abstract:

> Although gender violence is a significant cause of female morbidity and mortality, it is almost never seen as a public health issue. Recent World Bank estimates of the global burden of disease indicate that in established market economies gender-based victimization is responsible for

one out of every five healthy days of life lost to women of reproductive age. On a per capita basis, the health burden imposed by rape and domestic violence in the industrial and developing world is roughly equivalent, but because the total disease burden is so much greater in the developing world, the percentage attributable to gender-based victimization is smaller.[59]

The doubled calculation-as-declaration and declaration-as-calculation of VAW are both strikingly matter-of-fact and confounding. I admit that I glazed over these words in my first reading and then was subsequently befuddled when I tried to make clearer sense of their meaning and possible implications. What was being measured here exactly? Or what exactly was being calculated for comparison? Who or what is the burdened subject?

One year earlier, in 1993, the World Bank had commissioned the publication of *World Development Report 1993: Investing in Health* (hereafter referred to as *Investing in Health*) under its Health, Nutrition and Population Division. Although it was not yet evident in 1994 when *The Hidden Health Burden* was published, *Investing in Health* would prove to be enormously consequential in introducing several concepts and measures for the calculation and comparison of health on a global scale. The 1993 report opens by announcing an epochal *demographic* shift: "Over the past forty years, life expectancy has improved more than during the entire previous human history." This worldwide increase in life expectancy was attributed to both decreases in infant mortality and the success of new vaccines for smallpox, measles, and polio. As the report explains, "Not only do these improvements translate into direct and significant gains in well-being, but they also reduce the economic burden imposed by unhealthy workers and sick or absent schoolchildren." The authors proposed a new method of measuring this *economic burden* of disease, which would account not only for the numbers of deaths and especially premature deaths but also for "many diseases and conditions that are not fatal but that are responsible for great loss of healthy life." This negative quantification of the *loss* of "healthy life" in a single global index was very different from Sen's conceptualization of human development as centered on "human well-being" and "functionings and capabilities to function, the range of things a person could do and be in her life." Pointing to chronic depression and polio-related paralysis as two examples, the authors of *Investing in Health* explain, "These conditions are common, can last a long time, and frequently lead to significant demands on the health system."[60] The economic burden was thus twofold as a loss of worker productivity and as a cost borne by a singular, generic "health system."

To retrace the genesis of this new metric even further back, in 1990 the World Bank and the World Health Organization had undertaken "a joint exercise" in an attempt to "quantify the full loss of healthy life" to various diseases. They classified 109 categories of diseases based on the International Classification of Diseases, which encompassed "all possible causes of death and about 95 percent of the possible causes of disability." Deaths were calculated not in terms of the number of individual persons or occurrences but in the number of *years of life lost*, which was defined as "the difference between the actual age at death and the expectation of life at that age in a low-mortality population."[61] In addition, this joint exercise yielded a method of calculating the number of *healthy* years of life lost because of disease, illness, and injury, which were labeled controversially as *disability*. *Disability* was deployed as a catchall rubric covering both communicable diseases and noncommunicable illnesses such as cancer as well as "neuropsychiatric disease" and a separate category of "injuries" that were further divided into three perplexing categories: "Motor vehicle," "Intentional," and "Other."

As explained in a section titled "Measuring the burden of disease," the calculation of this *disability* was more complex if no less problematic. The "expected duration of the condition (remission to death)" was multiplied by "a severity weight that measured the severity of the disability in comparison with the loss of life."[62] The 109 diseases were collated into six classes of "severity of disability" so that the number of cases of a disease in a given year that did *not* result in death could still be calculated in terms of the years of healthy life in the future that would be lost as a result of living with the disability. There was also a relative weighting of the value of a year of life at different ages, steeply increasing from birth (0) to age 15 with a peak value between 20 and 30 years of age and steadily decreasing below 1 in the early 50s (figure 4.1). Adding up those two losses, the report introduced into global governance a new metric called the *disability-adjusted life year* (DALY):

DALY = YLL (years of life lost) + YLD (years lived with disability)

DALY was a measure of the GBD calculated in terms of "the *present value of the future years* of disability-free life that are lost as the result of the premature deaths or cases of disability occurring in a particular year." This odd temporality demands further deliberation: "The global disease burden measures the present value of the *future stream* of disability-free life lost as a result of death, disease, or injury in 1990. It is thus based on events that occurred in 1990 but includes the loss of disability-life in future years."[63] As the authors calculated, "Worldwide, 1.36 billion DALYs were lost in 1990."[64] This figure was disaggregated into 66 percent of DALYs lost to premature death and 34 percent DALYs lost to disability.

Violence against Women 143

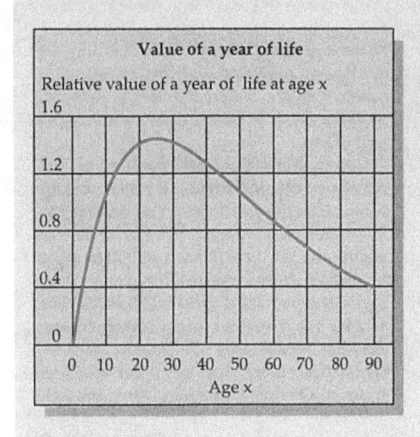

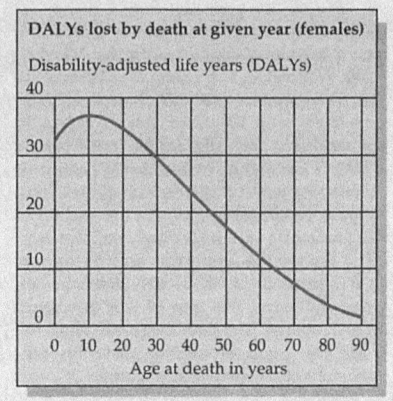

Box figure 1.3 Age patterns of age weights and DALY losses

Value of a year of life	DALYs lost by death at given year (females)
Relative value of a year of life at age x	Disability-adjusted life years (DALYs)

Source: World Bank data.

FIGURE 4.1. Photo of "Box figure 1.3" illustrating age patterns of DALY ("Disability-Adjusted Life Years") in *Investing in Health: The 1993 World Development Report of the World Bank*.

Beyond imposing years of illness and suffering on individuals, diseases and injuries resulted in both individual and aggregate labor *non*-productivity and further entailed additional resource and time demands on the health-care sector. In addition to measuring the GBD, DALY would also measure "the effectiveness of health interventions, as indicated by reductions in the disease burden."[65] Thus, it "makes sense" that the World Bank played a key role in developing and disseminating this metric in global governance. There was also a distinctive U.S. provenance to this World Bank initiative. Christopher Murray, an American health economist, physician, and public health professor at Harvard, and Alan Lopez, an Australian statistician at the WHO, are credited as inventing and then later refining the DALY calculus. According to Katherine E. Kenny, "Although the World Bank's Health Sector Priorities Review began in the late 1980s, it received renewed attention under Lawrence Summers' tenure as chief economist of the World Bank beginning in 1991."[66] By then, Murray and Lopez had already begun to develop the DALY calculus. In 1990 the World Bank had tapped Murray to advise the organization on a $50 million loan to China for a tuberculosis-control program. Alan Lopez also served as editor of the WHO's *World Health Statistics*. The World Bank appointed another American researcher and economist, Dean Jamison, then at the University of California, Los Angeles, as the chief editor of the 1993 issue of its annual *World*

Disease burden per 1,000 population

Sub-Saharan Africa	
India	
China	
Other Asia and islands	
Latin America and the Caribbean	
Middle Eastern crescent	
Formerly socialist economies of Europe	
Established market economies	
World	

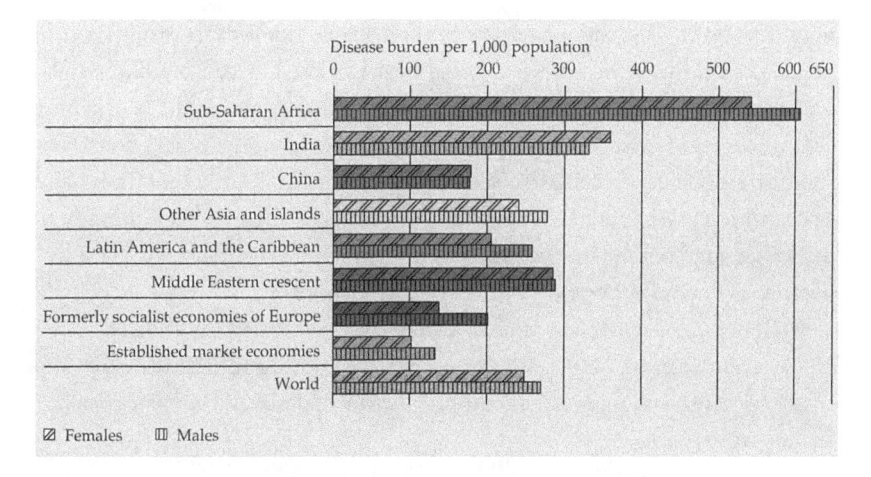

▨ Females   ⊞ Males

FIGURE 4.2. Photo of "Figure 1.5" illustrating "Disease burden by sex and region" in *Investing in Health: The 1993 World Development Report of the World Bank*.

Development Report. Jamison, in turn, tapped Murray and Lopez to head the research team.[67]

The "worldwide" estimates of the GBD and DALY are disaggregated into two sexes and eight regions (figure 4.2). The regional demarcations are an oddly mixed bag of national, geographical, and economic distinctions: sub-Saharan Africa, India, China, Other Asia and islands, Latin America and the Caribbean, Middle Eastern crescent, Formerly socialist economies of Europe (FSE), and Established market economies (EME). The separate demarcation of India and China from the oddly designated "Other Asia and islands" is never explained.[68] Although one can make some reasonable conjectures such as the large population size of China and India or the relative availability of health data for each site, what I would note is how the category of "Asian women" becomes discombobulated and even meaningless through such a regime of global calculation. The report further divides these eight regions into two "demographic" groupings. Whereas the FSE and EME countries are characterized by "relatively uniform age distributions" and "older populations," the other six regions are deemed as "demographically developing," with their age distributions skewing younger.

There is limited but still some focused attention to *violence against women* as a significant cause and manifestation of "sex" differences in both GBD and DALY in *Investing in Health*. Table 1.1, titled "Burden of disease by sex, cause, and type of disease," features three disease categories: communicable diseases, non-communicable diseases, and injuries. Below the table, the authors mindfully

Violence against Women   145

note that "even as broad a measure as the GBD does not capture all the consequences of disease or injury ... some health-related factors are likely to be underreported. A clear example is violence against women, much of which goes undetected—but not unsuffered." A few pages later, the report notes that there is a distinctive "female disadvantage" in disease burden in China and India, which is attributed to their "large numbers of 'missing' (and presumed) dead women in relation to the expected population balance between the sexes" because of female infanticide and sex-selective abortion.[69]

Violence against women is most explicitly, albeit briefly, addressed at the end of chapter 2, on "Households and health." Noting specifically how "domestic violence and rape" constitute a "category of danger to women's health," the report explains:

> Although this has only recently been viewed as a public health issue, it is a significant cause of female morbidity and mortality, leading to psychological trauma and depression, injuries, sexually transmitted diseases, suicide, and murder. Rape and domestic violence cause a substantial and roughly comparable disease burden per capita to women in developing and industrial countries. These problems account for about 5 percent of the total disease burden among women ages 15–44 in developing countries, where the burden from maternal and communicable causes overwhelm that from other conditions. In industrial countries, where the total disease burden is much smaller, this share rises to 19 percent.[70]

There is no explanation of why only rape and domestic violence were chosen or how they might be aligned with each other under "households."

It is clear that this attentiveness to violence against women was a considerate recognition of and response to feminist international activism and knowledge production, which I discussed earlier in the chapter. Noting several different endeavors ranging from women's NGOs in Africa, a campaign on family violence launched in 1991 by the American Medical Association, and a project by the Colombian Ministry of Health, the report acknowledges in familiar language that "these efforts come on the heels of almost two decades of organizing efforts by women around the world; in Latin America alone there now nearly 400 separate organizations working to reduce violence against women." A half-page box on "Violence against women as a health issue" briefly mentions figures for a wide range of VAW, including figures on Papua New Guinea based on the Bradley study. Lori Heise's contribution to *Investing in Health* is acknowledged in two places. First, the report describes a special consultation "focused on the health outcomes of violence against women for the global burden of disease exercise" convened on February 12, 1993, in Washington, D.C. Both Heise and Christopher Murray were in attendance.[71] Heise's chapter in *The Health of Women* (1993) is also listed in the bibliography of *Investing in Health*.

The following year, Heise, Pitanguy, and Germain would adapt the DALY metric in their World Bank report *Violence against Women: The Hidden Health Burden*. Chapter 4 is titled "Health Consequences of Gender-Based Violence" and opens: "A growing body of research has emerged in recent years of the mental and health consequences of violence against women and the burden it places on health care systems." Acknowledging that "much of this research is from the industrial world," the authors could still confidently declare that "when this literature is considered together with estimates of the prevalence of gender-based violence in different parts of the world, the magnitude of the violence-related health burden begins to become clear." The paper continues: "Perhaps the best estimate of this burden comes from a modeling exercise undertaken by the World Bank to inform its policy annual, the *World Development Report*, which in 1993 focused on health. For this effort, the Bank staff and outside experts estimated the healthy years of life lost to men and women due to different causes.... From this analysis, broken down by region and age group, rape and domestic violence emerge as a significant cause of disability and death among women of reproductive age in both the industrial and the developing world."[72] Although Heise, Pitanguy, and Germain characterize the GBD/DALY as a somewhat speculative "modeling exercise," their 1994 paper, also published by the World Bank, affirmed this methodology and extended its relevance to violence against women but now in a semiofficial document authored by women researchers and, in Heise's case, a feminist activist associated with the Center for Women's Global Leadership.

The Hidden Health Burden contains table 5 (figure 4.3), in which the authors have inserted the category of "Rape and domestic violence" into the GBD figures from *Investing in Health*. Table 5 features this explanation at the bottom: "Rape and domestic violence are included here for illustrative purposes. They are *risk factors* for disease conditions, such as STDs, depression, and injuries, not diseases in and of themselves." Appendix C, which focuses on the report's methodology, further explains how the DALY metric could be used to measure and quantify the burden of "gender-based victimization": "To equate morbidity and mortality, the global burden of disease (GBD) exercise assigns 'disability weighting factors' (between 0.02 and 0.9) to conditions based on their interference with normal enjoyment of life and functioning. A rating of 0.02 represents minimal interference with well-being and productivity, and weightings of 0.6 and higher represent major life dislocations, with 0.9 appropriate only for

FIGURE 4.3. Photo of "Table 5: Estimated global health burden of selected conditions for women age 15 to 44," which lists and calculates "rape and domestic violence," in *Violence against Women: The Hidden Health Burden* (Washington, DC: World Bank, 1994).

Table 5 Estimated global health burden of selected conditions for women age 15 to 44

Condition	Disability-adjusted life years lost (millions)
Maternal conditions	29.0
Sepsis	10.0
Obstructed labor	7.3
STDs (excluding HIV)	15.8
Pelvic inflammatory disease	12.8
Tuberculosis	10.9
HIV	10.6
Cardiovascular disease	10.5
Rape and domestic violence*	9.5
All cancers	9.0
Breast	1.4
Cervical	1.0
Motor vehicle accidents	4.2
War	2.7
Malaria	2.3

a. Rape and domestic violence are included here for illustrative purposes. They are *risk factors* for disease conditions, such as STDs, depression, and injuries, not diseases in and of themselves.
Source: World Bank 1993.

conditions just short of death, such as coma." From there, the authors are able to extrapolate that "since domestic violence and rape are not diseases per se, the GDB [sic] frames gender-based victimization as a risk factor that increases the incidence of certain other morbidities and conditions, such as physical traumas and depression. Thus, the calculation of DALYs lost to gender-based victimization begins with the GDB [sic] estimates of DALYs lost due to each condition and then estimates the percentage of the total for that condition attributable to domestic violence and rape. (An analogy would be estimating the proportion of disability resulting from emphysema, lung cancer, and heart disease that can be attributed to smoking.)"[73]

Even though this was an *estimation* based on an already speculative "modeling exercise," Heise, Pitanguy, and Germain proceed to make several assertions of material fact. In a section titled "Effects of violence against women on the health care system," they write that "violence affects women's health—and the health of society at large—by *diverting scarce resources* to the treatment of a largely preventable social ill. Considering the prevalence of abuse and the nature of its health effects, it is reasonable to conclude that victimization represents *a significant drain* on available health resources." Some of Carrillo's

Appendix table C.1 Disability-adjusted life years lost to women age 15 to 44 due to conditions attributable to domestic violence and rape

Relevant conditions	Total DALYs lost to women age 15 to 44 (millions)	Share attributable to domestic violence and rape
STDs (excluding HIV)	15.8	2 percent
HIV	10.6	2 percent
Abortion	2.5	10 percent
Depression	10.7	50 percent of difference between women and men
(men age 15 to 44)	5.4	
Alcohol dependence	0.9	10 percent
Drug dependence	1.1	10 percent
Post-traumatic stress disorder	2.1	60 percent
Unintentional injuries	6.7	20 percent of total burden minus burden attributable to motor vehicle accidents and occupational injuries
Suicide	5.5	30 percent
Homicide	0.9	60 percent
Intentional injury	1.2	90 percent
Total	58.0	6 percent

Source: World Bank data.

FIGURE 4.4. Photo of "Appendix table C.1: Disability-adjusted life years lost to women age 15 to 44 due to conditions attributable to domestic violence and rape," in *Violence against Women: The Hidden Health Burden* (Washington, DC: World Bank, 1994).

earlier work is reproduced in chapter 5, titled "Implications of Gender Violence for Health and Development." But now the language has been slightly altered to read "Gender violence, through its effects on a woman's ability to act in the world, can serve as a *brake* on socioeconomic development."[74] Note the distinction between the now-specified "socioeconomic development" from the older governance frame of "women in development." In appendix table C.1 (figure 4.4), Heise, Pitanguy, and Germain further tabulate the DALYs *in millions* "lost to women age 15 to 44 due to conditions attributable to domestic violence and rape," which selects eleven "relevant conditions" ranging from STDs and HIV to abortion, depression, alcohol and drug dependence, post-traumatic stress disorder, and both unintentional and intentional injury. They compute the percentage of DALYs lost to these conditions, which can be attributed to domestic violence and rape: ranging from 2 percent for STDs and HIV to 90 percent for "Intentional injury." Finally, they add up each column to arrive at a total of 58 million DALYs, with 6 percent attributable to domestic violence and rape.

A notable shift in the definition of violence against women occurs between Heise's 1993 article in the *World Health Statistics Quarterly* and the 1994 World Bank report. In the 1993 article, Heise endorses and even quotes directly from the expansive definition of VAW put forth by the special working group convened by the Commission on the Status of Women, which was adopted in the 1993 Declaration on the Elimination of Violence against Women (DEVAW). Appendix B of *The Hidden Health Burden*, titled "Definition of violence against women," which appears to have been solely authored in its repeated "I" authorial position, and I would attribute to Heise, is explicitly critical of the recently passed DEVAW, charging that it "avoids making difficult distinctions by offering a tautology in place of a definition." Though acknowledging the "appeal of a broad definition that ... would permit many violations of women's rights to be addressed under the rubric of violence," the author points to a risk that the "descriptive power" and "explanatory power" of *violence* might be lost in such capaciousness: "Calling everything violence—poverty, pornography, trafficking in women, lack of access to schooling—makes it easier to discount the issue entirely and to justify inaction on the specific forms of abuse, such as rape and wife assault. (It is rather like the justification that since everything causes cancer anyway, one might as well smoke.) This is not to say that unequal pay and lack of access to safe abortion, for example, are not violations of women's human rights, but we must ask what explanatory power is gained by calling these violations violence." Appendix B concludes by proposing a narrower but still very broad definition of *violence against women* as "any act of verbal or physical force, coercion, or life-threatening deprivation, directed at an individual woman or girl, that causes physical or psychological harm, humiliation or arbitrary deprivation of liberty and that perpetuates female oppression."[75] The author emphasizes that this has an important advantage: "By referring to acts directed at an individual girl or woman, it helps distinguish between acts of violence and harmful policies that may damage the health of women as a class but are not directed at a particular individual (for example, lack of investment in women's health research)."

Recalling the strategic choice of violence against women as the most capacious rubric for registering women as a class, how might we make sense of this individualizing contraction? I would like to suggest that the institutionalization of violence against women (or any specific category of injury) through particularly sanctioned methods of proper documentation and measurement created openings for a select cohort of feminist experts, who, in turn, became invested in their own individual institutional and epistemological authority within that particular power/knowledge nexus. One final thought is to historicize this particular feminist investment in the GBD and DALYs in the early 1990s, when the ambitions and confidence—and its ethnocentric blind spots—of earlier U.S. feminist theories and concepts about universal gender subordination had been effectively challenged by antiracist, anti-imperialist feminisms. But these inter-feminist insights and contestations could not be transferred into and be made legible and significant under this new paradigm of making violence against women count in and for global governance. Both the concerted feminist efforts to elucidate and catalogue the numerous and multifarious "acts of violence and harmful policies that may damage the health of women as a class" *and* the feminists critiques aimed at disabusing the presumption of women as a universal, monolithic category became inconsequential in the determined prioritization of the unburdening of economic development and health care systems.

5

TRUTH DISCLOSURE

This chapter considers the demand for the disclosure of "truth" about the Japanese military "comfort system." Many have rightly heralded the courage of the survivors in telling their stories publicly as the catalyzing force in exposing this history in the early 1990s, but the "comfort women" problematic presents a challenge for aligning truth with knowledge and justice due to the multisited, relational processes of recording, suppression, forgetting, remembering, witnessing, and disclosure across differently scaled yet linked national, regional, and international publics.[1] For example, in Japan, as Yoshimi Yoshiaki points out, "Any military personnel with wartime experience knew of the existence of comfort women."[1] He then adds that it was represented quite early on in Japanese literature and film: "In 1947, the writer Tamura Taijiro took up the issue of Korean comfort women in his novel *Shunpuden* (*A Prostitute's Story*), which was later made into a movie." Elazar Barkan points to the 1965 publication of *Memoirs of a Korean Comfort Woman* by the Modern History Research Society of Japan, which was attributed to a pseudonymous Kim Chun Ja.[2] Ienaga Saburō's 1968 book, *Taiheiyō Sensō (The Pacific War)*, briefly but strikingly mentions what he calls the "comfort girls." Senda Kakō's 1973 book, *Military Comfort Women (Jugun Ianfu)*, has been identified by some as an especially significant early text, whereas others point to Korean *zainichi* scholar Kim Il-myon's 1971 article and 1976 book, *Tenno no Guntai to Chosenjin Ianfu (The Emperor's Forces and the Korean Comfort Women)*. In 1979 Japanese director Yamatani Tetsuo completed an eighty-seven-minute documentary film titled *Okinawa no Harumoni (An Old Lady in Okinawa: Testimony of a Military Comfort Woman)*, which featured interviews he had conducted over a two-year period with Pae Pong Gi (1915–1991). Yamatani also edited and published a full transcript of his interviews as a book under the same title, *Okinawa no Harumoni* (1979). Given the existence of these multiple accounts that span almost the entire postwar period, Yoshimi soberly points out, "Thus it can't be said that people were completely unaware of the issue until recently. Rather, social concern about its gravity was never widespread."[3]

There was certainly enduring knowledge about the Japanese military "comfort system" in Korea, most painfully in the embodied memories of the survivors but also in many others who lived through the colonial period and never forgot the mandatory drafting of Korean girls and women. Indeed, Yun Chung-ok was compelled to conduct research by her own memories of being caught up in the *Chongshindae* mobilization as a young woman. In addition to an investigative team research trip to Japan in February 1988 with two other member of Korean Church Women United (KCWU), Yun made additional research trips to Thailand and Papua New Guinea in 1989. A four-part series of articles that she authored was published in the South Korean daily *Hankyoreh* in January 1990. Thus, rather than a total suppression or forgetting, this history was not considered internationally noteworthy and widely investigated until the 1990s. There is a difference between knowing *about* and knowing *as* under heterogeneous and shifting conditions of intelligibility and significance.

I am specifically interested in tracking the representations of the "comfort system" in their transpacific relay into English-language publications that circulated in the U.S. and internationally. I have already pointed to two very different instances: Sean O'Callaghan's 1968 book, *The Yellow Slave Trade: A Survey of the Traffic in Women and Children in the East*, and Matsui Yayori's translated essays in the 1970s. There were several fleeting mentions in historical accounts of World War II. The first English translation of Ienaga's book, *The Pacific War* (1978), includes these three sentences: "Korean women were also mobilized by the thousands and shipped off to the battlefronts as 'comfort girls' for Japanese troops. Called *Chōsenpi* (*pi* was soldiers' slang for 'comfort girl'), they were a sexual outlet for the soldiers. The women were brought right to the front lines for fornication between combat operations, and apparently many were killed in the fighting."[4] Acknowledging that some of the awkwardness of these words can be attributed to the problem of translation, this matter-of-fact description now appears anachronistic and even obtuse in its use of terms like *fornication*. The "comfort girls" make a second, more extended appearance later in Ienaga's book in a chapter on "The Horrors of War," oddly following an account of suicide attacks by Japanese soldiers:

> A military psychology insensitive to human life, to the individual's right to survive, conceived of the special attack idea.
>
> The military's attitude toward civilians was similar. Since human rights were totally ignored within Japan, it was not likely that they would be respected on the battlefield. Prostitutes were a case in point. Prostitution is by its very nature a violation of women's rights to a decent occupation and livelihood. Prostitutes for the military, euphemistically called "comfort girls," were placed in double jeopardy. Large numbers were sent to the front line "comfort stations" to service the troops, including some who had been tricked or forced into the job. The soldiers queued up in long lines for their few minutes of "comfort"; the girls took them on one after another, probably never getting off their backs from one customer to the next. "Comfort girls" wounded in the fighting were apparently sometimes abandoned or shot to prevent capture. Many of the women were Korean, but Japanese prostitutes and ordinary girls were also induced or tricked into service at the front.[5]

Considering that Ienaga's book was first published in Japan in 1968, his clear acknowledgment of "human rights" and "women's rights" is quite remarkable. He also notes the use of deception and force in the recruitment of the girls and women and, more strikingly, the likelihood that the Japanese soldiers murdered some of them. However, the interchangeable deployment of *prostitutes*, *the girls*, *"comfort girls,"* and *women* jams up in the odd syntax of that last sentence and raises the question of whether the term *ordinary girls* refers only to Japanese girls and women.

This brief reference in *The Pacific War* was an early indication that the Japanese military "comfort system" would turn up in other English-language histories and remembrances of the war. It is described at greater length in Louis Allen's 1984 book, *Burma: The Longest War*, which details the actions of the British Army. In the U.S. the World War II sightings of "comfort girls" began to be mentioned in the reminiscences and memoirs of veterans who served in the military in Asia and the Pacific Islands. This specific body of war literature includes the recollections of an extraordinary group of U.S. veterans: Asian American and specifically Japanese American men who served as U.S. military intelligence specialists in the Asia-Pacific War. Even before the U.S. formally declared war on Japan following the attack on Pearl Harbor in December 1941, the U.S. military leadership had been closely monitoring Japan's expansionist drive in the Asia-Pacific and identified a problematic lack of Japanese-fluent personnel: "As tensions rose between the U.S. and Japan, these former language officers realized the U.S. needed qualified Japanese linguists if the country were to successfully prosecute a war against Japan. . . . In June 1941, Major Carlisle C. Dusenbury, a former Japanese language student working in the Intelligence Division of the War Department, suggested using Nisei to solve the linguist problem. Lieutenant Colonel Wallace Moore, a former missionary who had served in Japan, agreed and subsequently planned the organization of the Army's first Japanese language school."[6] The students of the Military Intelligence Service Language School (MISLS) were mostly Nisei: second-generation Japanese Americans. Some of them were already enlisted by December 1941, both as volunteers and also in response to the Selective Training and Service Act of 1940, which required all men between twenty-one and thirty-six to register with their local draft boards. But many of the six thousand plus Japanese Americans who graduated from the language school and are referred to as "MISers" were carefully screened and personally recruited from the various concentration camps in which Japanese Americans were interned. The U.S. military also strategically enlisted the linguistic services of a smaller number of Korean Americans and Chinese Americans for deciphering intercepted communications, translating captured documents, and performing intelligence work in combat areas, which included eavesdropping on Japanese soldiers' conversations, interpreting battlefront commands, producing and broadcasting propaganda, negotiating peaceful surrender, and interrogating Japanese prisoners of war (POWs). These U.S. military-trained Japanese language specialists were also assigned to work with Allied forces over a large geographical area from Alaska to Australia.

By 1944, there were 150 Japanese American soldiers working in the China-Burma-India theater of operations, where two teams of Nisei interpreters would meet and interrogate a group of Korean women who had been taken to Burma in 1942 to toil in the Japanese military "comfort stations." This remarkable encounter between Asian American military linguists and Korean women who had been captured in North Burma and detained as prisoners of war (POWs) was recorded in several U.S. military documents and photographs that were discovered in the early 1990s. Other documents were subsequently located by diligent researchers, and the U.S. National Archives continues to yield a wide variety of textual records, including photographs and, most recently, filmed footage of captured Korean women in China. This chapter excavates and reconsiders this U.S. military archive of Korean "comfort women," which I divide into three interconnected and overlapping sets of texts:

- black-and-white photographs taken by the U.S. Army Signal Corps
- POW interrogation reports of the "captured" Korean women
- memoirs by and published interviews with the Asian American military intelligence personnel published in the 1980s

The first two sets of texts were produced earlier in time, but the peculiar terms and conditions of their composition, circulation, and archiving rendered them insignificant and they went largely unnoticed until the transnational justice and redress movement was inaugurated in the early 1990s. Thus, the third group of texts preceded and, I would argue, constituted a distinctive yet also internally heterogeneous channel of recall, which would connect in fascinating ways with the scholarly research, survivor testimonies, cultural representations, and governmental reports that were issued in the 1990s. By framing these memoirs as *Asian American* compositions, I would argue that they offer an important counterpoint to the large volume of Korean American cultural and scholarly productions that are cast from a diasporic, elegiac distance.[7] These U.S. military photographs and POW reports allow us to think of the Korean women in the coeval *and* irretrievable time-space of their capture through U.S. military actions and bureaucratic protocols, which call for a more genealogical method. My intent is not to demonstrate the greater truth value of these U.S. archival documents because, as I will demonstrate, they are also strategically composed, culturally specific, and genre-bound texts that have been subject to multiple decodings and appropriations.

U.S. SIGNAL CORPS PHOTOGRAPHS

Beginning in the late 1970s, the history of Japanese Americans who served in U.S. and Allied military intelligence during World War II was documented in a range of publications, largely because of the veterans' own efforts to recall and record their wartime work and experiences and to share these memories with one another and a broader audience. An important early instance was a 1979 book titled *Yankee Samurai: The Secret Role of Nisei in America's Pacific Victory*.

Although Joseph Daniel Harrington is the credited author, the book is largely a compendium of vignettes culled from the memories of and, in some cases, already written accounts by many Nisei veterans, and Harrington duly acknowledges how several Nisei veterans played a crucial role in assisting him with research, putting him in touch with interviewees, and prodding him toward the completion of the book. The Nisei veterans also began to write and publish their own individual memoirs. *Yankee Samurai* briefly mentions "comfort girls" to several places, and, most remarkably, it features possibly the earliest appearance of a photographic image of Korean "comfort women" in an English-language book.[8] It is a tightly cropped reproduction of a now familiar U.S. Army Signal Corps photograph (SC 262580—figure 5.1), which was taken on August 14, 1944, of two Korean women who are seated on the ground with downcast eyes and another woman behind them. To either side of the women are two uniformed Asian American male soldiers, whose bodies fill the left and

Capt. Chan and Comfort Girls with Sgt. Grant Hirabayashi. Myitkyina, Burma. August 1944.

FIGURE 5.1. Photo of cropped image of the US Signal Corps Photograph #262580 (August 14, 1944) of two Korean women being interrogated by Won-Loy Chan and Grant Hirabayashi with a third woman and Robert Honda in the background, in Myitkyina, and the accompanying caption, as featured in Won-Loy Chan's 1986 memoir, *Burma: The Untold Story*.

right edges of the frame. The caption provided in *Yankee Samurai* reads "Charlie Chan (l) and Grant Hirabayashi interrogate 'comfort girls.' A detachment of them was captured after Myitkyina, Burma, was overcome."[9]

After being assigned to and graduating from MISLS in Camp Savage in Minnesota as a Japanese intelligence specialist, Won-Loy ("Charlie") Chan arrived at the Allied headquarters in Ledo, India, in April 1943. He was serving as "the officer-in-charge of the POW interrogation point and document processing center" at the Myitkyina airstrip in north Burma in August 1944 when the women were captured.[10] Grant Hirabayashi was a Kibei who, along with thirteen other Japanese American linguists trained at Camp Savage, volunteered to join a ground combat unit for a dangerous mission "behind enemy lines" in North Burma: the 5307th Composite Unit, Provisional, more famously known as the Merrill's Marauders. In addition to the photograph, *Yankee Samurai* mentions that Hirabayashi and Chan interrogated the "comfort girls" in two different points in the book. Harrington even offers his own jocular close reading of the photograph of the women with Chan and Hirabayashi: "A lad of religious bent, totally out of place in the roughneck Army, even Hirabayashi had to admit that the Japanese had some novel ideas for fighting a war. A picture of him and 'Charlie' Chan at Myitkina (sp?) reminded the author of a cartoon showing two Roman legionnaires coming out of a city they've just helped destroy. One is carrying loot, the other has a struggling female slung over a shoulder. The second is saying to the first, 'The pay is lousy, but fringe benefits are terrific!'"[11] The Korean women are further dehumanized and disappeared through the heterosexist, fetishized spectacle of militarist fraternity.

In 1986 Won-Loy Chan published his own account as a book titled *Burma: The Untold Story*. Although it is largely a conventional war memoir, the book contains a remarkable section subtitled "The Comfort Girls," which provides a detailed account of his encounter with and interrogation of the Korean women in Myitkyina. The episode was considered significant enough by the book's publisher to merit a separate index entry for "Korean 'comfort girls,'" and it was also featured in the book cover description. Chan's account is markedly detailed, especially considering that the memoir was published in 1986, two years before the tourism seminar on Jeju Island when Yun Chung-ok presented her research and five years before the lawsuit by Kim Hak-sun captured international news headlines. Chan begins plaintively: "There are no records of the Korean comfort girls. No one knows how many of these unfortunate young women were forced into prostitution by the Imperial Japanese forces during the World War II." But then he continues with this lengthy description:

Truth Disclosure 159

Estimates run as high as 200,000. Mostly daughters of Korean farmers and peasants—although some came from the city slums and some may have practiced the oldest profession previously—between 1935 and 1945, they were rounded up by the Kempei Tai and sent to China, Burma, Guam, Malaya, the Philippines, the Dutch East Indies, in fact anywhere in the vast Pacific theatre of war where Japanese troops were garrisoned. Thousands were killed during the bloody fighting in the Pacific, Southeast Asia, and elsewhere. Following the Japanese surrender, many were repatriated by the Allies, eventually returning to Korea. The Japanese destroyed all records of this chapter in the history of the Imperial forces. Only a few photos remain today.

The comfort girls were organized by the Japanese into what they euphemistically called the Women's Volunteer Labor Corps. They were grouped down to platoon level of about fifty girls each. Some were exclusively for the pleasure of Japanese officers. Others serviced NCOs while the least attractive were forced to cater to the lowly private soldier of the Emperor. Each platoon-sized group was commanded by a Mama-san, usually a middle-aged Japanese woman who spoke Korean. When the girls weren't engaged in their primary occupational specialty or were ill, they acted as the washerwomen and barracks maids in the troop rest areas.

No one knows what has become of those who survived the war. Most would be in their early or mid-sixties today. United Nations troops in Korea between 1950 and 1953 reported that some of the girls continued to practice the profession after returning to Korea. Some also did that on Okinawa. For the vast majority, however, the stigma and shame resulting from what they had been forced to do prevents research and the absence of official records leaves one to conjecture as to the fate of those still living.[12]

Amazingly, Chan does not cite any sources here, but much of this account accords with or rather previews the large volume of archival research and witness testimonies that would be subsequently produced in the 1990s and beyond.[13] I will return to examine some more particular details in Chan's account later in this chapter, but for now I want to mark it as an early and clear instance in which the Japanese military "comfort system" and the Korean women that it forcibly recruited and displaced appear in print as an indelible part of *Asian American* memories of the Asia-Pacific war. These errant and minoritized inscriptions have not been but should be inducted as significant event-texts in U.S. histories of World War II.

As Chan points out in the above passage, "Only a few photos remain today." This reinforces his earlier pronouncement that "there are no records of the Korean comfort girls." Both statements work to enhance the shock effect and truth value of the large reproductions of three photographs of the Korean women (two of them with Chan), which are featured in *Burma: The Untold Story*. One photo (figure 5.1) is the same one that appears in *Yankee Samurai*, but here it is not as tightly cropped as it was in Harrington's book and is captioned differently, foregrounding the Chinese American authorial subject: "Capt. Chan and Comfort Girls with Sgt. Hirabayashi, Myitkyina Burma August." The second photo (figure 5.2) shows a much larger group of the seventeen Korean women; it also includes two other Japanese American military linguists identified as Howard Furumoto and Robert Honda. The third photo (figure 5.3), dated a week earlier on August 3, 1944, shows a lone Korean woman being interrogated and is captioned "Kim, the first 'Comfort Girl' taken prisoner at Myitkyina. With Kim is Karl Yoneda of the OWI and a Japanese soldier." All three photos were taken by the same U.S. Army combat photographer, Frank W. Shearer, who was assigned to the 164th Signal Photo Company.[14] The pictures were

Capt. Chan, Sgts. Howard Furumoto, Grant Hirabayashi, and Robert Honda, with Comfort Girls. Myitkyina, Burma. August 1944.

FIGURE 5.2. Photo of cropped image of the U.S. Signal Corps #III-SC-262579 of Korean women and Asian American soldiers in Myitkyina and the accompanying caption, as featured in Won-Loy Chan's 1986 memoir, *Burma: The Untold Story*.

Truth Disclosure 161

Kim, the first "comfort girl" taken prisoner at Myitkyina. With Kim is Karl Yoneda of the OWI and a Japanese soldier. 3 August 1944.

FIGURE 5.3. Photo of cropped image of the U.S. Signal Corps photograph of Karl Yoneda's interrogation of a Korean woman identified as "Kim" in Myitkyina and the accompanying caption, as featured in Won-Loy Chan's 1986 memoir, *Burma: The Untold Story*.

subsequently catalogued at the National Archives, where they were later rediscovered by journalists and researchers in the 1990s.

By now, all three photos have been reprinted in many other texts, news stories, and countless websites. The large group photo (figure 5.2) has been most widely circulated, achieving a kind of iconic status. It was perhaps most notably featured as the wraparound cover image of the 1995 English translation of Yoshimi Yoshiaki's book *Comfort Women: Sexual Slavery in the Japanese Military during World War II*.[15] Like most others, I have taken these photographs as visible evidence of the "truth" of the Japanese military "comfort system." At the same time, I have long been preoccupied by how they attest to the extraordinary meeting and assembly of *these* two groups of Asian American and Korean subjects in a makeshift military enclosure in North Burma. On further inspection, these photos are the cruel and astounding trace of several intercutting histories of power, knowledge, violence, and exigency as well as their indifferent and arbitrary documentation.

A clearer reproduction of the large group photo from the U.S. National Archives brings new details into view (figure 5.4). There is another female figure dressed in a kimono in the more shaded bottom right corner and two more women behind her, who were all cropped out in the close-up reproduction centering Chan that was featured in *Burma: The Untold Story*. The structure's now visible slanted roof and its more distinct barbed wires emphasize the carceral conditions of this setting. The requisite Signal Corps caption sheet for this photo indicates that it was taken on August 14, 1944, and contains these notes under "Location & Subject": "Capt. Chan [####] San Francisco, Cal. 1012 Jackson St., in charge of prisoners of war at Myitkyina Burma with the captured Comfort Girls of the Japanese garrison at Myitkyina."[16] Although the composition and framing suggest that the scene was self-consciously posed and strategically arranged, there is enough unevenness and heterogeneity to imbue a certain degree of extemporaneity and indeterminacy. There is no singular focal point or single punctum but rather a crowded, disorienting jumble of bodies and faces bearing partial, restricted visibility and many disparate-looking positions. It could be—and has been—read as a snapshot of rescue and liberation. But, as the Signal Corps caption announces, this is a record of incarceration. This time-space is also a switching point from the "Japanese garrison" of an occupied Burma to the "Ledo Stockade" of a colonized India, where these women will go after this photo

FIGURE 5.4. Reproduction of the original U.S. Signal Corps Photograph #III-SC-262579 of Korean women and Asian American soldiers in Myitkyina. (Source: US National Archives photo no. III-SC-262579.)

Truth Disclosure   163

has been taken and where they will be further confined and interrogated by the United States Office of War Information—Psychological Warfare Branch.

What if we were to zoom out from this cropped framing, not just optically but also in terms of the broader historical, geopolitical, cultural, and governmental forces that came to bear upon the assembly of these bodies in this time-space, the production of this photographic image, and its subsequent archiving, forgetting, and late retrieval? First, they attest vividly to the U.S. military's cotemporaneous awareness of the existence of the "comfort stations," notably in and through such direct face-to-face encounters with the abused and traumatized women on the Asia-Pacific battlefield. Second, they are also the visible record of the cruel induction and strategic use of Asian Americans and specifically Japanese Americans by the U.S. as especially qualified and exemplary agents of "military intelligence" and "psychological warfare" against the Japanese military during World War II. Third, approached as the execution of a particular U.S. military practice of documentation and archiving, they suggest how the selective priorities and methods of this cosmology and episteme contributed to the effacement and unfathomability of the Korean women who were *captured* within its frame. Fourth, we would have to consider their "discovery" in the early 1990s as conditioned by several competing desires and discrepant genres for remembering the role of the U.S. military in the Asia-Pacific War, including the ambivalent attachments of certain militarized Asian American subjects.[17]

U.S. POW INTERROGATIONS AND MILITARY INTELLIGENCE REPORTS

These U.S. Signal Corps photographs were part of a larger "discovery" of U.S. military documents in the early 1990s. They were initially hailed as providing credible, third-party attestation of the existence of the Japanese military "comfort stations," despite the Japanese government's denials. On December 21, 1991, two weeks after the first lawsuit filed by survivors made international headlines, South Korea's Yonhap News Agency reported that the U.S. embassy in Seoul had conveyed a U.S. military document from World War II to the South Korean Ministry of Foreign Affairs: "The declassified document, entitled *Interrogation Bulletin No 2*, is a report by a U.S. Army psychological warfare team between August and September 1944 from India and Burma based on interviews with Japanese prisoners of war."[18] I have not been able to obtain any more information about how and why this intergovernmental exchange took place, but I am curious about who initiated the process and whether it was specifically requested by the South Korean representatives or independently located and then transmitted by authorized agents of the U.S. government. There is an intriguing background story or several stories there. The thirteen-page document, issued by the South East Asia Translation and Interrogation Center (SEATIC), summarizes the interrogation of several Japanese military and civilian POWs first in Burma and later at the Red Fort in Delhi and concludes with a three-page-long section titled "A Japanese Army Brothel in the Forward Area." The source is identified as "M.739, a civilian brothel-owner, captured with his wife and 20 Army prostitutes near Waingmaw on 10 August 1944," but a prefatory note indicates that the following account is also based on "O.W.I. Interrogation at Ledo Base Stockade of 20 Korean 'comfort girls,' Report dated 21 Sept. 1944."

In early January 1992 the news broke that Yoshimi Yoshiaki had located several documents in the archives of the Library of the National Institute for Defense Studies at the Defense Agency in Tokyo that showed direct Japanese military involvement in the management of the "comfort stations." Then, on January 26, 1992, a Kyodo News Service dispatch from Washington, D.C., announced the discovery of "two reports by Americans who interrogated 20 Korean women forced into prostitution in the Myanmar town of Myitkyina. They show two Japanese brothel owners operated on detailed instructions from the Japanese military."[19] One of these documents was a *Japanese Prisoner of War Interrogation Report, No. 49* (hereafter referred to as OWI *Interrogation Report No. 49*), issued by the U.S. Office of War Information's Psychological Warfare Team (OWI-PWB) on "20 Korean Comfort Girls," which was authored by Technical Sergeant Alex Yorichi. This report is dated October 1, 1944, but notes that the interrogation of the twenty Korean female POWs had been conducted earlier, from August 20 to September 10, following their "date of capture" on August 10 (figure 5.5). After being captured by a group of ethnic Kachin soldiers, the women were initially confined at the Allied military headquarters in Myitkyina until they were transferred on August 15, the day after the two photos with Chan and Hirabayashi were taken, to the Ledo Stockade in India for further interrogation, processing, and eventual repatriation. Although there is a discrepancy between the dates cited in the *Bulletin No. 2* (September 21 versus October 1), it is clear that *Interrogation Report, No. 49* predated and served partly as the basis of the account that appears under the heading of "A Japanese Army Brothel in the Forward Area" at the end of SEATIC *Bulletin No. 2*.[20]

On February 5, 1992, the Kyodo New Service reported on a third incriminating U.S. military document that it had just obtained from Grant Goodman, a

Truth Disclosure 165

```
                    UNITED STATES OFFICE OF WAR INFORMATION
                           Psychological Warfare Team
                    Attached to U.S. Army Forces India-Burma Theater.
                                    APO 689

   Japanese Prisoner        Place interrogated:      Ledo Stockade
   of War Interrogation     Date interrogated:       Aug. 20 - Sept.10, 1944
   Report No. 49.           Date of Report:          October 1, 1944
                            By:                      T/3 Alex Yorichi

   Prisoners:               20 Korean Comfort Girls
   Date of Capture:         August 10, 1944
   Date of Arrival          August 15, 1944
   at Stockade:
```

PREFACE:

   This report is based on the information obtained from the interrogation of twenty Korean "comfort girls" and two Japanese civilians captured around the tenth of August, 1944 in the mopping up operations after the fall of Myitkyina in Burma.

   The report shows how the Japanese recruited these Korean "comfort girls", the conditions under which they lived and worked, their relations with and reaction to the Japanese soldier, and their understanding of the military situation.

FIGURE 5.5. Photo of the title page of *Japanese Prisoner of War Interrogation Report No. 49*, written by Alex Yorichi for the US Office of War Information, Psychological Warfare Team, in 1944. (Source: US National Archives.)

Japan historian at Kansas University who had served as a Japanese translator for the U.S. Army during World War II, first at the Allied Translator and Interpreter Section (ATIS) headquarters in Manila and later in Tokyo. Goodman had kept a personal bound copy of an ATIS report titled *Amenities in the Japanese Armed Forces* (hereafter referred to as the ATIS *Amenities* report), which contains an extensive section on the "comfort system."[21] Goodman was impelled to locate his copy of this document after reading about Yoshimi's important discoveries in the Japanese military archives and the Japanese government's denials of official involvement. Goodman contacted Miura Junji, a reporter with the Washington Bureau of the Kyodo News Agency, and provided him with a copy. The discovery of the ATIS *Amenities* report was soon reported in several newspapers; an article in the *Japan Times* characterized it as "the most detailed account yet on the controversial brothel operation run and abetted by the Japanese military in occupied Asian territories."[22]

These U.S. military archival disclosures and discoveries were marshaled to confirm both Korean and Japanese scholarly research and the survivors' testimonies. They were featured significantly as "evidence" and bibliographical sources in several key early publications on the subject.[23] The OWI *Interrogation Report No. 49* was included in the South Korean government's first official publication by its Inter-Ministerial Working Group on the Comfort Women Issue, *Military Comfort Women under Japanese Colonial Rule Interim Report* (July 1992). The 1994 book-length report by the International Commission of Jurists [ICJ], *Comfort Women: An Unfinished Ordeal*, also references the *Interrogation Report No. 49* and quotes extensively from the 1945 *Amenities* report as well as Won-Loy Chan's 1986 memoir.[24] Characterizing it as "among the most detailed sources on the system," George Hicks summarizes the OWI *Interrogation Report No. 49* at length in his 1995 monograph, *The Comfort Women*.[25]

Reading each document closely alongside and against the others, it becomes clear that these are also records of the beginnings of U.S. military intervention into and occupation of Asia. They incriminate the U.S. military as an early knowing subject, selective scribe, and indifferent preservationist of the atrocities of the Japanese military "comfort system." This was duly observed in several early publications. Ustinia Dolgopol and Snehal Paranjape, the two authors of the 1994 ICJ report, pointedly note these unsettling power/knowledge implications: "A disturbing facet of this story is that the Allied Powers had compiled extensive documentary and other evidence, immediately after the war, about the comfort stations, the manner in which the women were recruited, and the vicious nature of the control the Japanese military had over the women. They also knew that comfort stations had been established throughout the Asia-Pacific Region and that Dutch, Korean, Chinese, Taiwanese, Filipino, Indonesian, Malaysian and Burmese women had been victimized."[26] George Hicks also questions this early awareness and tacit tolerance:

> The comfort women were not unknown to the Allies, who had repatriated many. The United States Army had even, as mentioned, made a study group of comfort women, and Allied soldiers had been known to take advantage of them. Only the Dutch took action against the Japanese for forced prostitution—but on behalf of Dutch women only. Indonesian women who were also captured for comfort stations did not figure in the Batavia Trials, a reflection of racist bias just as the failure of the Allies to try those responsible for the comfort system is a reflection

of sexism. There is a niggling thought that the sufferings of the comfort women did not matter enough for an issue to be made out of them.[27]

Hicks does not provide any more information about this intriguing U.S. Army "study group," and I have not been able to locate any more information about its formation and operation. I do want to point to a certain persistence and continuity that connect this indifference to the *Asian* female victims of the "comfort system" and the earlier indifference to Asian women in the League of Nations trafficking inquiries.

Yuki Tanaka has elaborated most extensively on this particular, uneasy truth of the early U.S. military knowledge and nonintervention in his 2003 monograph. Chapter 4 is pointedly titled "Why did the U.S. forces ignore the comfort women issue?" and Tanaka calls attention specifically to the ATIS *Amenities* report as evidence that "well before the end of World War II, the U.S. armed forces became aware of the comfort women system organized by the Japanese Imperial forces." Later on, reducing the charge from a willful disregard to a cognitive incapacity, Tanaka asks: "Why was awareness of the comfort women issue as a serious war crime clearly lacking in the mind of the leaders of the Allies forces?" Tanaka attributes this lack or inability to racism and sexism: "One reason probably lies in the fact that the majority of the women victims of this enforced military prostitution were Asians and were therefore neither white women nor civilians of Allied nations." Tanaka also underscores "military ideology, regardless of its nationality, [which holds that] women are morally obliged to offer amenities to soldiers" and whereby "military men are generally quite insensitive towards the services rendered by women."[28] Finally, Tanaka also describes at length the U.S. military's use of organized prostitution and regulated VD checks as a similar instance of official tolerance and active coordination.

As indicated in the passages quoted above, in his attempt to demonstrate how the U.S. and Allied militaries were complicit in and also culpable for the rape and sexual exploitation of women, Tanaka tends to disregard crucial differences and hierarchies among military personnel. There is an important difference and large power gap between "military men" and "the leaders of the Allied forces," but especially, I would argue, in this particular case of the Japanese American military intelligence personnel. Stating that the OWI *Interrogation Report No. 49* "clearly refers to the violation of these Korean women's human rights by the Japanese forces" and thus supports the "claims that most of these women were deceived into becoming prostitutes for the Japanese forces," Tanaka adds, "However, it seems that the American interrogators did not regard it as a serious war crime against humanity, and had no intention of prosecuting the Japanese officers of the 114th Infantry Regiment for sexual exploitation of these women."²⁹ This sentence attributes a generic subject-position to "the American interrogators" and assumes its unity with "the leaders of the Allied forces," but it is critical to understand that these were Japanese American subjects who acted as interrogators and translators of Korean women categorized and treated as Japanese POWs. So many books and articles on the "comfort women" problematic cite these and other U.S. POW interrogation reports as incontrovertible evidence and official archival sources, but no one has paid any sustained attention to the peculiar fact that it was mostly Nisei and Kibei soldiers, many of them recruited from the U.S. concentration camps to be trained at the Military Intelligence Service and Language School, who conducted the interrogations and composed the reports.

Tanaka gets closer when he points to the myopic instrumentalism and constrained terms of U.S. military intelligence, within which the Korean women and the Japanese American interrogators were both caught up. Referring specifically to the SEATIC *Psychological Warfare Interrogation Bulletin No. 2* (rather than the OWI *Interrogation Report No. 49*, which is the only document based on the direct interrogation of the women), Tanaka asks, "Why did a Psychological Warfare Team interrogate these comfort women?"

> U.S. Psychological Warfare Teams were formed for the purpose of gathering as much information as possible concerning the psychological conditions of Japanese soldiers in the battlefield. A particular function was to conduct thorough interrogations of Japanese POWs, to find out how they perceived the ongoing war and under what conditions they would decide to surrender. Such information was forwarded to the Foreign Morale Analysis Division in the Office of War Information, to be analyzed by such prominent psychologists and anthropologists as Ruth Benedict, Clyde Kluckhohn, and John Embree. These specialist opinions were taken into account in producing various propaganda leaflets designed to persuade Japanese soldiers and civilians to surrender rather than fight to the death. Tens of thousands of these leaflets were printed and scattered from the air throughout the Pacific region, in particular during the fiercest battle of World War II in the Okinawa islands.³⁰

Tanaka does not reflect further upon the blind spots, silences, and distortions created by the very structure of this racist and ethnocentric transpacific feedback loop. He merely concludes that "it is presumed, therefore, that the interrogation of comfort women was not regarded as an important task for the U.S. Psychological Warfare Teams. Such interrogation could provide only secondary information on the psychology of members of Japanese military forces." Interestingly, Tanaka supports this contention by citing a personal interview he conducted with Grant Hirabayashi: "He explained that only a brief interrogation was conducted, simply because these women had unexpectedly fallen into the hands of U.S. forces. According to Hirabayashi, only a summary memorandum was recorded in this case, in contrast to normal POW procedures in which every question and answer was precisely recorded. In other words, information obtained from these women was not highly valued by the Americans."[31] It's unclear what this "summary memorandum" was, but if there is such a document that was written up by Hirabayashi or Chan, it has not yet been located. What we have instead is a book-length memoir written by Chan (*Burma: The Untold Story*) and videotaped testimony and a transcribed speech by Hirabayashi.[32] Neither Chan nor Hirabayashi was assigned to the Psychological Warfare Branch.

The OWI *Japanese Prisoner of War Interrogation Report No. 49* was authored by Alex Yorichi, who belonged to a ten-person team with the OWI-PWB, which included nine Japanese Americans: "Koji Ariyoshi, journalist and team captain; Kenji Akune, interrogator/translator; Chris Ishii, former Walt Disney cartoonist; Clarke Kawakami, former *Domei* correspondent; Masao Kitsuta, a Kibei, interrogator/translator; Edgar Laytha, a Hungarian, writer, and Japanese linguist; Sam Sasaki, a Kibei, interrogator/translator; Kenji Yasui, a Kibei, former Tokyo University student; Karl Yoneda, a Kibei, former *Rodo Shimbun* editor; and Alex Yorichi, a University of California graduate."[33] As this list demonstrates, half of these men were Kibei (Japanese Americans born in the U.S. but sent to Japan for a period of schooling and then returned), and many of these men had a history of journalism and media production, making them specially qualified for the task of "psychological warfare." Recall that Yoneda was the one photographed interrogating a Korean woman identified as "Kim" in one of the Signal Corps photos featured in Won-Loy Chan's book (figure 5.3).

Here, we must pause to note that although much has been made of the evidentiary "truth" value of these surviving military documents, there are countless more documents and records that have been destroyed or misplaced. First, as many have already pointed out, the Japanese destroyed much of the incriminating records of its military expansion, including its very detailed records concerning the establishment and operation of the "comfort stations."[34] It is likely that the intensive Allied bombings during the war also destroyed some documents both in Japan and throughout the vast Asia-Pacific territory that the Japanese army invaded and occupied. But the U.S. military and other

Allied forces also destroyed, lost, and mishandled many documents that it did seize, both in the various battlefronts and later in Japan during the U.S. occupation. This was partly the result of a sometimes murky division of military intelligence command among the Allies. The South East Asia Translation and Interrogation Center (SEATIC) was first established in New Delhi as a British-run agency responsible for deciphering, translating, and publishing captured Japanese documents and prisoner-of-war interrogations related to the China-Burma-India theater, which were shared among the Allied nations. The U.S. and Australia jointly commanded a parallel agency called the Allied Translator and Interpreter Section (ATIS), which "served as a centralized Allied intelligence unit for the translation of intercepted Japanese communications, interrogations and negotiations in the SWPA [South West Pacific Area] between September 1942 and December 1945."[35] According to military historian Edward Drea, "The compartmentalization of the war in Asia also diminished the possibility that one nation would end up with the lion's share of Japanese documentation. British Empire forces, for example, took charge of Japanese materials in Southeast Asia. Returning colonial authorities in Indochina and the Dutch East Indies gathered material for their war crimes trials. The Chinese and Russians also gathered and kept many documents."[36]

There was a particular nonsignificance and illegibility of the Japanese military "comfort system," which further reduced the likelihood that incriminating documents would have been preserved. As Drea further explains, "During World War II and its immediate aftermath, not all areas of Japanese war criminality were explored in depth. For example, while the 'comfort women' issue is of great current importance, the U.S. government did not systematically collect or create records related to the topic during or after the war. As a consequence, there are very few documents pertaining to the topic in the archives." Although there was some knowledge of what Drea labels as "the Imperial Japanese Army's field brothel system," he contends, "However, the scope of the brothel network (particularly in China) and the Japanese Army's official sponsorship of the system were not well understood. Licensed prostitution was legal in prewar Japan, and Allied officials viewed the small part of the overseas system they uncovered as an extension of homeland practices. Prosecuting Japanese soldiers for rape, a notorious crime everywhere the army set foot, took precedence over investigating the circumstances of 'comfort women,' who were seen as professional prostitutes, not as unwilling victims coerced into brothels by employees of the Japanese military."[37] To be clear, this is Drea's *interpretation* of the possible reasons for the non-recognition and non-prosecution of the "comfort system" in the immediate aftermath of their discovery by Allied forces and military leaders. His reference to prewar licensed prostitution in Japan and characterization of Allied perception that this system was merely "an extension of homeland practices" thus attribute this non-recognition to an overarching exclusion of Japan and the Imperial Army *and* its Asian victims from prevailing categories of intelligibility and standards of judgment. But, as I will show below, the impressions and memories of the Asian American military interrogators are more heterogeneous and ambivalent than the "Allied officials" that Drea names as categorically and uniformly perceiving the women as "professional prostitutes."

Pointing specifically to how the 1945 *Amenities* report had been declassified quite early in the 1960s, Drea writes that "although available to the public for years, it received little attention until the 'comfort women' issue focused attention on these wrongdoings in the 1990s."[38] Thus, Drea suggests that it was not the inaccessibility of such archival evidence but an absence of will by researchers and also a broader lack of public interest and concern about this history. I would add that the *mis*-categorization and forgetting of the "comfort women" can be partially attributed to the differences among but also the staggered relay of the three military documents among the various U.S. and Allied military agencies. Here it is important to note that although Hirabayashi, Chan, and Yoneda are prominently featured in the Signal Corps photographs of the Korean women, *Interrogation Report No. 49* was written by Alex Yorichi, who belonged to the ten-person OWI-PWB team, and it is the only document based on the author's direct interrogations of the twenty Korean women.

The U.S. Office of War Information [OWI] was established by executive order on June 13, 1942, and charged with the monitoring and dissemination of both domestic and foreign news, and coordinating various forms of propaganda. This involved monitoring Japanese publications and broadcasts but also analyzing information derived from interrogating POWs and captured military documents.[39] Its Psychological Warfare Branch engaged in various methods and tasks, including drafting the standard questionnaires that were used in the interrogation of Japanese POWs. When read alongside and against one another, it becomes easier to see how each document was composed within specific parameters of ordering, formatting, diction, and citation. Indeed, in some respects the three reports seem to belong to distinctive genres of military documentation. Each document, especially *Japanese Prisoner of War Interrogation Report No. 49*, also bears traces of distinctive authorial decisions and edits along this military chain of circulation and reinscription.

From the dozen or so POW interrogation reports of the Japanese soldiers that I have been able to access,[40] it is apparent that they followed a standard outline, based on the questionnaire, with some small deviations. As one *Psychological Warfare Bulletin* noted, the interrogation of Japanese POWs was "based on questionnaires prepared by Morale Analysis Section, OWI, Washington."[41] An opening, general "Evaluation" set forth a summary impression of the POW, followed by a biographical "History" and a separate section titled "Military History." Some reports would also include a section titled "Circumstances of Capture." Then there was a long section on "Information & Propaganda," followed by "General Ideas," which were further subdivided into subsections, as in this example from *Japanese Prisoner of War Interrogation Report, No. 23*:

INFORMATION & PROPAGANDA:
Leaflets:
News:
Radio:
Morale:
Food:
Medical Care:
Officer Relations:
Air Attacks & Support:
Lectures:

GENERAL IDEAS:
Suicide:
Japan:
Allies:
Axis:
War:
Treatment:[42]

As demonstrated by this template, a primary aim of the interrogations was to assess the effectiveness of the various "psychological warfare" methods used by the U.S. military. There was an almost absurd feedback loop, resembling a kind of audience research. A concluding section titled "SUPPLEMENT: Reactions to OWI Leaflets shown to POW" sometimes contained itemized reactions to specifically named OWI leaflets and even included a subsection titled "Suggestions by the POW," in which the Japanese POWs provided advice on the effective content and form of propaganda.

The sectional outline of *Japanese Prisoner of War Interrogation Report, No. 49* composed by Alex Yorichi is clearly different from the OWI-PWB template. It begins with a rather scholarly "PREFACE" and then proceeds as follows:

RECRUITING;
PERSONALITY;
LIVING AND WORKING CONDITIONS;
PRICE SYSTEM;
SCHEDULES;
PAY AND LIVING CONDITIONS;
REACTIONS TO JAPANESE SOLDIERS;
SOLDIERS REACTIONS;
REACTION TO THE MILITARY SITUATION;
RETREAT AND CAPTURE;
PROPAGANDA;
REQUESTS;

Although the initial "discovery" of this OWI interrogation report in 1992 by the Kyodo News Agency was hailed as further corroboration of the role of the Japanese Imperial Army in the recruitment and transport of the women from Korea and the establishment, operation, and strict regulation of the "comfort stations," the document has subsequently been upheld as proof of radically different interpretations of the truth of the "comfort system." These differently preferred and negotiated decodings are made possible by the report's voluble pronouncements and deep contradictions. The final paragraph of the preface reads as follows: "A 'comfort girl' is nothing more than a prostitute or 'professional camp follower' attached to the Japanese Army for the benefit of the soldiers. The term *comfort girl* is peculiar to the Japanese. Other reports show the 'comfort girls' have been found wherever it was necessary for the Japanese Army to fight. This report however deals only with the Korean 'comfort girls' recruited by the Japanese and attached to their Army in Burma. The Japanese are reported to have shipped some 703 of these girls to Burma in 1942."[43] The "other reports" point to an established written record and awareness of the Japanese "comfort system."

Bear in mind that the author of these words is Technical Sergeant Alex Yorichi. From what I have been able to find, these are the few biographical details of his life leading up to his deployment to Burma. Born on November 23, 1920, in the small town of Trowbridge in Sutter County, California, Yorichi attended the University of California, Berkeley. Given these dates, he might have recently graduated or was still a student when the evacuation order was issued. Yorichi and his widowed father were first interned at the Tanforan Assembly Center and then at the Topaz War Relocation Center, both in Utah. The June 6, 1942, issue of the Japanese American camp journal

Tanforan Totalizer lists Yorichi as a staff member in charge of circulation, and he was also later a staff writer for the *Topaz Times*. Two months later, Yorichi enlisted in the U.S. Army and was assigned to Camp Savage in Minnesota, where he was in the December 1942 class of the Military Intelligence Service Language School.

Yorichi's opening categorical declaration—"A 'comfort girl' is nothing more than a prostitute or 'professional camp follower'"—has been often cited, especially by deniers and revisionists, as official, documentary "proof" that the women were indeed paid prostitutes, *not* the "sex slaves" that survivors, activists, and feminist scholars claim. The revisionists have also pointed to select phrases and sentences in the section on LIVING AND WORKING CONDITIONS, such as describing how the women (actually they are referred to as "girl" or "girls" throughout) "transacted business" and "lived in near-luxury in Burma in comparison to other places." Other positive details follow: "They lived well because their food and material was not heavily rationed and they had plenty of money with which to purchase desired articles. They were able to buy cloth, shoes, cigarettes, and cosmetics to supplement the many gifts given to them by soldiers who had received 'comfort bags' from home. While in Burma they amused themselves by participating in sports events with both officers and men, and attended picnics, entertainments, and social dinners. They had a phonograph and in the towns they were allowed to go shopping."[44]

On the other hand, many scholars and commentators have also cited this same report as official, documentary "proof" of the duplicitous, coercive, and exploitative nature of the Japanese military "comfort system." For example, much of the section on RECRUITING appears largely to corroborate survivors' claims of being misled by the Japanese procurers and further compelled by poverty and family hardships. It also describes official Japanese military involvement in the transport of the women to Burma:

> Early in May of 1942 Japanese agents arrived in Korea for the purpose of enlisting Korean girls for "comfort service" in newly conquered Japanese territories in Southeast Asia. The nature of this "service" was not specified but it was assumed to be work connected with visiting the wounded in hospitals, rolling bandages, and generally making the soldiers happy. The inducement used by these agents was plenty of money, an opportunity to pay off the family debts, easy work, and the prospect of a new life in a new land, Singapore. On the basis of these false representations many girls enlisted for overseas duty and were rewarded with an advance of a few hundred yen.[45]

Yorichi's translation of "comfort service" and the additional scare quotes around "service" signal a skepticism toward the euphemism, and he clearly denotes the "false representations" that were used in their recruitment. Noting that "the majority of the girls were ignorant and uneducated," Yorichi adds, "a few had been connected with the 'oldest profession on earth.'" The details of the graduated price system as well as the scheduling of the specific times and days in which certain military ranks and divisions were given priority and/or permission to use the "comfort stations" also clearly demonstrate that the Japanese military strictly regulated the operation of the comfort stations. The report also notes that the women described how they were "well supplied with all types of contraceptives" and were subject to weekly physical examinations by a Japanese Army doctor. Although each woman was supposed to be paid a percentage (40–50 percent) of what the soldiers paid, the report notes that "many 'masters' made life very difficult for the girls by charging them high prices for food and other articles." Finally, an appendix in OWI *Report No. 49* lists the individual names, ages, and hometowns of the twenty women followed by the names and ages of the married "Japanese civilians" who recruited them and managed the "comfort house": Kitamura Tomiko (thirty-eight) and Kitamura Eibun (forty-one).[46] The women's names are clearly butchered, but the list still demonstrates some effort at individual identification.

In contrast to this focus on the twenty Korean women, the SEATIC *Psychological Warfare Bulletin No. 2* includes information culled from the interrogations of several other Japanese POWs captured in Burma, and the concluding section, titled "A Japanese Army Brothel in the Forward Area," reiterates some details from *Interrogation Report No. 49* but is more focused upon information derived from Kitamura Eibun, who is here referred to as "M.739, a civilian brothel-owner." Also, the interrogation of "M.739" took place not at the Ledo Stockade, where Yorichi interrogated the Korean women, but at the Combined Services Detailed Interrogation Centre (CSDIC [I]) at the Red Fort in Delhi. The CSDIC (I) was part of a far-flung network of British intelligence centers, but the title page of *Bulletin No. 2* bears the signature of U.S. Army Colonel Alexander Swift, who was the superintendent of the SEATIC in November 1994, when the bulletin was issued.

The ATIS *Amenities* report was even further removed in time and space from the initial encounter with and direct interrogations of the Korean women. An earlier draft was prepared in February 1945 by ATIS, then based in Manila, and published again in November 1945 after the headquarters of the Supreme Commander for the Allied Powers (SCAP) had moved to Tokyo. By then, the U.S. had acquired many more documents about the Japanese military "comfort system." An extensive and detailed account of Japanese military regulations surrounding fees, daily and weekly schedules, and mandated health checks at the "comfort stations" appears under the rubric of "Brothels" in the second section of the *Amenities* report titled "Amusements," along with "Athletics," "Movies," and "Geisha and Entertainment Troupes." The subsection on brothels is further subdivided into geographic locations: Manila, Burma, Sumatra, and "Southwest Pacific Area." The Burma portion is mostly a verbatim re-presentation of the account presented in "A Japanese Army Brothel in the Forward Area" in SEATIC *Bulletin No. 2* with a few slight revisions, most notably the replacement of "M.739" with the even more anonymous and generic "prisoner of war." This is followed and supplemented by four brief excerpts that contain explicit references to the "comfort system" in the interrogations of Japanese POWs. The twenty "Korean Comfort Girls" captured in Myitkyina undergo a certain mutation and gradual erasure at each step in this chain of documentation, circulation, and recitation.

There is a conflicting and somewhat confusing archival mesh created by the Signal Corp photographs and the three U.S. and Allied military intelligence documents. Some of this blurring can be attributed to the different aims and priorities of POW interrogation for different military branches and divisions operating under very diverse geographical, infrastructural, and material circumstances. For example, Chan and Hirabayashi encountered and interacted with the women in the more frenetic battlefront, shortly after intensive combat. In addition, Hirabayashi, Honda, and Furumoto had all been attached to a ground combat unit that had been subject to a long, grueling, and lethal campaign "behind enemy lines" in northern Burma. In contrast, the ten-person OWI-PWB team, which included Karl Yoneda and Alex Yorichi, arrived in Ledo, Assam, near the India-Burma border in March 1944. The OWI office was housed in a two-story bungalow, where the Psychological Warfare Branch team worked on drafting propaganda leaflets to persuade Japanese soldiers to surrender, which were dropped in North Burma and also read out loud in radio broadcasts. On July 23, 1944, Karl Yoneda and Kenny Yasui were flown to the front lines to conduct live broadcasts for Japanese soldiers. This explains how Yoneda was there in Myitkyina on August 3 when the Allied forces took the town and was photographed interrogating the woman identified as "Kim"; Yoneda then returned to Ledo on August 6. The twenty Korean women were captured on August 10 and brought to the provisional military intelligence headquarters in Myitkyina, where they were detained in a separate makeshift tent for POWs. Although the Signal Corps records indicate that the women were photographed with Chan and Hirabayashi in Myitkyina on August 14,

1944, it is unclear on which day(s) they were interrogated in this four-day span and also on how many occasions. In contrast, Yorichi interrogated the Korean women *after* they had been transported to the Ledo Stockade near the OWI-PWB headquarters there. Thus, even though Chan, Hirabayashi, and Yoneda all seem to agree, in retrospect, that the information that was yielded from the two different sets of interrogations of the Korean women was deemed as "low-value," the more immediate, chaotic conditions of the battlefront may explain why Yorichi's writing up of *Report No. 49* is so much more detailed, opinionated, and, at times, even extemporaneous.

The traces of Yorichi's singular authorial impressions as well as the extraordinary and radically attenuated conditions of this writing up of "20 Korean Comfort Girls" as *Japanese Prisoner of War Interrogation Report No. 49* in the U.S. military archive fade away as the document becomes habitually invoked and thus validated as truthful record and evidence. But of what? The photos will also become untethered from the pained, forcible conditions and preconditions of *this* assembly of *these* Korean women and *these* Japanese American soldiers at this place and time. Both the capture and documentation *and* the effacement and illegibility of the Korean women encountered on the battlefronts by the U.S. military are the symptoms and consequences of a peculiarly enfolded frame of comprehension, categorization, and prioritization. Rather than fixate upon and identify with the Korean women, I propose instead to re-*think* both *Interrogation Report No. 49* and the Signal Corps photographs as distinctive yet unruly *American* compositions, which betray the U.S. state's incoherent mix of racist mass incarceration and denaturalization of Japanese Americans with its imperialist investment in and militarized commitment to Asia. To do this, we have to make an undisciplined generic switch. If we reread these U.S. military documents alongside personal and avowedly personal and self-interested Asian American veteran recollections of their improbable encounters and interactions with these women, we can discern the conventional but also leaky and occasionally flouted boundaries of the POW interrogation report and the warfront photograph, which constitute the nationalist and imperialist U.S. military archive.

ASIAN AMERICAN WAR COMPOSITIONS

Before I discuss the veterans' writings and oral recollections, I want to point out how these accounts were importantly preceded by the U.S. military's own strategic public representation of their heroic contributions at the close of

World War II. One still common narrative of these Nisei linguists is that their contributions were officially suppressed and largely forgotten, especially in contrast to the celebration of the 442nd and 100th Nisei-only combat units that fought in Europe. But there was actually some limited press coverage of their accomplishments during the war, especially in the Japanese American press but also in military periodicals such as the *CBI Roundup* and in some mainstream newspapers. The Allied campaign against the Japanese Imperial Army in North Burma in 1944 was notable for several historic, geopolitical, and ideological reasons. The Japanese invasion and occupation of Burma were significant as the westernmost extension of its territorial expansion across the Asia Pacific and a specifically pointed usurpation of British colonial rule. The deployment of U.S. soldiers to Burma was also hailed as the "first" time that U.S. military combat troops had landed on the Asian mainland. Back in the U.S., by 1944 there had been several legal challenges to and public criticisms of the unconstitutional removal and incarceration of Japanese Americans in concentration camps. As other U.S. soldiers returned home from the European, Asian, and Pacific battlefronts, many of them attested to the bravery and camaraderie of Japanese American soldiers who served alongside them, and several openly criticized the racist dispossession and mistreatment of Japanese Americans by their own government. In April 1945 the War Relocation Authority published a seventeen-page mimeographed pamphlet titled *Nisei in the War against Japan*, which reproduces many of these favorable news stories about the Japanese American soldiers and some supportive letters to the editor.

The crucial role of Nisei linguists in the brutal Burma campaign figured significantly in the deliberations about removing the ban on publicizing the fact that Japanese American soldiers were deployed to work on military intelligence throughout the Asia-Pacific. An article in the November 22, 1945, issue of the now renamed *India-Burma Theater Roundup* announced the official lifting of a veil of secrecy on "the exploits of the American-born Japanese and the important role they performed in the re-conquest of Burma," which had been imposed "to protect the relatives of the Nisei in Japan from retaliation."[47] The article quotes from a statement by Colonel G. F. Blunda, the commanding officer of the SEATIC: "Each Nisei was as valuable as a company of Infantry in Burma, despite the fact they weren't combat troops. Many Allied soldiers are returning safely to their homes because the Nisei lighted the darkness in front of them by interrogating prisoners and translating documents." He continued: "The value of the Nisei was that they supplied the missing link—understanding of the shades of meaning of the Japanese language, written and spoken—between the enemy and the British and U.S. Intelligence officers responsible for evaluation of information gathered from various sources."

Against such instrumentalist commendation, which both obfuscates and justifies the inhumane terms and conditions of the induction and deployment of these Nisei soldiers, I would stress how the Asian American veterans' varied recollections and representations pose an additional complication to the "full disclosure of the truth" about the Japanese military "comfort system." These archival records and personal remembrances attest to how these women became refigured as objects of fascination, contempt, and pity, but also a fleeting mutuality in and through the layering and crossing of Japanese and U.S. patriarchies, racisms, and imperialisms. To take the photographs in chronological order, Karl Yoneda, who appears in Photograph 3 (figure 5.3) interrogating a Korean woman identified as "Kim" on August 3, 1944, briefly mentions the Korean women in his fascinating 1983 memoir, *Ganbatte: Sixty-Year Struggle of a Kibei Worker*. In his account of the long Allied siege of the town of Myitkyina from May to early August 1944, Yoneda recalls that "ex-mine workers among the enemy soldiers had dug elaborate trenches and built a bunker able to withstand direct bomb hits. Some two thousand enemy troops, holding forty so-called Korean 'comfort girls' captive were entrenched there." On July 23, 1944, Yoneda and another member of his OWI-PWB team, Kenji (Kenny) Yasui, were dispatched to Myitkyina for "broadcast duty in no man's land" to persuade the Japanese soldiers inside the siege to surrender. After a "general attack" was ordered on August 3, several surviving Korean women were taken into custody along with other Japanese POWs. The next day, Yoneda conducted "spot interrogations of thirty-one of the POWs on their reactions to our OWI leaflets and frontline broadcasts," but, contrary to the Signal Corps photographs, Yoneda does not indicate that he ever conducted a direct interrogation of "Kim" or of the twenty Korean women. Instead, Yoneda writes, "The Korean women had to be interrogated too. Sergeant Yorichi was called 'Lucky Boy' because he was detailed for that assignment."[48] Given this disclosure, it is puzzling why this particular photograph of Yoneda and "Kim" was taken at all and archived by the U.S. military, reemerging much later in Won-Loy Chan's 1986 memoir as one of the three photographs.

Chan's book does include some more details about the woman identified as "Kim" in a chapter on "The Battle for Myitkyina." As he recalls the date of her *capture*, "I immediately began processing POWs, who were being brought in in increasing numbers. Of the prisoners brought in on 3 August, none attracted more attention and curiosity than did a young Korean female who answered to the name of Kim. Morris Force Kachins had captured her in a bunker along with a Japanese soldier." This is immediately followed by the three-page section titled "The Comfort Girls":

> Kim was a "comfort girl" and looked the part in an above-the-knee length dress that was obviously all she was wearing. We put MP guards around her and Sgt. Karl Yoneda of the OWI asked me if he could ask her a few questions. Since we were overwhelmed with legitimate POWs to question, I said yes. I never did learn what Karl asked her or what she answered. I asked her a few routine questions later, but it was readily apparent that she had no valuable information. The next day we put her on a plane for Ledo to be turned over to the British who were responsible for all POWs and civilians.[49]

There is no POW interrogation report on a woman named "Kim," but the OWI-PWB *Japanese Prisoner of War Report No. 48* is based on the interrogation of a Korean nurse identified by the Japanese name Miyamoto Kikue. Composed by Technical Sergeant Kenjiro Akune of the ten-person OWI-PWB team, the report is dated September 4, 1944, and the "Date of Capture" is listed as "About August 3, 1944." Although the report indicates that the interrogation of "Miyamoto" took place on August 8 at "Combat Headquarters," there is also a baffling notation at the outset under "CIRUMSTANCES OF CAPTURE," which reads "Captured in the company of 'the Korean Comfort Girls' when Myitkyina fell."[50] But the *Japanese Prisoner of War Report No. 49* lists their date of capture as August 10. The capitalization, definite article, and single quotation marks all gesture to both an already established notoriety about this group of twenty Korean women who had been captured separately and transported to Ledo by the time that Akune drafted *Japanese Prisoner of War Report 48*. The quotation also suggests a certain self-consciousness about the problem of translation and proper English terminology to be used. My guess is that "Miyamoto" is likely the same person as "Kim" in the photograph with Karl Yoneda and briefly described in Chan's book.

Chan's account, composed from a physically removed and retrospective position of a U.S. Army veteran writing in the 1980s, does provide several specific and troubling details about what was *not* included in these POW interrogation reports. Noting that twenty-one women were still at Myitkyina on August 3, when the Allied forces took the town, he speculates that "how many had attempted to raft down the Irrawaddy could not be determined. Undoubtedly, many who tried were killed by Allied marksmen from the river banks along with the fleeing Japanese troops. Others probably died from starvation and exposure in the jungles of north Burma." A couple sentences later, Chan adds that "in various stages of dress and undress, they could have caused a small riot among both Chinese and American troops who hadn't seen a female in quite some time. However, a quick-thinking American military police officer immediately segregated them from the male prisoners, found clothing that more adequately covered them and got them into tents inside a guarded barbed-wire enclosure, where they were protected from victor and vanquished alike."[51] Both passages attest to the lethal physical and sexual violence against the women by U.S. and other Allied soldiers during and after the war, but they also betray the uncontroversial terms of their frank disclosure in this English-language publication as late as 1986.

There is some discrepancy between Chan's book and Akune's *Japanese Prisoner of War Report No. 48* about the actual date that the twenty (or possibly twenty-one) Korean women were first apprehended by Allied forces. According to Chan, he first learned of a group of twenty women on the morning of August 8, 1944, when Grant Hirabayashi, who had been temporarily assigned to assist Chan in Myitkyina, came to him: "'Captain,' he said, 'you aren't gonna believe this, but I've got about twenty female, I think Korean, POWs down at the center and I need help.' Along with sergeants Howard Furumoto and Robert Honda, Grant and I went down to the improvised female POW processing point. A GI MP guard opened the gate and let us enter. Inside a large British-style tent with the sides rolled up because of the heat were the female prisoners."[52] However, the *Japanese Prisoner of War Interrogation Report No. 49* lists the women's "date of capture" as August 10, 1944. The account that Chan presents in *Burma: The Untold Story* is most likely an amalgam of his own memories and the recollections of the Nisei soldiers, especially Grant Hirabayashi, who has given very similar, almost identical accounts of the encounter with the Korean women in several published and videotaped interviews. As Chan acknowledges, Hirabayashi acted as the main interrogator of the women, and Chan also thanks him for "providing anecdotal material" for his book.[53] Chan's representation of the twenty women is nevertheless quite detailed:

> They were dressed for the most part in ill-fitting, shapeless, and not very clean dresses or baggy pants and blouses. . . . The girls were young, eighteen to twenty-four was my guess. Some, despite their makeshift clothing and lack of even rudimentary grooming, were still attractive. Their expressions varied. One or two appeared defiant, but most wore looks of fear and anxiety. Some obviously had tears in their eyes or running down their cheeks, while some with their heads bowed low appeared to

be praying. None exhibited the coquetry usually attributed to camp followers. I'd heard stories of female prostitutes serving with the Japanese and had only half believed them. But here they were.

Although his rendering of the women is largely sympathetic up to this point, Chan also shows no qualms about displaying the inane heterosexism of militarized masculinity when he then adds: "Could they have any intelligence information that would be of help to us? After all, it is said that a man is most vulnerable during the act of love." Later, when he points out how one of the women identified a Japanese officer from some photos shown to them, Chan adds this: "(I got the feeling that the young woman who made the identification had known the good Colonel Maruyama very well indeed!)." He then blithely concludes that "aside from that we got nothing of value." I want to draw attention to Chan's assessment of the twenty Korean women's limited Japanese language proficiency. To reinforce his point that he and the Nisei interrogators "got nothing of value," Chan adds, "The girls (Koreans all) spoke some Japanese, but it was of the bedroom and kitchen variety and extremely limited. When you added that to their confusion, fear, and general lack of education, the answers they gave weren't worth much."[54]

Given what Chan recalls about their "extremely limited" Japanese, it is worth asking how Alex Yorichi was later able to glean so much detailed information from the Korean women for his OWI-PWB report. One possibility is that one or both of the Kitamuras may have served as interpreter, as Kitamura Tomiko did in the earlier interrogation of the twenty women by Hirabayashi and Chan in Myitkyina. However, rather than uphold Yorichi's report as more accurately representing the Korean women based on direct interrogation of the women, I propose to categorize the *Japanese Prisoner of War Interrogation Report No. 49* as a generically aberrant "Asian American" composition. I propose to reread it as a tangled, fascinating personal essay of Yorichi's assumptions and impressions as inscribed in compliance with but also at times in refractory excess of the given OWI-PWB template.

In contrast to Yoneda, Chan, and Hirabayashi, there is no extended memoir or videotaped testimony by Alex Yorichi. Indeed, there is very little postwar trace of Yorichi, who passed away in 1987 at the age of sixty-six. His relative anonymity may have something to do with the fact that he continued to work in military intelligence. Yorichi conducted and composed several other POW interrogations, and in a few instances Yorichi and Yoneda jointly signed off on the interrogation report. Some members of the OWI-PWB team, namely Karl Yoneda and Kenny Yasui, were flown to the front lines, where they conducted live broadcasts addressed to Japanese soldiers over speakers, but none of these accounts mention that Alex Yorichi was ever present in Myitkyina.

Returning to the *OWI Report No. 49*, I want to focus on a couple of details that have not received much attention. The most interesting and editorialized writing appears in the section on PERSONALITY. Yorichi writes the following:

> The interrogations show the average Korean "comfort girl" to be about twenty-five years old, uneducated, childish, and selfish. She is not pretty either by Japanese or Caucasian standards. She is inclined to be egotistical and likes to talk about herself. Her attitude in front of strangers is quiet and demure, but she "knows the wiles of a woman." She claims to dislike her "profession" and would rather not talk either about it or her family. Because of the kind treatment she received as a prisoner from American soldiers at Myitkyina and Ledo, she feels that they are more emotional than Japanese soldiers. She is afraid of Chinese and Indian troops.[55]

This construction of a composite *average* Korean "comfort girl" is outrageous, especially if we remember the extraordinary circumstances of the meeting of this Japanese American male interrogator with this group of Korean women as POWs. But this writerly rendering of a generic female subject allows Yorichi to make several absurd claims and clichéd characterizations, which turn attention to the author and the impossible genre in which he must compose. The negative assessment of their appearance by "Japanese or Caucasian standards" is also striking and raises questions about whether such judgments are warranted in a POW report. Given that the Korean women are so written off by the report, it is doubly problematic that its characterization of the women has come to take such a significant place in the contemporary contests over the truth of the Japanese military "comfort system."

The *Japanese Prisoner of War Interrogation Report No. 48* of Miyamoto Kikue, a twenty-eight-year-old Korean nurse assigned to the Second Field Hospital of the Japanese Imperial Army, offers a stark contrast to Yorichi's composite characterization of the twenty women. Although it begins by noting that Miyamoto was "captured in the company of 'the Korean Comfort Girls' when Myitkyina fell," the summary evaluation written by Kenjiro Akune of the OWI-PWB team is quite different from Yorichi's report: "The most valuable information given by the POW was about the discrimination against Koreans by the Japanese. She is happy to be a POW of the Allies, because she knows that they treat her better than the Japanese did. Since she was in the Japanese Hospital, she overheard many interesting things about the military and she has given much information that most soldiers didn't even know."⁵⁶ This interrogation report offers a uniquely detailed glimpse of Miyamoto's singular biography and her clear-eyed and spirited analysis of the recent history of Japanese colonization and imperial expansion, which forcibly brought her to Burma. There are several long passages of Miyamoto's translated statements. For example, under the standard section on "leaflets," the report quotes her as saying that "I didn't care about such things too much, for it didn't matter who took hold of Korea. Till now, Koreans were treated very badly. Even if some other country took over, we can't be treated much worse. There are many anti-Japanese movements in Korea. I was going to hide out with such a group. But my mother, finding out about my plan got scared that I would be killed and locked me up so that I could not go away with the anti-Japanese group. I believe this group is somewhere out in this area." Later, Miyamoto expresses her angry resentment about and even defiance toward her oppressive treatment "as a Korean" by Japanese doctors and nurses at the field hospital: "Once I got so mad, I told them I was going to become a POW. The doctor said go ahead. If the enemy ever catches you, they will rape you and kill you. That was one reason I was afraid when I was caught; but nothing happened; instead I got and am getting good treatment."⁵⁷ I find Miyamoto to be a very differently moving and intriguing figure that merits additional archival research and a more in-depth exploration and accounting than I can give here. But I also want to caution against the desire to uphold her as an exceptional model figure of agency or resistance, which can be readily co-opted as proof of differently preferred overarching narrations and characterizations of the women who were violently but also differentially inducted and exploited by the Japanese imperial war machine. Instead, the *Japanese Prisoner of War Interrogation Report No. 48* offers an interesting counter-text of compositional heterogeneity to Yorichi's report, the document that immediately follows in the serial order of the U.S. military archive.

Turning back to *Japanese Prisoner of War Interrogation Report No. 49*, a very fleeting yet most moving trace of the twenty women's voices—restored to the plural "they" from the generic composite—appears in a final section of the report on REQUESTS: "They asked that leaflets telling of the capture of the 'comfort girls' should not be used for it would endanger the lives of other girls if the Army knew of their capture. They did think it would be a good idea to utilize the fact of their capture in any droppings planned for Korea."⁵⁸ As summarized earlier in the report, the women had described how they had become separated from a larger group of sixty-three people during the final Japanese retreat from Myitkyina. In the SEATIC *Bulletin No. 2*, which is based on the interrogation of Kitamura Eibun, the Japanese male proprietor, he recalls that there were

Truth Disclosure 185

three "comfort houses" at Myitkyina: his own house, comprising twenty-two Korean women; another house of twenty Korean women; and a third house with twenty-one "Chinese girls, who had been purchased from Canton on the same conditions as the Koreans." This larger group of sixty-three women had evacuated from Myitkyina on July 31 but became separated around August 7 during the many days of heavy Allied bombing of the area:

> The 20 Chinese girls remained behind in the jungle, and gave themselves up to Chinese troops. One party of about 20 Korean girls followed on in the wake of the Japanese troops, and were seen by another prisoner of war on 19 August, a small disconsolate group still following on. M.739's party took shelter in an abandoned native house where they remained for two days while prisoner of war tried to construct a raft; with them was a wounded Japanese soldier. On 10 Aug., the house was surrounded by a number of Kachins under the command of an English officer, and they were captured. Of the original party of 63 girls, 4 had died during the journey and 2 had been shot, mistaken for Japanese soldiers.[59]

The captured women's concern for the "other girls" could be in reference to this "small disconsolate group still following on," with whom the twenty Korean women would have been familiar, if not intimate with, as co-captives and possibly friends in the "comfort station" at Myitkyina. We should acknowledge and honor the grace of their caring and concern for the unaccounted women amid the residual shock of their capture and the uncertainties of their transitional incarceration by the U.S. and Allied armies.

The "other girls" could also have been the much larger group of women that disembarked with them earlier in Rangoon in 1942 and who would have been scattered across the various Japanese garrisons in Burma and nearby areas of China. Less than a month later, on September 3, 1944, another group of Korean women "surrendered" to Allied Chinese forces in the Sung Shan (Songshan) hills in Yunnan, China. They too were photographed by the U.S. Signal Corps, and the photograph would also feature prominently in the contemporary, ongoing "comfort women" debates (figure 5.6). The November 30, 1944, issue of the *CBI Roundup*, a newspaper published by the army for the soldiers in the China-Burma-India campaign, featured an article titled "Jap 'Comfort Girls,'" written by Walter Rundle, a United Press correspondent. Ten Japanese and Korean women had been captured by Chinese troops at Sung Shan after being subject to months of intense bombing. With "a Japanese-speaking Chinese student who had escaped from Manchuria" acting as interpreter, Rundle interviewed the four surviving Korean women, who were all from Pyongyang. The

FIGURE 5.6. Reproduction of U.S. Signal Corps Photograph #111-SC-230147 of four Korean women survivors and a Chinese soldier in the aftermath of the Allied bombing of Sung Shan. (Source: U.S. National Archives photo no. 111-SC-230147.)

women spoke of how they were recruited under false pretenses and through economic necessity: "With propaganda posters and speeches the Japs began a recruitment campaign for 'WAC' organizations which they said were to be sent to Singapore to do noncombatant work in rear areas—running rest camps for Japanese troops, entertaining and helping in hospitals. All four said they needed money desperately." Their living and working conditions differ markedly from what was set forth in *POW Interrogation Report No. 49:* "Among other duties, they had to wash Japanese soldiers' clothing, cook their food and clean out the caves in which they lived. They said they were paid nothing and received no mail from home. When Chinese troops attacked Sungshan, the girls lived below ground in caves. Fourteen of the original 24 were killed by shellfire. They said they had all been told they would be tortured if captured by the Chinese and all admitted they had believed such stories."[60] C. Sarah Soh reads the difference between the women's states in the two photos from Myitkyina and Sung Shan as visible proof of the heterogeneity of material conditions in the Japanese "comfort stations," which, in turn, affirms her own aim to contest the "paradigmatic narrative" of victimhood and abjection.[61] However, both photos from Myitkyina were taken four days *after* the women were initially "captured" on August 10. As for the Sung Shan photo (figure 5.6), an earlier article in the *CBI Roundup* provides a clearer picture of the massive Allied bombing that the women in this photo had been subject to: "Sungshan, Gibraltar of the Burma Road, just west of the Salween River, fell after three months of continuous assault during which the 2,000 defenders were virtually exterminated. Only a handful of prisoners were taken, including five women. In one instance, the Chinese literally blasted the Japs off the top of their mountain fortress by planting dynamite under their positions."[62] The discordant smile of the Chinese soldier indicts the blithe disregard of the women's humanity on all sides of the warfront. Finally, another inhuman detail of Signal Corps photo #230417 appears in the bureaucratic notations following the caption, "Prisoners of war: Japanese women"—"photo released by Bureau of Public Relations, U.S. War Department." How and why was this photo made to be circulated? At the end of his account of his interrogation of the Korean women in Myitkyina, Won-Loy Chan briefly notes that "the Allied press made a big thing of the comfort girls in sensational releases."[63] Whose interests and what aims were served by such Allied public relations?

The U.S. National Archives continues to reveal new, more astonishing materials for the persistent researchers of the "truth" of the history of the Japanese military "comfort system," which includes the harrowing survival of some women and the violent deaths of others on the multiple battlefronts of the Asia-Pacific War. In July 2017 a research team supported by the Seoul Metropolitan Government and the Seoul National University Human Rights Center discovered the "first filmed evidence of 'comfort women' found in U.S. archives."[64] Most recently, in February 2018, the same research team announced the discovery of a nineteen-second film clip of a mass grave of thirty Korean women in Tengchong, China, near the border with Myanmar. The footage had been filed on September 13, 1944, by a cinematographer with the U.S. Army 164th Signal Corps.[65] How could we, how must we, reckon with this unfolding archive of these inhuman *American* compositions of the capture of and traffic in Asian women?

JUST COMPENSATION

On August 31, 1994, recently elected Japanese Prime Minister Murayama Tomiichi announced a two-part "Peace, Friendship, and Exchange Initiative" to commemorate the upcoming fiftieth anniversary of the end of World War II on August 15, 1995. Acknowledging at the outset that "Japan's actions in a certain period of the past not only claimed numerous victims here in Japan but also left the peoples of neighboring Asia and elsewhere with scars that are painful even today," Murayama added that "it is imperative for us Japanese to look squarely to our history with the peoples of neighboring Asia and elsewhere. Only with solid basis of mutual understanding and confidence that can be built through overcoming the pain on both sides, can we and the peoples of neighboring countries together clear up the future of Asia-Pacific." To that end, he pledged 100 billion yen over ten years to "support historical research" and fund "exchange programs to promote dialogue and mutual understanding." Murayama then turned to address "the issue of wartime 'comfort women,' which seriously stained the honor and dignity of many women." In addition to expressing his "profound and sincere remorse and apologies," he proposed "to find out, together with Japanese people, an appropriate way which enables a wide participation of people so that we can share such feelings." This vague pronouncement led into the next numbered point, which framed these "feelings" in anticipation of another historic event in 1995: "Knowing that the Fourth World Conference on Women is scheduled to be held in Beijing next year to formulate new guidelines for the advancement of women toward the 21st century, the government intends to place even greater emphasis on economic cooperation in such fields as the advancement of women and the enhancement of women's welfare, including, for example, vocational training centers for women, particularly in relation to the neighboring Asian countries and areas."[1]

Following Murayama's August announcement, the Subcommittee to Address the Wartime Comfort Women Issue was appointed and later submitted "The First Report on the So-Called Wartime Comfort Women Issue" (hereafter the "First Report" on December 7, 1994. Opening with the acknowledgment that "the Government of Japan now recognizes that there existed in the past a great number of comfort women," the report goes on to admit that "comfort stations were established at the demands of the Japanese military authorities at that time, with the then-military being directly or indirectly involved in the establishing and managing of those stations and the transfer of comfort women." While straining to demarcate these as events that happened *in the past*, the report goes on to acknowledge that "the women were recruited against their will, through coaxing, coercion and the like" and further notes that "it is clear that government officials and others in authority also directly took part in their recruitments." In explaining why the government was soliciting voluntary private donations from "a broad spectrum of the Japanese population" for a special fund to redress the actions of "military authorities" and "government officials," the report was clear to remind readers that "with regard to the question of restitution or the right to demand material compensation as a result of issues arising from the past war, including the so-called wartime comfort women issue, the Japanese Government has always acted in good faith and in view of international law and the practice of diplomacy in accordance with the stipulations of the San Francisco Peace Treaty, bilateral peace treaties and other relevant accords." The report proceeds to explain, "Showing the atonement of the Japanese people, through expressions of apology and remorse to the so-called wartime comfort women, it is important not only to restore their honor, which was affronted, but also to indicate in Japan and abroad our country's strong respect for women."[2]

The question of restitution for the "comfort system" and specifically regarding material compensation for its victim-survivors was thus enfolded into the general protection and promotion of "women's welfare" at this pivotal moment between the celebrated success of the Global Campaign for Women's Human Rights at the 1993 Vienna Conference and the upcoming 4th World Conference on Women in Beijing. If the growing force of the "women's rights as human rights" movement fortified activists' demands for admission, apology, and compensation, it also provided a generic globalist banner for both the past atrocity and its contemporary redress. Immediately following the confirmation of "our country's strong respect for women," the "First Report" interposes this reminder: "It must be noted that problems of offending the honor and dignity of women still exist in many parts of the world. It is important that we Japanese remain concerned about these problems and promote efforts to eliminate them worldwide." The invocation of "the world" reshuffles and transposes the Japanese "comfort system" problematic onto a more impersonal and distant global horizon of injured womanhood, even as "we Japanese" enacts a willful erasure of the long history of bilateral and inter-Asian feminist efforts, including those organized by many Japanese activists, writers, scholars, and lawyers, to publicize the issue and demand justice for the survivors. Then too, the enlisting of the *voluntary* participation of "the Japanese people" in paying into what subsequently came to be referred to in English as the Asian Women's Fund (AWF) was consistent with and even bolstered the Japanese government's repeated refusal to make direct state compensation to the survivors. The AWF eventually offered an atonement package that would include a lump-sum payment, an official letter of apology, and provisions for medical care for the surviving women. The Japanese government would cover the administrative costs of the AWF and release relevant government records and documents. On August 15, 1995, six Japanese national newspapers carried a full-page advertisement announcing the formation of the Asian Women's Fund and soliciting contributions to this peculiar public/private entity.

Rather than mollify the survivors and activists, the Asian Women's Fund inaugurated a contentious debate about the proper terms and conditions of reparation, which persists to this day. The various projects of the AWF would themselves become the target of protests and international criticism. Some dismissed the monetary payments to individual survivors from private donations as "hush money," intended mostly to quell protests and tamp down negative international publicity.³ There was also considerable opposition to the AWF within Japan by those who saw it as weak-willed capitulation to outside pressures. Some pointed out that other nations, including the United States and South Korea, were also guilty of sexual crimes against women during wartime and military occupation.

The differential responses to the AWF's offer of monetary compensation brought into critical relief significant economic disparities among the most affected Asian nations, which further problematizes the generic categories of "Asian women" and even "Asian 'comfort women.'" The advent of South Korea and Taiwan as regional and international economic powers by the early 1990s was evident in how South Korean and Taiwanese survivors were offered alternative payments and material support via domestic fund-raising and state welfare provisions. In 1993 the South Korean Ministry of Health and Welfare initiated a process of verifying claims by survivors and officially recognizing them as "victims of Japanese military sexual slavery," which entitled them to a one-time payment of 5 million won (around $5,000) as well as "a monthly subsidy and free medical care, and . . . the right to rent public housing."⁴ In 1996, the Taiwanese government established a fund for Taiwanese victims and survivors. Survivors in the Philippines were not offered a comparable alternative, and several women, including most notably Maria Rosa Luna Henson, decided to accept the AWF monetary payment. Thailand responded that "individual compensation to former comfort women would (a) expose and embarrass them, (b) produce an endless string of bereaved families seeking compensation, and (c) it was therefore preferable to pay the state."⁵ On January 15th, 1997, the AWF and the Department of Social Welfare and Development (DSWD) of the Republic of the Philippines signed a memorandum of understanding (MOU) whereby "the AWF and the DSWD will provide good and services in the medical and welfare fields to those who underwent immeasurable and painful experiences and suffered incurable physical and psychological wounds as 'comfort women,' with a view to supporting their livelihood and well-being." The MOU then clarified the different roles of the two agencies in what was oddly named as the "Lolas in Crisis Situation Project." The AWF will "provide the necessary financial resources" while the DSWD would be charged with "the implementation of the Project."⁶ Indonesia provided yet another different response because of its own distinctive history of Japanese bilateral aid and economic investment. According to a memorandum of understanding signed with the Department of Social Affairs (DSA) of the Indonesian government on March 24, 1997, the AWF pledged to provide 380 million yen to be utilized and distributed by the DSA for the "promotion of social welfare services for elderly people in Indonesia."

Although the targeted constituency was broadened to "elderly people," there was this specific provision under Article 2: "The DSA shall assure that the Project be implemented in the regions where former 'wartime comfort woman' seem to exist. The Project shall be implemented in such a manner that priority be given to women."[7]

The most impassioned resistance to the AWF unfurled in South Korea, from where the largest number of women had been forcibly conscripted. There have been published accounts of survivors being cajoled and sometimes threatened into refusing the AWF payments by other survivors, activists, and supporters; the few individual women who decided to accept the funds were harshly criticized and sometimes ostracized. According to Chungmoo Choi, "In January 1997, one week prior to the visit of the Japanese minister of Foreign Affairs [to South Korea], the [Asian Women's] Foundation delivered promissory notes to a few Korean comfort women who agreed to receive the private fund. A few activist groups in South Korea protested that this was the Foundation's attempt to divide the victims and the activists, and tried to penalize these women by petitioning the South Korean government to stop its monthly living cost assistance payments, which the women had received since 1993."[8] On April 21, 1998, the Cabinet of the recently elected President Kim Dae-jung announced that the South Korean government would stop seeking direct compensation from the Japanese government. As the *New York Times* reported, "Instead, South Korea will pay each of the 152 registered 'comfort women' $22,700, which will be supplemented by $4,700 each from victims' rights organizations."[9]

Despite its generic, pseudo-philanthropic naming, the Asian Women's Fund prods us to think about the calculations and the monetization of justice *for* women alongside and against the calculations of violence *against* women, discussed in chapter 4. In framing the AWF as "an already compromised solution to the shortcomings of the earlier Cold War redress," Lisa Yoneyama suggests that "insofar as the Asian Women's Fund was a redress effort attempted within the bounds of Cold War formations, the rejection of its rationale can be read as signaling the impossibility of justice without a thoroughgoing makeover of state-to-state reparations agreements, international protocols, military alliances, and other arrangements that have shaped post–World War II Asia and the Pacific."[10] This chapter will attempt to map some of these "other arrangements." Both the AWF's hybrid monetization of atonement and the differently fraught responses unfolded within several strata of binational, regional, and international diplomacy and economic relations and must be critically registered within those broadly determining but also provisionally negotiated and renegotiated frames. This will entail that we also bring into view the determining role of the U.S., the World Bank, and the International Monetary Fund in shaping the uneven political economy of the Asia-Pacific after World War II.

This chapter frames the making of Japan's regional economic hegemony and the uneven development trajectories of the other Asian nations in terms of shifting modalities of U.S. empire in Asia in the second half of the twentieth century. I have already described the significant role played by the U.S. military as part of the Allied forces fighting in the Asia-Pacific in chapter 5. After the end of World War II, the U.S. played an active role in shaping Japan's postwar economic recovery, including limiting the amount of Japan's war reparations to the other Asian nations that it invaded and occupied. Then U.S. military expenditures in the Korean War (1950–53) helped boost several key Japanese industries that were just beginning to rebuild. South Korea, in turn, recovered from the devastations of Japanese colonization and a civil war, and its economy grew significantly through the provision of U.S. foreign aid and military expenditures related to the Vietnam War. These multiply enfolded and cross-cutting relations of protection, reparation, aid, and strategic cooperation were crucial to what came to be widely hailed and later disparaged as the "Asian miracle." By the early 1990s, Japan had taken a leading economic position in the Asia-Pacific and was also playing a more prominent role in global governance, including the United Nations and the World Bank. Prime Minister Murayama's framing of the Asian Women's Fund in terms of "economic cooperation in such fields as the advancement of women and the enhancement of women's welfare" and the specific example of job training for women in "neighboring Asian countries and areas" tacitly affirmed Japan's regional economic leadership and enhanced standing in global governance, which were both being called into question by newly activated reminders of its colonial atrocities and wartime crimes.

This chapter opens by unpacking how the U.S. strategically facilitated Japan's postwar recovery and regional economic ascendance through different bilateral negotiations of reparations, aid, and trade with South Korea, Taiwan, the Philippines, and Indonesia. In addition to covering over national differences, the broad and positive figuration of an "Asian miracle" justified and obfuscated the brutal disciplining and exploitation of female labor, including sexual labor for the U.S. military and international sex tourism, which were crucial to the linked yet uneven economic growth of these countries in the 1970s and 1980s. As I suggested earlier in chapter 4, an unintended consequence of the spectacular focus on the physically and sexually violated Asian female body, which was made so prominent and stirring with the global campaign to focus on violence against women in the 1990s, was to shift critical attention away from these myriad forms of economic dispossession and labor exploita-

194   Chapter 6

tion. Instead, the increased presence and active participation of some Asian women in the broader "women's rights as human rights" campaign through numerous NGOs and various agencies, commissions and working groups of the United Nations could be framed as evidence of the socioeconomic advancement of "Asian women" as part and parcel of the "Asian miracle."

The second section tells a less sanguine, more contentious account of globalization and global governance by tracing how "Asian miracle" and its variant of "East Asian miracle" became highly charged designations in a debate about two contrasting models of government and economy, an "Asian model" distinguished by strategic state planning and intervention and the "Washington Consensus" paradigm of a greatly reduced state that mainly facilitates the international flow of goods and capital. Neoliberalization, the global drive toward privatization, deregulation, and financial liberalization, which began in the 1970s, greatly accelerated with the internationalization of capital markets in the 1990s and unleashed a series of linked financial crises. A currency crisis in Thailand in July 1997 soon expanded regionally to what has been referred to alternately as the "Asian economic crisis" or "Asian financial crisis" of 1997–98. In the early 1990s the U.S. actively promoted the financial liberalization of Asian markets and then played a leading role in the figuration and the management of the "Asian crisis" in ways that clearly protected the interests of Wall Street and other private U.S. investors. This political-economic repositioning of the U.S. was closely interrelated with a complementary shift in the mission and actions of the Bretton Woods institutions, especially the World Bank and the IMF.

The third and final section points to how remembering the multiply uneven effects of development, globalization, and financialization on different women across Asia can serve as a feminist method for contesting the Asianization of both economic miracle and economic crisis. But I also caution against the pitfalls of producing yet another fixation of a distinctly Asian female misery. Instead, I call for careful accounting for multiple formations and unaccustomed permutatons of Asian women in a coeval time-space of intra-Asian and transpacific economic interpenetration and concerted collaboration, which also problematize East/West and Asian/American boundaries.

FROM "JAPANESE MIRACLE" TO "ASIAN MIRACLE"

The word *miracle* was first deployed to distinguish Japan's impressive recovery and unprecedented economic growth after the devastations of World War II.[11] As a strategic Pacific base for the U.S. military, Japan and its economic recovery were crucial to U.S. geopolitical interests in the Asia-Pacific region, and the U.S. played a key role in securing certain specific terms and conditions of that recovery. As Chalmers Johnson sums up, "From approximately 1950 to 1975, the United States treated Japan as a beloved ward, indulging its every economic need and proudly patronizing it as a star capitalist pupil."[12] This patronage entailed large ethnocentric blind spots about the organization of the Japanese government and civil society but also regarding Japan's imperialist enterprises and atrocities. In his elucidating 1995 book, *Buying Power: The Political Economy of Japan's Foreign Aid*, David Arase diagnoses how a crucial U.S. *mis*-reading of Japan's political-economic structure enabled Japanese civilian bureaucracies to maintain continuity in their power to set and steer economic policy. The U.S. Occupation authorities "incorrectly assumed that like U.S. bureaucracies, Japanese economic bureaucracies were politically neutral instruments, and so the Occupation purge and reform efforts never targeted them." Arase points to Okita Saburo as one illustrative figure of this continuity, who also hearkens back to Japan's prewar imperialist expansion across Asia. Born in Dairen, Manchuria, in 1915 and having worked in the Greater East Asia Ministry, "where he turned his skills to economic planning for colonial development and the war effort," Okita would later go on to join the Ministry of Foreign Affairs and become "a key architect of Japan's postwar economic miracle."[13]

But the more notable figure of continuity is Kishi Nobusuke, the maternal grandfather of Abe Shinzo. Kishi oversaw the economic development of the Japanese puppet state of Manchuko after the territory in Manchuria was seized in 1932 and served as Japan's Minister of Commerce and later in the Munitions Ministry during the Asia-Pacific War. As historian Michael Schaller pointed out in a short yet searing 1995 article, Kishi "had overseen the forcible conscription of hundreds of thousands of Korean and Chinese laborers and been responsible for military production."[14] Although he was imprisoned for three years (1945–1948) as a "Class A" war criminal, Kishi was never tried and was ultimately released in December 1948. He would go on to become the thirty-seventh Prime Minister of Japan (1957–60). As clearly indicated in the article's title, "America's Favorite War Criminal," Schaller writes: "A small but influential group of private Americans . . . identified Kishi as among those best suited to lead the new Japan. In 1947, *Newsweek* foreign affairs editor Harry Kern, *Newsweek* Tokyo bureau chief Compton Packenham, corporate lawyer James L. Kauffman, the retired Joseph C. Grew, and Eugene Dooman, a retired diplomat who served under Grew in Tokyo, took the lead in creating the 'American Council on Japan' (ACJ) with the aim of changing occupation policy." Grew had served as U.S. Ambassador to Japan from 1932–41, and then as Under

Secretary at the State Department. He played a significant role in advocating for Japan to retain the emperor system after its defeat and surrender. Kishi was elected to the Japanese Diet in 1953 as the end of the Korean War inaugurated the long Cold War and the U.S. zeal to contain communism in Asia. According to Richard J. Samuels's account of Kishi's rise to political power, Kishi was present at a meeting in August 1954, when then U.S. Secretary of State John Foster Dulles (1953–59) "told Japanese Foreign Minister Shigemitsu Mamoru that the U.S. had a strong interest in the consolidation of the conservative camp; he [Dulles] may even have made further U.S. support conditional on its coming to pass."[15] When Kishi became prime minister in 1957, he "reasserted his loyalty to America's Cold War strategy, pledging to limit contact with China and, instead, to focus Japanese economic attention on exports to the United States and mutual development of Southeast Asia." With the approval of President Eisenhower and Secretary of State Dulles, the CIA covertly channeled funds to secure Kishi's power within the Liberal Democratic Party (LDP); Schaller estimates that "sums as high as $10 million may have been spent annually between 1958 and 1960."[16] Long after the end of formal occupation in 1952, the U.S. government continued to shape Japan's political power structure.

Another important U.S. intervention was to set a limit on war reparations that Japan would be compelled to pay to its former colonies and other Asian nations that it had invaded and brutalized. Even though the 1951 San Francisco Peace Treaty called on Japan to pay war reparations, it "did not specify the amount or type of reparations, allowing Tokyo to negotiate a separate agreement with each country."[17] Arase outlines the distinctive features of the first reparations agreement that Japan signed with Burma in November 1954: "This reparations agreement had two precedent-setting differences from the provisions of the San Francisco Peace Treaty. First, it allowed Japan to provide goods in fulfilling its reparations obligations. This would allow Japan to turn the reparations obligation into a subsidy for Japanese capital goods exports. Second, it shifted the rationale for the transfer of goods from Japan's war guilt to concern for Burma's 'economic recovery and development' and for the 'improvement of social welfare.' This developmental rationale for reparations allowed Japanese reparations (*baisho*) and reparations-like payments (*jun-baisho*) to be incorporated in Western statistics on ODA."[18] Here we see an early co-constitution of reparations and development aid but also the malleability of these numbers for different and just-emerging statistical registers in global governance. In addition to enabling such arrangements to minimize the financial burden on the Japanese state in the immediate postwar period, U.S. military spending during the Korean War ended up benefiting private Japanese firms in a variety of sectors. The U.S. played this vital role in structuring and later securing Japan's regional economic hegemony in order to prevent its political rapprochement and to delimit its trade relations with Communist China. It may seem unfathomable now, but Secretary of State Dulles "believed that American consumers would shun Japanese products as merely 'cheap imitations of our own.' The only 'solution for Japan,' Dulles argued, was to sell goods to and obtain raw materials from 'presently underdeveloped areas such as Southeast Asia.'"[19] Or, as William R. Nester describes this intra-Asian, transpacific arrangement, "American policy in East Asia was to build up an integrated, stable political economic system with Japan acting as the region's 'economic workshop.'... Washington promoted a triangular economic division of trade between the United States, Japan and Southeast Asia in which America would provide high technology and capital goods, Japan intermediate and consumer goods and Southeast Asia raw materials and energy." As Nester sums up even more strongly, "Washington used every possible means to promote Japan's economic penetration of Southeast Asia, including tying American aid to the region to the purchase of Japanese goods and services. Officials in every American embassy in the region had the sole responsibility for promoting Japanese trade."[20] The U.S. also aided the entry of Japan into the United Nations and the Organization for Economic Cooperation and Development (OECD) in 1964.

The intermeshed triangulation of South Korea's economic development with its diplomatic normalization with Japan and military cooperation with the U.S. in the 1960s offers another illuminating scene of U.S.-Asia and intra-Asian entanglements. As Jung-en Woo points out in her brilliant 1991 monograph, *Race to the Swift: State and Finance in Korean Industrialization*, "Seoul in 1960 was the site of the largest U.S. aid operation, providing a quarter of the Korean GNP in military and economic assistance combined."[21] Under the newly elected Kennedy administration, the National Security Council introduced "a new Korean policy (NSC 6018)," which reduced U.S. aid amounts and called for South Korea to undergo economic restructuring centered on export-oriented industrialization supported by both foreign direct investment and other sources of bilateral aid. A steep reduction in U.S. aid to South Korea from $383 million in 1957 to $192.8 million in 1961 compelled the recently coup-installed regime of General Park Chung-hee toward several linked economic, diplomatic, and military actions, including the signing of the 1965 normalization treaty with Japan. We should bear in mind that it is this 1965 treaty that has been insistently invoked by the Japanese government in its refusal of formal compensation to the former Korean "comfort women" and other Korean victims of its colonial-era atrocities.

The signing of the Korea-Japan normalization treaty in 1965 coincided with the escalation of U.S. military involvement in Vietnam. Several fledgling South Korean conglomerates benefited from lucrative contracts for large-scale construction projects and military logistics financed by the U.S., so "the Vietnam War was not only a cornucopia of huge invisible earnings and immense U.S. assistance, but an incubator of new industries before testing the fires of international competition."[22] Although this was somewhat reminiscent of the earlier Japanese economic gains during the Korean War, the direct and extensive military participation of South Korean soldiers in the U.S. war in Vietnam distinguishes this particular vector of U.S.-Asia and intra-Asian violence. According to Iain Pirie, "Park, eager to prove Korea's worth as an ally, was quick to offer troops to assist in the anti-communist crusade, in return of course for considerable financial support from the U.S."[23] South Korea sent more than three hundred thousand soldiers to Vietnam, which was "more men per capita than any nation in the world, including the United States." Calculating that the U.S. paid South Korea more than $1 billion from 1965 to 1970, Woo convincingly argues that "the Brown Memorandum, dated March 4, 1966, is the governing document—and an astonishing one—laying out the arrangements for American utilization of Korean forces, which the Pentagon was to coordinate with AID [Agency for International Development]. Although the two had always worked closely together, the link between economic development and war-induced profits was never so lucid as in this memorandum."[24] Thus, U.S. military interventions in Asia and against Asians were crucial motors of both Japanese and Korean economic "miracles."

In the 1970s, virulently anti-communist South Korea and Taiwan began to partially displace Japan as the "star capitalist pupil" of the United States. These "first-generation NICs" ("newly industrialized countries") were also held up by the World Bank and the IMF as models of export-oriented development for other countries in Asia, Latin America, and Africa. With its earlier economic ascendance and expanding reserves, Japan, in turn, became an important source of both bilateral aid and foreign direct investment (FDI) throughout Asia. The already blurred lines between *reparations* and *aid* became more fungible and flexible. Recall that an important precursor to Japanese foreign aid was the series of war reparations that it negotiated in the 1950s and 1960s. Arase points to key differences between U.S. and Japanese foreign aid: "Unlike the United States, which from the beginning took up foreign aid as a weapon against the spread of communist influence in the decolonizing world, Japan undertook what would only in retrospect be called foreign aid because of its obligation to make war reparations to neighboring developing countries

Just Compensation 199

victimized in World War II. Confronted by its own need for recovery and development, Japan invented a distinctive pattern of economic cooperation with the developing world that at its core is intended to contribute to Japan's own developmental plans." While fulfilling certain important "diplomatic needs" and accruing "political capital" in the international community through doling out aid, as Arase makes very clear, this system of *keizai kyōryoku* ("economic cooperation") worked to "advance Japanese economic interests."[25]

Even in cases where the matter of war reparations was not a factor, early Japanese foreign aid was concentrated in Asia because of geographical proximity but also the fact that many of these countries possessed natural resources necessary for Japan's continued economic development. For example, the first yen loan to India in 1958 was to develop iron ore mining in Goa. In the mid-1960s, Japan began to provide large aid packages to Indonesia, which "enjoys high-priority status in Japan's ODA disbursement due to its commercial shipping lanes, which are indispensable to Japan."[26] Loans were usually made with certain conditions: they had to be used to purchase Japanese goods and machinery necessary for specifically approved projects. Japan would also provide technical training and assistance, which further worked to ensure that Japanese firms and consultants would be hired and retained for these projects. These countries could also become future markets for Japanese exports.

As economic self-interest began to overshadow postwar reconciliation, there was increasing criticism of Japanese aid as overly harsh and self-serving. Arase and several others cite John White's 1964 analysis, *Japanese Aid*, as a significant early instance of this international scrutiny. In a deeply suspicious and at times baldly racist assessment, White outlined Japan's dual political-economic objectives of achieving parity with the U.S. and European nations while extending and augmenting its dominant position in Asia. White notably drew these historical, affective, and material distinctions to explain the differences between Japanese aid to Indonesia and Japanese aid to South Korea: "Indonesia has been spotted as the essential element in a purely Asian alignment (i.e. non-western rather than anti-western) in which Japan would have more scope than she has now.... South Korea, formerly the most closely bound of Japan's dependencies, still harbours too much resentment against Japan to fit easily into the picture of some kind of Japanese sphere of influence: while South Korea's lack of raw materials makes it a less interesting prospect than Indonesia for Japanese investors."[27] What South Korea did possess was geographical proximity and a harshly disciplined, low-paid labor force for Japanese offshore manufacturing and for sex tourism. The inter-Asian feminist protests of the 1970s critically resisted this neocolonial "invasion of Japanese capital."

There were several important recalibrations of Japanese ODA in the 1970s. The 1973 oil crisis exposed Japan's dependence on importing natural resources and engendered "worries about resource nationalism in the developing world."[28] Beginning with an agreement signed with Indonesia in 1975 with plans to construct a dam, a power station, and an aluminum processing plant on the Asahan River in Sumatra, Japan embarked upon a carefully coordinated program of "resource diplomacy," which was characterized by "a strengthened connection between Japan's economic aid to industrialization in resource-exporting developing countries and the assured supplies of resources secured in exchange for such aid; and the simultaneous uses of such assistance as an internal aid to the overseas activities of Japanese industry in large-scale resource development ventures."[29] Japanese firms sent technology, equipment, and expert personnel to Indonesia, and Indonesia provided a disciplined, low-wage labor force, which, in turn, gave an important boost to those sometimes-flagging Japanese industries. The Asahan aluminum plant in Indonesia was "the clearest single example of the flexible use of ODA to aid a domestic industry facing extinction after the oil shock."[30] The Nixon administration's normalization of relations with China also pushed Japan to begin dispensing more aid to China.[31] In 1978 Japan signed "a ten-year long-term trade agreement featuring Chinese oil and coal in exchange for Japanese plants and equipment."[32] Though extracting natural resources from these distant places, Japanese firms did not have to contend with the local devastation and pollution created by their projects.

The increase in Japanese ODA was partially a response to pressures from the U.S. for Japan to play a greater part in national defense and regional security. As Dennis Yasumoto sums up this division of military and economic expenditures, "The Japanese held to their pledge to remain a nonmilitary power and proposed a Japanese definition of defense-burden sharing: Tokyo would support the military role of the U.S. through nonmilitary contributions, whether increased financial support for American troops on Japanese soil or increased aid to strategic nations and regions."[33] But in the context of Japan's growing trade surpluses in the 1980s and an increasingly rancorous "trade war" with the U.S., there was growing and widespread criticism of Japan's self-serving aid practices. Rather than ease the harsh conditions of its aid for the borrowing countries in Asia, this conflict was resolved with a bilateral agreement to placate the U.S.: "In 1978 the government in a joint communiqué with the U.S. announced its intention to untie Japanese aid loans. U.S. firms would now be able to compete for Japanese-aid funded contracts in developing countries, a move (according to some Japanese officials) specifically intended to benefit U.S. firms and the U.S. economy."[34] Thus, rather than relieving pressures on the borrowing nations, this move only expanded the possible beneficiaries of these loans to include a few American companies. Even after making these special concessions, Japan emerged in 1985 as the world's largest creditor, and it overtook the U.S. as the largest donor of foreign aid in 1988.

In addition to the disbursement of aid and direct investment, Japan carved out its regional economic leadership through several multilateral and intergovernmental entities. In 1965 Japan had been the second largest (after India) *borrower* from the World Bank; by 1990, when it repaid its final loan payment to the World Bank, Japan had already overtaken the U.S. as the largest *donor* of ODA.[35] Well before then, in 1966, with the strong support of the U.S., Japan had spearheaded the establishment of the Asian Development Bank (ADB) as part of "a very determined effort by the Japanese government to restore national prestige and re-emerge as a regional leader" after its defeat in World War II.[36] Although Japan was not successful in its effort to have the ADB headquarters located in Tokyo rather than in Manila, the ADB presidency has always been held by a Japanese representative, and other means of Japanese control were achieved through "ruthless use of bilateral programs to influence other Asian countries during the final negotiation in Manila." Pointing to how "61 percent of all ADB loans went to the six strongest developing members: Korea, Taiwan, Singapore, Hong Kong, Thailand, and Malaysia, with Korea claiming the largest share," Woo adds that "not so insignificantly, the East Asian countries receiving the most ADB loans also happened to be destination countries for Japanese private investment."[37]

These intra-Asian financial arrangements set the stage for the establishment of the sex tourism industries in South Korea, Thailand, and the Philippines. Here I would recall the Ewha students' letter and the Korean women's airport and hotel protests in the early 1970s, and situate them within a broader regional political economy that was crucially shaped by both U.S. foreign policy and U.S.-dominated international financial institutions, especially the World Bank, but also related offshoots such as the Asian Development Bank. This dependence upon Japanese aid, loans, and private investment also partly explains why these formerly colonized or occupied countries did not press claims for compensation for past Japanese atrocities until the 1990s. Thus, I would argue that, rather than a forgetting, the Japanese military "comfort system" was made illegible as an extraordinary atrocity and even rendered unremarkable in and through these binational, regional, and global transactions of reparation, aid, and capital investment. The naming of a generic, overarching "Asian miracle" obfuscated significant intra-Asian differences and inequalities.

As Japan consolidated its regional power and influence, it also took on a more prominent and assertive role in global economic governance. There

202 Chapter 6

was an escalating struggle within the World Bank, specifically between Japan and the United States, about the proper role of state guidance and interventions in economic development. Given its growing financial contributions to the World Bank and the enhanced international standing and regional leadership they secured, Japan began to articulate criticisms of the reigning neoliberal orthodoxy of the Washington Consensus along with a more assured advocacy of its own distinctive, state-guided path to economic growth and stability. Since the early 1980s, the World Bank had been intensifying structural adjustment programs (SAP) comprising deregulation, cuts in public spending, privatization of state resources, and openness to foreign investments as conditions of lending. By the end of the decade, the World Bank turned its attention to the financial sector and convened a Task Force on Financial Sector Operations, which endorsed extensive financial liberalization. The World Bank's annual *World Development Report* for 1989 was subtitled *Financial Systems and Development*, and featured chapter titles that moved from asking "Why does finance matter?" to pointing "Toward more and open financial systems." The report opens by establishing at the outset that "although countries differ in the scale of government intervention and in the extent to which they have already stabilized and restructured their economies, most have decided to rely more upon the private sector and market signals to direct allocation of resources" and goes on to note, two paragraphs later, "In the past, governments' efforts to promote economic development by controlling interest rates, directing credit to priority sectors, and securing inexpensive funding for their own activities have undermined financial development."[38] *World Development Report 1989* concludes, "This Report has tried to specify the prerequisites for building an efficient financial system capable of mobilizing and allocating resources on a *voluntary* basis. Such a system would continue to make mistakes and waste resources. But it would probably make fewer mistakes and waste fewer resources than the interventionist approach followed in many developing countries today."[39] This clear endorsement of non-intervention was a barely veiled criticism of state coordination by Japan but also other countries whose economic growth in the 1980s comprised the "Asian Miracle." In 1991, in response to pressure from the Japanese Ministry of Finance (MOF), the World Bank commissioned a multi-country study of the role of state guidance in Indonesia, Thailand, and Malaysia, along with Japan, South Korea, Singapore, Taiwan, and Hong Kong. In return, Japan agreed that it would not oppose what eventually became Operational Directive 8.30, Financial Sector Operations (February 1992), which championed financial deregulation.[40]

The final World Bank report published in 1993 and titled *The East Asian Miracle: Economic Growth and Public Policy* was a muddled product of U.S.-Japan contestation and compromise. In his fascinating, detailed account of the political economy underwriting this textual production, including its highly strategic and negotiated conceptualization, writing, revision, and editing by an international but largely U.S.-dominated team, Robert Wade describes the "Japanese challenge" to the reigning Washington Consensus as motivated by several ideological and material reasons. First was the domestic criticism of Japanese foreign aid as "not paying enough attention to Japan's national interest." Second, Wade cites the specific "organizational interest" of Japan's Ministry of Finance in the face of explicit criticism of its directed credit to specific sectors and industries deemed important for national economic growth. Characterizing this practice as "what MOF considered its greatest post-war achievement," Wade explains: "Directed credit was its principal industrial policy instrument in the post-war renaissance of Japan; effective use of directed credit is the foundation of its claim to have played a major role in the 'miracle.'" Wade identifies the third reason for Japan's challenging the neoliberal paradigm as "national material interest" and regional dominance: "Interventionist policies can potentially help Japanese firms and the Japanese government consolidate profits and influence in the region." Wade's fourth and final explanations are the most interesting. He begins by identifying Japanese "nationalism" as "the desire to overcome a sense of being judged inferior by representatives of other states—or in this case, multilateral financial institutions." But he goes on to a more specific, detailed feature of this dynamic as a bilateral struggle between Japan and the U.S. or, perhaps more accurately, Japanese versus U.S. hegemony in and through the World Bank: "Japan cannot constantly bow to foreign—that is, U.S.—pressure. It needs to be seen asserting its own views on appropriate rules for the international economy. These cannot be free-trade rules, for the free-trade ideology is already led by the U.S. It can differentiate its principles from those of the U.S. by basing them on its own experience of economic nationalism." As for the U.S., which has "used the Bank as an instrument of its own external infrastructural power to a greater degree than any other state," Wade points out the critical role of the U.S. university and, more specifically, "American academic economics" in that institutional hegemony: "The President of the Bank has always been an American; Americans are greatly over-represented at professional levels in the Bank relative to the U.S.'s shareholding; some two thirds of World Bank economists are certified by U.S. universities—and 80 per cent by North American and British universities."[41] In the end, *The East Asian Miracle: Economic Growth and Public Policy* made some modest acknowledgments of the effectiveness of state planning and strategic in[...] stances, but it largely affirmed the neoliberal Washin[...] was slightly toned down as a "market-friendly" approac[...]

The U.S. versus Japan ideological rivalry coexisted [...] eral agreements, preferential concessions, and freed capi[...] two countries. I am especially interested in how explicit [...] served funds *for* women often served as a more amicable, [...] over these negotiations. In the 1990s the Asian Developme[...] several national reports on women, including "Women in De[...]opment: Vietnam" (1994) and "Women in Development: Cambodia" (1996). On January 11, 1995, shortly after the establishment of the World Trade Organization, U.S. President Clinton and Japanese Prime Minister Murayama agreed to "include Women in Development (WID) as a new area of cooperation under the U.S.-Japan Common Agenda for Cooperation in Global Perspective."[42] Here I would recall that in June 1995, right before the Asian Women's Fund was officially inaugurated, Japan's Chief Cabinet Secretary Kozo Igarashi issued a statement that pledged that, in addition to providing direct compensation to the surviving women, "the Fund will, through the use of government funding and other funds, support those who undertake projects that address contemporary problems, such as violence against women."[43] Then, in 1996, during Special Rapporteur Coomaraswamy's investigative mission to Japan, North Korea, and South Korea, representatives of the office of the Japanese Prime Minister again stated as one of the five goals of the AWF: "Support projects by NGOs in the Asian region and, in countries from which 'comfort women' victims were drawn, in the field of the elimination of contemporary forms of violence against women, such as trafficking and prostitution."[44] Thus, we might make different sense of the peculiar naming of the Asian Women's Fund and this beneficent goal in several ways. First, they attest to the success of the longer and broader feminist efforts to name these specifically gendered injuries, which had achieved clear meaning and resonance in global governance by 1995. Second and more troublingly, this gesture hitched the Japanese military "comfort system" onto a more generic international horizon of one of many forms of violence against women and their nongovernmental amelioration. Third, this framing of the Asian Women's Fund reaffirmed Japan's leadership in the "Asian region," not just in terms of economic development but also in the arena of philanthropic pro-women projects but also novel public/private arrangements of fundraising and redistribution. The super-visibility of Asian women as mobile subjects and worthy beneficiaries of global civil society in the early 1990s trailed after and vindicated the unfettering of capital movements in a newly "borderless" world.

Just Compensation 205

The upbeat appraisal of several Asian economies along with the deregulation of the financial sector attracted unprecedented international investments, much of which had been redirected from the U.S., where interest rates remained low through the early 1990s. However, the naming of the "Asian miracle" elided an important distinction between industrial productivity and macroeconomic performance versus foreign capital flows into these countries. This increased their indebtedness and exposure to the vagaries of capital markets rather than self-sufficiency and solvency. Unlike foreign direct investments (FDI) in machinery, plants, and other infrastructure, portfolio investments in stocks, bonds, currencies, and derivatives are much easier to withdraw quickly if the terms become unfavorable. After the Mexican crisis of 1994, investors turned even more toward Asia. By raising their interest rates above the U.S. rates and pegging the value of their currencies to the U.S. dollar, several Asian countries provided a lucrative and safe alternative for investors. Between 1994 and 1996, over $220 billion was pumped into Thailand, Indonesia, Korea, Malaysia, and the Philippines, and the total foreign debt of these five countries doubled in a three-year period to $275 billion by June 1997. Just in 1996, there was a net capital inflow of $93 billion into these economies. Such massive influx of foreign capital increases the value of local currencies; this makes imports cheaper, fueling a consumption boom, but also makes exports more expensive, leading to an account deficit. The suddenly bloated foreign debt soon exceeded each country's foreign-currency reserves. More consequential still was the fact that much of this foreign debt were mostly short-term loans, with 62 percent of them set to mature in one year or less and a sizable number of loans with a repayment window of ninety days or less.[45]

But there were notable exceptions to this capitulation to "the private sector and market signals." China emerged in the 1990s as a leading export manufacturer *without* financial liberalization. Currency devaluations by China in 1990 and 1994 and later by Japan raised the value of exports from other Asian countries.[46] In 1995 Japan and the U.S. struck an accord whereby the yen depreciated 60 percent against the dollar by April 1997, thereby lowering the prices of Japanese exports to the U.S. and stimulating demand. Chalmers Johnson frames this as a "deal intended to help re-elect President Clinton the following year . . . [by keeping] U.S. interest rates at politically desirable levels."[47] U.S.-Asia trade pacts are thus enmeshed in U.S. domestic political power struggles. In return, Johnson continues, "The Clinton Administration also agreed to take a dive on the auto talks, abandoning its efforts to impose duties on Japanese luxury cars; the Administration shut up about America's billion-dollar-a-week trade deficit with Japan." This was *not* a case of fiscal or trade policy dictated by market signals.

Certain U.S. political interests may have been advanced, but the currency devaluations hurt the export competitiveness of Thailand and Indonesia, whose currencies were pegged to the dollar, and further compromised their ability to meet foreign debt obligations. The collective rush to invest in Asia turned to a panicked retreat after July 2, 1997, when Thailand became the first country to fail to meet its foreign loan payments and floated its baht. Investors realized that many firms were carrying high debt loads and that several countries did not have enough foreign-currency reserves to cover a massive flight of capital. The earlier competitive dash to invest in Asian markets and economies reversed into a rush to get out quickly before others could do so. Foreign lenders called in their loans and stopped extending new credit. The Philippines, Malaysia, and Indonesia floated their currencies shortly thereafter.

Many Western commentators were quick to blame the "meltdown" on a specifically Asian pathology of "crony capitalism," characterized by excessive government intervention in industrial growth and banks, widespread nepotism and favored protection of specific firms, and a lack of transparency. As the concerned editors of a special issue of the *Cambridge Journal of Economics* explained, "We were, we felt, witnessing a revival of Orientalism, in which all manner of fantasies and prejudices are projected onto Asia, with no concern for their veracity . . . 'cronyism,' for example, was becoming the modern substitute for 'Oriental despotism' or 'Asiatic absolutism.'"[48] Indeed, it was a distinctly *American* moment of triumph and self-congratulation. In an article in the February 13, 1998, edition of the *New York Times* bearing the blunt title "Greenspan Sees Asian Crisis Moving World to Western Capitalism," the chairman of the Federal Reserve is quoted as testifying before the Senate Foreign Relations Committee: "What we have here is a very dramatic event towards a consensus of the type of market system which we have in this country." As Chalmers Johnson critically noted ten days later in *The Nation*, "With East Asia's economic troubles in mind, many Americans have entered the last years of the twentieth century in a mood of truly obscene jingoism, or what the Germans call *Schadenfreude*, the malicious pleasure of gloating over the misfortunes of others."[49] Quoting an array of commentators from U.S. Federal Reserve Chairman Alan Greenspan to financier George Soros to IMF Deputy Managing Director Stanley Fisher, Robert Wade articulated an especially lively depiction of these dynamics: "The tone of voice ranges from gloating, to sanctimonious, to schoolmasterly. It is not hard to imagine the offense of Japanese, Korean, and other Asian policy-makers at the triumphalism of Westerners who picture the Asian political economy as a system whose movement toward America-without-the-ghettoes the current crisis has simply accelerated."[50] Some seized upon the 1997–98 crisis to effect a further bifurcation of the so-called "Asian model" from the Washington consensus in what Chalmers Johnson characterized as "the clash of capitalisms."[51]

Such hyperbolic figurations precluded a careful account of several interrelated political and economic processes conditioning the crisis. The first broad context was the crises-ridden globalization of finance capitalism, which began in the 1960s, partially yet importantly with the massive U.S. military spending (through borrowing) during the Vietnam War. Then the OPEC oil boom of the 1970s made an even larger pool of money available for international circulation. In the 1980s the invention and proliferation of new financial instruments such as credit default swaps and derivatives, intended to manage the growing risks such as currency fluctuations in international markets, also created new channels of investment. These financial instruments came to function increasingly as vehicles of speculation and outsized bets, generating more commissions and profits for some but also intensifying volatility and uncertainty. Contrary to the prevalent figuration of Asian capital markets as overly protected and underdeveloped in the 1990s, many Asian firms were very much actively integrated into this transnational circuit of speculative capital and offshore finance. The oversupply of money circulating in an unevenly integrated circuit of established and emerging markets created a hazardous scene well before 1997–98.[52]

Another related global shift was toward more private lending to developing countries. Recall the affirmative yoking together of "financial systems" and "development" in the 1989 *World Development Report*. Framing the 700 percent rise in "net private capital inflows," including portfolio investments (bonds and equities), into developing countries in the 1990s against a decrease of "net official capital inflows" from foreign governments and international financial institutions (IFIs) such as the IMF and the World Bank, Diane Elson has usefully summarized this conjuncture as a "delinking of social goals and international finance."[53] But as we have seen in the previous chapter, the World Bank had itself become invested in estimating the economic costs of illness and social problems such as violence against women. Thus, rather than a delinking of the two, I would say that there was a partial absorption and subordination of social goals to the instrumental calculations and speculative logic of international finance. Whereas the IFIs were at least nominally committed to the alleviation of poverty or restoring national economic soundness, private investors were motivated by quick returns and easy entry and exit from these emerging markets. Volatility is exploited and capitalized upon by foreign investors who have no ties or commitments to the specific countries that are adversely affected by their decisions. But the myriad adversities wrought by such indifference and cruelty were not as amenable to the spectacle of suffering and sexual endangerment, which was so effectively but also narrowly marshaled for some Asian women.

A third connecting thread across these crises was the moral hazard created by their management and rescue by governments and the IMF. Rather than formulate necessary limits and rules in order to discourage such overexposure to risk, they repeatedly bailed out private lenders and investors and shifted the costs onto the public, which encouraged further risky investments and lax lending practices. Palma points to the Thai government's 1996 bailout of the Bangkok Bank of Commerce in Thailand and the World Bank loan of $307 to Indonesia in 1992 to bail out its state-run banks as local precedents that created the expectation that the Asian governments and IFIs would continue to come to the rescue.[54] These macro-level public-private transactions and protections must be considered alongside and against the calculations of female injury and the debates over efficient public expenditure and proper compensation, which were discussed in the previous chapters. Banks and private investors get bailed out with public funds; individual victims of state-coordinated violence get compensated through private donations. A critical feminist method should dispute both transactions.

The currency and debt crises in Thailand and Indonesia came to be figured as a more encompassing "Asian financial crisis" in October 1997 when Taiwan, which had large foreign-exchange reserves, devalued its currency partially to discourage such a panicked withdrawal. Although Taiwan would not become one of the countries later subject to the IMF bailouts, the devaluation activated a categorical shift on the part of international investors: "After Taiwan, the conceptual category of 'Asian financial crisis' came into being. Capitalists began to sell the Hong Kong dollar and the Korean won."[55] The persistent "Asianization" of the crisis as a localized structural problem of "crony capitalism" misses how investors were fueled by such blunt mappings of "Asian" sameness, with little or no regard to substantive differences in economic fundamentals among these countries. The figurations of financial "contagion" as the "tequila effect" of the 1994 Mexican crisis and the "yellow fever" of the 1997–98 crisis implicate the enduring import of racialization under finance capitalism.[56]

The "Asian crisis" was and is also a story about the U.S. and significant political and economic shifts conditioning the ascent of Wall Street in Washington. First, investment practices shifted from individual savings and domestic stocks and bonds to international markets: "In 1993 alone, U.S. investors bought more foreign equities—about $68 billion—than in the whole decade of the 1980s."[57] The U.S. also took an active role in promoting free trade and financial liberalization throughout the Asia-Pacific region. In the early 1990s, American mutual funds alone invested $4 billion to $5 billon per year in Asian markets. According to Chalmers Johnson, "At annual meetings in different Pacific Rim countries, [the U.S.] insistently propagandized that the Asian 'tiger economies' open up to global market forces." On November 2, 1993, President Bill Clinton convened the first APEC (Asia-Pacific Economic Cooperation) Economic Leaders' Meeting on Blake Island. Then, at the 1994 APEC meeting in Bogor, Indonesia, the U.S. representatives enjoined the other attendees to commit to "free trade and investment in the Pacific."[58]

In 1993 the U.S. Department of the Treasury successfully convinced the Clinton administration to pressure South Korea toward greater financial liberalization *against* the opposition of its own Council of Economic Advisers.[59] South Korea had been able to weather earlier external shocks in the 1970s and 1980s because of strict government oversight of and intervention into banking and finance, including restricting borrowing by Korean firms only for productive investments rather than speculation and increasing government spending to enable firms to generate needed revenue. However, in 1994, in response to pressure from the U.S. and in order to join the Organization for Economic Cooperation and Development (OECD)—dubbed "the club of rich nations"—the South Korean government abolished its Economic Planning Board, loosening restrictions on both foreign borrowing by Korean banks and the movement of foreign capital investments into and out of the country.[60] By 1997, Korean banks and corporations had incurred $160 billion in foreign debt.[61] Many of these loans were short-term, so repayment was due within twelve months or less in some cases. Several Korean banks, flush with this new capital, began to make speculative investments in junk bonds in Russia and Latin America. They did so under the assumption that the Korean won–U.S. dollar exchange rate would stay stable: "As the won fell, the banks began to sell foreign securities in order to boost liquidity. Their sell-off helped to spread the financial contagion."[62]

The "Asianization" of the 1997–98 crisis also obscured a third story about the changing mission and role of the World Bank and the IMF in the post–Bretton Woods era. Diane Elson lucidly contextualizes the crisis within "a surreal financial architecture" of a reoriented IMF and especially the World Bank, from promoting important "social goals" to mandating "sound finance" through open markets on the part of debtor nations. I have already discussed the neoclassical orthodoxy reigning at the World Bank throughout the 1980s and fortified through its "market-friendly" neutralization of the challenge from Japan in the early 1990s. Since the 1970s, the IMF has increasingly imposed certain conditions upon borrowing countries, which have included privatization of public enterprises, lifting trade restrictions, opening up of capital markets, and cutting public expenditures. Rather than stabilizing and ensuring the solvency of developing economies, the IMF increasingly became an auditor for private capital. Even as the IMF has intensified surveillance of certain developing countries and imperiled economies, demanding that they demonstrate greater *transparency*, as Elson pointedly clarifies, "the emphasis is mainly on transparency towards international investors, rather than towards their citizens."[63] I would even argue that the IMF's selectively targeted demand for accountability and transparency props up the fiction that there is a supranational agency, which could and indeed does account for a definite standard of sound finance and foolproof measure of transparency.

The "Asian crisis" could thus be reframed as a story about the damaging force and expanding repertoire of IMF interventions. Several analysts have pointedly accused the IMF of creating the crisis by championing what Walden Bello characterizes as "indiscriminate capital account liberalization" and holding up Indonesia and Thailand as models for rapidly opening up to foreign investments in the 1990s.[64] Then the IMF's blanket diagnoses of "immature institutions" and "lack of transparency" prodded and amplified investors' panic. Others accused the IMF of worsening the crisis through its blunt macroeconomic restructurings that combined cutting public expenditures and raising taxes and interest rates. In January 1998, in a rare public disagreement between the leaders of the Bretton Woods institutions, Joseph Stiglitz, the chief economist at the World Bank, openly criticized the IMF's approach as contradictory to both its prior advice to Japan to widen its deficits and the U.S. government's rescue of the U.S. savings-and-loans industry.[65]

The 1997–98 crisis would also prove to be the occasion wherein the IMF would demonstrate its overarching commitment to protecting private capital interests. Several Asian governments, including Thailand and Malaysia, which had opposed the liberalization of financial services during the WTO negotiations of 1996–97, were compelled to approve the agreement in December 1997: "Either they signed or their receipt of IMF bail-out funds would be complicated."[66] In turn, the IMF, along with the World Bank and the WTO, were able to strengthen their standing in the eyes of "the owners and managers of capital" through these actions "both as organizations that can get them out of the crisis without serious losses and as organizations that can cajole Asian governments to reshape their domestic economies in line with Western models."[67] In his examination of IMF actions in South Korea, Ha-Joon Chang points to a "mission creep" whereby the IMF extended its reach beyond its original purpose of dealing with problems in maintaining current account balances to dictate domestic budgetary and monetary policies, "including hitherto-untouched areas such as corporate governance system and labor law . . . issues that it has neither the mandate nor the expertise to deal with."[68]

The active role of U.S. officials in dictating the terms of the "bailouts" affirmed both U.S. power within the IMF and Wall Street's influence on U.S. economic and foreign policy. Wade and Veneroso thus offer the expanded term "Wall Street-Treasury- IMF Complex" to identify this newly fortified political-economic bloc.[69] Early on in the crisis at a G7 meeting in September 1997, Japan, with the backing of several other Asian countries, proposed the creation of a $100 billion Asian Monetary Fund (AMF) comprising a $50 billion contribution from Japan and the rest from the other still healthy economies of the region, Taiwan and Singapore. This was roundly rejected by the IMF and the U.S., then represented by Deputy Treasury Secretary Lawrence Summers. After his stint as Vice President of Development Economics and Chief Economist at the World Bank, Summers joined the Clinton administration and was appointed as Deputy Treasury Secretary under Robert Rubin in 1995. As Kristen Nordhaug explains this U.S. rejection, an Asian Monetary Fund would have drained deposits from the U.S. Treasury and hurt the domestic economy: "Concern about the U.S. reliance on East Asian holdings of Treasuries may have been equally important. If regional central banks led by the Bank of Japan had sold out from their huge holdings of Treasuries to finance this costly operation, the interest rates on Treasuries and U.S. long-term interest rates would probably have soared and halted the U.S. economic upturn."[70] Back in the United States, in arguing for additional contributions to the IMF before the Senate Foreign Relations Committee on February 13, 1998, Alan Greenspan, along with Lawrence Summers and Treasury Secretary Robert Rubin, testified that "the IMF had succeeded in using its bailouts to force nations to open their markets and transform their economies."[71] Or, as Bruce Cumings painted in a more coercive picture in a 1998 article, "Sources in Washington acknowledged that several reforms had been specifically demanded by U.S. Treasury officials, in keeping with former U.S. Trade Representative Mickey Kanter's view that the IMF could be a 'battering ram' for American interests."[72]

But here we should be mindful that only particular American interests—namely heavily exposed Wall Street firms and private investors—were being protected and promoted by the U.S. government. For instance, $2 billion of J. P. Morgan's exposure to Korea involved derivative contracts: "This perhaps explains why Morgan was at the forefront of the move to convert Korean banks' short-term debt into sovereign debt."[73] This conversion to sovereign debt holds the government responsible for repayment with funds raised partly but crucially from collecting taxes and also cutting public expenditures. Pointing out that "the thing our government most seemed to fear was that contracts to buy our weapons might now not be honored," Chalmers Johnson recounts how then U.S. Secretary of Defense William Perry traveled to the Asian countries to secure these payments.[74] In light of this, we might consider an alternately expanded name: the Wall Street-Treasury-Defense-IMF complex. Such unabashed promotion of a very narrow set of U.S. financial and military interests also announced the attenuation of the Cold War protector-sponsor role of the U.S. in Asia. As Cumings more forcefully characterized this break, "The deep meaning and intent of the American and IMF response to the Asian liquidity crisis is to close the historical chapter in which the sheltered 'developmental states' have prospered."[75] From a different angle, considering how the IMF bailout funds would go to the foreign banks that had made "shaky and imprudent loans" and not the people or domestic firms in the most negatively affected countries, Johnson flatly declared that "the ultimate in crony capitalism is actually the U.S. dominated International Monetary Fund (the IMF)."[76] Several observers have repeatedly used the term *fire sale* to refer to how investors rushed back in to buy up the devalued Asian firms and assets in the aftermath of the IMF interventions.[77] When several of these Asian economies demonstrated faster-than-expected signs of economic upturn, the "recovery" was interpreted as affirmation of the IMF reforms and financial liberalization. However, the recovery of certain Asian economies had much to do with their breaking away from the IMF-mandated program of financial liberalization and social disinvestment. In 1998 both Korea and Thailand reinstated some state interventions such as extending low-interest loans to at-risk businesses.

ASIAN WOMEN AS DIFFERENTIAL METHOD

The interlinked and mutually reinforcing Asianizations of both miracle and crisis can be broken up by focusing on the contiguous yet differential exploitation of women's labor in specific countries. The export-led industrialization of many Asian economies in the 1960s and 1970s was crucially powered by the super-exploitation of women's labor in the free trade zones and special economic zones throughout Asia. In addition, as the inter-Asian feminist network pointed out in the early 1970s, women's sexual labor in U.S. military prostitution and international sex tourism had been crucial to the economic development of many countries in the region, including South Korea, Thailand, and the Philippines. In an editorial published in the June 1980 issue of *Asian Women's Liberation*, Suzuyo Takazato of the Asian Women's Association clearly traced these linkages:

> While Japanese corporations make enormous profits by using Asian women as cheap labor [in Japanese-controlled factories], thus making the Japanese economy prosper as the result of extremely severe exploitation, Japanese men go to these Asian countries in order to buy women. Furthermore, Japanese capital has moved into local tourist industries, which sell women as a commodity. On the one hand, Japanese capital is selling local women in these countries. On the other hand, Japanese men are buying the same women as a commodity. Thus, the exploitation of Asian women by Japanese men is two-fold and their human rights are completely violated.[78]

Citing this passage in her 1984 article, Elaine Kim remapped the distinctly gendered and sexual contours of the so-called "flying geese" model of Japan-led regional industrialization: "Japanese sex tourism flourished first in Taiwan and then in South Korea, where facilities and female companionship were less expensive. Now Japanese men are turning their attentions toward the Philippines and Southeast Asia, including Malaysia and Indonesia, where prices are even lower."[79]

Low-paid women's labor was later crucial to the expansion of clerical sectors and service economies linked to the global expansion of finance capitalism into Asia. Foreign investment in Korean capital markets, which began as early as 1981, led to the growth of female workers, especially young unmarried women, in clerical jobs. In the late 1990s, as wages and the standard of living rose in South Korea, labor-intensive production was relocated to other countries with a lower-paid labor force while foreign direct investment was channeled toward the growing service and retail sector. There was an especially marked increase in women's employment in the new global chain and department stores. Married women were preferred by these global retail chains because they could influence their neighbors and were also less prone to unionization.[80] Meanwhile, as the Korean won rose in exchange value, more Korean men began to travel to other countries in Asia and Southeast Asia as sex tourists and to seek marriage partners in China, Vietnam, and the Philippines.

Thanh-Dam Truong has been especially insightful by using a focus on Asian women's labor in the 1990s to *broaden* the temporal and geographical frame of analysis. She suggests that rather than an anomaly or localized failure, "The trends characterizing women's experiences in crisis situations are manifestations of a deeper problem that had emerged in times of economic growth, i.e. the gendered logic of industrial organization in East and South East Asia." The much-touted "flexibility" of the regional workforce was made possible by a concomitant hardening of gendered ideologies that further feminized "caring work" and reproductive labor while upholding male sexual privilege and male workers' need for "sexual comfort," which, in turn, rationalized the proliferation of sex industries. Indonesia offered an especially tumultuous and complicated scene of sexual labor exploitation and sexual violence. According to Johan Linquist, "With the emergence of the Growth Triangle in the early 1990s, prostitution rapidly expanded on Batam and neighboring islands, as primarily Singaporean men began to take the short ferry trip across the border. This process reached its peak in 1998 at the height of the financial crisis, as the Indonesian rupiah dropped to as little as one sixth of its previous value in relation to the Singapore dollar."[81] In May 1998 the currency devaluation, unemployment, and food shortages generated by the financial crisis set off mass riots, which included targeted rapes of Indonesian-Chinese women, which briefly captured international headlines. Truong concludes that "if a gender analysis had been part of the evaluation of ANICs' industrial transformation, the outcomes of this transformation would not have received the label of a miracle, and the crisis might possibly have been anticipated."[82]

There were several contemporary attempts to point to how macroeconomic policies and bilateral agreements were specifically harmful to women. To take one notable but under-credited instance, in a 1995 essay titled "Economic Development and Asian Women" Matsui Yayori aligns domestic violence with "the impact of unequal development" as "a form of structural violence" affecting a diverse range of women. Reporting on the Asian Women's Tribunal on Women's Human Rights, which was convened in December 1994 at Chulalongkorn University in Thailand by the Asian Pacific Forum on Women, Law, and Development (APWLD), Matsui conveys testimony from women who were being displaced by large infrastructural development projects, including dam and tourist resort construction, logging, export-oriented manufacturing, and large-scale shrimp farming, which were imposed by structural adjustment programs (SAP) and funded by "international financial institutions, private capital, and ODA from Japan and other nations."[83] Importantly, Matsui also pointed to several examples of women's concerted resistance to these projects.

There were distinctively gendered but also differentiated repercussions for women workers in the aftermath of the 1997–98 financial crises, which contest the geographical bounding of Asian women within Asia and the very categorical designation of "Asian women" or "Asian women workers." As one article recalled, "In Thailand, 95 percent of those laid off from the garment sector were women; in the toys' sector, it was 88 percent. In South Korea, 86 percent of those who lost their financial services and banking jobs were female."[84] Specific local and national responses to the crises proceeded unevenly across gender and class differences. In the Philippines the "women-specific impact" of the crisis included higher rates of unemployment and a turn toward more income generation in the informal economy. Women constituted the majority of the workers in two of the three most negatively affected industries, garment manufacturing and electronics. In addition, the agricultural sector, which also employed more women than men, cut two hundred thousand jobs in the first quarter of 1998. Cuts in public health care further increased women's burden of caring for sick family members.[85] Finally, the austerity measures entailed large job cuts in the public sector, the largest employer of women.[86]

In Korea, where the IMF-mandated restructurings also led to massive layoffs, more women than men were laid off, especially in the service sectors. One out of five female white-collar workers was laid off. Married women were targeted for layoffs by a refortified patriarchal logic of the male head of household as the primary breadwinner. But as Cho pointed out, "In reality, women were pushed into the labour market at lower wages on behalf of unemployed husbands."[87] At the same time, such gender-specific response to crisis also produced new female figures such as the "IMF *chonyo* (IMF maiden)," referring to the predicament of single women who delayed marriage plans because married women would be first to be targeted for layoffs. The international financial institutions and their interventions do not merely act upon or on behalf of preexisting "Asian women" from above and afar; their policies and priorities also shape and materialize newly and distinctly gendered, classed, and sexual subjects.

The 1997–98 crisis also accelerated the migration of women workers across and also beyond Asia. This has had differentially marked impacts on specific countries, which further contests the "Asianization" of the crisis. Facing a labor shortage with its rapid economic development in the 1980s, South Korea began a program to recruit foreign workers in 1991 called the Industrial and Technical Training Programme for Foreigners (ITTP), which followed the model set earlier by Japan. South Korea's economic growth also fed a boom in the country's sex industry in the 1990s, which "started to diversify into new forms that included prostitution carried out not just in places like brothels, but also the pandering of sex in bars and restaurants, as well as in hotels, public bathhouses,

216 Chapter 6

and massage parlours." This increased the demand for foreign women workers. In 1994 the South Korean government created the E-6 or entertainer visa, which was "to provide singers, musicians, and dancers to the Korean entertainment industry." The crisis and its management greatly rerouted this labor migration. As Lee recounts, "About 100,000 migrant workers left South Korea at the end of 1997 alone due to the economic crisis and the curtailments required for South Korea to receive its IMF bailout package." However, with the onset of recovery, there was an even more pronounced gender imbalance in E-6 visa holders among migrant workers: "Even though the number of male entertainers has been declining since 1997, the demand for foreign female entertainers has more than doubled since South Korea's recovery from the crisis at the end of 1998."[88]

The case of Filipina migrant workers in Hong Kong offers another illustrative instance of these complex and dynamic shifts. The number of Filipina domestics in Hong Kong increased more than twofold over the 1990s from 66,000 in 1991 to 140,000 by 1999. Although there had long been ethnocentric biases against these Filipina migrants, antipathy toward these women was further "fueled by the Asian economic crisis."[89] Rising local unemployment provoked calls for cutting the minimum wage for domestic workers and enacting new measures of surveillance and deportation. A new immigration control policy dubbed "Operation Hoover" soon went into effect, whereby young foreign women suspected of prostitution were detained and interrogated, a measure intended to thwart these migrant women workers from extending their stays in Hong Kong. None of these groups of women targeted for firing, exploitation, detention, and expulsion were able to capture and hold the attention of the transnational public sphere in the ways in which the "sex slave" continued to do throughout the end of the 1990s and well into the twenty-first century.

Truong asserts that rather than disprove the moniker of "Asian miracle," as Alan Greenspan and others declared, the 1997–98 crisis posed a challenge of "whether the miracle can stand as a miracle of social transformation rather than merely industrial transformation."[90] If this challenge had been taken up, as she suggests, by reopening "the discussion on the relationship between polity and economy, economic performance and governance," the "Asian crisis" could have produced critical insights against further neoliberalization. However, as Tani Barlow incisively points out, the much-lauded visibility of Asian women's nongovernmental activism and induction into global governance in the 1990s was marshaled as an indicator of the salutary effects of globalization even in the midst of the economic crisis. Pointing to a chapter titled "Prospects for Women" in an April 1998 ESCAP report titled *Asia and the Pacific into the*

Twenty-First Century: Prospects for Social Development, Barlow notes: "Thus, the report concluded, while the impact of the finance crisis had hit Southeast Asia most strongly and had adversely affected women there, not only were indicators high relative to other regions, globalization has had the most positive effect on the regional women's movement."[91] A contradictory diagnosis was presented two years later in a 2000 report on violence against women, in which Special Rapporteur Coomaraswamy framed the 1997–98 crisis as the *result* of earlier structural adjustment programs that "have led to increased impoverishment, particularly amongst women, displacement and internal strife resulting from the political instabilities caused by devaluing national currencies, increasing debt and dependence on foreign direct investment."[92] She continued: "The crisis in ASEAN countries is an indicator that globalization policies can result in disaster if not properly managed." However, immediately following this warning, there was a slide into revitalizing old and tried figures of female vulnerability: "The economic crisis in East Asia has resulted in many women being trafficked to escape from sudden poverty."

As I have tried to show in chapter 2, divergent registers of the "traffic in women" are envisioned and enacted under the obligatory but also self-congratulatory banner of bilateral cooperation as much as international competition and enmity. We can see this by considering key events between the June 1993 Vienna World Conference and the triumph of the Wall Street–Treasury-IMF complex in 1998 as contemporaneous and interrelated, even if "Asian women" appear to be visible only in some instances. In March 1993 the administration of South Korea's first democratically elected president, Kim Young-sam, announced that it would not demand official compensation from Japan: "Instead, Korea demanded that the Japanese government take moral responsibility for investigating the issue."[93] In August 1993 the Kim Young-sam administration initiated its *segyehwa* (globalization) campaign, which included forging new economic relations of cooperation with Japan. In November 1993 Japan's Prime Minister Hosokawa Morihiro made an apology during a visit to South Korea. On January 11, 1995, a few months ahead of the UN conference in Beijing, U.S. President Clinton and Japanese Prime Minister Murayama agreed "to include Women in Development (WID) as a new area of cooperation under the common U.S.-Japanese Agenda for Cooperation in Global Perspective."[94] In August 1995, the Asian Women's Fund was formally established. In April 1998, in the midst of the financial crisis and IMF-mandated restructurings, the government of the newly elected South Korean President Kim Dae-jung offered to pay 31.5 million won ($26,000) to any surviving Korean "comfort woman" who had *not* accepted money from the Asian Women's Fund. It also declared that it would not press for direct compensation from the Japanese government. As a *New York Times* article on April 22, 1998, bearing the headline, "Seoul Won't Seek Japan Funds for War's Brothel Women," relayed, "Yang Mi Kang, a spokeswoman for the Korea Council for Women Drafted for Military Sexual Slavery in Japan, said today that the council was pleased that at a time of economic hardship, the Government had decided to dip into its budget to give the women, many in their 70's and 80's, a means of support."[95] In October 1998 President Kim Dae-jung visited Japan, where he and Japanese Prime Minister Keizo Obuchi cosigned "The Korea-Japan Economic Cooperation Agenda 21," which articulated a "future-oriented relationship" between the two countries.

The co-constitutive enfolding of official apologies and conditional reparations in the "comfort women" case with bilateral and multilateral trade negotiations demands that critical feminist analysis resist and rethink the charge of the endangered and violated female body as well as the ready recourse to its monetary calculation. Late in the writing and editing of this chapter, I was alerted to a sizable and substantive international disparity in the Asian Women's Fund when I reread the April 1998 *New York Times* article. Harada Shinichi, then spokesman for the Asian Women's Fund, explained the reasoning for different amounts of sums distributed to different national groups of survivors: "He took pains to stress that the money—$23,000 apiece for the women from South Korea and Taiwan and $9,200 for those from the Philippines, paid out over five years—was for medical and welfare expenses and was not to be regarded as compensation.... Mr. Harada said the difference in the amounts given to women from the Philippines and those from South Korea and Taiwan was due to differences in costs of living in the three countries. He said, for example, that 3 million yen would buy three houses in the suburbs of Manila, while it would not even cover the down payment on a small house outside Seoul." It's easy to be outraged by the unabashed calculation of amounts of this not-compensation to differential "costs of living" pegged to real estate markets as yet another expression of Japanese official disregard for the women, especially if we consider that this was uttered in the midst of a financial crisis resulting in severe economic dislocations and harsh retrenchment measures in both South Korea and the Philippines. But, as I have tried to show in this chapter, we should strive to make critical sense of the Asian Women's Fund in terms of a longer history of bilateral, regional multinational and global transactions that made such inhuman expressions of false equivalence and currency exchange thinkable, speakable, and publishable.

ENDURING
MEMORIALS

On December 28, 2015, in a joint press conference of their respective foreign ministers, the governments of Japan and South Korea announced that they had signed what was widely hailed as a "landmark agreement" related to the ongoing dispute about the proper terms of apology, redress, and memorialization regarding the Japanese military "comfort system" during World War II.[1] In what has come to be referred to alternately as the *"comfort women" agreement*, the *"comfort women" settlement*, and, more crassly, the *"comfort women" deal*, Japan's Prime Minister Abe Shinzo expressed "anew his most sincere apologies and remorse," and the Japanese government pledged to pay 1 billion yen ($8.3 million) as a "one-time contribution" toward a foundation that would be established and overseen by the South Korean government to support "projects for recovering the honor and dignity and healing the psychological wounds of all former comfort women." The South Korean government, then headed by Park Geun-hye, its first woman president and daughter of the military dictator Park Chung-hee, who had earlier signed the 1965 Treaty on Basic Relations between Japan and the Republic of Korea, pledged its cooperation in the implementation of these projects. Both governments confirmed that "this issue is resolved finally and irreversibly" and further pledged to "refrain from accusing or criticizing each other regarding this issue in the international community, including at the United Nations." The absolute, sweeping declaration—"the issue is resolved *finally* and *irreversibly*"—belies the many contradictions, misalignments, reversals, and reshufflings that have punctuated the irresolvability of a constellation of accusations, grievances, demands, denials, and desires that cannot be distilled as a single *issue*.

The conventionally generic language and abstracted terms of interstate negotiations and their neatly monetized calculations were betrayed by the co-presence of a determinedly concrete and intractable figure. The second of three numbered points in the statement of South Korea's Foreign Minister demurred: "The Government of the ROK acknowledges the fact that the Government of Japan is concerned about the statue built in front of the Embassy of Japan in Seoul from the viewpoint of preventing any disturbance of the peace of the mission or impairment of its dignity, and will strive to solve this issue in an appropriate manner."[2] The shift in the wronged subject of *dignity* from "all former comfort women" to "the Government of Japan" in the statement projects an odd, counterbalanced commensurability in this struggle and transaction. But only one of these parties had been able to negotiate on their own behalf in this binational settlement. The agreement was met immediately by criticism, denunciation, and more protests, especially over the lack of consultation with the surviving women and the NGOs that had been advocating on their behalf since the early 1990s. As Kim Kun-ja, a ninety-year-old survivor, told South Korean Vice Foreign Minister Cho Tae-yul on the following day: "We're the victims. Why should the government rashly reach a deal? We won't accept it."[3] The Korean Council decried the agreement as a product of "humiliating diplomacy," and Amnesty International released a brief statement: "The women were missing from the negotiation table, and they must not be sold short in a deal that is more about political expediency than justice."[4] Several observers questioned the monetary sum of 1 billion yen, which was to cover 100 million won as individual compensation for 46 still-living Korean survivors and 20 million won to the surviving heirs of 199 deceased women. There was an especially impassioned condemnation of the South Korean government's capitulation to the long-standing displeasure among some Japanese about the bronze statue.

The bronze life-size statue of a young Korean female figure seated next to an empty chair was installed on December 14, 2011, as a "Peace Monument" in front of the Japanese Embassy in Seoul. This was timed to commemorate the one-thousandth weekly "Wednesday Demonstrations" led by the Korean Council for the Women Drafted for Military Sexual Slavery. This timing was also significant in anticipation of the twentieth anniversary of the protests on January 8, 2012. The statue, commonly referred to in Korean as *Sonyeosang* ("Girl Statue"), was designed by an artist couple, Kim Seo-kyung and Kim Eun-sung. They had initially planned on a simple "memorial stone" but were provoked to design the more elaborate and figural sculpture after they heard of the Japanese government's opposition to any monument at that location.[5] This statue has been replicated and installed in multiple locations throughout South Korea but also in the U.S. (2013), Canada (2015), Australia (2016), and Germany (2017), along with other statues and memorials to the "comfort women" in the Philippines and Taiwan.[6]

In this final chapter I move to consider the proliferation of physical memorials as a supplement and a rejoinder to the virtualization of both activism *and* redress across multiple forums and communication media. The "comfort women" redress movement offers an instructive yet vexing case study for tracking the various *media* through which social movements and conflicts appeared and circulated within and across domestic and transnational public spheres in the 1990s and up to the present. Key early moments involved staging press conferences, releasing "statements," and publishing "open letters" by activist groups. Once survivors came forward, they provided compelling live testimonials, which were reported by both domestic and then international news media. Official Japanese government denials and demurrals, in turn, prompted another round of criticisms and rearticulated demands. The world-changing expansion of the internet in the 1990s provided a crucial tool for disseminating updates, organizing protests, and publicizing conferences and new scholarship. I would also include the various reports and comments released by the United Nations and other international organizations and NGOs to this list of transnational cyber-publicity. Both official reports and activist documents became widely accessible through multiple websites of the United Nations, individual governments, and nongovernmental organizations. The past atrocity as well as the unfolding social movement began to be represented artistically in literary works and also in painting, film/video, sculpture, public art, and multimedia installations, which received more news coverage.[7] As the "comfort women" issue came to be prolifically represented across these visual media, the expanding repertoire of images has also highlighted the pitfalls of

Enduring Memorials   223

objectification, numbing spectacle, aestheticization, and decontextualization. There has been much recitation, reassemblage, and what Bolter and Grusin have termed "remediation."[8]

One of the most bewildering event/texts of this multisided, multisited struggle occurred on March 27, 2007, with the launch of the Digital Museum for the Comfort Women Issue and the Asian Women's Fund (hereafter the Digital Museum) (figure 7.1). A striking feature in the continuing transnational struggle for justice is the place of museums, both real and virtual, in activist demands for redress but also as an effective tool of education and remembrance.[9] As Murayama Tomiichi, the former prime minister of Japan (1994–96) who first announced the establishment of the Asian Women's Fund and later served as its final president, declared in a press conference to introduce the Digital Museum, "We hope that this virtual memorial hall long remembers the comfort women issue, and will help promote reconciliation between Asian citizen [sic] and the Japanese. We also hope that Japanese citizens and people around the world would likewise visit this site and pass down their insights on the issue of comfort women to the generations that follow."[10] The Digital Museum is a fascinating virtual repository and remediation of the knotty political-economic-social-cultural contours of the "comfort women" problematic. It entered an already crowded field of websites dedicated to documenting and, in some cases, debunking the "true history" of the Japanese military "comfort system." That it is a technologically mediated and politically partial *hypertext* is apparent at the very outset from the spectral, computer-generated building façade on its home page. Its awkward English moniker, strange form, and voluminous content bear the impossibilities of both refusing and securing redemption across multiple languages, conflicting ideological frames, and uneven, shifting political economies. As a response to compounded demands for apology, reparation, and transparency, its tone veers between contrite and self-congratulatory, and its archival curation is meticulous in documenting certain facets while obfuscating other key knowledges.

Rather than decry it as a partial and distinctly fabricated composition—as are all other representations of the issue—this chapter seeks to think through the strange scaffolding and multiple contradictions of the Digital Museum as enacting the communicational possibilities and exigencies of the age of mixed-media politics. One useful way of unpacking and remapping its contents is through different, albeit overlapping geographical-linguistic-juridical frames of production, circulation, and reception: (1) national; (2) bilateral, such as between Japan and South Korea; (3) regional or intra-Asian; and (4) international. These demarcations are admittedly heuristic, especially given how digi-

FIGURE 7.1. Photo of the home page of the Digital Museum for the Comfort Women Issue and the Asian Women's Fund, http://awf.or.jp/index.html.

tal citation and remediation often collapse and blur them, but they are useful for deconstructing the political-archival-cultural-corporate contours of the Digital Museum, which gathers, collates, and reframes some texts while leaving out many others in the ever-growing and incalculable archive of the "comfort women" problematic.

TRANS-MEDIA RELAYS

Before moving on to discuss the Digital Museum, I want to map several key media sightings and relays in the long, multisited, and circuitous recall and composition of the Japanese military "comfort system." First, I would point to the archival black-and-white photos, some often blurry and worn, which have circulated as visible evidence of the truth of the historical event. These photographs have been reproduced and dispersed across print media, including newspapers and books, but also in documentaries, artworks, and websites. I have already discussed in chapter 5 the photographs that were taken by the

Enduring Memorials   225

U.S. Signal Corps in Burma and China in 1944. But long before their rediscovery in the U.S. National Archives in the early 1990s, another set of photographs played an important role in the early excavation of the "comfort system" in Japan. According to Chunghee Sarah Soh, Japanese journalist Senda Kako first became interested in researching the military "comfort system" in 1965 while he was working as a reporter for the *Mainichi Shimbun* and conducting research for his 1967 book, *Nihon so Senreki (Japan's War Chronicle)*, in the *Mainichi* archives: "In the process of selecting photographs for the book from more than twenty thousand taken by *Mainichi* photojournalists who reported on the Japanese military during the Fifteen-Year War, Senda came across a number of strange pictures of women marching together with the troops. Some of them showed the women carrying trunks on top of their heads, which Senda recognized as a traditional manner of carrying things among Korean women. One picture taken right after Japan's defeat showed the women wearing kimonos, while another showed one woman with a Japanese hairstyle being stared at contemptuously by a Chinese."[11] The first photograph, of two women crossing a river, was subsequently published in the volume of Korean survivors' testimonials compiled by the Korean Council, *True Stories of the Korean Comfort Women* (1995). A large reproduction of this photograph accompanied a reprinted excerpt of Kim Tokchin's testimonial in the journal *Index on Censorship*. The caption reads "Crossing the Yellow River, 1940s: the snap that started the search in 1962, when Senda Kako, a Japanese journalist with *Mainichi Shimbun*, discovered this photograph in the Japanese War Archives. On discovering there were comfort women from Korea, he began the first research into forced prostitution during World War II."[12]

Television was another important medium of publicity and provocation. Many have pointed to the August 1991 press conference in which Kim Hak-sun testified about her experiences in the "comfort system" as the decisive beginning of international awareness of the problem and the redress movement. According to one account, Kim Hak-sun "became determined to break her silence" while "watching the news on TV, when she was enraged by the denial of a Japanese politician of the existence of the military's 'comfort women' and 'comfort houses.'"[13] What is suggestive for me about this detail is how it prods us to consider Kim as an engaged viewer and critical reader of the televisual. Another pivotal early development, Yoshimi's discovery of incriminating archival documents in Japan, was also partially spurred on by television. Yoshimi became interested in the issue after watching an interview that Kim Hak-soon gave to the NHK (Japan Broadcasting Corporation) about her pending lawsuit, during which she declared that "I wanted to sue for the fact that I was trampled upon by the Japanese military and have spent my life in misery. I want the young people of South Korea and Japan to know what Japan did in the past." As Yoshimi later recalled, "Those words inspired me to begin researching the comfort women issue."[14]

On August 18, 1992, the Korean Council held a press conference at the Palais des Nations in Geneva with Hwang Geum-joo, a Korean survivor, testifying. The international television coverage of the issue hailed more women in other places to come forward. Kim Yong-Sil, one of the first survivors from North Korea to do so, testified at the International Public Hearing Concerning on War in 1993: "This year, it was a great shock to me to see on TV former 'comfort women' disclosing their past. That encouraged me. After long and deep thought, I made up my mind to bring to light the atrocities committed by the Japanese army."[15] In a 2001 interview broadcast on the Australian Broadcasting Channel, Jan Ruff-O'Herne, a Dutch survivor, described how she was motivated by seeing a Korean survivor testify on television: "In 1992, 50 years on, I remember hearing on the news that the war in Bosnia had broken out, and women were being raped. Then I saw on television the Korean comfort women. The South Korean comfort women were the first ones to speak out. And I watched them here in my living room. And they wanted justice and compensation and an apology, more than anything else. They wanted an apology from the Japanese government. And they weren't getting anywhere. They were getting nowhere. And I thought, 'I must back up these women. Now it's time to speak out.'"[16] Given the timing of 1992, it is possible that Ruff-O'Herne was referring to the televised coverage of Hwang Geum-joo's testimonial in Geneva.

Radio played a pivotal role in locating survivors the Philippines.[17] Maria Rosa Henson was moved to come forward after hearing "Nelia Sancho and a colleague from Gabriela ... discussing sex slaves of the Japanese army on Philippine AM radio DZRH in August 1992 with broadcaster Ducky Paredes." Although she was initially reluctant, Henson decided to contact Paredes after hearing a second interview given by Sancho. The Task Force on Filipino "Comfort Women" (TFFCW) and the Asian Women's Human Rights Commission (AWHRC)—Philippine Section organized a press conference with Henson on September 12, 1992.[18] In a detailed account of the multimedia campaign to locate survivors by the task force, Indai Lourdes Sajor recalls that in addition to coverage in the seven major daily newspapers, several television shows featured their efforts. The TFFCW also began monitoring Japanese and international news outlets, including TV Asahi, NHK, Mainichi Television, the Kyodo News Agency, the *International Herald Tribune*, *Newsweek*, and *Asiaweek*.[19]

Enduring Memorials 227

The "comfort women" history and contemporary redress movement soon came to be widely documented on independently produced video and film. Video Juku, a Tokyo-based organization that both produces and distributes videos for purchase online, describes itself on its website as "a women's group that creates documentaries in order to achieve a society free of violence and discrimination against women" and is part of "a bigger movement to record testimonies of the former comfort women of the Japanese military."[20] The group has produced *We Shall Always Remember: Tribute to KANG Deuk-Kyung Halmoni* (1997); *Memories of Da-niang: Testimonies of the Chinese Grannies* (1999); *The Testimony of Rosalind: The Former "Comfort Woman" in Malaysia* (dir. Tokunaga Risa, 2000); and *"Comfort Women" Recorded in Photographs: The Testimony of Paku Yonsim in North Korea* (dir. Aono Emiko, 2000). In 2001 Video Juku produced a sixty-eight-minute documentary, *Breaking the History of Silence: The Women's International War Crimes Tribunal on Japan's Military Sexual Slavery*. The following year, it produced a thirty-three-minute video on the Hague Final Judgment delivered on December 4, 2001. In addition, the website lists for purchase several other videos: *One Truth: A Hainanese "Comfort Woman" Testifies* (dir. Foo Choo Wei, 1998); *Burma's Vanished "Comfort Women"* (dir. Morikawa Machiko, 1999); and *Testimony by Ha Sang Suk (the Former Korean "Comfort Woman" in Muhan, China)* (dirs. Noriko Seyama and Suda Kaori, 2000).

Several longer, feature-length documentaries have been shown in theaters and film festivals and broadcast on television internationally. In 1995 Korean feminist filmmaker Byun Young-joo directed the ninety-eight-minute *Murmuring (Nateunmoksori)*, which is also distinguished as the first documentary film to be shown in commercial theaters in South Korea. It was also screened at several international film festivals. *Murmuring* was the first of a trilogy that went on to include *Habitual Sadness* (1997) and *My Own Breathing* (1999). According to Chungmoo Choi, *Habitual Sadness* was "made at the request of the comfort women themselves."[21] Also in 1999, Dai Sil Kim-Gibson's documentary *Silence Broken: Korean Comfort Women* screened at several conferences and international film festivals; it was also broadcast in May 2000 on PBS.

When a group of Korean survivors began making drawings and paintings as "art therapy," these artworks also began to circulate in traveling exhibits. These survivors' artworks added a group of especially wrenching but also angry and defiant images to this ever-expanding and mobile catalogue of visual representations of the Japanese military "comfort system." In the fall of 2000, an exhibit called "Quest for Justice: The Story of Korean 'Comfort Women' as Told Through Their Art" traveled throughout the United States and also appeared in Toronto.[22] At what was titled "The World Conference on Japanese

Military Sexual Slavery" in October 2007 at the University of California at Los Angeles, attendees could purchase canvas bags and posters featuring the survivors' artworks. These drawings and paintings have been published in numerous books and articles and showcased in documentaries. They continue to proliferate across various websites and videos in cyberspace.

CONTENDING WEBSITES

The internet has functioned as an especially dynamic staging ground and an expanding archive of multimedia contestations around the issue. Indeed, one could compose an interesting, situated history of the medium's key technological innovations and their political uses by social movements in the 1990s and beyond by tracking how the "comfort women" problematic was staged in the rapidly changing cyber realm. There have been several websites devoted specifically to the "comfort women" case. For much of the 1990s, Chunghee Sarah Soh and Jerry Boucher maintained a site titled "Comfort Women: A Web Reference," which included several links to other relevant sites.[23] The Washington Coalition for Comfort Women Issues has long maintained an English-language website at www.comfort-women.org.[24] The websites of other nongovernmental organizations have also publicized and recorded specific protests, hearings, inquiries, and tribunals. These sites also solicit donations both on behalf of direct aid to the surviving women and to sustain the organizations. Many other international organizations have addressed the topic on their websites but do not focus exclusively on it, including the Center for Women's Global Leadership, Solidarity Philippines Australia Network, Amnesty International, and V-Day. More recently, activists and supporters have used social networking sites such as Facebook and Instagram to commemorate past events as well to publicize current events and mobilize future actions.

The advocacy websites have proliferated alongside ideologically conflicting websites, which demand careful cross-site analysis and contextualization of "comfort women" in cyberspace. In their assessment of the large number of websites that emerged in the 1990s to debate Japan's role in World War II, Tessa Morris-Suzuki and Peter Rimmer discern a clear dichotomy between websites with a "critical view of the Japanese state's responsibility for wartime misdeeds" and those espousing a "'revisionist position' (which disputes the reality or minimizes the importance of these misdeeds)." They insightfully observe how these opposing websites focus on and showcase very different *kinds* of material. The "critical" websites include a diverse range of evidence including official documents, archival photographs, and survivors' testimonials, but the "revisionist" websites are largely focused on debunking the testimonials provided by the surviving women and also a few Japanese veterans through honing in on small inconsistencies, especially about whether the women were forcibly recruited. Warning against the fragmenting and polarizing tendency of these contested representations, Morris-Suzuki and Rimmer argue for a more "balanced" approach that "combin[es] the Internet with other media (including books, TV documentaries or video) to provide a wider analysis of the social structures at work in shaping history."[25] I would argue that it is impossible and futile to attempt to *balance* the radically opposed interests and interpretations of these contending websites. But I do agree with Morris-Suzuki and Rimmer in their call for a "wider analysis," which includes situating the "comfort women" problematic within a broader history of varied and changing media technologies and their political uses.

The website hosted by the Korean Council (www.womenandwar.net) has long presented a rich, dynamic example of both cyber-activism and cyber-memorial. It has included many of the conventional features of NGO and INGO sites, including the organization's history, a signature campaign, a newsletter, interviews with survivors, and a portal for monetary contributions.[26] The home page has centrally featured a regularly updated roll of news on significant activities such as the Asian Solidarity Conference on the Issue of Military Sexual Slavery by Japan, which was most recently convened in Seoul for its fifteenth meeting in March 2018. For much of the 2000s the Korean Council website was divided into four sections: "About Us," "Wednesday Demonstration," "War & Women's Human Rights Center," and a "Cyber Memorial."

The first "Wednesday Demonstration" in front of the Japanese Embassy in Seoul was held on January 8, 1992, to protest the impending visit of Japanese Prime Minister Kiichi Miyazawa, and they have been repeated weekly since. Much photographed and filmed, the "Wednesday Demonstration" has become the signature tactic of the Korean Council. A time line of significant moments in its history illustrates how the target of the protest on a specific Wednesday has shifted to an expanding cluster of publications, public statements by politicians, and media productions, which span national-bilateral-regional-transnational frames. The demonstration on July 20, 1994, "protested against the Japanese government's plan to compensate the survivors through the private fund of 'Asian Women's Fund,' which would allow the Japanese government to avoid its responsibility for the issues." The Asian Women's Fund was singled out again on May 3, 1995, and on May 29, 1996. For the two-hundredth demonstration, on January 17, 1996, the protesters "demanded the Japanese government's prompt acceptance of the report on the issues of Military Sexual Slavery by Japan by the United Nations special rapporteur." The June 3, 1998, demonstration targeted a Japanese film, *Pride, the Moment of Destiny*, which "depicted the A-class World War II criminal Tojo Hideki as a hero." The protest on February 28, 2001, spotlighted the omission and reduced coverage of the "comfort women" history in Japanese middle school textbooks, and the protest on April 10, 2002, was aimed at Japanese high school textbooks. As part of the "Global Day of Action for Justice to Comfort Women," August 10, 2005, was heralded as a "Worldwide Wednesday Demonstration" day, with allied demonstrations held in sixty different locations.

As evident in that litany, the Korean Council has long been actively invested in the proper remembrance of the past across various media. At one point, the "Cyber Memorial" comprised four sections with the following headings: "Remember the Past," "Rise for Justice," "Move to the Future," and "Establishment of the Museum." The first section, "Remember the Past," was divided into four further sub-pages titled "Photos," "Victims," "Testimonies," and "Paintings," which was a cyber-gallery of nine drawings and paintings by Korean survivors. The twenty-one black-and-white photographs began with a photo of Japanese written script identified as "Comfort station rules by the commissary in the battle line in China, 1933" and included photos of the interior of a "comfort station" and a line of waiting Japanese soldiers outside another station.[27] The "Testimonies" section contained the individual stories of eight women, and the "Rise for Justice" section presented images of contemporary protests.

In June 2001 the Korean Council formed an "affiliated organization" called the War and Women's Human Rights Center (WWHRC) with a broadened objective of performing research, monitoring, and advocacy on other historical occurrences of violations of women's human rights in armed conflict in Korea and elsewhere. Its inaugural project was holding the "1st Open Symposium for Writing a History Book from the Korean and Japanese Women's Point of View" in October 2001. Then, in December 2001, the WWHRC published testimonies and "opened the Cyber Reference Lab for Military Sexual Slavery issues and women's human rights." Under the rubric of the WWHRC, the Korean Council worked across print and visual media in several registers, including setting up a "Multimedia Department" in March 2003 and holding two symposia on writing history books in June and October. In December 2003 the Korean Council also produced a film, *History of the Activities for the Japanese Military Sexual Slavery by Japan Issues*, and an educational video, *War and Women*.[28]

The Korean Council also used its website to raise funds for the construction of a War and Women's Human Rights Museum. As Yun Chung-ok explained, the purpose was to "re-create the history of the 'sex slaves' in order to ensure that this cannot happen again to future generations of women, and to educate and increase the number of peace-loving people who deeply value human rights." The goal was buttressed by the expressed desire for a museum by two pictured survivors. Hwang Geum-joo disclosed that she had been setting aside 100,000 won of her monthly stipend from the South Korean government in order to contribute to the museum construction fund. Gil Won-ok's account was even more enthusiastic and hopeful: "The fact that even though I will die, the victimization I suffered won't be forgotten—even in the midst of my suffering, it makes me feel so fortunate that I've survived for this long." She added that "I hope that our descendants will be able to see and learn as much as possible about our history at the museum so they won't be deceived the way we were, they won't have to suffer through the same ordeals, and so they don't ever have to live through such bleak, dangerous times."[29] All three statements bespeak an abiding faith in museums as effective channels of historical recreation, moral education, and perpetual remembrance. The website also listed these three projected functions of the War and Women's Human Rights Museum:

1   Introduces the development and methods of the campaign to settle issues involving real facts about the Japanese military "sex slaves" and the history of the relationship between war and women's human rights.
2   Will take its place in the ranks of famous sites in Korean feminist history.
3   Will become a base for international exchange between women and the development of feminist issues.[30]

The three numbered goals are not as easy to distinguish or align; the materials necessary for one enterprise would exceed the rubric of the other two. The particular complexities of the first goal, which are quite vast and far-flung, extend beyond the explicitly ethno-national borders of the second goal. On the other hand, the specific history of Japanese military sexual slavery in World War II is at risk of being rendered as one among many subjects in a too generic horizon of women and feminism under the third goal.[31] On May 5, 2015, after nine years of planning and fund raising, the War and Women's Human Rights Museum opened at Seongsan-dong in Seoul.[32]

With the "brick-and-mortar" museum constructed, along with its own dedicated website, the current iteration of the Korean Council website (January 2019) has greatly reduced the cyber-memorial component. It now features three sub-pages. The "What Is Japanese Military Sexual Slavery System" sub-page features three black-and-white photographs: a straw mat inside a "comfort station," the U.S. Signal Corps photograph of Park Young-sim and three other women alongside the Chinese soldier (see figure 5.6 in chapter 5), and Kim Hak-sun at the August 14, 1991, press conference. The following sub-page, "History of the Movement," features two lists of demands, the first directed at the South Korean government and the second at the Japanese government. The first list of demands is largely a direct response to the 2015 bilateral agreement:

1. Annulment of the 2015 Korea-Japan agreement and return of the 1 billion yen provided by the Japanese government.
2. Cancellation of the certification of the Foundation for Reconciliation and Healing established with the 1 billion yen from the Japanese government.
3. Investigation of the process through which the 2015 Korea-Japan agreement was reached.
4. Inclusion of an accurate treatment of the Japanese military sexual slavery issue in schools and social education curriculum.[33]

In June 2016 a new activist formation called the Foundation for Justice and Remembrance for the Issue of Military Sexual Slavery by Japan was established with the explicit goal of having the 2015 bilateral agreement annulled.[34] In August 2016 twelve Korean survivors sued the South Korean government, each seeking 100 million won, for signing the 2015 deal and thereby failing to hold Japan legally responsible for its military "comfort system." In July 2018 the Korean Council merged with the Foundation for Justice and Remembrance. The full name of this new organization is the Korean Council for Justice and Remembrance for the Issues of Military Sexual Slavery by Japan.

THE DIGITAL MUSEUM

The Digital Museum for the Comfort Women Issue and the Asian Women's Fund is not the first virtual museum to address the issue. The South Korean government has long maintained an "e-Museum of the Victims of Japanese Military Sexual Slavery," which is operated by the Ministry of Gender Equality and Family.[35] The Digital Museum presents an interesting supplement and contrast to the e-Museum and the website of the Korean Council. The Digital

Museum illustrates that as much as the internet has been crucial for publicizing injuries and demanding justice, it has also become a virtual portal for exhibiting atonement. Recall that the early demands by the Korean Council called for governmental acknowledgment of the factualness of this history, an official apology, full disclosure, memorialization, and history education. Over its twelve years in operation, the Asian Women's Fund produced numerous publications about the comfort women issue but also on other issues of women's human rights, including violence against women, trafficking, labor migration, and HIV/AIDS. It even produced a thirty-minute video on its own activities. A website would thus seem to a wide-ranging and flexible, if not ideal, medium for preserving and making these materials available to public view. As for the demand for compensation, the Digital Museum relays both a careful accounting of the different sums dispensed to individual survivors as well as the total sum spent by each country on medical care and social service projects; it supplements those monetary figures with narrative, photographic, and audiovisual displays of the payments and their appreciative receipt.

In February 2008, Wada Haruki, identified as the "original proponent and executive managing director" of the Digital Museum, composed a short article that was translated into English and published online by the *Asia-Pacific Journal*.[36] As Wada explains, the idea of a permanent *digital* museum was activated partly in response to the conservative movement within Japan to retract and revise the 1993 Kono Statement, which began in 1996 and continued throughout the 2000s:

> Looking back over these events, the Asian Women's Fund decided to set up a digital museum, "The Comfort Women Issue and the Asian Women's Fund." The first purpose was to have the understanding arrived at by the government of Japan and the Asian Women's Fund on the Comfort Women question preserved permanently and become the basis for the way the Japanese people understand the matter. The government has released the materials it had collected on the Comfort Women problem. The second purpose was to clarify the way in which the Asian Women's Fund was initiated, how it conducted its business, and what it accomplished. To that end, by providing detailed explanation of the Fund, and preserving and publishing as much as possible of related materials, we have made it possible for them to be subjected to critical study.[37]

The first purpose, permanent preservation, echoes a standard museum function, but we must ask this: preservation of what? Far from being a material object or even a significant historical event, *it* here is "the understanding arrived at by the government of Japan and the Asian Women's Fund of the Comfort Women question." Thus, what has been preserved is both a cognitive achievement of and an agreement between two different parties. But the second stated purpose is a clarification about the origin and actions of only one of those two parties, the AWF, which already anticipates that "the Fund" will be subject to "critical study."

The choice to name the website as the Digital Museum for the Comfort Women Issue and the Asian Women's Fund and to integrate certain conventional museum features—such as the naming of the sections as "halls"—invites scrutiny. The home page presents a front facade of a computer-generated two-story building (figure 7.1). There is no discussion of the website's conceptualization and design even as it bears the proprietary "Copyright(c) Asian Women's Fund. All rights reserved" at the bottom of almost every page. What is the aim and function of rendering its portal as the front entry to a virtual building that simulates an offline, real-world museum? One could say that it tries to fulfill a key demand by survivors and NGOs for a memorial. The image visually buttresses the naming of the website as a *museum*, which harnesses its multiple valences as enduring repository of heritage, historical knowledge, and cultural achievement, on the one hand, and as effective mechanism of remembrance, exhibition, pedagogy, and enculturation, on the other.[38] Another obvious frame of reference is the proliferation of Holocaust museums and memorials. The "museum" designation also aligns the website with the many peace museums throughout Japan, including the Women's Active Museum on War and Peace, which was established in the summer of 2005 to mark the sixtieth anniversary of the end of World War II. As Arjun Appadurai and Carol Breckenridge have pointed out, the meanings and forms of museums are further brought into critical relief when considered within a postcolonial, transnational frame: "Today, museums reflect complex mixtures of state and private motivation and patronage, and tricky transnational problems of ownership, identity, and the politics of heritage. Thus museums, which frequently represent national identities both at home and abroad, are also nodes of transnational representation and repositories for subnational flows of objects and images. Museums, in concert with media and travel, serve as ways in which national and international publics learn about themselves and others."[39]

A *digital* museum avoids several practical and political problems of an emplaced structure. Aside from the construction and maintenance costs of a material building, the wide compass of the past atrocity and the current transnational redress movement complicates the choice of geographical location. More significantly, the virtual form circumvents the possibility that a physical museum, especially if it housed the carefully edited artifacts and texts of the extant five halls of the Digital Museum, would very likely become the target *and* physical location of future protest actions. To point that out is not to criticize or cast suspicion on the virtuality of the Digital Museum. As Elisa Giaccardi reminds us, "All museums are virtual, independent of information technologies. Museums extract each piece from an environment that, as the site of origin, is deemed to hold some significance. The piece is then transferred to a new site, the museum, in which the relationships with its original environment and time are recreated. In this sense, museums are virtual because they collect pieces that work as a switch to 'something else.'" Considering this traffic in artifacts across space and time, Giaccardi also adds that the "pieces placed and arranged within a museum" are also virtual: "They present the ambiguity of being physically tangible as a museum piece, but also being subject to change according to different perspectives in which they can be interpreted and displayed."[40]

Pressing "Next" on the home page takes the visitor to what looks like a large wall plaque, bearing a message, dated March 2007, by Murayama, the former Japanese Prime Minister and the final President of the Asian Women's Fund (figure 7.2). The message begins with a lengthy quotation from Murayama's statement on August 15, 1995, and then continues in a retrospective register:

> On the morning of that day, an appeal of the Asian Women's Fund (AWF) for national atonement for the former comfort women was made public in full-page advertisements which appeared in six national newspapers.
>
> Thus the AWF started its activities to atone for those women made to be "ianfu" by joint efforts of the government and the people, and to tackle the problems of honour and dignity of women in a contemporary world. We have finished our activities finally as of March 2007.
>
> In keeping a record of our awareness of the comfort women issue and of our atonement project so that people can learn a lesson from history, we have decided to establish a digital museum "The Comfort Women Issue and the Asian Women's Fund." I sincerely hope that everyone who visits this museum will not forget this history, and will redouble their commitment to reconciliation and cooperation in Asia and the world.[41]

This "origin story" presages several of the quandaries enacted in the rest of the Digital Museum. The first revolves around temporal demarcation: August 1995 to March 2007. Here, August 15, 1995, commemorates two linked yet very different events: the fiftieth anniversary of the end of World War II but also the publication of the first nationwide call for private donations to the AWF. The

To our visitors

"During a certain period in the not too distant past, Japan, following a mistaken national policy, advanced along the road to war, only to ensnare the Japanese people in a fateful crisis, and, through its colonial rule and aggression, caused tremendous damage and suffering to the people of many countries, particularly to those of Asian nations. In the hope that no such mistake be made in the future, I regard, in a spirit of humility, these irrefutable facts of history, and express here once again my feelings of deep remorse and state my heartfelt apology. Allow me also to express my feelings of profound mourning for all victims, both at home and abroad, of that history."

I stated these words of apology in the statement of the Prime Minister "On the occasion of the 50th anniversary of the War's End" dated August 15, 1995. On the morning of that day, an appeal of the Asian Women's Fund (AWF) for national atonement for the former comfort women was made public in full-page advertisements which appeared in six national newspapers.

Thus the AWF started its activities to atone for those women made to be "ianfu" by joint efforts of the government and the people, and to tackle the problems of honour and dignity of women in a contemporary world. We have finished our activities finally as of March 2007.

In keeping a record of our awareness of the comfort women issue and of our atonement project so that people can learn a lesson from history, we have decided to establish a digital museum "The Comfort Women Issue and the Asian Women's Fund". I sincerely hope that everyone who visits this museum will not forget this history, and will redouble their commitment to reconciliation and cooperation in Asia and the world.

March 2007

President of the Asian Women's Fund
Tomiichi Murayama
村山富市

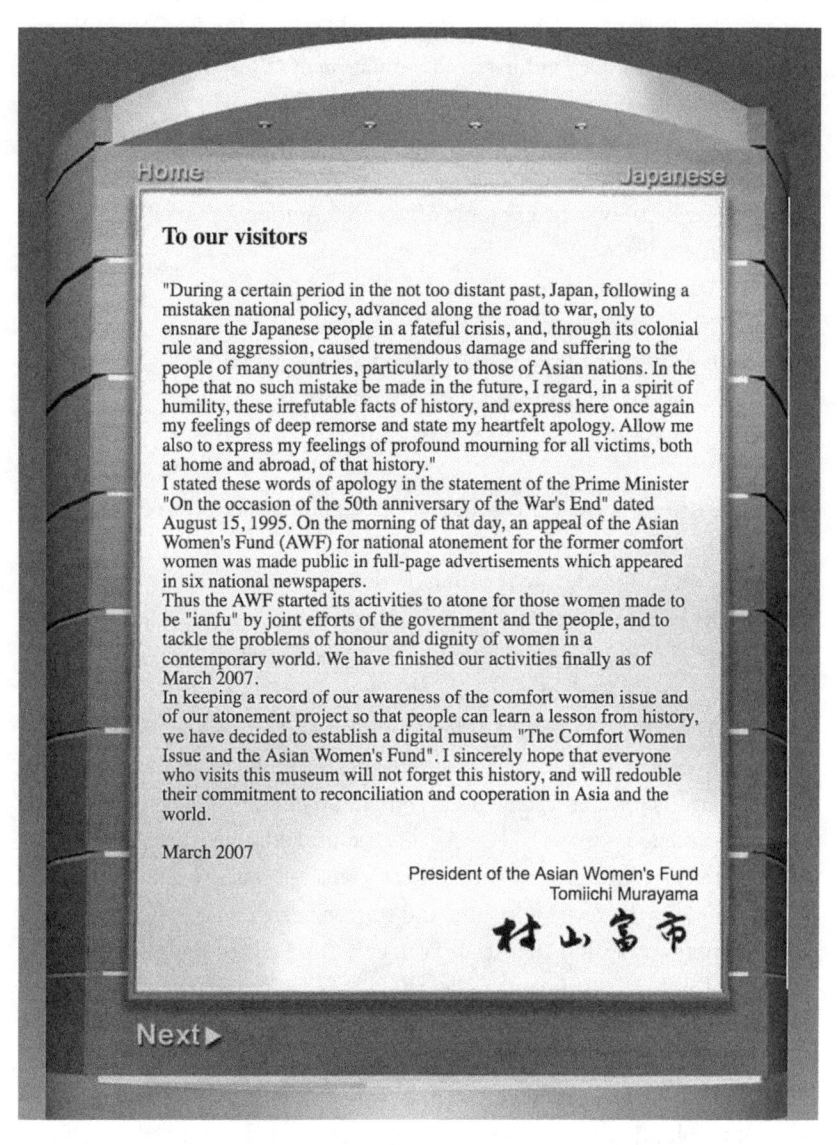

FIGURE 7.2. Photo of the preface page of the Digital Museum for the Comfort Women Issue and the Asian Women's Fund, http://awf.or.jp/e-preface.htm.

detailing of "full-page" and "six national papers" underscores the super-visible scale of this outreach. There is no explanation of why the activities of the AWF were terminated in March 2007, but the Digital Museum promises to extend the "record of our awareness of the comfort women issue and of our atonement project" indefinitely well beyond this date. Finally, Murayama's "welcome" statement uses the awkward passive nomination of "those women made to be 'ianfu'" alongside "former comfort women."

That the primary mission of the Digital Museum is the exhibition of the Asian Women's Fund in virtual form is clarified early on in a Guide Map (figure 7.3), which lists the contents of five different halls:

Hall I: Japanese Military and Comfort Women
Hall II: Establishment of the Asian Women's Fund
Hall III: Atonement Project of the Asian Women's Fund
Hall IV: Various Efforts regarding the Comfort Women Issue
Hall V: The Asian Women's Dignity Project

At the bottom of the page is this disclaimer: "The views expressed in the exhibitions of this museum were all formulated on the responsibility of the Asian Women's Fund." But who are the subjects that must or could bear "responsibility" for this peculiar historical-economic-political-cultural formation? Then, too, who or what are the agencies that can accredit such an enterprise?

Rather than a clear-cut diagnosis of success or failure, I propose to read the Digital Museum in terms of different and conflicting responsibilities under changing terms and conditions of international publicity and transnational justice. First, its form and some of its content are *responsive to* demands for official acknowledgment and full disclosure. It must address a transnational public produced and sustained by the "critical" websites, but also a more skeptical public hailed by the revisionist sites and the recursive denials of coercion and official sanction. In 1999 the Asian Women's Fund edited and published five volumes of archival documents under the title *Seifu Chousa "Jugun Ianfu" Kankei Shiryou Shuusei (Compilation of Government-Collected Documentary Materials Relating to Wartime "Comfort Women")*, and all of these volumes can be downloaded via the archives sub-page of the Digital Museum.[42] The volumes range from 581 pages (volume 1) to 291 pages (volume 5). Most of the archival documents and photographs that are featured on other pages of the website are credited to this source with the shortened title *Shiryoushusei*. All of the documents in volumes 1–3 are typed or handwritten in Japanese. The very end of volume 4 has three pages with some English text that appears in some tables listing

To our visitors

Hall I : Japanese Military and Comfort Women
- Who were the Comfort Women?/ Number of Comfort Stations and Comfort Women/ Their life in comfort stations
- Women made to become Comfort Women
  - Philippines/ South Korea/ Taiwan/ Netherlands/ Indonesia/ Other countiries

Hall II : Establishment of the Asian Women's Fund
- How did the Comfort Women Issue come to light?
- Establishment of the AWF and the basic concept of its projects

Hall III : Atonement Project of the Asian Women's Fund
- Projects by country or region
  - Philippines/ South Korea/ Taiwan/ Netherlands/ Indonesia
- Testimonies of the victims
- Messages from Japanese contributors
- Memoirs of the persons who have engaged themselves with the AWF
- Closing of the Asian Women's Fund

Hall VI:Various Efforts regarding the Comfort Women Issue
- Discussions in international organizations, Eg. United Nations
- Lawsuits in Japanese Courts
- Attempts at legislation in the Japanese Diet

Hall V : The AWF's Women's Dignity Project
- Round Table: Aim and effect of the project
- Promotion/Support/Communication/Research

Archives
- Historical documents regarding the Comfort Women issue
- Materials regarding the Asian Women's Fund
  - Documents of the Japanese Government and the AWF
  - Protocols of board meetings and attached materials
  - Publications and videos issued by the Asian Women's Fund

The views expressed in the exhibitions of this museum were all formulated on the responsibility of the Asian Women's Fund.

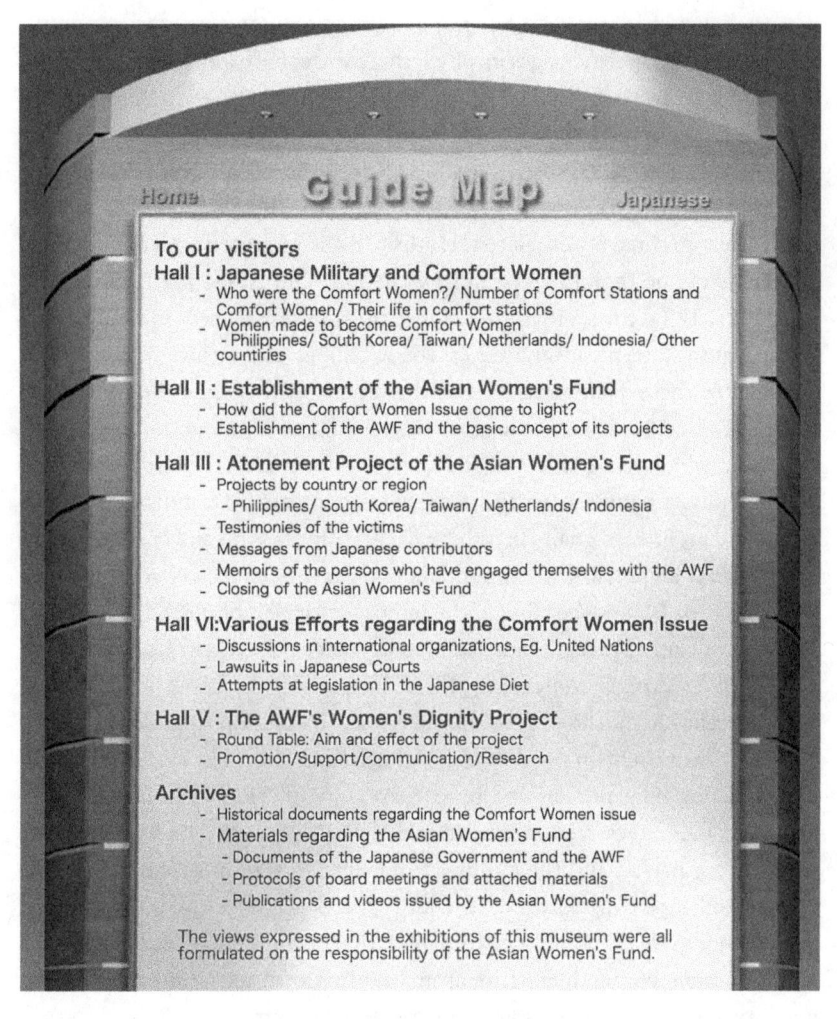

FIGURE 7.3. Photo of the "Guide Map" of the Digital Museum for the Comfort Women Issue and the Asian Women's Fund, http://awf.or.jp/e-guidemap.htm.

different female occupations, including "Prostitute" and "Comfort Girl." Volume 5 features copies of the English-language interrogation reports of Japanese prisoners of war grouped according to the three different agencies: the Allied Translator and Interpreter Section (ATIS), the South East Asia Translation and Interrogation Center (SEATIC), and the United States Office of War Information (OWI). But only the OWI *Japanese Prisoner of War Interrogation Report No. 49* is reproduced in its entirety. For the most part, volume 5 includes reproductions of only the specific pages in which there was some explicit mention of the "comfort system"—almost always referred to as "brothels"—which produces a somewhat disjointed reading experience but also reframes the significance of these archival traces.[43] Rather than provide insights into the organization and conditions of the "comfort system," their repeated though truncated appearances attest to three other related "truths": (1) the interest in and documented awareness of the "comfort system" by the U.S. and Allied militaries during World War II, (2) the archiving *and* forgetting of these records in the U.S. and Great Britain after the war, and (3) the assiduous excavation, reproduction, and relay of these documents to the cyber-public by the Asian Women's Fund and the Digital Museum in the present. The digital reproduction of archival materials, which bears traces of their original form as fuzzy black-and-white photographs or handwritten and redacted documents from military and governmental archives, signals their unmediated transmission and creates the impression that all possibly relevant documents have been located and rendered to public view. Second, because of the intense criticisms of the Asian Women's Fund, the Digital Museum must assiduously *account for* its efforts to publicize and fulfill its various atonement projects, especially the cases of acceptance and appreciation on the part of the survivors. In addition to enumerating its monetary disbursements and resource allocations, the Digital Museum demonstrates due diligence on and by the AWF. In addition to historical documents, the Archives section also includes important AWF communications with various parties and the minutes from all of its staff meetings. These two responsibilities of disclosure and fiscal-operational accountability exist in tension alongside and against a third operation of the Digital Museum, which *arbitrates among* contending national and transnational accounts of the history, invalidating and criticizing some and upholding others.

Hall I ("Japanese Military and Comfort Women") exhibits a fascinating mix of transparency, accountability, justification, and pointed skepticism. The first page introduces the contents: "In this hall, it is to be described how the comfort station [sic] were made in the war time, and how the victims were brought there." The repeated passive verb form is peculiar and especially suspect in the last instance. This subject-less locution is repeated throughout the Digital Museum. Anticipating objections to the decision to use the contested term *comfort women* in the name of the Digital Museum, the first section, titled "Who Were the Comfort Women?," begins with this densely layered explanation:

> The so-called "wartime comfort women" were those who were taken to former Japanese military installations, such as comfort stations, for a certain period during wartime in the past and forced to provide sexual services to officers and soldiers. Authors who wrote about these women in the postwar Japan called them *"jugun ianfu* (comfort women joining the army)." And when the Japanese government first faced the issue of these women, it adopted this term, *"jugun ianfu,"* and the AWF, when it started in 1995, it used this term as well. But in historical wartime documents we only find the term *"ianfu* (comfort women)." Therefore, we now always use this term *"ianfu* (comfort women)."[44]

The brief reference to coercion is counterbalanced by the use of the less damning and more equivocal term *sexual services*, as well as the temporal specification of "a certain period." The decision to stick to *ianfu* as a gesture of historical and archival accuracy is supported with a large image of an official military document dated June 27, 1940, which was issued and stamped by Yoshihide Hayashi, commander of the Hayashi Regiment, Shioda Corps, Expeditionary Army in South China, which was reproduced in *Shiryoshushei*. An English translation of the document, provided in a hyperlinked window, reads: "This man is a manager of the comfort station attached to our regiment, who has returned to Japan in order to take back comfort women. As comfort women are indispensable to give comfort to the men of our regiment, I would like to ask those related to these activities to assist women to come abroad." The three characters of *ianfu* in the photo reproduction are underlined in red. Several other Japanese archival documents follow, which individually but also as a whole clearly illustrate official military knowledge about and coordination of the "comfort system." This corrects the early government denials but also supports the 1993 Kono Statement and counters the later qualifications and demurrals by Japanese politicians, which continue to provoke new protests and charges of unfinished atonement.

However, the authorial position of the Asian Women's Fund is not wholly aligned with the survivors and activists, especially regarding their emphasis on force and deception in the recruitment of the girls and women. The odd locution of "Women Were Collected" is the title of a sub-page of Hall I, which starts out with a rather elliptical note that "the military would often designate certain people as business agents and commission them to bring women from Japan," followed by a "request to support women traveling to provide comfort to the Imperial Army," which was sent by the chief of police at the Shanghai Consulate-General to the chief of Nagasaki Marine Police in December 1937. The following, detailed account of how this "collection" of women unfolded first in Japan and Taiwan and later in Korea and China connects the Digital Museum in a fascinating yet also questionable way back to the League of Nations and specifically to the 1921 Convention for the Suppression of Traffic in Women and Children. According to this narrative, in response to the request for women from Shanghai, "In early 1938, agents canvassed in different parts of Japan, hoping to employ 3,000 women to serve in the Imperial Army's comfort stations in Shanghai. Their efforts were criticized by the police in different parts of Japan, who equated the agents' efforts with kidnapping unsuspecting women and said that they were tarnishing the honor of the Imperial Army." The story continues: "The reaction of the Director of the Police Bureau of the Home Ministry was to issue a memorandum on February 23, 1938, stipulating that all recruited women had already to be involved in prostitution in Japan, be at least 21 years of age, and obtain permission from their parent or guardians to go overseas."[45] A photo reproduction of an announcement from the Adjutant of the Ministry of War, dated March 4, 1938, avowing that "in the future, armies in the field will control the recruiting of women and will use scrupulous care in selecting people to carry out this task" is followed by the comment that "the stipulation that the women must be at least 21 was made because the International Convention for the Suppression of Traffic in Women and Children, which Japan had ratified, prohibited the prostitution of minors."

Further down this page, when the discussion moves to "how were women collected in Taiwan and Korea," there is more doubt and equivocation about whether "the rules in effect in Japan" were duly applied by the authorities and followed in practice. Citing the research of historian Zhu Delan about an effort to recruit women from Taiwan and take them to work in military "comfort stations" in Hainan in 1939, which confirmed that these women were "at least 21 years old and already involved in prostitution," the authors add rather vaguely: "In this case, it would appear that the rules in effect in Japan were also applied when recruiting from Taiwan, although whether they were always followed is unknown. Because in ratifying the International Convention for the Suppression of Traffic in Women and Children in 1925, the Japanese government excluded the colonies from its application."[46] The following page is quite explicit in indicating that these stipulations were most likely *not* followed in Korea. Although the authors begin by stating that "it is natural to assume that, in the beginning, the women from Korea were already involved in prostitution," they add, "over time, women from poor families mainly came to be taken." The passive construction is intermingled and counterbalanced with statements of greater certitude: "They were enticed in a variety of ways. There are clear evidences that, even in the early days, some were told lies about what their work would be. It is recognized that those recruiters often resorted to coaxing and intimidating those women to be recruited against their own will, and there were even cases where administrative/ military personel [sic] directly took part in the recruitments." Most incriminating of the fact that the 1921 Convention was flouted with respect to Korean girls and women is a photocopy of the records of the examination for "sexual diseases" by the Japanese Military Medical Office in Ilolio on June 23, 1942, which lists the ages of the girls and women that were examined at two "comfort stations." Two were only sixteen years old, three were eighteen, two were nineteen, and two others were twenty. As the authors of the Digital Museum text clearly point out, "many women were taken from Korea were under the age of 21, something not allowed in Japan. Some were no more than 16 or 17, and had been in no previous contact with the world of prostitution."[47]

The following sub-page, titled "The Pacific War and Spreading of Comfort Station," extends this accounting of the active role of the Japanese military in the forceful and duplicitous recruitment of girls and women and their transportation to the new territories that the Japanese Imperial Army was conquering and annexing, such as Borneo and Burma. The archival documents of the U.S. military and specifically the Office of War Information Psychological Warfare Team's *Japanese Prisoner of War Interrogation Report No. 49* make a prominent appearance at the bottom of this page. A block quotation from the report is bookended by two statements that support the claims of survivors that they did not knowingly volunteer for the Japanese military "comfort system": "It appears that the women and girls were not clearly told they would be required to serve as comfort women," and then, "In such cases the agents tricked them, basically recruiting them against their will."[48] This repeated acknowledgment of the deceptive methods of recruitment used by *private* agents is notably offset by the matter-of-fact characterization of the Kitamuras, who were identified in the OWI interrogation report as "Japanese Civilians," but are described here in the Digital Museum as "a Korean couple, operating a restaurant in Seoul."[49]

The *Japanese Prisoner of War Interrogation Report No. 49* is referenced again in a later sub-page titled, "Life in the Comfort Stations." This section opens starkly, "Women at comfort stations were forced to render sexual services to many officers and men, their human dignity trampled upon." Two reproductions of black-and-

Enduring Memorials 243

white photographs taken by Murase Moriyasu of Japanese soldiers waiting in line outside and posted signs inside a "comfort station" in China are followed by this ambiguous summary of whether the women had been paid, a sore point of contention in the ongoing debates: "In ordinary comfort stations soldiers were paying a certain sum of money directly or indirectly. The sum of money was usually divided into halves between proprietor and comfort women. But it was not clear whether the sum of money was handed to women surely." The authors then add, "The records of a prisoner-of-war interrogation conducted by the U.S. military include the claim that, at a comfort station run by a Korean manager in Myitkyina, Burma, the women were free to go on outings, participated in sports, and had picnics, giving the impression that the comfort woman had an elegant lifestyle. However, we might take into account the fact that these were testimonies before the U.S. military interrogators." The note of qualification and skepticism at the end raises but also further confuses the question about the credibility of these statements and their transcription. The harrowing U.S. Signal Corps photograph #III-SC-230147 of four Korean women survivors and a Chinese soldier in the aftermath of the Allied bombing of Sung Shan (fig. 5.6, chapter 5) appears at the bottom of the sub-page, but it is captioned here as "Korean women who survived and were protected in Lameng, Yunnan."[50]

Hall II ("Establishment of the AWF") contains two sub-pages, the first titled "How did the Comfort Women Issue come to light?" and a second that details the establishment of the Asian Women's Fund. In answer to the first question, the sub-page begins with "It cannot be said that people in Japan were completely unaware that there were comfort women during wartime. But there was almost no awareness of the issue as a social problem."[51] Thus, a key distinction is introduced between a simple knowledge of the past phenomenon ("something happened") and a mediated awareness of that past as "a social problem." To unpack that distinction further, the opening sentence obscures three different temporal-epistemological-interpretive frames: (1) contemporaneous awareness of the existence of comfort stations and comfort women in the past, (2) historical memory in the aftermath of that past and on to the present, and (3) present-day interpretations of that history as an "issue" and a "social problem" that must be dealt with in several conflicting ways. These frames of awareness and memory map unevenly onto the ambiguous category of "people *in* Japan" rather than "people of Japan" or "Japanese people." It is unclear whether that choice expresses a shorthanded acknowledgment of the existence of non-Japanese persons (especially but not exclusively Koreans and Taiwanese) who were in Japan during the war as imperial subjects, migrants, conscripted soldiers, and factory workers. More specifically, it could a acknowledging the differential historical consciousness of the *zainichi* (Kor Japanese) as "people *in* Japan" but not "people *of* Japan."

The following paragraph shifts locations to what people *in* Korea must have known and could have suppressed:

> When a campaign for girls to join a girls volunteer labor corps (during the war, girls were mobilized to work at factories mostly munition industries) was launched in Korea in 1943, toward the end of the war period, the rumor spread that corps members would be forced to become comfort women. The Governor-General's office denied the rumors, saying they were being spread maliciously and intentionally without foundation, but this only caused people to believe the rumors even more. This shows that the existence of the comfort women system was not unknown in Korea in 1945. Even after liberation, however, the issue was probably something people preferred not to discuss.[52]

Again, there is an assertion that in Korea, and perhaps even *especially* in Korea, many people were aware of the comfort stations and the forced and deceptive recruitment of Korean girls and women. The concluding sentence, while more speculative, nevertheless asserts that some Koreans had knowledge of the comfort stations during and after the war and thus also implicates them in the forgetting and suppression of the history. Although it points to the significance of democratization in South Korea after 1987 as an important precondition and briefly mentions the 1990 publication of Yun Chung-ok's article in the Korean daily *Hankyoreh*, there is no acknowledgment of the longer history and broader network of Korean feminist activism and scholarship that I described in chapter 1. Instead, this account of how the issue "came to light" singles out the August 1991 press conference by Kim Hak-sun as "the decisive moment" and features a black-and-white photograph of a tearful Kim. The authors then note that "these developments created a shock in Japan, and a movement promoted mainly by women quickly gained ground in the country." This gendered particularization further disregards the longer and earlier antiwar, anti-imperialist, and feminist movements in Japan.[53]

These authorial choices and demurrals are counterbalanced by diligently accounting for the efforts of the Japanese government and the Asian Women's Fund. Much of Hall II is devoted to discussing the various Japanese government-sponsored inquiries and their findings, beginning with the Kato Statement of July 6, 1992, which offered a detailed admission of government involvement but did not admit the use of force in the procurement of the women. In response to

ernment conducted further research and interviewed people
volvement in the comfort stations, including sixteen Korean
n this expanded inquiry, Chief Cabinet Secretary Yohei Kono
nt on August 4, 1993, which acknowledged that the women
ainst their own will, through coaxing coercion, etc."[54] The
lso includes an English translation of the "First Report on the So-Called Wartime Comfort Women Issue," which was drafted by the Subcommittee to Address the Wartime Comfort Women Issue and released publicly on December 7, 1994. However, the qualified imprint of stubborn dissent is parenthetically notated by specifying the document as part of the "(Ruling Parties' Project to Deal with Issues Fifty Years after the War)."[55]

A conspicuous feature of this narrative of growing publicity and official acknowledgment is the detailed enumeration of archival effort and official disclosure: "Finally 117 documents from the Defense Agency, 54 documents from the Ministry of Foreign Affairs were discovered with 19 documents from the National Archives, [of] the United States." A separate "Archives" section offers for download the full five-volume Japanese language publication of 260 relevant archival documents. Granted that this makes the documents available to interested and even skeptical Japanese-literate visitors, the fact that there was no effort to translate or even outline their contents raises questions about the extra-linguistic effect of their inclusion. Rather than offering new insights, the sheer size and length of the five volumes, which range from 294 to 581 pages, solicit belief in a thorough research effort and their unmediated publication. However, they also proclaim a privileged and contingent access to those archives that the AWF enjoyed as a private/public entity.

A second section of the Archives section, titled "Materials regarding the Asian Women's Fund," contains links to full-text translations of the major statements, press releases, official apologies, reports from inquiries, and resolutions by the Japanese government on the comfort women issue as well as major communications and documentation of activities by the Asian Women's Fund. The protocols, minutes, and documents from fifty meetings of the Asian Women's Fund between 1995 and 2001 are all available for download. This provision of administrative documents transfigures the Digital Museum from a charged memorial into a flattened registry of bureaucracy. Marilyn Strathern has drawn attention to the proliferation of "new accountabilities" and "audit regimes" in diverse institutional matrices of late modernity. "That there is culture on the make here," she argues, "is evident from the concomitant emergence, and dominance, of what are deemed acceptable forms." She explains, "Only certain social practices take a form which will convince, one which will persuade those to whom accountability is rendered—whether it is 'the government' or the taxpayer/public—that accountability has indeed been rendered." Pointing to the transnational proliferation of these sanctioned forms and practices, Strathern adds, "Audit regimes accompany a specific epoch in Western international affairs . . . when transparency of operation is everywhere endorsed as the outward sign of integrity."[56] Considered alongside Appadurai and Breckenridge's characterization of museums as "nodes of transnational representation and repositories for subnational flows of objects and images," I would press for a broader regime of visibility and accountability wherein the matter of national heritage is not limited to the preservation and display of cultural artifacts but also involves the exhibition of political-economic redemption within a transnational frame. The Digital Museum instantiates the predicament of atonement—that which one must properly and convincingly exhibit but can never adequately or fully accomplish—in such virtualized registers of the truth and justice.

As I have pointed out, the Digital Museum does not always display contrition or even neutrality. Some instances demonstrate a very partial, self-interested authorship that corrects and chides other, prior accounts and also provides its own distinct conclusions and judgments. Even as the Digital Museum presents key archival evidence of official sanction and involvement, there are also specific places where their truth value is questioned and even explicitly rejected. The subpage on "The Establishment of Comfort Stations" focuses upon General Yasuji Okamura, who is featured in a black-and-white portrait and directly quoted in shaded block text from a 1970 Japanese publication where he admitted, "To speak frankly, I am an initiator of the comfort women project." However, the preceding description of his involvement is more tentative:

> It was *apparently* Yasuji Okamura, at that time the Vice Chief of Staff of the Shanghai Expeditionary Force, who first promoted the establishment of comfort stations for the Japanese army. There were *apparently* a number of reasons for establishing them: Japanese military personnel had raped Chinese civilian women in occupied areas on numerous occasions, and the military hoped to prevent a worsening of anti-Japanese feelings on the part of the Chinese people; there was a need to prevent the spread of venereal diseases among officers and men, as otherwise military effectiveness would be reduced; and it was also feared that contact with Chinese civilian women could result in the leaking of military secrets.[57]

Some may read these repeated equivocations as part and parcel of the long tangle of admissions, denials, and minimizations. However, one could argue that they are also accounting for the persistent contestations over the "truth" of this history and the motivations of its various actors.

Elsewhere, the authors are more direct in questioning and invalidating specific claims. A sub-page titled "Number of Comfort Stations and Comfort Women" in Hall I provides an extended discussion of the varying calculations by Japanese, Korean, and Chinese researchers of the total number of women conscripted. It goes on to contest Kim Il-myon's estimate that 80 to 90 percent of them were Korean: "A careful reading of all available documents shows that many of the women were indeed from Korea, but probably not the overwhelming majority. After all, many of the women were Japanese."[58] This sub-page also targets the 1998 United Nations McDougall report and a specific passage from its appendix: "Between 1932 and the end of the Second World War, the Japanese Government and the Japanese Imperial Army forced over 200,000 women into sexual slavery in rape centers throughout Asia." This is immediately followed by another quote from the McDougall report, which estimated that 25 percent of the women survived. Pointing out that these numbers are taken from "a 1975 [sic] statement by Seijura Arafune, Liberal Democratic Party member of the Japanese Diet, that 145,000 Korean sex slaves had died during the Second World War," the page argues: "None of Arafune figures have any basis whatsoever. It is most unfortunate that Special Rapporteur McDougal [sic], who held a responsible position working for a United Nations organization, relied on such an untrustworthy source. Professor Su Jiliang learned of Arafune's speech from the paper written by Kim Il Myon, accepted it, and used the figure of 142,000 Korean comfort women to estimate that there were 200,000 Chinese comfort women, out of the 360,000 to 410,000 he estimated to have existed in total. Regrettably this mistaken conjecture, too, is simply based on Arafune's inflammatory remarks."[59] Thus, although the Digital Museum includes links to the full text of the 1998 MacDougall report, along with the 1996 Coomaraswamy report in Hall IV under "Discussions in the international organizations, e.g., United Nations," the passage above pointedly undermines their legitimacy and authority in another hall.

Against the temptation to judge such contestations and resignifications as bespeaking a bad-faith commitment to truth and reconciliation, I would steer analytical energies to how the three conflicting tasks of responsiveness, accounting, and arbitration, which I outlined earlier, are exhibited in the mixed-media form of the Digital Museum. This is most evident in Hall III, on the various atonement projects undertaken by the Asian Women's Fund, which is neatly schematized in its opening graphic (figure 7.4).

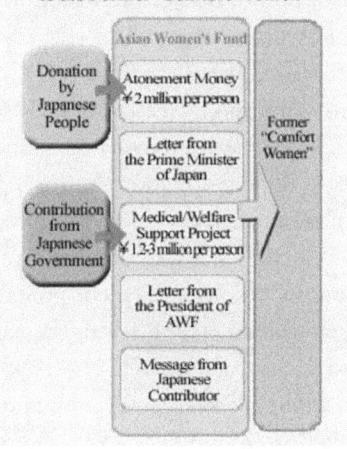

FIGURE 7.4. Photo of the "Hall III: Atonement Project of the Asian Women's Fund" sub-page of the Digital Museum for the Comfort Women Issue and the Asian Women's Fund, http://awf.or.jp/e3/index.html.

According to this unidirectional flow of private and public funds, the "former 'comfort women'" are clearly and, I would add, simply *recipients* of things and services from the two clearly distinguished giving subjects. A photograph of an official letter of apology from the prime minister is prominently featured. There is also a photograph of a pile of letters sent in by individual Japanese donors and translations of some of the earnest messages accompanying the donations.[60] The hall also details the various projects undertaken in each of the countries, providing visual evidence and documentation of AWF efforts and accomplishments, including photocopies of the newspaper advertisements announcing the Asian Women's Fund in South Korea and the Philippines.[61] The visitor can also download the three-page "Memorandum of Understanding between the Department of Social Affairs of the Republic of Indonesia and the Asian Women's Fund concerning Promotion of Social Welfare Services for Elderly People in Indonesia," as well as another MOU between the AWF and the Project Implementation Committee of the Netherlands (PICN) on July 15, 1998.

The reports on South Korea and Taiwan stand in marked contrast to the reports on the Philippines and the Netherlands. The South Korea and Taiwan accounts detail a concerted resistance to the successful implementation of the atonement projects, which is largely attributed to opposition from the two leading NGOs, the Korean Council and the Taipei Women's Rescue Foundation. Both reports allege that survivors were misled into believing that the acceptance of AWF package would compromise or invalidate pending lawsuits for reparations. Nevertheless, the report on Korea includes a link to a video of seven Korean survivors accepting the letter of apology on January 11, 1997. The Philippines report features a photograph of local activist Nelia Sancho and credits her work with LILA-Pilipina in locating and organizing two hundred survivors. It recalls how even though LILA-Pilipina had initially rejected the AWF and its atonement projects, it moved to support several individual women who opted to accept the monetary compensation. A most striking visual documentation of survivors accepting the atonement package appears in the Philippines report. A color photograph shows Maria Rosa Henson, Anastasia Cortez, and Rufina Fernandez holding up copies of the letters from the Japanese Prime Minister and the President of the Asian Women's Fund. This photograph is followed by this block quotation from Henson: "Many other former comfort women and Japanese people in support groups criticized me, saying that I would never regain my human dignity without compensation from Japan itself. There's no contradiction in accepting benefits from the AWF and continuing with the lawsuit, and there's nothing stopping me from doing both." Because she had been such a prominent figure, Henson's acceptance of the moneys was especially significant for both the Asian Women's Fund and other survivors and activists. The Netherlands report features a photograph of Marguerite Hamer-Monod de Froideville, who served as the president of PICN, alongside a quotation from her statement marking the end of the AWF atonement projects in July 2001:

> Although the Project was established not until 53 years after the end of the War, and although no money in the world can ever compensate for what they had to endure in their young days, yet it did indeed bring a sort of peace to the victims, and a kind of justice to them, which they needed. Their lives really have been improved thanks to the AWF, not only because of the financial compensation in the form of the Project money, but also because of the recognition of the wrong doings of the past Mr. Hashimoto's letter has conveyed to them.[62]

Hall III also includes a sub-page titled "Voices of the victims-recipients of the project of the AWF." It relays the recollections of Ms. Mitsuko Shimomora, then Director of the Asian Women's Fund, of her meeting with an unnamed Korean survivor on October 29, 1997, when she delivered the apology and the compensation.[63] This account contrasts sharply to the representation of this act on the Korean Council website, which notes that on January 11, 1997, "'Asian Women's Fund' paid the 'atonement money' to the seven former Korean Military Sexual Slavery by Japan secretly."[64] The Digital Museum then narrates the story of appreciation, forgiveness, and satisfaction expressed by Taiwanese victims upon receipt of the apology and compensation. Finally, the page posts the appreciative notes from four Dutch survivors. The category of "victims-recipients" is an interesting re-signification of the women that stands in contrast to "survivors" or "activists."

Although the digital medium and museum format hold out the promise of open-ended, far-flung engagements, the marked contradictions of this Digital Museum make it liable to multiple refusals and enclosures. Six months after its launch, an article on the Digital Museum was posted on *Japan Times Online*. Dated September 28, 2007, and titled "Web Site Documents Wartime Sex Slaves," the article opened with "A digital museum was recently launched on the Internet to document the activities of a disbanded semiofficial relief organization for former World War II sex slaves, who were euphemistically called 'comfort women.'"[65] The characterization of the Asian Women's Fund as "a disbanded semiofficial relief organization" demotes its significance and authority by casting it back into a finished pastness. This strange locution is repeated in the caption to the accompanying photograph, which is an odd mix of multiply layered images. It is a photograph of two different pages from the Digital Museum. The screen on the left is on the sub-page titled "The Life in Comfort Stations," which features the U.S. Signal Corps photograph (see figure 5.6 in chapter 5) of Korean women in China, which was taken by U.S. soldiers at the end of the war and is housed in the U.S. National Archives. The close-up color portrait on the right is of Kimiko Haneda and appears on a sub-page on "Testimonies of victims" under "Atonement Project of Asian Women's Fund"; Haneda's story is featured as a representative of South Korea along with Maria Rosa Henson representing the Philippines and an unnamed "Taiwanese victim." Notably, all three women are identified as "a recipient of the atonement project of the AWF." Insofar as it stages the perspectival positioning of a generic, everyday computer user, the peculiar composition of the monitors with the keyboard in the foreground pushes both the Digital Museum and the images of the women to the background. The photograph dramatizes how the sheer surfeit, mundane adjacencies, and unmoored malleability of the "comfort women" issue in cyberspace have entailed a blurring of protest and redress but also of who was and is the victim, who was and is the perpetrator, who was and is the jury and adjudicator.

RECOURSE TO MATTER

A widely circulated photograph of the installation of the *Sonyeosang* on December 14, 2011 (figure 7.5), presents a stark and poignant juxtaposition between the young female figure, forever suspended in youth but also pulsating an indeterminate subjectivity—the neutral and blank facial expression and the upright, almost too proper seated position are offset by those clenched fists—and the four elderly women with their fists raised in protest and their four distinctive faces projecting a range of different emotions and intentions.[66] How might we make critical sense of this resolute *re*-materialization and defiantly embodied crowding alongside and against the virtualization and the individualized receipt of apology and atonement of the Digital Museum? Then too, how is it that this statue would come to figure so centrally in a "landmark" and "irrevocable" state-to-state agreement four years later, in 2015?

In addition to the recurring denials and demurrals by the Japanese government, there were also several new, unforeseen political and legal developments bridging these three event-texts from 2007 to 2011 to 2015. Although I have not been able to locate an explicit explanation of why the Asian Women's Fund

FIGURE 7.5. Photo of Korean survivors/activists and the *Sonyeosang*/Statue of Peace in Seoul at the one-thousandth Wednesday Demonstration in December 2011.

ceased its operations in March 2007, I would point out that Abe Shinzo had been elected as prime minister in July 2006. As I pointed out in chapter 1, on March 1, 2017, Prime Minister Abe made this statement to reporters, which signaled a disavowal of the use of forcible recruitment by the Japanese military in the 1993 Kono Statement: "There is no evidence to prove there was coercion, nothing to support it. So, in respect to this declaration, you have to keep in mind that things have changed greatly."[67] Although Abe would abruptly resign a few months later, his brief first tenure as prime minister emboldened Japanese conservatives and specifically those who believed that Japan had been too responsive to activists' demands and international criticisms regarding its military "comfort system."

There was increasing domestic criticism of the South Korean government for its lukewarm support of the redress movement. On August 30, 2011, four months before the statue was installed, the Korean Constitutional Court ruled by a vote of six to three that the South Korean government's failure to act responsibly to resolve the "comfort women" dispute was itself unconstitutional. The ruling also declared that the South Korean government was obligated to enter into arbitration on behalf of the "comfort women" when conventional diplomatic efforts had failed. At a binational summit meeting in Kyoto in December 2011, South Korean President Lee Myung-bak strongly demanded that Japan settle the issue. Although this can be read as a gesture of support, I want to draw attention to its timing in the aftermath of the South Korean court ruling *against* the South Korean government in August 2011. According to one account of this bilateral exchange, Japanese Prime Minister Noda Yoshihiko "counterattacked" in response to Lee's demand: "He demanded that President Lee remove the bronze statue of a young girl seated across the road in front of the Japanese Embassy in Seoul. . . . Lee immediately rejected Noda's demand and warned that second and third statues might be erected if Japan failed to resolve the issue."[68] Thus, the statue came to be deployed as a pawn in inter-state negotiations well before the so-called "landmark agreement" in December 2015.

Abe's election for the second time as Japan's prime minister in 2012 reenergized the "anti-comfort women movement" in Japan and internationally. There was a concerted effort to reformulate the acceptable language for naming and describing the Japanese military "comfort system." There has also been a coordinated attack on the veracity and credibility of various non-Japanese accounts of the "comfort women" history, specifically in the English-language documents of global governance and U.S. textbook representations. As McNeill and McCurry report, "In January of [2014] Abe pledged to 'correct' the international record on comfort women, citing a U.S. textbook that refers to Japan's wartime military brothels. His close confidant, Inada Tomomi, policy chief of the Liberal Democratic Party, expressed outrage in the Diet that American children were being taught 'that our ancestors were a group of rapists, murderers, and kidnappers.' Such accusations violated 'the rights of Japanese children living in the U.S.,' she said."[69]

On September 19, 2014, a group called "The LDP Committee on Reevaluation of Global Information Strategy Headquarters for Regional Diplomatic and Economic Partnership," chaired by Harada Yoshiaki, adopted a resolution declaring that "the 'forced relocation' of the so-called 'comfort women' is rejected as a fact, and so is *sexual abuse*."[70] The resolution went on to declare that the committee "not only denies the responsibility of the Japanese military but also rejects the violation of human rights at the 'comfort stations' itself." Framing this resolution as "the first concrete step towards the denial of 'forced removal,'" Nishino and Nogawa point to a significant detail related to the Asian Women's Fund:

> It was revealed that the Ministry of Foreign Affairs had removed the "Appeal for Donations for the Asian Women's Fund" from the MOFA

homepage. Chief Cabinet Secretary Suga explained in a press conference on October 15 that the homepage was reorganised because it contained a mixture of government and nongovernment documents. But the removal was prompted by a question in the House of Representatives Budget Committee by the aforementioned Mr. Yamada, a member of the House of Representatives, on the following phrase in the appeal: "the act of forcing women, including teenagers, to serve the Japanese armed forces as 'comfort women.'"[71]

The year 2014 also saw a coordinated attack on the *Asahi* newspaper's reporting on the "comfort women" issue in the 1990s. According to a 2015 account by two concerned British journalists, David McNeil and Justin McCurry, the other major Japanese newspapers, namely the conservative *Sankei* and the *Yomiuri Shimbun*, began to publicly criticize the *Asahi*. A four-part series in 2014 in the *Japan News*, the English-language online edition of the *Yomiuri*, asserted that "the Asahi's stories on the comfort women issue over the decades have been a significant factor in the entrenchment of the distorted view that 'the Japanese military systematically and forcibly took away women to serve as comfort women' for its soldiers."[72] On August 5, 2014, the *Asahi Shimbun* published a correction and retraction of its early reporting on the "comfort women" system. By December 2014, a third-party committee convened to review the *Asahi* controversy concluded in its report: "There were careless and indiscreet descriptions as the articles gave the impression that she was forcibly taken away."[73]

In January 2015 approximately 8,700 people filed a class-action lawsuit against the *Asahi Shimbun* in Tokyo District Court. As reported in the *Japan Times*, "the plaintiffs, including researchers, journalists and lawmakers, are demanding ¥10,000 in compensation to each person, arguing that the newspaper 'damaged Japanese people's personal rights and honor.'"[74] Then, in February 2015, another lawsuit was filed against the *Asahi Shimbun* by more than 2,000 plaintiffs demanding that the newspaper "place international advertisements apologising for its coverage of wartime sex slavery, saying it has stained Japan's reputation."[75] The discrediting of the 135-year-old *Asahi* was intended to influence international news coverage and to reframe the "comfort women" issue in the broader transnational public sphere. As McNeill and McCurry recount, "After the *Asahi*'s retraction, we were approached by several Japanese news organizations asking the same question: Wasn't the *Asahi* coverage of Yoshida's testimony on the comfort women issue a major influence on reporting by foreign correspondents?" As McNeil and McCurry explain—and others have also pointed out—this attack on the *Asahi* was connected to "a sustained campaign to discredit the Kono statement, as the region nears the 70th anniversary of the end of World War II this summer."[76]

At the United Nations, the Abe administration has demanded changes to the 1996 Coomaraswamy Report. In October 2014 the Japanese government sent Sato Kuni, its ambassador on human rights, to New York to make a direct request to Coomaraswamy to retract aspects of her 1996 report. Coomaraswamy rejected this request. According to a *New York Times* article about this request, "Calls by right-wing politicians and activists to challenge the women's stories have increased sharply since August, when a major liberal newspaper, the *Asahi Shimbun*, printed a front-page retraction of several articles it published on the issue in the 1980s and 1990s."[77] A *Japan Times* article on the requested revision provides more details: "Coomaraswamy's report was considered controversial in Japan because she concluded that the brothel system should be described as 'military sexual slavery,' given 'the status or condition of a person over whom any or all of the powers attaching to the right of ownership are exercised.' This use of the terms 'sex slavery' and 'sex slaves,' now widely used by Western media outlets and activists, have upset right-leaning Japanese politicians and scholars who allege that working conditions at the 'comfort stations' were no different from those at state-regulated brothels that existed before and after the war in many countries, including Japan."[78]

While the struggle over the proper terminology continues in the UN Commission on Human Rights, another avenue of re-materialization has wended through the UNESCO Memory of the World Register. On June 1, 2016, an international alliance of NGOs from eight different countries including South Korea, Japan, Taiwan, and the Philippines submitted an application to UNESCO for 2,744 documents and archival records related to the Japanese wartime "comfort stations" to be included (figure 7.6). According to Shin Heisoo, these files, audiotapes, and videotapes could be distinguished as "the largest volume in UNESCO's Memory of the World Register."[79] This application followed an earlier application by the Chinese government for the UNESCO registry to include documents and artifacts related to the Nanjing Massacre and Japanese military sexual slavery in China. In October 2015 UNESCO approved the inclusion of only those documents related to the Nanjing Massacre. The government of Japan, in turn, lodged a protest of their inclusion. On November 5, 2015, Hiroshi Hase, Japan's Minister of Education, Culture, Sports, Science and Technology, addressed the General Conference of UNESCO and called for the body to "swiftly improve governance and transparency" of the registration process.[80]

all > International

Group seeking UNESCO registration of comfort women archival materials

Posted on : Jun.2,2016 15:31 KST Modified on : Jun.2,2016 15:31 KST

Materials from several countries being collected to preserve the voices of comfort women

Fourteen civic groups from South Korea, Japan, and six other countries and a UK war memorial requested UNESCO Memory of the World registration for archival materials related to the drafting of comfort women by the Japanese Imperial Army.

A group calling itself the International Solidarity Committee for Joint UNESCO Memory of the World Registration of Records Related to Japanese Military Comfort Women held a press conference at the Franciscan Education Center in Seoul on June 1 to announce that it had filed a request the day before with Memory of the World headquarters for the listing of 2,744 related materials. The records include 660 submitted by South Korea related to the comfort women.

Left, materials documenting the cases of comfort women from the Philippines, provided by the Lila Pilipina Lolas Center. Right, treatment records for a survivor from a Daegu hospital.

Audio tapes of testimonies by former comfort women

FIGURE 7.6. Screen shot of a June 2, 2016, *Hankyoreh* news website article, "Group seeking UNESCO registration of comfort women archival materials," featuring photographs of boxes of documents and audiotapes of testimonies by survivors. Source: *Hankyoreh*, http://english.hani.co.kr/arti/english_edition/e_international/746527.html.

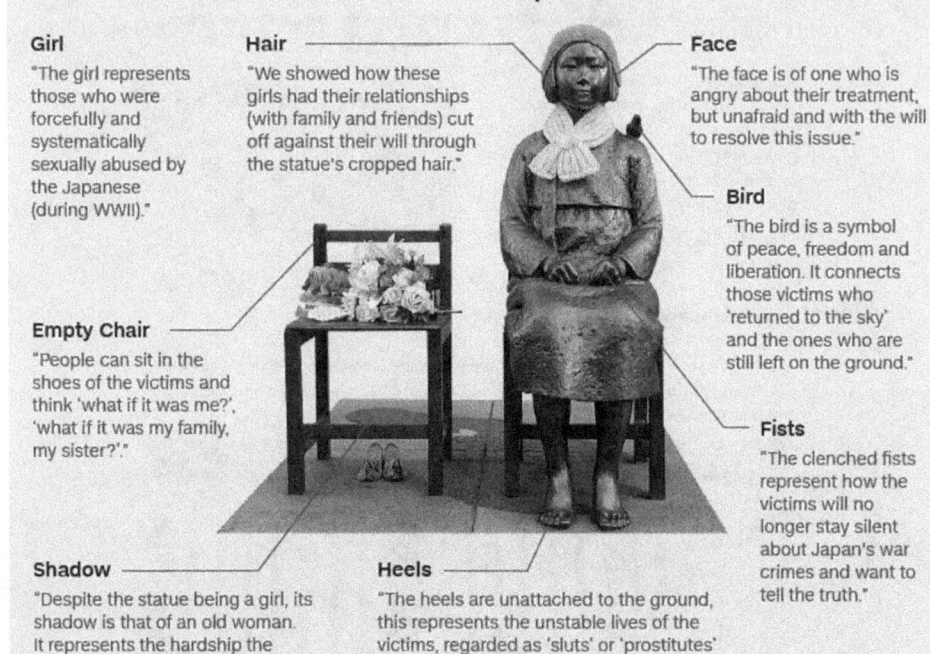

'Comfort women' statue explained

Girl
"The girl represents those who were forcefully and systematically sexually abused by the Japanese (during WWII)."

Hair
"We showed how these girls had their relationships (with family and friends) cut off against their will through the statue's cropped hair."

Face
"The face is of one who is angry about their treatment, but unafraid and with the will to resolve this issue."

Bird
"The bird is a symbol of peace, freedom and liberation. It connects those victims who 'returned to the sky' and the ones who are still left on the ground."

Empty Chair
"People can sit in the shoes of the victims and think 'what if it was me?', 'what if it was my family, my sister?'."

Fists
"The clenched fists represent how the victims will no longer stay silent about Japan's war crimes and want to tell the truth."

Shadow
"Despite the statue being a girl, its shadow is that of an old woman. It represents the hardship the victims had to suffer all this time."

Heels
"The heels are unattached to the ground, this represents the unstable lives of the victims, regarded as 'sluts' or 'prostitutes' and treated coldly by society."

CNN Source: CNN interview

FIGURE 7.7. CNN infographic of "'Comfort women' statue explained," noting the artists' intended meanings of several details of the *Sonyeosang*/Statue of Peace statue, which was featured as part of an article titled "Why This Statue of a Young Girl Caused a Diplomatic Incident," February 10, 2017. Source: CNN, https://www.cnn.com/2017/02/05/asia/south-korea-comfort-women-statue/index.html.

How might we begin to make critical sense of this intense re-investment in matter and materiality and their multilateral contestation alongside and against the proliferation of statues and memorials?[81] I would frame both as a supplement and a rejoinder to the dematerialization and fungibility of the issue across digital media and journalism but also in what is presumed to be the more official, durable sphere of global governance. As demonstrated in an infographic posted on the CNN website (figure 7.7), the *Sonyeosang* statue is encoded with many specific details that are aimed at producing a specifically preferred reading, one that would coherently contain several disparate but familiar archetypes: the innocent, virginal girl; the defiant victim; the peaceful activist; the aging and unconsoled *halmoni*; and the sympathetic ally. Inasmuch as these captions detail an assiduous attempt to direct and constrain the meanings of the figure through these precise, permanent etchings, they also betray its openness to multiple meanings *and* nonmeanings. The preference for and tendency toward younger figurations of the victims of the "comfort system" needs to be critically analyzed.[82] We should be mindful of the specific political-economic geographical location and physical surroundings of each site of its installment. Beginning with the placement of the first public memorial in Palisades Park in New Jersey in October 2010, there have been additional memorials built in Eisenhower Park in Westbury, New York (June 2012), Glendale, California (July 2013), and most recently in San Francisco (2017). Considered alongside other memorials in the U.S., the *Sonyeosang* expresses very specific ethnic but also patriarchal and hetero-normative attachments and a limited repertoire of strategies for laying claim to civic and political citizenship for some Korean/Americans, strategies that do not align with other Korean/American and Korean diasporic visions of belonging, kinship, and deserving humanity.[83] The question should not be reduced to a simplistic and moralistic binary of whether one supports or opposes these memorials and their unending proliferation. Rather, I would ask how these avowals of care and concern for the "comfort girl" might open out and extend to other, contemporary, and more immediate victims of sexual violence, state racism, compulsory, uncompensated labor, and forced removal and detention in each and every site of their moving commemoration. This is not a betrayal of or departure from the innumerable casualties and determined survivors of the Japanese military "comfort system" but rather a remembering and honoring of the demonstration of care and concern for each other enacted before us by the twenty Korean women under U.S. captivity.

NOTES

INTRODUCTION: TRAFFIC IN ASIAN WOMEN

1. "Japan-Korea Renew Feud over Imperial Apology," *Washington Post*, May 15, 1990; "Japanese Express Remorse to Korea," *New York Times*, May 25, 1990.
2. Kazuko Watanabe, "Militarism, Colonialism, and the Trafficking of Women: 'Comfort Women' Forced into Sexual Labor for Japanese Soldiers," *Bulletin of Concerned Asian Scholars* 26, no. 4 (1994): 3–17. According to Kim Pu Ja, she and other members were moved to form Yosong Net by a presentation that Yun Chung-ok had given in Japan in 1990. "Looking at Sexual Slavery from a Zainichi Perspective," *Voices from the Japanese Women's Movement*, AMPO-*Japan Asia Quarterly Review* (Armonk, NY: M. E. Sharpe, 1996), 157.
3. Jutta Joachim, "Shaping the Human Rights Agenda: The Case of Violence against Women," in *Gender Politics and Global Governance*, ed. Elizabeth K. Meyer et al. (Lanham, MD: Rowman and Littlefield, 1999), 151.
4. Indai Lourdes Sajor, "Military Sexual Slavery: Crimes against Humanity," in *Peace, Justice and Freedom: Human Rights Challenges for the New Millennium*, ed. Gurcharan Singh Bhatia et al. (Edmonton: University of Alberta Press, 2000), 165.
5. United Nations, Department of Economic and Social Affairs, *Study on Traffic in Persons and Prostitution* (1959), 24.
6. Kathleen Barry, *Female Sexual Slavery* ([1979] New York: New York University Press, 1984), 40, 7 (emphasis in original).
7. United Nations, *Report of the World Conference of the United Nations Decade for Women: Equality, Development and Peace: Copenhagen*, July 14–30, 1980. A/CONF.94/35 (1980), 103.
8. Jean Fernand-Laurent, *Report of the Special Rapporteur on the Suppression of the Traffic in Persons and the Exploitation of the Prostitution of Others* (Geneva: United Nations, 1983), 6.
9. Charlotte Bunch and Shirley Castley, "Introduction," to *International Feminism: Networking against Female Sexual Slavery*, ed. Kathleen Barry et al. (New York: International Women's Tribune Centre, 1984), 8.

10. Kathleen Barry, "The Network Defines Its Issues: Theory, Evidence and Analysis of Female Sexual Slavery," in *International Feminism: Networking against Female Sexual Slavery*, ed. Kathleen Barry et al. (New York: International Women's Tribune Centre, 1984), 22, 23 (emphasis in original).

11. A noteworthy but understudied exception was the International Tribunal on Crimes against Women, which was convened in Brussels in 1976. See *The Proceedings of the International Tribunal on Crimes against Women*, ed. Diana E. H. Russell and Nicole Van den Ven (Millbrae, CA: Les Femmes, 1976).

12. United Nations, *The Nairobi Forward-Looking Strategies for the Advancement of Women* (New York: United Nations, 1985), para. 258.

13. Charlotte Bunch, "Women's Rights as Human Rights: Toward a Re-vision of Human Rights," *Human Rights Quarterly* 12 (1990): 488-89.

14. Center for Women's Global Leadership, *International Campaign for Women's Human Rights: 1992-1993 Report* (New Brunswick, NJ: Center for Women's Global Leadership, 1993), 1.

15. "This period encompasses four significant dates: November 25, December 1, December 6, and December 10. November 25 is International Day against Violence against Women, which was declared by the first Feminist Encuentro for Latin America and the Caribbean in 1981. This date was chosen to commemorate the lives of the Mirabel sisters, who were murdered on that date in 1960 by the Trujillo dictatorship. December 1 is World AIDS Day. December 6 is the anniversary of the Montreal massacre, when fourteen women engineering students were gunned down for being 'feminists,' according to the man who killed them. December 10 is International Human Rights Day, the date on which the Universal Declaration of Human Rights was proclaimed in 1948. Taken together, the sixteen days reflect the mourning and hope that characterizes the victimization and activism of women." Susan E. Roche, Katy Biron, and Niamh Reilly, "Sixteen Days of Activism against Gender Violence," *Violence against Women* 1 (1995): 273-74.

16. Margaret E. Keck and Kathryn Sikkink, *Activists beyond Borders: Advocacy Networks in International Politics* (Ithaca, NY: Cornell University Press, 1998), 166.

17. Cambodian Women's Association, *Selling Noodles: The Traffic in Women and Children in Cambodia* (Phnom Penh: Cambodian Women's Association, 1996).

18. Dorothy Q. Thomas, Sidney Jones, Women's Rights Project, and Asia Watch, *A Modern Form of Slavery: Trafficking of Burmese Women and Girls into Brothels in Thailand* (New York: Human Rights Watch, 1993). See also Asia Watch and Women's Rights Project, *Double Jeopardy: Police Abuse of Women in Pakistan* (New York: Human Rights Watch, 1992). This report on the trafficking of Bangladeshi women into Pakistan for sex work was coauthored by two staff members of two Human Rights Watch (HRW) subdivisions: Dorothy Q. Thomas, director of the then recently formed Women's Rights Project, and Patricia Gossman, South Asia research associate of Asia Watch, which had been established earlier in 1985. HRW would later publish *Rape for Profit: Trafficking of Nepali Girls and Women to India's Brothels* (1995) and *Owed Justice: Thai Women Trafficked into Debt Bondage in Japan* (2000). Although HRW's reports would go on in subsequent years to focus on other countries and regions,

including the United States, Greece, Bosnia and Herzegovina, Togo, Kyrgystan, Guinea, and Papua New Guinea, it is clear that Asia and Asian women were the focus of much of their anti-trafficking work in the 1990s.

19. Examples include the Cambodian Women's Association, *Selling Noodles*; and S. Skrobanek, N. Boonpakdee, and C. Jantateero, *The Traffic in Women: Human Realities of the International Sex Trade* (London: Zed, 1997). For a longer list of texts, see chapter 3.

20. The first chapter of Yayori Matsui's 1996 book, *Women in the New Asia: From Pain to Power*, is titled "Trafficking in Women." The book was first published in Japan as *Onnatachi go Tsukuro Asia* (Tokyo: Iwanami Shote, 1996). It was translated by Noriko Toyokawa and Carolyn Francis and published in English by Zed Books in 1999. See also Kazuko Watanabe, "Trafficking in Women's Bodies, Then and Now: The Issue of Military 'Comfort Women,'" *Women's Studies Quarterly* (1999). In Chilla Bulbeck's essay "Women's Movements in the Asia-Pacific," section 8.4 is on "The International Traffic in Women," in *Culture and Society in the Asia-Pacific*, ed. Richard Maidment and Colin Mackerras (London: Routledge, 1998), 163–84. Lora Jo Foo's 2002 Ford Foundation report, *Asian American Women: Issues, Concerns, and Responsive Human and Civil Rights Advocacy*, contains a chapter titled "The Trafficking of Asian Women."

21. Because the UN allowed only representatives from nongovernmental organizations with consultative status to attend and speak at these meetings, the Korean Council participated successively under three accredited international NGOs: World Council of Churches (WCC), the World Alliance of Reformed Churches (WARC), and then the Asian Pacific Forum on Women, Law and Development. The demands for investigation and compensation received support from other NGOs, including the Coalition against the Traffic in Women (CATW).

22. Charlotte Bunch and Niamh Reilly, *Demanding Accountability: The Global Campaign and Vienna Tribunal for Women's Human Rights* (New York: Center for Women's Global Leadership and the United Nations Development Fund for Women, 1994), 35.

23. Donna J. Sullivan, "Women's Human Rights and the 1993 World Conference on Human Rights," *American Journal of International Law* (1994): 156.

24. Linda Chavez, *Contemporary Forms of Slavery, Preparatory Document Submitted by Mrs. Linda Chavez on the Question of Systematic Rape, Sexual Slavery, and Slavery-like Practices during Wartime* (September 7, 1993): 1–2. The proceedings of the International Public Hearing on Traffic in Women and War Crimes against Women included a statement by Vesna Kesic of the Center for Women Victims of War and Zagreb Women's Lobby (Croatia). Asian Women's Human Rights Council, *In the Court of Women II: Asia Tribunal on Women's Human Rights in Tokyo: Proceedings of the International Public Hearing on Traffic in Women and War Crimes against Women* (Quezon City, Philippines: Asian Women's Human Rights Council, 1994), 56–58.

25. Radhika Coomaraswamy, *Preliminary Report Submitted by the Special Rapporteur on Violence against Women, Its Causes and Consequences, Ms. Radhika Coomaraswamy, in Accordance with Commission on Human Rights Resolution 1994/45* (E/CN.4/1995/42 22) (United Nations Economic and Social Council, November 22, 1994), 68–69. The

other subcategory was "custodial violence against women," which includes "custodial rape," defined as "rape in any state-owned institution" (63).

26. Here, too, the Korean Council and Shin Heisoo played a significant role. According to Shin, "I felt that the most effective way to persuade her would be visiting her in her home country. I met Ms. Coomaraswamy at her office at the International Center on Ethnic Relations in Colombo. After a two-hour conversation, the Special Rapporteur willingly accepted my request and agreed to take the issue of 'comfort women' as the subject of her first mission" (18). As Shin thus proudly adds, "Now the Korean Council had successfully secured two Special Rapporteurs committed to work on the 'comfort women' issue." Shin Heisoo, "Seeking Justice, Honour and Dignity: Movement for the Victims of Japanese Military Sexual Slavery," in *Global Civil Society 2011, Globality and the Absence of Justice*, ed. Martin Albrow et al. (Basingstoke, UK: Palgrave Macmillan, 2011), 18.

27. Radhika Coomaraswamy, *Report on the Mission to the Democratic People's Republic of Korea, the Republic of Korea and Japan on the Issue of Military Sexual Slavery in Wartime. Report Submitted to the 52nd Session of the UN Commission on Human Rights* (E/CN.4/1996/53/Add.1) (New York: UN Economic and Social Council, Commission on Human Rights, Economic and Social Council, January 4, 1996), 4.

28. Shin Heisoo, "The Situation of the Comfort Women: An Update," in *Without Reservation: The Beijing Tribunal on Accountability for Women's Human Rights*, ed. Niamh Reilly (New Brunswick, NJ: Center for Women's Global Leadership, 1996), 43.

29. Ustinia Dolgopol, "Knowledge and Responsibility: The Ongoing Consequences of Failing to Give Sufficient Attention to the Crimes against the Comfort Women in the Tokyo Trial," in *Beyond Victor's Justice? The Tokyo War Crimes Trial Revisited*, ed. Yuki Tanaka et al. (Leiden Martinus Nijhoff, 2011), 245.

30. Radhika Coomaraswamy and Lisa M. Kois, "Violence against Women," in *Women and International Human Rights Law*, ed. Kelly D. Askin et al. (Ardsley, NY: Transnational, 1999), 178.

31. Coomaraswamy, *Preliminary Report*, 69.

32. Siriporn Skrobanek, Nattaya Boonpakdi, and Christina Janthakeero, *The Traffic in Women: Human Realities of the International Sex Trade* (London: Zed, 1997), 17; Louise Brown, *Sex Slaves: The Trafficking of Women in Asia* (London: Virago, 2000), 8.

33. Katharine H. S. Moon, "South Korean Movements against Militarized Sexual Labor," *Asian Survey* 39 (1999): 315.

34. Chih-Chieh Chou, "An Emerging Transnational Movement in Women's Human Rights: Campaign of Nongovernmental Organizations on 'Comfort Women' Issue in East Asia," *Journal of Economic and Social Research* 5, no. 1 (2003): 175.

35. Moon, "South Korean Movements against Militarized Sexual Labor."

36. Laura Hein, "Savage Irony: The Imaginative Power of the 'Military Comfort Women' in the 1990s," *Gender and History* 11 (1999): 336, 340, 343.

37. In a cogent 2007 essay, Tani Barlow articulates a particularly skeptical assessment of the super-visibility of Asian women in global governance. According to Barlow, Asian women's NGOs joined a dense web of power/knowledge that brought together "interested academics, health providers, activists, and NGO

officials" in meetings and consultations with intergovernmental agencies such as ESCAP, the World Bank, and the Commission on the Status of Women. Pointing to the 1995 Fourth Women's World Conference in Beijing and the 2000 Women's International War Crimes Tribunal on Japan's Military Sexual Slavery in Tokyo as two especially prominent and celebrated moments of women's activism in Asia, Barlow suggests, "If we consider [these two events] as examples of what André C. Drainville calls 'efforts to judicialize transnational politics,' then the gender concept becomes more clearly a policy category that seeks to mitigate damage unleashed in global economic restructuring—to, in a sense, create a language of redress." Barlow further suggests the "possibility that the UN matrix operates as a major dis/enabling platform." Tani Barlow, "Asian Women in Reregionalization," *positions: east asia cultures critique* 15, no. 2 (2007): 292, 311.

38. Yoshimi Yoshiaki, *Comfort Women: Sexual Slavery in the Japanese Military during World War II*, trans. Suzanne O'Brien (New York: Columbia University Press, 2000), 34.

39. Some early reviewers of the manuscript understandably expressed a certain weariness with my opening the book with the extended, dry recitation of key events, actions, and documents in international feminist activism and global governance. But in putting forth this chronicle of accretion and conglomeration at the beginning, I seek to show that a positive, focused account of emergence, presence, participation, and significance is mindfully fabricated, and its descriptiveness and easy coherence can also be quieting and mis-orienting.

CHAPTER 1: ASIAN WOMEN AS METHOD?

1. Kuan-Hsing Chen, *Asia as Method: Toward Deimperialization* (Durham, NC: Duke University Press, 2005). Chen acknowledges that the idea had been previously articulated by Takeuchi Yoshimi, the Japanese scholar of China, in a 1960 essay titled "Asia as Method." Though acknowledging "vast differences . . . at the level of thought and lifestyle between Japan and China," Takeuchi also noted "the internal division within Japan of the Asian and the non-Asian": "At present, Japan is in some ways more western than the West. . . . But the fact is that similar examples can all be found in colonial situations. As a colony, for example, Shanghai was also more western than the West." Takeuchi Yoshimi, *What Is Modernity? Writings of Takeuchi Yoshimi* (New York: Columbia University Press, 2005), 161.
2. Chen, *Asia as Method*, 63, 20.
3. Chen, *Asia as Method*, 226, 223.
4. Chen, *Asia as Method*, 212.
5. Kuan-Hsing Chen and Chua Beng Huat, "Introduction: The Inter-Asia Cultural Studies: Movements Project," in *The Inter-Asia Cultural Studies Reader*, ed. Chen and Chua (Abingdon, UK: Routledge, 2007), 1.
6. Chen, *Asia as Method*, 10.
7. Chungmoo Choi, "Guest Editor's Introduction," *positions: east asia cultures critique* 5, no. 1 (1997): v–vi.

8. Hyunah Yang, "Revisiting the Issue of Korean 'Military Comfort Women': The Question of Truth and Positionality," *positions: east asia cultures critique* 5, no. 1 (1997): 66–67, emphasis in original.
9. Yang, "Revisiting the Issue," 63. As Yang acknowledges, "In this connection, I find useful the current analysis of the war in the former Yugoslavia for conceptualizing collective rapes inflicted by one ethnic group on another."
10. Yang, "Revisiting the Issue," 64.
11. Lisa Yoneyama, *Cold War Ruins: Transpacific Critique of American Justice and Japanese War Crimes* (Durham, NC: Duke University Press), 140.
12. Yuki Tanaka, *Japan's Comfort Women: Sexual Slavery and Prostitution during World War II and the US Occupation* (New York: Routledge, 2002).
13. Yoneyama, *Cold War Ruins*, 8.
14. Lisa Lowe, *The Intimacies of Four Continents* (Durham, NC: Duke University Press, 2015), 39, emphasis in original.
15. Quoted in Matsui Yayori, *Why I Oppose Kisaeng Tours: Exposing Economic and Sexual Aggression against South Korean Women*, trans. Lora Sharnoff (Tokyo: Femintern, 1975), 2.
16. Quoted in Matsui, *Why I Oppose Kisaeng Tours*, 18. Later, in September 1973, the Women's Committee of the National Christian Council of Churches (Japan) drafted a supportive response: "Predominantly male tourists from Japan are behaving in Korea on the most culturally debasing animal levels. Such behavior must come from a total lack of conscience and respect for human rights as well as a complete lack of repentance about our past aggression against neighboring countries." Reprinted in *Isis International Bulletin* (November 1979): 26.
17. Chungmoo Choi, "The Discourse of Decolonization and Popular Memory: South Korea," *positions: east asia cultures critique* 1, no. 1 (1993): 77–102.
18. Quoted in Matsui, *Why I Oppose Kisaeng Tours*, 11. For another account of these protests, see Takahashi Kikue, "*Kisaeng* Tourism," *Isis International Bulletin* 13 (November 1979): 23–25. This article was published in September 1975 in a booklet titled *Tourism: The Asian Dilemma*. Takahashi ends the essay with a section titled "Responsibility of the Japanese": "The old anti-Japanese feeling harbored by Koreans since the colonial period remains to this day; conclusion of the Japan-ROK treaty and recent Japanese incursions into the Korean market have done nothing to assuage that feeling. On top of all that, the Japanese rush on the flesh for sale in Korea is just adding fuel to the fire of anti-Japanese sentiment. Japanese seem unconcerned about the conduct of their government during the period of colonization; and in effect, they are launched on another invasion of South Korea—this time economic instead of military" (25). Noting that Japanese travel agencies were not so blatantly marketing prostitution in their tour packages to the US or Europe as they were with the South Korean "*kisaeng* tours," Takahashi explains: "It is a result of racial discrimination and a mistaken sense of superiority, based on collusion between the governments of both countries; economic assistance in return for economic invasion by Japan, with all the ugly ramifications" (25).
19. Matsui, *Why I Oppose Kisaeng Tours*, 2.

20. Matsui, *Why I Oppose Kisaeng Tours*, 3.
21. Matsui, *Why I Oppose Kisaeng Tours*, 7.
22. Matsui, *Why I Oppose Kisaeng Tours*, 7. Matsui cites as her source Senda Natsumitsu, *Jūgun Ianfu (Prostitutes Who Accompanied the Army)* (Futabasha, no date), 16n4.
23. Matsui, *Why I Oppose Kisaeng Tours*, 7.
24. Matsui, *Why I Oppose Kisaeng Tours*, 30.
25. "Declaration of the Asian Women's Liberation Committee in Japan," *Asian Women's Liberation* 1 (1977): 2.
26. "Who Are We?," *Asian Women's Liberation* 1 (1977): 4.
27. Alice Yun Chai, "Asian-Pacific Feminist Coalition Politics: The *Chŏngshindae/Jūgunianfu* ('Comfort Women') Movement," *Korean Studies* 17, no. 1 (1993): 67–91.
28. According to Elaine H. Kim, "After the South Korean government banned the Korean women's group, members of the Japan-based Asian Women's Association continued the lobbying effort by calling meetings with the Japan Association of Travel Agents and the Japan Travel Bureau, contacting Japanese Diet representatives, organizing workshops and lectures, and publishing print materials on prostitution tourism and women's enfranchisement. The Manila-based Third World Movement against the Exploitation of Women and Women's Friend Group in Bangkok have also been working to draw attention to the problems of sex tourism, particularly Japanese sex tourism." Elaine H. Kim, "Sex Tourism in Asia: A Reflection of Political and Economic Inequality," *Critical Perspectives of Third World America* 2, no. 1 (1984): 230n1.
29. See Chai, "Asian-Pacific Feminist Coalition Politics." According to C. Sarah Soh, "The transnational comfort women originated in South Korea in the early 1970s as a women's campaign against international sex tourism. The campaign targeted Japanese male visitors, and eventually evolved into a postcolonial dispute between Japan and Korea in the early 1990s." "Japan's National/Asian Women's Fund for 'Comfort Women,'" *Pacific Affairs* 76, no. 2 (2003): 214. Given the multiple erasures and significant delay between the early protests in the 1970s and the international redress movement in the 1990s, I would characterize their relationship as one of productive but also provisional connections rather than a single, continuous trajectory from a definitive origin.
30. Chai, "Asian-Pacific Feminist Coalition Politics," 79.
31. Kim Puja, "Looking at Sexual Slavery from a *Zainichi* Perspective," in *Voices from the Japanese Women's Movement*, ed. AMPO-*Japan Asia Quarterly Review* (Armonk, NY: M. E. Sharpe, 1996), 157.
32. Yoneyama, *Cold War Ruins*, 28.
33. Susan Brownmiller, *Against Our Will: Men, Women and Rape* (New York: Fawcett Columbine, 1975), 63.
34. Quoted in Brownmiller, *Against Our Will*, 64.
35. Brownmiller, *Against Our Will*, 93, 99. Although Brownmiller devotes more space to covering the Vietnam War, even this account is partial and spotty given that she relied largely upon U.S. military records and the anecdotal observations of the journalist Peter Arnett. At the end of that chapter, Brownmiller thus offers this

apology: "I am sorry that it is not within the scope of this book to explore the lives of Vietnamese women who became 'Occupation: prostitute' as a direct result of the foreign military presence in their country. It is a story that should be told in detail.... I have dwelt on official U.S. military prostitution, and the concomitant concern for control of venereal disease..." (96).

36. Barry, *Female Sexual Slavery*, 75.
37. Quoted in Barry, *Female Sexual Slavery*, 75–76.
38. Barry, *Female Sexual Slavery*, 76.
39. This omission of the Japanese military "comfort system" during World War II was partially redressed in Barry's 1995 book, *The Prostitution of Sexuality*, which includes a section titled "The Military Market: Korea." As Barry notes, "Korean and other Southeast Asian women were deployed to Japanese 'comfort stations,' a version of U.S. military R & R" (127). There are significant differences between the two, and it is additionally perplexing to characterize the earlier Japanese military "comfort system" as a categorical version of the latter U.S. military R & R. Even in this 1995 book, it is striking that Barry never uses the term *sexual slavery*. Instead, Barry deploys a range of descriptions to refer to the Japanese military "comfort system" as "sex marketing of massive populations of women during wartime" (127), "sexual incarceration" (128), and "Korean prostitution for occupation forces" (129). The term *military sexual slavery* appears only in Barry's recitation of the full English name of the Korean Council, but the language of service and prostitution is manifest in several places. The lengthy passage from Matsui's essay about the R.A.A. is again re-cited in full but is followed up with this modification of the line of continuity between the Japanese military "comfort stations" to Japanese sex tourism: "Korean prostitution for occupation forces, first Japanese and then U.S., later turned into military prostitution for U.S. forces in Korea and then developed into sex tourism for Japanese businessmen" (130).
40. Cynthia Enloe, *Does Khaki Become You? The Militarization of Women's Lives* (Boston: South End, 1983), 31.
41. Enloe, *Does Khaki Become You?*, 32 (emphasis in original), 37, 41–42.
42. Gayle Rubin, "The Traffic in Women: Notes on the 'Political Economy' of Sex," in *Toward an Anthropology of Women*, ed. Rayna Reiter (New York: Monthly Review Press, 1975), 163, 174, 176.
43. As Rubin writes, "Far from being an expression of natural differences, exclusive gender identity is the suppression of natural similarities. It requires repression: in men, of whatever is the local version of 'feminine' traits; in women, of whatever is the local version of 'masculine' traits ... a rigid division of personality" ("The Traffic in Women," 180).
44. Rubin, "The Traffic in Women," 198–99. In her 1984 essay "Thinking Sex: Notes for a Radical Theory of the Politics of Sexuality," Rubin recasts the earlier spatiotemporal division and overlays it with a separation of sexuality from gender: "'The Traffic in Women' was inspired by the literature on kin-based systems of social organization. It appeared to me at the same time that gender and desire were systematically intertwined in such social formations. This may or may not be an accurate

assessment of the relationship between sex and gender in tribal organizations. But it is surely not an adequate formulation for sexuality in Western industrial society." Gayle Rubin, "Thinking Sex: Notes for a Radical Theory of the Politics of Sexuality," in *Pleasure and Danger*, ed. Carole Vance (Boston: Routledge and Kegan Paul, 1984), 307.

45. Gayle Rubin and Judith Butler, "Sexual Traffic," *Differences: Journal of Feminist Cultural Studies* (1994): 99.
46. Emma Goldman, "The Traffic in Women," in *The Traffic in Women and Other Essays on Feminism* (New York: Times Change, 1970), 19.
47. Goldman, "The Traffic in Women," 20, 24, 27.
48. Charlotte Bunch and Shirley Castley, "Introduction," in *International Feminism: Networking against Female Sexual Slavery*, ed. Kathleen Barry, Charlotte Bunch, and Shirley Castley (New York: International Women's Tribune Centre, 1984), 9.
49. Sister Mary Soledad Perpiñan, "Confronting Prostitution Tourism: The Third World Movement against the Exploitation of Women," *Canadian Woman Studies/Les Cahiers de la Femme* 7, nos. 1–2 (1986): 127.
50. Kathleen Barry, "The Network Defines Its Issues: Theory, Evidence and Analysis of Female Sexual Slavery," in *International Feminism: Networking against Female Sexual Slavery*, ed. Kathleen Barry et al. (New York: International Women's Tribune Centre, 1984), 17. Other named participants included Jyotsna Chatterji (India), Nimalka Fernando (Sri Lanka), Mallika Dutt (India), and Sudara Sereewat (Thailand).
51. Fernand-Laurent, *Report of the Special Rapporteur on the Suppression of the Traffic in Persons and the Exploitation of the Prostitution of Others*, 13.
52. Barry, *Female Sexual Slavery*, xiii.
53. United Nations Non-governmental Liaison Service, *Female Sexual Slavery and Economic Exploitation: Making Local and Global Connections: Report of a Consultation Organized by the Non-governmental Liaison Service (New York), San Francisco, California, October 25, 1984* (New York: United Nations Non-governmental Liaison Service, 1985), 1.
54. United Nations Educational, Scientific and Cultural Organization (UNESCO), *International Meeting of Experts on the Social and Cultural Causes of Prostitution and Strategies for the Struggle against Procuring and Sexual Exploitation of Women—Final Report*. Madrid, Spain, March 18–21, 1986, 3.
55. Kathleen Barry, "Keynote Address: Women's Rights as Human Rights," in *Women Empowering Women. Proceedings of the Human Rights Conference on the Trafficking of Asian Women*, ed. Aurora Javate de Dios (Manila: Coalition against Trafficking in Women-Asia, 1993), 23.
56. UNESCO, *International Meeting of Experts*, 3.
57. Kathleen Barry, *The Prostitution of Sexuality* (New York: New York University Press, 1996), 4.
58. Indai Lourdes Sajor, "Military Sexual Slavery: Crimes against Humanity," in *Peace, Justice and Freedom: Human Rights Challenges for the New Millennium*, ed. Gurcharan Singh Bhatia (Edmonton: University of Alberta Press, 2000), 165.

59. Maki Kimura's recent monograph, *Unfolding the "Comfort Women" Debates: Modernity, Violence, Women's Voices* (New York: Palgrave Macmillan, 2016), posits that under the hegemony of Western imperialism and the specific ideology of Orientalism, the "comfort system" has been wrongly cast as unique to Japan by attributing its formation to a primitive, barbaric Japanese culture and pointing to premodern antecedents of licensed prostitution in Japan. Against this "cultural imperialist paradigm," which is fixated on Japan, Kimura points to how regulated prostitution was first developed in France and Great Britain and its colonial territories and then later introduced to Japan in the immediate aftermath of its opening to foreign trade with the U.S. and the European nations. Specifically, she dates the establishment of red-light districts in Japan following the 1854 Treaty of Kanagawa, which was signed between Japan and the United States. According to Kimura, it is this distinctly modern and transnational development that would later serve as the foundation for the Japanese military "comfort system." Kimura further argues via a detour into Hannah Arendt that "evil is an integral part of the Enlightenment" (49) and that violence is central in and to modernity. I would point out that there is a fine but important distinction between arguing for the nonexceptionality of the atrocities committed by the Japanese Imperial Army and relativizing and downplaying the definite shape and gruesome extent of those atrocities. Framing the "comfort system" as one of many instances of violence in modernity should still demand careful attention to the heterogeneous and unequal forms of agency and responsibility among the variously empowered and commanding Japanese and non-Japanese subjects in committing, rationalizing, forgetting, and disavowing its atrocities.
60. Alice M. Miller, "Sexuality, Violence against Women, and Human Rights: Women Make Demands and Ladies Get Protection," *Health and Human Rights* 7, no. 2 (2004): 30–31, 33.
61. Pamela Thoma, "Cultural Autobiography, Testimonial, and Asian American Transnational Feminist Coalition in the 'Comfort Women of World War II' Conference," *Frontiers: A Journal of Women's Studies* 21, no. 1/2 (2000): 29.
62. Margaret D. Stetz, "Representing 'Comfort Women': Activism through Law and Art," *IRIS* 45 (2002): 26, 84.
63. "Abe Rejects Japan's Files on War Sex," *New York Times*, March 2, 2007.
64. "Japan Court Rules against Sex Slaves and Laborers," *New York Times*, April 28, 2007. Here it is important to keep in mind, once again, that there was not and has never been a univocal, homogeneous Japanese position on the "comfort women" issue, including the matter of forcible recruitment. As this same article reported, Japan's Supreme Court rejected two lawsuits for monetary compensation on behalf of Chinese survivors: "But in a striking rebuke to nationalist politicians who have tried to play down Japan's wartime crimes, the court acknowledged the historical facts of sex slavery and forced labor, two practices that continue to fuel anger in Asia six decades after the war's end. In its 16-page ruling in a sex slavery case, the court acknowledged that Japanese soldiers had abducted two teenage Chinese girls and forced them to work as sex slaves for months, contradicting Mr. Abe's recent denial of the practice."

65. "Shinzo Abe's Optimistic Vision," *Washington Post*, March 25, 2007.
66. Chunghee Sarah Soh, *The Comfort Women: Sexual Violence and Postcolonial Memory in Korea and Japan* (Chicago: University of Chicago Press, 2008), xi–xii, xvii, 246.
67. Soh, *The Comfort Women*, xii.
68. See Chunghee Sarah Soh, "The Korean 'Comfort Women': Movement for Redress," *Asian Survey* 36, no. 12 (1996): 1226–40; and "Human Rights and the 'Comfort Women,'" *Peace Review* 12, no. 1 (2000): 123–29.
69. Soh, *The Comfort Women*, xii.
70. Chunghee Sarah Soh, "Prostitutes versus Sex Slaves: The Politics of Representing the 'Comfort Women,'" in *Legacies of the Comfort Women of World War II*, ed. Margaret Stetz and Bonnie B. C. Oh (Armonk, NY: M. E. Sharpe, 2001), 76, emphasis mine.
71. Chunghee Sarah Soh, "From Imperial Gifts to Sex Slaves: Theorizing Symbolic Representations of the 'Comfort Women,'" *Social Science Japan Journal* 3, no. 1 (2000): 67, emphasis mine.
72. Soh, *The Comfort Women*, 77.
73. Soh, "From Imperial Gifts to Sex Slaves," 68.
74. Karen Parker and Jennifer F. Chew, "Compensation for Japan's World War II War-Rape Victims," *Hastings International and Comparative Law Review* 17 (1994): 498.
75. Kazuko Watanabe, "Militarism, Colonialism, and the Trafficking of Women: 'Comfort Women' Forced into Sexual Labor for Japanese Soldiers," *Bulletin of Concerned Asian Scholars* 26, no. 4 (1994): 4.
76. UN Economic and Social Council, Commission on Human Rights, 50th Session, *Contemporary Forms of Slavery—Systematic Rape, Sexual Slavery and Slavery-Like Practices during Armed Conflict. Final report submitted by Ms. Gay J. McDougall, Special Rapporteur* (E/CN.4/Sub.2/1998/13), June 22, 1998 (masthead), 56.
77. Suzanne O'Brien, "Translator's Introduction," in Yoshimi Yoshiaki, *Comfort Women: Sexual Slavery in the Japanese Military during World War II*, trans. Suzanne O'Brien (New York: Columbia University Press, 2000), 213.
78. Chai, "Asian-Pacific Feminist Coalition Politics," 75.
79. Yun Chung-ok, "In Memory of Yayori Matsui," *Inter-Asia Cultural Studies* 4, no. 2 (2003): 191. As Yun explains in greater detail in reference to the 2000 Tribunal, "[Matsui] was in favor of Emperor Hirohito standing as a defendant because he was at the summit of a patriarchal family-based state, Japan. However, she could not agree with the view that the victimized Asian countries held so strongly. It was the view that Emperor Hirohito was the highest person responsible for the systematic atrocities, which were the fruition of his policy of segregation, in addition to the system which discriminated against women. In other words, Matsui viewed the problem only from the point of view of gender." Lisa Yoneyama summarizes these persistent "internal differences": "The difference between the universalist, gender standpoint feminism and the (post)colonial, anti-imperialist feminism also had to be negotiated among the Tribunal's organizers." Yoneyama, *Cold War Ruins*, 260n27.
80. Kim Puja, "'Ianfu' mondai to datsu shokuminchi shugi," in *Rekishi to sekinin: "Ianfu" mondai to 1990 nendai*, eds. Kim Puja and Nakano Toshio (Tokyo: Seikyūsha, 2008). Cited in Kimura, *Unfolding the "Comfort Women" Debates*, 47.

81. See "Vietnamese women raped in wartime seek justice for a lifetime of pain and prejudice," *Independent*, September 11, 2017.
82. Kandice Chuh, "Discomforting Knowledge: Or, Korean 'Comfort Women' and Asian Americanist Critical Practice," *Journal of Asian American Studies* 6, no. 1 (2003): 9.

CHAPTER 2: TRAFFIC IN WOMEN

1. Lenore Manderson and Margaret Jolly, "Sites of Desire/Economies of Pleasure in Asia and the Pacific," in *Sites of Desire, Economies of Pleasure: Sexualities in Asia and the Pacific*, ed. Lenore Manderson and Margaret Jolly (Chicago: University of Chicago Press, 1997), 17.
2. Andrea Marie Bertone, "Sexual Trafficking in Women: International Political Economy and the Politics of Sex," *Gender Issues* 18, no. 1 (2000): 8.
3. Louise Brown, *Sex Slaves: The Trafficking of Women in Asia* (London: Virago, 2000), 3–4.
4. Aurora Javate de Dios, "Introduction," in *Women Empowering Women: Proceedings of the Human Rights Conference on the Trafficking of Asian Women* (Quezon City, Philippines: Coalition against Trafficking in Women-Asia), 1.
5. Cecelia Hoffman, "Foreword," in *Women Empowering Women: Proceedings of the Human Rights Conference on the Trafficking of Asian Women*, ed. Aurora Javate de Dios (Manila: Coalition against Trafficking in Women-Asia, 1993), 1.
6. Kathleen Barry, "Keynote Address: Women's Rights as Human Rights," in *Women Empowering Women: Proceedings of the Human Rights Conference on the Trafficking of Asian Women*, ed. Aurora Javate de Dios (Manila: Coalition against Trafficking in Women-Asia, 1993), 21. Barry makes some slight but significant modifications, most notably the substitution of "Asian woman" with the broader "woman of color," when these assertions appear later in her book *The Prostitution of Sexuality*. Under the heading "The Social Construction of Sexuality: Stages of Dehumanization," Barry outlines the stages as 1. *Distancing*, 2. *Disengagement*, 3. *Dissociation*, and 4. *Disembodiment* and *Dissembling*. She notes under 3. *Dissociation*, "In prostitution, customer demand includes specification of color and cultural characteristics, which are advertised and sold. Racism, which like sexual exploitation is an objectification that dehumanizes, is a foundation of the prostitution industry. A woman of color in prostitution is expected to be not only a sexed body but a 'colored' one also—from which she must also dissociate as that, too, is part of herself that she exchanges. Race is that which is bought with sex. And so it goes through different cultures . . ." (34–35).
7. This "Profile of CATW" appeared on the inside back cover of *Trafficking in Women and Prostitution in the Asia Pacific* (Manila: CATW-Asia Pacific, 1996).
8. Global Alliance Against Traffic in Women (GAATW), Cambodian Women's Development Association (CWDA), and International Organization for Migration (IOM). *Two Reports on the Situation of Women and Children Trafficked from Cambodia and Vietnam to Thailand* (Bangkok: GAATW, CWDA, IOM, 1997), 6.

9. Annuska Derks, *Trafficking of Cambodian Women and Children to Thailand* (Phnom Penh: Center for Advanced Study, International Organization for Migration [IOM], 1997).
10. League of Nations, Covenant of the League of Nations, April 28, 1919, art. 23c.
11. "International Conference of Traffic in Women and Children"—"Final Act," *League of Nations Journal* (July/August 1921): 596.
12. Quoted in Barbara Metzger, "Towards an International Human Rights Regime during the Inter-war Years: The League of Nations' Combat of the Traffic in Women and Children," in *Beyond Sovereignty: Britain, Empire and Transnationalism, c. 1880–1950*, ed. Kevin Grant et al. (New York: Palgrave Macmillan, 2007): 59.
13. League of Nations, *Report of the Special Body of Experts on Traffic in Women and Children* (Geneva: League of Nations, 1927), 8.
14. Metzger, "Towards an International Human Rights Regime," 56.
15. Paul Knepper, *International Crime in the 20th Century: The League of Nations Era, 1919–1939* (New York: Palgrave Macmillan, 2011), 96.
16. Florence Brewer Boeckel, "Women in International Affairs," *Annals of the American Academy of Political and Social Science* 143 (1929): 234.
17. Antoinette Burton, *Burdens of History: British Feminists, Indian Women, and Imperial Culture, 1865–1915* (Chapel Hill: University of North Carolina Press, 1994), 130.
18. Philippa Levine, *Prostitution, Race, and Politics: Policing Venereal Disease in the British Empire* (New York: Routledge, 2003), 38. Levine also points out that there was some variation in how infected women were treated, including expulsion and cutting off their hair: "In other colonies, the means chosen were less dramatic and ritualized, but still focused on women's mobility: the governing assumption was that knowing women's whereabouts and having the ability to register, detain, or expel them bodily was desirable" (39).
19. Eileen Scully, "Pre-Cold War Traffic in Sexual Labor and Its Foes: Some Contemporary Lessons," in *Global Human Smuggling: Comparative Perspectives*, ed. David Kyle and Rey Koslowski (Baltimore: Johns Hopkins University Press, 2001), 81–82.
20. Scully, "Pre-Cold War Traffic in Sexual Labor and Its Foes," 79.
21. James Francis Warren, *Ah Ku and Karayuki-san: Prostitution in Singapore, 1870–1940* (Singapore: Oxford University Press, 1993), 34.
22. Scully, "Pre-Cold War Traffic in Sexual Labor and Its Foes."
23. Levine, *Prostitution, Race, and Politics*, 4, 39.
24. Edward J. Bristow, *Vice and Vigilance: Purity Movements in Britain since 1700* (Dublin: Gill and Macmillan, 1977), 82–83.
25. Levine, *Prostitution, Race, and Politics*, 104.
26. Burton, *Burdens of History*, 8, 136.
27. Levine, *Prostitution, Race, and Politics*, 104.
28. League of Nations, *Report of the Special Body of Experts on Traffic in Women and Children*, 8.
29. "Minutes of the International Congress on the White Slave Traffic Held at Westminster Palace Hotel on June 21st, 22nd and 23rd, 1899," 4IBS/1/1, Box FL192, Archives of the International Bureau for the Suppression of Traffic in Persons,

Women's Library, London. Quoted in Thomas Richard Davies, "Project on the Evolution of International Non-governmental Organizations," accessed May 1, 2012, www.staff.city.ac.uk/tom.davies/IBSTP.html.
30. Stephanie A. Limoncelli, "International Voluntary Associations, Local Social Movements and State Paths to the Abolition of Regulated Prostitution in Europe, 1875-1950," *International Sociology* 21, no. 1 (2006): 51.
31. Scully, "Pre-Cold War Traffic in Sexual Labor and Its Foes," 84.
32. Nora Demleitner, "Forced Prostitution: Naming an International Offense," *Fordham International Law Journal* 18 (1994): 166.
33. Metzger, "Towards an International Human Rights Regime during the Inter-war Years," 60.
34. International Convention for the Suppression of the Traffic in Women and Children (signed in Geneva, September 30, 1921), art. 14.
35. International Agreement for the Suppression of the White Slave Traffic (signed at Paris, May 18, 1904). Reprinted in League of Nations, *Report of the Special Body of Experts on Traffic in Women and Children*, Annex IV, 197.
36. "Traffic in Women and Children," *League of Nations Journal* (March/April 1921): 230.
37. "Questionnaire issued by the special body of experts on the traffic in women and children, on April 24, 1924." Reprinted in League of Nations, *Report of the Special Body of Experts on Traffic in Women and Children*, Annex II, 196.
38. Jessica R. Pliley, "Claims to Protection: The Rise and Fall of Feminist Abolitionism in the League of Nations' Committee on the Traffic in Women and Children, 1919-1936," *Journal of Women's History* 22, no. 4 (2010): 105-6.
39. The 1921 questionnaire included a supplementary section on "Colonies and Dependencies," which expressed a persistent worry about interracial sexual relations. As a parenthetical note in the section pointed out, "Reports have been received that it is the practice in certain Colonies for immigrant white men to have native women and girls procured for them for immoral purposes, and that these women and girls are provided for them by Chiefs or procurers."
40. Gail Hershatter, *Dangerous Pleasures: Prostitution and Modernity in 20th-Century Shanghai* (Berkeley: University of California Press, 1997), 38.
41. Grace Abbott, "Memorandum by Miss Abbott (United States of America)," included as Annex II of the *Report of the Special Body of Experts on Traffic in Women and Children* (Geneva: League of Nations, 1927), 50.
42. Angie C. Kennedy, "Eugenics, 'Degenerate Girls,' and Social Workers during the Progressive Era," *Affilia* 27 (2008): 28.
43. Although President Woodrow Wilson was a proponent of the League of Nations, there was strong opposition in the U.S. Congress, and the Treaty of Versailles was not ratified.
44. John D. Rockefeller Jr., "The Origin, Work and Plans of the Bureau of Social Hygiene," January 27, 1913, Rockefeller Archive Center, Office of the Messrs. Rockefeller Records, Series O, Box 9, Folder 67.
45. Alan M. Brandt, *No Magic Bullet: A Social History of Venereal Disease in the United States since 1880* (London: Oxford University Press, 1987), 39.

46. As Rockefeller described it, "In this Laboratory, it is proposed to study from the physical, mental, social and moral side each person committed to the Reformatory. This study will be carried on by experts and each case will be kept under observation for from three weeks to three months, as may be required. When the diagnosis is completed, it is hoped that the Laboratory will be in position to recommend the treatment most likely to reform the individual, or, if reformation is impossible, to recommend permanent custodial care." This experiment was envisioned with much broader applicability beyond shaping carceral conditions and sentencing at the Reformatory for Women. As Rockefeller also confidently proposed, "Furthermore, reaching out beyond the individuals involved, it is believed that thus important contributions may be made to a fuller knowledge of the conditions ultimately responsible for vice. If this experiment is successful, the principle may be proved to all classes of criminals and the conditions precedent to crime, and lead to lines of action not only more scientific and humane but also less wasteful than those at present followed." Here we see the dream of a perfect alignment of science, philanthropy, and economic efficiency.
47. See George J. Kneeland, *Commercialized Prostitution in New York City* (New York: Century, 1913); Abraham Flexner, *Prostitution in Europe* (New York: Century, 1914); and Howard B. Woolston, *Prostitution in the United States* (New York: Century, 1921).
48. Paul Knepper, "Measuring the Threat of Global Crime: Insights from Research by the League of Nations into the Traffic in Women," *Criminology* 50, no. 3 (2012): 783.
49. Johnson had previously served as the director of the Sanitary Corps of the National Army and published an essay titled "Eliminating Vice from Camp Cities" in 1918 in the *Annals of the American Academy of Political and Social Science*.
50. Roy Lubove, "The Progressives and the Prostitute," *Historian* 24 (1962): 328.
51. Roswell H. Johnson, "Adequate Reproduction," *Journal of Social Hygiene* 5 (1919): 223.
52. Harry H. Laughlin, "Eugenical Sterilization in the United States," *Journal of Social Hygiene* 6 (1920): 530–31.
53. Institute of Hygiene, presented to the General Education Board, May 17, 1915, Rockefeller Archive Center (RAC), Rockefeller Foundation, Record Group 1.1, Series 200L, Box 183, Folder 2208, emphasis in original.
54. John D. Rockefeller Jr., letter to Raymond B. Fosdick, June 18 1923, RAC, Rockefeller Boards, Bureau of Social Hygiene, Record Group: Traffic in Women III, Series Subpanel 2, Box 9, Folder 73.
55. Charles O. Heydt, letter to Grace Abbott, October 1, 1923, RAC, Rockefeller Boards, Bureau of Social Hygiene, Record Group: Traffic in Women III, Series Subpanel 2, Box 9, Folder 73.
56. William F. Snow, Letter to Grace Abbott, September 5, 1924, RAC, Rockefeller Boards, Bureau of Social Hygiene, Record Group: Traffic in Women III, Series Subpanel 2, Box 9, Folder 73. In another letter to Abbott, dated March 9, 1925, Snow discreetly referenced this funding arrangement: "As on previous occasions I am writing you direct at the request of the Director of the Social Section of the League (Dame Rachel Crowdy), because of the agreement made between the Treasurer and myself, as Chairman of this Special Body of Experts." Subsequently, Charles O.

Heydt sent checks for $10,000 (on March 24, 1923) and for $25,000 (on March 30) to Grace Abbott at her office at the Children's Bureau of the US Department of Labor in Washington, D.C., with a note indicating that the check would then be forwarded to Snow at the League of Nations.

57. William F. Snow, "The Program of the League of Nations Advisory Committee on the Traffic in Women and the Protection and Welfare of Children and Young People," *Proceedings of the Academy of Political Science in the City of New York* 12, no. 1 (1926): 412 (emphases mine), 414.
58. Snow, "The Program of the League of Nations Advisory Committee," 414.
59. League of Nations, *Report of the Special Body of Experts on Traffic in Women and Children* (1927), 5.
60. Dame Rachel Crowdy, "The Humanitarian Activities of the League of Nations," *Journal of the Royal Institute of International Affairs* 6, no. 3 (1927): 157.
61. "Review of *Report of the Special Body of Experts on Traffic in Women and Children*," *Social Service Review* 2, no. 1 (1928): 166–67.
62. Review of *Report*, 168.
63. John D. Rockefeller Jr., "Introduction," in Kneeland, *Commercialized Prostitution in New York City*, ix–x.
64. Bureau of Social Hygiene, *A Report to the Trustees Covering the Years 1928, 1929, 1930*, 67–68, RAC, Bureau of Social Hygiene, Series 1, Box 1, Folder 1.
65. "Minutes of Meeting of Executive Committee," September 29, 1930, RAC, Bureau of Social Hygiene, RG: Minutes 1917–, Series 1, Box 3, Folder 42.
66. League of Nations, *Enquiry into Traffic in Women and Children in the East* (1932), 15. As the mis-naming and labeling of "Keijo" and "Fusan" indicate, there was an unquestioned recognition of Koreans and Korean women specifically as Japanese imperial subjects. Indeed, a section D. titled, "Women of Japanese Nationality as Victims of International Traffic," lays out the incoherent tangle of nationality, ethnicity, and race in early global governance: "In order to obtain a picture of the possible extent of international traffic in women of Japanese nationality, it will be convenient to recall, first of all, the numbers of Japanese, Korean and Formosan prostitutes as they have been indicated to the Commission in the various places visited outside the Japanese Empire. For the reader who is not familiar with the ethnographic conditions of the Japanese Empire, it should be mentioned that under 'Japanese' are to be understood persons of Japanese race, under 'Koreans' those of Korean race, and under 'Formosans' persons of Chinese race who, as inhabitants of Formosa, are Japanese nationals" (62). The facile ("convenient") confidence of this pseudo-social scientific ("ethnographic") taxonomy betrays the blithe non-consideration of Japanese imperial force and colonization of Korea and Taiwan in this early document of global governance. More troublingly, it portends and partially preconditions the persistent illegibility of "Asian women" as an effect of multiple layers of Japanese, European, and U.S. territorial ambitions and negotiated sovereignties.
67. Ruth Topping, "Survey of Traffic in Women and Children," December 23, 1931, RAC, Bureau of Social Hygiene, Series 3, Sub-Series 2, Box 10, Folder 203.

68. John Farnham, "Interview with Dr. Snow and Dr. Clarke, December 29, 1931," 1, RAC, Bureau of Social Hygiene, Series 3, Sub-Series 2, Box 10, Folder 203.
69. Knepper, "Measuring the Threat of Global Crime," 21–22.
70. Farnham, "Interview," 2.
71. League of Nations, *Enquiry into Traffic in Women and Children in the East* (1932), 18.
72. League of Nations, *Enquiry into Traffic in Women and Children in the East* (1932), 21.
73. League of Nations, *Enquiry into Traffic in Women and Children in the East* (1932), 21.
74. League of Nations, *Enquiry into Traffic in Women and Children in the East* (1932), 22.
75. League of Nations, *Enquiry into Traffic in Women and Children in the East* (1932), 21.
76. Pliley, "Claims to Protection," 101–2.
77. International Convention for the Suppression of the Traffic in Women of Full Age (signed in Geneva on October 11, 1933), emphasis mine.
78. Knepper, *International Crime in the 20th Century*, 95.
79. Pliley, "Claims to Protection," 96. Pliley concludes that "feminist abolitionists carved out a space in the [Advisory Committee] to have their voices heard" and "produced the momentum resulting in the 1927 trafficking study" (105).
80. Katarina Leppanen, "Movement of Women: Trafficking in the Interwar Era," *Women's Studies International Forum* 30, no. 6 (2007): 527.
81. Stephanie A. Limoncelli, *The Politics of Trafficking: The First International Movement to Combat the Sexual Exploitation of Women* (Palo Alto, CA: Stanford University Press, 2010), 73–74.
82. Marlou Schrover, "History of Slavery, Human Smuggling and Trafficking 1860–2010," in *Histories of Transnational Crime*, ed. Gerben Bruinsma (New York: Springer, 2015), 59.
83. *International Review of Criminal Policy* (1958): 138.
84. United Nations Department of Economic and Social Affairs, *Study on Traffic in Persons and Prostitution* (1959): 3–4, 2, 24.

CHAPTER 3: SEXUAL SLAVERY

1. UN Economic and Social Council (ECOSOC), *Report of the First Session of the Ad Hoc Committee on Slavery to the Economic and Social Council*, UN Doc. E/1660, E/AC.33/9, March 27, 1950, 1.
2. UN ECOSOC, *Report of the First Session*, 6.
3. Hans Engen, *Slavery. Concise Summary of the Information Supplied with Resolutions 238 (IX), 276 (X), 388 (XIII), 475 (XV) and 525 A (XVII). UN Doc. E/2673. February 9, 1955*, 9.
4. According to Suzanne Miers, "By spelling out the various forms of exploitation under attack, the 1956 Supplementary Convention against slavery made it more difficult to get agreement on measures to enforce the treaty or even to monitor

progress." *Slavery in the Twentieth Century: The Evolution of a Global Problem* (Walnut Creek, CA: AltaMira, 2003), 358.
5. Quoted in John P. Humphrey, "The United Nations Sub-commission on the Prevention of Discrimination and the Protection of Minorities," *American Journal of International Law* 62, no. 4 (1968): 870.
6. Humphrey, "The United Nations Sub-commission," 871.
7. Miers, *Slavery in the Twentieth Century*, 360. According to Miers, "Women's organizations played an increasingly vociferous role in this campaign. Their support was welcomed by the Anti-Slavery Society, whose own membership had declined, leaving it in greater financial straits than usual. Together, they got slavery placed on the agenda for the 1960 session of the ECOSOC" (359). The group of NGOs also included the Associated Country Women of the World, the International Alliance of Women, the International Council of Women, the International Federation of Women Lawyers, and the World Young Women's Christian Association (369n21).
8. Miers, *Slavery in the Twentieth Century*, 360–61.
9. Mohamed Awad, *Report on Slavery* (New York: United Nations, 1966), 6.
10. Awad, *Report on Slavery*, 123, 198, 301, 302.
11. Awad, *Report on Slavery*, 7. Awad then adds that "the request for replies to such a questionnaire probably also has a psychological effect in that it brings some to Member States the interest which the United Nations retains in such a vital question."
12. Quoted in Miers, *Slavery in the Twentieth Century*, 364.
13. Miers, *Slavery in the Twentieth Century*, 367.
14. Awad, *Report on Slavery*, 303.
15. Miers, *Slavery in the Twentieth Century*, 307.
16. Mohamed Awad, *Question of Slavery and the Slave Trade in All Their Practices and Manifestations, Including the Slavery-Like Practices of Apartheid and Colonialism*, UN doc. E/CN.4/Sub.2/322, July 16, 1971, paras. 226–29.
17. Sean O'Callaghan, *The Yellow Slave Trade: A Survey of the Traffic in Women and Children in the East* (London: Blond, 1968), 7. There are two other fleeting references to the "comfort system" in the book. In chapter 9 ("The Boryokudan of Japan"), O'Callaghan describes meeting an American expat named Carl who reminded him of how "during the war the Japanese organized brothels in Hong Kong, as indeed they did in every other country they occupied" (80). Carl also briefly pointed to a group he called "sister girls": "When war broke out in the Pacific the sister girls were all drafted into the army and sent to the forward battle areas to entertain the troops" (82).
18. Stephen Barlay, *Sex Slavery: A Documentary Report on the International Scene Today* ([1968]; London: William Heinemann, 1977), 13, 17.
19. Kathleen Barry, *Female Sexual Slavery* ([1979]; New York: New York University Press, 1984), 7, emphasis in original.
20. Barry, *Female Sexual Slavery*, 72.
21. Kathleen Barry, "International Feminism: Sexual Politics and the World Conference of Women in Copenhagen," *Gender Issues* 1, no. 2 (1981): 49.

22. Susan Jeanne Toepfer and Bryan Stuart Wells, "The Worldwide Market for Sex: A Review of International and Regional Legal Prohibitions regarding Trafficking in Women," *Michigan Journal of Gender and Law* 2 (1994): 108–9n156.
23. Fernand-Laurent, *Report of the Special Rapporteur*, 4, 5.
24. Fernand-Laurent, *Report of the Special Rapporteur*, 6, emphasis mine.
25. Fernand-Laurent, *Report of the Special Rapporteur*, 7. Referencing this particular passage, Jean Allain writes that "the equating of prostitution to slavery was made most explicit in 1983, by Jean Fernand-Laurent." *Slavery in International Law: Of Human Exploitation and Trafficking* (Leiden: Martinus Nijhoff, 2013), 346.
26. Benjamin Whitaker, *Slavery: Report* [updating the report on slavery to the subcommission in 1966] (New York: United Nations, 1984), E/CN.4/Sub.2/1982/20/Rev.1, 13.
27. Third World Conference on Women, *Nairobi Forward-Looking Strategies to the Year 2000: Report of the World Conference to Review and Appraise the Achievements of the United Nations Decade for Women: Equality, Development and Peace*, UN Doc. A/CONF.116/28/Rev.1, 1986.
28. Kathleen Barry, "The Network Defines Its Issues: Theory, Evidence and Analysis of Female Sexual Slavery," in *International Feminism Networking against Female Sexual Slavery*, ed. Kathleen Barry et al. (New York: International Women's Tribune Centre, 1984), 123.
29. Fernand-Laurent, *Report of the Special Rapporteur*, 13.
30. Judy Klemesrud, "A Personal Crusade against Prostitution," *New York Times*, June 24, 1985.
31. Fernand-Laurent, *Report of the Special Rapporteur*, 14.
32. UN Commission on Human Rights, *Report of the Working Group on Slavery of the Subcommission on Prevention of Discrimination and Protection of Minorities*, March 8, 1988, E/CN.4/RES/1988/42, line 3.
33. Nora Demleitner, "Forced Prostitution: Naming an International Offense," *Fordham International Law Journal* 18 (1994): 165–66.
34. Miers, *Slavery in the Twentieth Century*, 64.
35. Claude E. Welch Jr., "Defining Contemporary Forms of Slavery: Updating a Venerable NGO," *Human Rights Quarterly* 31, no. 1 (2009): 85.
36. Welch, "Defining Contemporary Forms of Slavery," 86n54.
37. Suzanne Miers, "Slavery and the Slave Trade as International Issues, 1890–1939," *Slavery and Abolition* 19, no. 2 (1998): 19.
38. Miers, *Slavery in the Twentieth Century*, 100–101.
39. Jean Allain, "The Legal Definition of Slavery into the Twenty-First Century," in *The Legal Definition of Slavery into the Twenty-First Century*, ed. Jean Allain (London: Oxford University Press, 2012): 200–201, 203.
40. League of Nations, "Memorandum Dated May 31, 1923 by Secretary-General Proposing That Council Should Entrust Permanent Mandates Commission with Preparation of Report to 5th Assembly on Question of Slavery," LoN C-385-1923, VI, 1–2.
41. Miers, *Slavery in the Twentieth Century*, 107.

42. League of Nations, Temporary Slavery Commission, *Report of the Temporary Slave Commission Adopted in the Course of Its Second Session, July 13th–25th, 1925*, A.19.1925, VI, 25 (July 1925), 2.
43. Miers, *Slavery in the Twentieth Century*, 108.
44. Miers, *Slavery in the Twentieth Century*, 128.
45. The Secretary-General, *Memorandum of the Secretary-General on the Terms of Reference of the Ad Hoc Committee on Slavery, Delivered to the Economic and Social Council*, UN Doc. E/AC.33/4 (February 3, 1950). Quoted in Jean Allain, "The Definition of Slavery in International Law," *Howard Law Journal* 52, no. 2 (winter 2009): 252.
46. Quoted in Allain, "The Definition of Slavery in International Law," 252.
47. UN ECOSOC, *Report of the First Session*, 3.
48. Awad, *Report on Slavery*, 10, 304, 312.
49. Miers, *Slavery in the Twentieth Century*, 392.
50. Kathryn Zoglin, "United Nations Action against Slavery: A Critical Evaluation," *Human Rights Quarterly* 8, no. 2 (1986): 321. This was especially opportune for the Anti-Slavery Society. Benjamin Whitaker, who had been a member of the society, was one of the five official expert members of the first Working Group, but Colonel Montgomery of the Anti-Slavery Society was also invited to attend its early meetings. Clarifying that the establishment of the Working Group "should not be credited primarily to the Commission or general international concern about slavery, but rather to the concentrated lobbying efforts of the Anti-Slavery Society," Zoglin adds, "In fact, in the view of numerous observers, the Working Group is almost the private creation of the Anti-Slavery Society" (314). We can see in this vital but occluded overlap between the nongovernmental and the intergovernmental the afterlife of the earlier coordination of anti-trafficking in the League of Nations and the determined work of the international voluntary organizations before that in shaping the 1905 agreement and the 1910 convention.
51. Zoglin, "United Nations Action against Slavery," 317–18, 315.
52. Kathleen Barry, *The Prostitution of Sexuality* (New York: New York University Press, 1995), 4.
53. United Nations, *Information Received from Non-governmental Organizations Pursuant to Commission on Human Rights Resolution 1989/35: Note* (Geneva: United Nations, 1989), 8.
54. *Report of the Working Group on Contemporary Forms of Slavery in Its Sixteenth Session*, UN Doc E/CN/CN4/Sub2/1991/41, August 19, 1991, 11, 6–7, 40.
55. Zoglin, "United Nations Action against Slavery," 326.
56. Chin Sung Chung, "The Origin and Development of the Military Sexual Slavery Problem in Imperial Japan," *positions: east asia cultures critique* 5, no. 1 (1997): 238.
57. UN Commission on Human Rights, *Contemporary Forms of Slavery: Report of the Working Group on Contemporary Forms of Slavery at Its Seventeenth Session*, E/CN.4/Sub.2/1992/34, June 23, 1992, 17.
58. Because the Korean Council did not have the necessary UN accreditation, Shin spoke under the auspices of another NGO with Category II consultative status, the Commission of the Churches on International Affairs of the World Council of

Churches. Here, we can see another connection to the significant role of international ecumenical organizations in both the 1970s protests against Japanese sex tourism and the 1990s redress movement regarding the Japanese military "comfort system."

59. UN Sub-Commission on Prevention of Discrimination and Protection of Minorities, 44th Session, *Summary Record of the 8th Meeting, 10 August 1992*, E/CN.4/Sub.2/1992/SR.8, December 7, 1992, 5.

60. This gathering has been referred to alternately as the "Asian Conference for Solidarity to Asian Women Drafted for Sexual Services by Japan" (AWHRC 1994), the "Asian Solidarity Conference on the Military Comfort Women Issue" (Hicks 1994), and the "Asian Solidarity Conference on 'Comfort Women' Issues" (Matsui 2002).

61. UN Sub-commission on Prevention of Discrimination and Protection of Minorities, 44th Session, *Summary Record of the 8th Meeting*, 6. The Third World Movement against the Exploitation of Women (TW-MAE-W) also appeared on the "roster" of this session with six members present, including the Filipina survivor, Maria Rosa Luna Henson, and the activist Nelia Sancho, but there are no details about what they might have said in the summary record.

62. C. Sarah Soh, "Aspiring to Craft Modern, Gendered Selves: 'Comfort Women' and Chongshindae in late Colonial Korea," *Critical Asian Studies* 36, no.2 (2004): 182, 198.

63. See Katharine H. S. Moon, "South Korean Movements against Militarized Sexual Labor," *Asian Survey* 39 (1999): 310–27.

64. Thomas Kern and Sang-hui Nam, "The Korean Comfort Women Movement and the Formation of a Public Sphere in East Asia," in *Korea Yearbook (2009): Politics, Economy and Society*, ed. Rüdiger Frank et al. (Leiden: Brill, 2009), 241.

65. Chunghee Sarah Soh, *The Comfort Women Sexual Violence and Postcolonial Memory in Korea and Japan* (Chicago: University of Chicago Press, 2008), 71–72.

66. Margaret D. Stetz, "What the West Failed to Learn about War from the 'Comfort Women,'" in *Gender Violence: Interdisciplinary Perspectives*, ed. Laura L. O'Toole et al. (New York: New York University Press), 225.

67. Soh, *The Comfort Women*, 72.

68. Chunghee Sarah Soh, "From Imperial Gifts to Sex Slaves: Theorizing Symbolic Representations of the 'Comfort Women'" *Social Science Japan Journal* 3, no. 1 (2000): 61.

69. UN Commission on Human Rights, *Summary Record of the 30th Meeting, Held at the Palais des Nations, Geneva, on Monday, 17 February 1992: Commission on Human Rights, 48th Session*, E/CN.4/1992/SR.30/Add.1.

70. UN Commission on Human Rights, *Contemporary Forms of Slavery*, 16–17.

71. UN Commission on Human Rights, *Contemporary Forms of Slavery*, 17.

72. UN Sub-commission on Prevention of Discrimination and Protection of Minorities, 44th Session, *Summary Record of the 8th Meeting*, E/CN.4/Sub.2/1992/58, October 14, 1992, 23–24.

73. United Nations, Sub-commission on the Promotion and Protection of Human Rights, *Review of Further Developments in Fields with Which the Sub-commission Has Been*

Concerned. Written Statement Submitted by Liberation, September 3, 1992, E/CN.4/Sub.2/1992/NGO/26.

74. Theo van Boven, "Letter, 22 April, from the Special Rapporteur on the Right to Compensation and Rehabilitation for Victims of Gross Violations of Human Rights and Fundamental Freedoms to the Working Group on Contemporary Forms of Slavery." Quoted in Heisoo Shin, "Seeking Justice, Honour and Dignity: Movement for the Victims of Japanese Military Sexual Slavery," in *Global Civil Society 2011, Globality and the Absence of Justice*, ed. Martin Albrow and Hakan Seckinelgin (Basingstoke, UK: Palgrave Macmillan, 2011), 16.

75. Theo van Boven, *Study Concerning the Right to Restitution, Compensation and Rehabilitation for Victims of Gross Violations of Human Rights and Fundamental Freedoms: Final Report Submitted by Theo van Boven*, Special Rapporteur (Geneva: United Nations, 1993), 7–8.

76. Radhika Coomaraswamy, *Preliminary Report Submitted by the Special Rapporteur on Violence against Women, Its Causes and Consequences, Ms. Radhika Coomaraswamy, in Accordance with Commission on Human Rights Resolution 1994/5* (1994), 69.

77. Radhika Coomaraswamy, *Report on the Mission to the Democratic People's Republic of Korea, the Republic of Korea and Japan on the Issue of Military Sexual Slavery in Wartime* (Geneva: United Nations, 1996), 4.

78. UN Commission on Human Rights, *Contemporary Forms of Slavery*, 17.

79. Ustinia Dolgopol and Snehal Paranjape, *Comfort Women: An Unfinished Ordeal. Report of a Mission* (Geneva: International Commission of Jurists, 1994), 24.

80. Quoted in Chung Chin Sung, "The Issue of Military Sexual Slavery and the International Labour Organization," *Korea Journal* 42, no. 1 (2002): 269.

81. Chung, "The Issue of Military Sexual Slavery," 271.

82. International Labour Organization, "Observation (CEACR)—Adopted 2002, Published 91st ILC session (2003). Forced Labour Convention, 1930 (No. 29)—Japan (Ratification: 1932)."

CHAPTER 4: VIOLENCE AGAINST WOMEN

1. Radhika Coomaraswamy and Lisa M. Kois, "Violence against Women," in *Women and International Human Rights Law*, ed. Kelly D. Askin and Dorean Koenig (Ardsley, NY: Transnational, 1999), 178.

2. Charlotte Watts and Cathy Zimmerman, "Violence against Women: Global Scope and Magnitude," *Lancet* 359, no. 9313 (2002): 1236.

3. In 1990–91, the UNESCO Principal Office for the Asia and the Pacific, based in Bangkok, commissioned a pilot project in India and the Republic of Korea as part of its Major Programme Area VII—"Peace, Human Rights and the Elimination of All Forms of Discrimination"—and published the findings in 1993 as a 100-page report titled *Violence against Women: Reports from India and Korea*. The Asian Women's Human Rights Council (AWHRC), which was formed in 1986, organized several

hearings and tribunals focused on various aspects of violence against women. In 1993, along with the Simorgh Women's Collective, the AWHRC organized the first public hearing in Lahore, Pakistan, focused on "personal" violence against women. Subsequent public hearings convened in different locations and co-organized by different local feminist groups would focus on different themes. The theme of the 2nd Asian-Pacific Public Hearing, held in Tokyo, was "War Crimes and the Trafficking in Women." It was co-organized with the Women's Human Rights Committee of Japan. In December 1994 the United Nations Children's Fund (UNICEF) and the newly created Secretariat of State for Women's Affairs in Cambodia jointly organized a regional conference on "Intra-Familial Violence" in Phnom Penh, with twenty-one countries represented. The proceedings would be published in August 1995 as *Fire in the House: Determinants of Intra-familial Violence and Strategies for Its Elimination by the UNICEF East Asia and Pacific Regional Office* (Bangkok: UNICEF, 1995).

4. See my review of *Breaking the Silence against Women in Asia* in *Asian Journal of Women's Studies* 7, no. 4 (2001): 122–31.

5. The notable absence of the issue at the 1975 Mexico City conference prompted the organization of the 1976 International Tribunal on Crimes against Women in Brussels. More than two thousand women from forty countries, including India, Japan, the Philippines, South Korea, Taiwan, and Vietnam, gathered to testify about and to analyze a large range of phenomena. The published proceedings of this tribunal featured a substantive chapter on violence against women. In addition to sections on "Rape," "Woman Battering," "Assault," "Femicide," and "The Castration of Females: Clitoridectomy, Excision, and Infibulation," this wide-ranging chapter also includes "Forced Incarceration in Mental Hospital in Marriage," "Violent Repression of Nonconforming Girls," and "Brutal Treatment of Women in Prison." Under "Torture of Women for Political Ends," the chapter features testimony of a Korean-Japanese woman who had been detained for interrogation by the Korean Central Intelligence Agency (KCIA). See Diana E. H. Russell and Nicole Van de Ven, eds., *The Proceedings of the International Tribunal on Crimes against Women* (Millbrae, CA: Les Femmes, 1976).

6. Jutta Joachim, "Shaping the Human Rights Agenda: The Case of Violence against Women," in *Gender Politics and Global Governance*, ed. Elizabeth K. Meyer and Elisabeth Prügl (Lanham, MD: Rowman and Littlefield, 1999), 144.

7. Lori L. Heise, Alanagh Raikes, Charlotte H. Watts, and Anthony B. Zwi, "Violence against Women: A Neglected Public Health Issue in Less Developed Countries," *Social Science and Medicine* 39, no. 9 (1994): 1170.

8. Quoted in Margaret E. Keck and Kathryn Sikkink, *Activists beyond Borders: Advocacy Networks in International Politics* (Ithaca, NY: Cornell University Press, 1998), 177.

9. Keck and Sikkink, *Activists beyond Borders*, 178.

10. Connors worked as a law teacher and legal scholar in the UK and Australia before joining the United Nations as the chief of the Women's Rights Section in

the Division for the Advancement of Women in the Department of Economic and Social Affairs from 1996 to 2002. She went on to work in the Human Rights Division at the UN Office of the High Commissioner of Human Rights and served as its director of the Research and Right to Development Division until 2015.

11. Jutta Joachim, *Agenda Setting, the UN and NGOs: Gender Violence and Reproductive Politics* (Washington, DC: Georgetown University Press, 2007), 117, 116.

12. UN Committee on the Elimination of Discrimination against Women, *Violence against Women*, Committee on the Elimination of Discrimination against Women Eleventh Session, General Recommendation No. 19, at 1, UN Doc. CEDAW/C.1992/L.1/Add.15, 1992.

13. UN Commission on the Status of Women, Working Group on Violence against Women, *Elimination of Violence against Women: Report of the Secretary-General*, Commission on the Status of Women, Thirty-Seventh Session, Vienna, March 17–26, 1993 (E/CN/6/1993/12), 7–8.

14. UN General Assembly, *Declaration on the Elimination of Violence against Women*, December 20, 1993, A/RES/48/104, https://www.refworld.org/docid/3b00f25d2c.html, accessed December 7, 2007.

15. Heise, Raikes, Watts, and Zwi, "Violence against Women: A Neglected Public Health Issue," 1165.

16. Center for Women's Global Leadership (CWGL), *1991 Women's Leadership Institute Report: Women, Violence and Human Rights* (New Brunswick, NJ: Center for Women's Global Leadership, 1992), 26.

17. In 1992 Skrobanek characterized U.S. military- and tourism-geared prostitution as illustrative cases of violence against women. See Siriporn Skrobanek, "Exotic, Subservient and Trapped: Confronting Prostitution and Traffic in Women in Southeast Asia," in *Freedom from Violence: Women's Strategies from around the World*, ed. Margaret Schuler (New York: UNIFEM, 1992), 127–37.

18. CWGL, *1991 Women's Leadership Institute Report*, 8.

19. CWGL, *1991 Women's Leadership Institute Report*, 25.

20. Niamh Reilly, ed., *Without Reservation: The Beijing Tribunal on Accountability for Women's Human Rights* (New Brunswick, NJ: Center for Women's Global Leadership, 1996), 5.

21. Elisabeth Jay Friedman, "Gendering the Agenda: The Impact of Transnational Women's Rights Movement at the UN Conferences of the 1990s," *Women's Studies International Forum* 26, no. 4 (2003): 321.

22. Charlotte Bunch, "Women's Rights as Human Rights: Toward a Re-vision of Human Rights," *Human Rights Quarterly* 12 (1990): 492.

23. *Violence against Women*, UN Committee on the Elimination of Discrimination against Women, Eleventh Session, General Recommendation No. 19, at 1, UN Doc. CEDAW/C.1992/L.1/Add.15, 1992.

24. Alice M. Miller, "Sexuality, Violence against Women, and Human Rights: Women Make Demands and Ladies Get Protection," *Health and Human Rights* 7, no. 2 (2004): 24, emphasis mine.

25. Janet Halley, Prabha Kotiswaran, Hila Shamir, and Chantal Thomas, "From the International to the Local in Feminist Legal Responses to Rape, Prostitution/Sex Work, and Sex Trafficking: Four Studies in Contemporary Governance Feminism," *Harvard Journal of Law and Gender* 29 (2006): 337, 340.
26. Bunch, "Women's Rights as Human Rights," 491.
27. Charlotte Bunch, "The Global Campaign for Women's Human Rights: Where Next after Vienna?," *St. John's Law Review* 69, nos. 1–2 (1995): 175.
28. Bunch, "The Global Campaign for Women's Human Rights," 177–78.
29. Miller, "Sexuality, Violence against Women, and Human Rights," 25, 29. Miller cogently encapsulates the limits of this framing of rape as torture: "The distance that must be traveled to see a male torture victim as a reconstituted citizen/subjective holder of rights is shorter than the distance that must be traveled to see a raped woman as a citizen/rights holder" (29–30).
30. Charlotte Bunch, Samantha Frost, and Niamh Reilly, "Making the Global Local: International Networking for Women's Human Rights," in *Women's International Human Rights: A Reference Guide*, ed. Kelly D. Askin et al. (New York: Transnational, 1998), 97.
31. Joachim, *Agenda Setting, the UN and NGOs*, 125.
32. Roxanna Carrillo, "Violence against Women: An Obstacle to Development," in *Gender Violence: A Development and Human Rights Issue* (New Brunswick, NJ: Center for Women's Global Leadership, 1991), 34.
33. Christine Bradley, "Why Male Violence against Women Is a Development Issue: Lessons from Papua New Guinea." Occasional paper, UNIFEM, 1990. Cited in Lori L. Heise, "Reproductive Freedom and Violence against Women: Where Are the Intersections?" *Journal of Law, Medicine and Ethics* 21, no. 2 (1993): 206–16. Bradley's paper for UNIFEM was updated and included in the 1994 collection *Violence against Women*, ed. Miranda Davies (London: Zed, 1994): 10–27.
34. Bradley, "Why Male Violence against Women Is a Development Issue," 10–11.
35. Bradley, "Why Male Violence against Women Is a Development Issue," 24, 13, 15.
36. Bradley, "Why Male Violence against Women Is a Development Issue," 20.
37. William H. Draper III, "Foreword," in United Nations Development Programme (UNDP), *Human Development Report 1990* (New York: Oxford University Press for the United Nations Development Programme, 1990), iii.
38. UNDP, *Human Development Report 1990*, 1.
39. Draper, "Foreword," iii.
40. UNDP, *Human Development Report 1990*, 32.
41. James G. Speth, "Foreword," in United Nations Development Programme, *Human Development Report 1995* (New York: Oxford University Press for the United Nations Development Programme, 1995), iii.
42. UNDP, *Human Development Report 1995*, 72.
43. Sakiko Fukuda-Parr, "The Human Development Paradigm: Operationalizing Sen's Ideas on Capabilities," *Feminist Economics* 9, nos. 2–3 (2003): 305, emphasis mine.
44. Fukuda-Parr, "The Human Development Paradigm," 315n1.
45. UNDP, *Human Development Report 1990*, 6, emphasis mine.

46. Carrillo, "Violence against Women," 17, 20.
47. Carrillo, "Violence against Women," 21, 24, 29.
48. Carrillo, "Violence against Women," 29, 31.
49. Some of these publications include "Violence against Women: The Hidden Health Burden," *World Health Statistics Quarterly. Rapport trimestriel de statistiques sanitaires mondiales* 46, no. 1 (1992): 78–85; "Violence against Women," *World Health* 46, no. 1 (1993); "Violence against Women: The Missing Agenda," in *The Health of Women: A Global Perspective*, ed. Marge Koblinsky, Judith Timyan, and Jill Gay (Boulder, CO: Westview, 1993): 171–95; "Reproductive Freedom and Violence against Women: Where Are the Intersections?" *Journal of Law, Medicine and Ethics* 21, no. 2 (1993): 206–16; "Gender-Based Abuse: The Global Epidemic," *Cadernos de Saúde Pública* 10 (1994): S135–45; and "Violence against Women: Translating International Advocacy into Concrete Change," *American University Law Review* 44 (1994): 1207.
50. Keck and Sikkink, *Activists beyond Borders*, 179.
51. Quoted in Keck and Sikkink, *Activists beyond Borders*, 179.
52. Heise, "Violence against Women: The Missing Agenda," 173, emphasis mine.
53. Heise, "Violence against Women: The Missing Agenda," 185.
54. Heise, "Violence against Women: The Hidden Health Burden," 78.
55. Heise, "Violence against Women: The Hidden Health Burden," 78.
56. Heise, "Violence against Women: The Missing Agenda," 171.
57. Heise, "Violence against Women: The Hidden Health Burden," 78.
58. Heise, "Violence against Women: The Missing Agenda," 171, 184.
59. Lori Heise with Jacqueline Pitanguy and Adrienne Germain, *Violence against Women: The Hidden Health Burden* (Washington, DC: World Bank, 1994), ix.
60. World Bank, *World Development Report 1993: Investing in Health* (New York: Oxford University Press, 1993), 1, 26.
61. World Bank, *World Development Report 1993*, 26.
62. World Bank, *World Development Report 1993*, 26, box 1.3.
63. At this point, it would seem most evident to readers that I have drifted very far from the "comfort women" case, which threads through and spirals around this book. But this peculiar temporal orientation in which the *future* is folded into a generic global *present* and also quantified not once and for all, but on a repeated, annual basis, allows me to make a brief return/detour. Recall the demand for as well as the refusal of monetary compensation to victims-survivors for the multiple violations and abuses that were inflicted in the past and have continued to afflict and debilitate them into the present. Regarding the difficult challenge of calculating the proper amount of compensation, how might we think about and attempt to measure a "past stream of disability-free life lost as a result of death, disease, or injury"? Can and must this GBD method be oriented only to the future-in-the-present and not the past-in-the-present?
64. World Bank, *World Development Report 1993*, x (emphasis mine), 27 (emphasis mine), 24.
65. World Bank, *World Development Report 1993*, x.

66. Katherine E. Kenny, "The Biopolitics of Global Health: Life and Death in Neoliberal Time," *Journal of Sociology* 51, no. 1 (2015): 15.
67. Christopher Murray is an especially fascinating figure. Having earned a doctorate in international health economics from Oxford and then a medical degree from Harvard, he was appointed as an assistant professor of the Harvard School of Public Health before he began working with the World Bank and the World Health Organization in the early 1990s. Murray's work on health metrics later garnered the attention of Bill Gates, and in 2007 the Bill and Melinda Gates Foundation committed $105 million for the establishment of the Institute for Health Metrics and Evaluation (IHME) at the University of Washington in Seattle. In January 2017 the foundation pledged an additional $279 million to the IHME. According to a 2013 feature article on Murray, "While writing his dissertation at Oxford in the mid-1980s, he saw residents of some low-income countries—China, Costa Rica, Sri Lanka, and the state of Kerala in India—repeatedly trumpeted as healthier than others and, in terms of mortality rate improvement, doing even better than those in many wealthy Western nations." The article then points to the example of a 1985 study, *Good Health at Low Cost*, published by the Rockefeller Foundation, which singled out those four countries. See Jeremy Smith, "Life, Not Death, Is the Focus of New Health Metrics," *Discover*, June/July 2013, http://discovermagazine.com/2013/julyaug/18-international-health-metric-measures-years-lost. For more biographical information and an interesting account of the genesis of the World Bank project on GBD/DALYS, see the lively and largely positive and even heroic portrait of Murray in Jeremy N. Smith, *Epic Measures: One Doctor, Seven Billion Patients* (New York: Harper Wave, 2015). Smith describes the important role of Lawrence (Larry) Summers, who was then vice president of Development Economics and Chief Economist at the World Bank (1991–1993), in spurring the organization, "which was much better known for its economic expertise and loans for infrastructure," to take on this new matter of "health policy priority-setting." Taking on the POV of the hegemonic neoliberal Washington Consensus, Smith writes: "Part of the good of getting government out of doing everything was that this freed it to put more energy into what it was good at. Health care, for example.... Larry Summers wanted the World Bank to issue clear calls to action. 'I had become tired of what I regarded as platitudinous Bank prose, which constantly said, "This is an important area. Policies must take this into account,"' he recalls. The upcoming World Development Report, Summers told Dean Jamison and his staff, better 'have some bite.'" *Epic Measures*, 73–74.
68. I inquired directly about the rationale for these geographical and categorical divisions in an email to Christopher Murray. He replied promptly and courteously on October 25, 2016: "The division of the world into the 8 regions was actually based on a group discussion of those involved in the WDR 93. China and India were separated out because of their large size and broad policy interest in the two mega countries. So somewhat disappointingly, there was not high-level principled reason for the division of countries into the 8 regions except that they made sense. The most difficult and heterogeneous was actually other Asia and islands."

69. World Bank, *World Development Report 1993*, 25, 28.
70. World Bank, *World Development Report 1993*, 50.
71. World Bank, *World Development Report 1993*, 51, 175. An earlier consultation on "Women and Health" had been convened on December 7–9, 1992, in Windsor, England, organized by the London School of Hygiene and Tropical Medicine. This was a follow-up from a consultation on "Interventions for Nervous System Disorders," which had been convened in Washington, DC, on July 6–7, 1992. In addition to Heise and Murray, the 1993 consultation on "Violence against Women" was chaired by Helen Saxenian and also attended by Jacqueline Campbell, Walter Gulbinat, and Dean Kilpatrick.
72. Heise, Pitanguy, and Germain, *The Hidden Health Burden*, 17.
73. Heise, Pitanguy, and Germain, *The Hidden Health Burden*, 17, 48.
74. Heise, Pitanguy, and Germain, *The Hidden Health Burden*, 22, 24 (emphasis mine).
75. Heise, Pitanguy, and Germain, *The Hidden Health Burden*, 46, 47.

CHAPTER 5: TRUTH DISCLOSURE

1. Yoshimi Yoshiaki, *Comfort Women: Sexual Slavery in the Japanese Military during World War II*, trans. Suzanne O'Brien (New York: Columbia University Press, 2000), 33.
2. George Hicks, *The Comfort Women: Japan's Brutal Regime of Enforced Prostitution in the Second World War* (New York: W. W. Norton, 1994), 69. Hicks cites Kim Il-myon's 1976 book here. See also Elazar Barkan, *The Guilt of Nations: Restitution and Negotiating Historical Injustices* (Baltimore: Johns Hopkins University Press, 2001), 52.
3. Yoshimi, *Comfort Women*, 33.
4. Ienaga Saburo, *The Pacific War, 1931–1945* (New York: Random House, 1978): 158–59. Ienaga cites several publications here, including Tsuyama Akira's *Sensō dorei* (*War Slave*) and Tamura Taijrō's *Inago* (*Locust*), which, as Ienaga explains, "cannot be taken literally (correspondence with the author). However, it is a valuable source about the plight of Korean prostitutes with the army" (282n30).
5. Ienaga, *The Pacific War*, 184. Ienaga cites two sources here: "Fujii Shigeo, *Hi no maru butai* (*The Rising Sun Unit*). Nishguchi Katsumi's *Kuruwa* (*The Brothels*) is a work of fiction generally based on fact. Correspondence with the author" (287n12).
6. James A. Stone, "Interrogation of Japanese POWs in World War II: U.S. Response to a Formidable Challenge," *Interrogation: World War II, Vietnam, and Iraq*, ed. William C. Spracher (Washington, DC: National Defense Intelligence College, 2008), 35.
7. See Laura Kang, "Conjuring 'Comfort Women': Mediated Affiliations and Disciplined Subjects in Korean/American Transnationality," *Journal of Asian American Studies* 6, no. 1 (2003): 25–55. The affective, political, and aesthetic investments of Korean Americans were crucial in introducing and sustaining the "comfort women" problem in U.S. public consciousness through a broad range of events, actions, and textual productions. In that 2003 essay I sought to register and think through my ambivalence and reservations about this intense investment and

lively proliferation. An earnest overidentification with Korean "comfort women" combined with a visceral and often spectacular staging of *their* violated bodies and psyches to inhibit and displace questions about the contingent grounds of ethnic affiliation and diasporic attachment, but also a very particular U.S. grammar and political economy of representation, which enabled and celebrated these endeavors. This chapter proposes a very different way that Korean Americans but also other Asian Americans and others might *think through* the doubly bracketed figure of "Korean 'comfort women'" as a multiply significant subject of U.S. history, culture, and politics.

8. Joseph Daniel Harrington, *Yankee Samurai: The Secret Role of Nisei in America's Pacific Victory* (Detroit: Pettigrew, 1979), 312. Harrington briefly mentions the interrogation of the women by Chan and Hirabayashi and follows up later with this odd two-paragraph-long vignette: "Comfort girls may have had some Nisei wondering whether the enemy's ideas on how to wage war might be more compatible with the average infantrymen's wishes, but the linguists did turn use of them against the enemy." He proceeds to describe a Japanese military document discovered at Guadalcanal, which listed the time schedule of the "comfort stations" at its New Britain base: "This document was thoroughly analyzed, to develop when the maximum number of senior officers would be patronizing the girls. An air strike was then laid on for that hour. After that, according to John Anderton, 'Japanese leadership at Rabaul was never the same'" (228).

9. Harrington, *Yankee Samurai*, 312.

10. Won-Loy Chan, *Burma: The Untold Story* (Novato, CA: Presidio, 1986), 100.

11. Harrington, *Yankee Samurai*, 241–42.

12. Chan, *Burma: The Untold Story*, 93–94.

13. Chan's reference to the United States troops' reporting is significant, but I am not aware of any such documents that have been located.

14. A June 7, 1945, article on the photographers of the 164th Signal Photo Company titled "Photo Wallahs" mentions "T/4 Frank W. Shearer, New Kensington, Pa." as one of its photographers. A July 12, 1945, article in the *India-Burma Theater Roundup* identifies Sgt. Frank Shearer as a *Roundup* photographer. See also Lee Barker, "Click Wallahs of CBI," *Ex-CBI Roundup*, July 1952, www.cbi-history.com/part_vi_164th_sig_co.html.

15. The photo is featured again at the beginning of chapter 2, where the caption reads, "Comfort women taken into *protective* custody by the Allied Powers in Burma, August 1944" (76, emphasis mine). The same photo is also featured in Yuki Tanaka's *Japan's Comfort Women*, where it is captioned as "A group of Korean comfort women captured in Burma, who were interrogated by some bilingual Japanese-American soldiers in August 1944" (41).

16. The capitalization of "Comfort Girls" shows that, even in 1944, the category was understood as a recognized *proper* noun. Then, at the bottom, there is one other entry under "Taken For: Capt. Chan, g-2 (wants 2 prints)." This further suggests that Chan might have requested copies of this photograph for his own personal records and even requested the taking of the photo. If I were to caption the image, it

might read: "Twenty Korean women who were subject to sexual slavery by the Japanese Imperial Army for two years in Burma and the Japanese woman who operated the 'comfort house' being detained as Japanese prisoners of war by the US military. Crouching behind them are four uniformed Asian American men who have been selectively assigned to U.S. Army military intelligence."

17. I borrow this locution from Jennifer Terry's illuminating book, *Attachments to War: Biomedical Logics and Violence in Twenty-First Century America* (Durham, NC: Duke University Press, 2017).
18. Yonhap News Agency, "South Korea Publicizes U.S. Document on Japan's Recruitment of 'Comfort Girls,'" December 21, 1991, trans. in BBC *Summary of World Broadcasts*, December 23, 1991, LNAU.
19. Kyodo News Service, "U.S. Records Detail Army's Management of 'Comfort Women,'" January 26, 1992. According to a United Press International dispatch on the same day titled "Wartime Army Directly Involved in Brothels, Report Says," both records were "obtained by the Kyodo News Service." Under the title, "OTHER REPORTS ON KOREA; Japanese agency cites U.S. military records on 'comfort women,'" the BBC *Summary of World Broadcasts* on January 29, 1992, describes them as "photocopies of documents kept at the Washington Record Centre which were acquired by Kyodo News Service recently." LNAU.
20. According to a prefatory note to the section, "The following is derived from interrogation at C.S.D.I.C. (I) of M.739, and from O.W.I. Interrogation at Ledo Base Stockade of 20 Korean 'comfort girls,' Report dated 21 Sept. 1944." *Bulletin No. 2*, 10.
21. The second cover page notes R. K. Sutherland, lieutenant general, United States Army Chief of Staff, and also credits C. A. Willoughby, major general, G.S.C., Asst. Chief of Staff, G-2.
22. Antonio Kamiya, "War Brothels Were Strict, Report Shows. Under Military Rules, 'Comfort Women' Had One Day off a Month," *Japan Times*, February 5, 1992. Reproduced in full in Grant Goodman, "My Own Gaiatsu: A Document from 1945 Provides Proof," in *Legacies of the Comfort Women of World War II*, ed. Margaret Stetz and Bonnie B. C. Oh (Armonk, NY: M. E. Sharpe, 2001): 142–51.
23. Yoshimi Yoshiaki would include them in the compilation of archival documents that he edited and published in 1992, *Jūgun ianfu shiryō-shū* [A collection of documents on military comfort women] (Tokyo: Otsuki shoten, 1992).
24. Ustinia Dolgopol and Snehal Paranjape, *Comfort Women: An Unfinished Ordeal. Report of a Mission* (Geneva: International Commission of Jurists, 1994), 32–53. The authors acknowledge that copies of the documents they cite were provided to them by Yoshimi Yoshiaki.
25. Hicks, *The Comfort Women*, 137–40.
26. Dolgopol and Paranjape, *Comfort Women: An Unfinished Ordeal*, 16.
27. Hicks, *The Comfort Women*, 270.
28. Yuki Tanaka, *Japan's Comfort Women: Sexual Slavery and Prostitution during World War II and the US Occupation* (New York: Routledge, 2002), 84, 87.
29. Tanaka, *Japan's Comfort Women*, 85.
30. Tanaka, *Japan's Comfort Women*, 85.

31. Tanaka, *Japan's Comfort Women*, 85.
32. See the feature on Hirabayashi at the Veteran's History Project of the Library of Congress, http://memory.loc.gov/diglib/vhp-stories/loc.natlib.afc2001001.28498. Additional videotaped testimony by Hirabayashi can be found at Go for Broke: National Educational Center, www.goforbroke.org/ohmsviewer/viewer.php?cachefile=1999OH0067_01_Hirabayashi.xml, and Densho Digital Repository, http://ddr.densho.org/narrators/208.
33. Karl Yoneda, *Ganbatte: Sixty-Year Struggle of a Kibei Worker* (Los Angeles: Asian American Studies Center, 1983), 151.
34. Noting that there was a thirteen-day gap between Japan's decision to accept the Potsdam Declaration on August 15, 1945, and the arrival of Allied authorities on August 28, Daqing Yang writes that "on August 16, Imperial Headquarters ordered Japanese military units to destroy all secret documents, many of which are believed to have contained evidence of war crimes. The orders themselves were to be destroyed, and no reports on the implementation of the orders were to be made except by secure telephone." Acknowledging that such destruction of incriminating evidence is "standard practice," Yang adds that "various Japanese agencies—the military in particular—systematically destroyed sensitive documents to a degree perhaps unprecedented in history" and cites Tanaka Hiromi's estimate that "less than 0.1 percent of the material ordered for destruction survived." Daqing Yang, "Documentary Evidence and the Studies of Japanese War Crimes: An Interim Assessment," in *Researching Japanese War Crimes Records: Introductory Essays* (Washington, DC: Nazi War Crimes and Japanese Imperial Government Records Interagency Working Group and the National Archives and Records Administration, 2006), 23.
35. John Blaxland, "Intelligence and Special Operations in the Southwest Pacific, 1942–45," in *Australia 1944–45: Victory in the Pacific*, ed. Peter J. Dean (Melbourne: Cambridge University Press, 2015), 158.
36. Edward Drea, "Introduction," in *Researching Japanese War Crimes Records: Introductory Essays* (Washington, DC: Nazi War Crimes and Japanese Imperial Government Records Interagency Working Group and the National Archives and Records Administration, 2006), 10.
37. Drea, "Introduction," 15.
38. Drea, "Introduction," 15.
39. As one study of the OWI has pointed out, the executive order charged the agency with "a number of potentially conflicting functions": "It was to provide truthful information to the American public, and meanwhile to develop campaigns—like those on behalf of bond-buying or salvage—to secure certain actions by that public. At the same time it was to provide truthful information to overseas audiences, but that material had to be slanted for the purposes of propaganda." Allan Winkler, *The Politics of Propaganda: The Office of War Information, 1942–1945* (New Haven, CT: Yale University Press, 1978), 35.
40. A most interesting and helpful archival repository that I consulted on the MISLS was created by the Japanese American Veterans Association (JAVA) and is at https://

java.wildapricot.org. According to the historical account provided on the website, "JAVA was activated in 1992, some 17 years after the Freedom of Information Act allowed the Military Intelligence Service (MIS) activities in the Asia Pacific theater, classified secret, to be told." Three especially dedicated and persistent researchers performed a bulk of this archival labor: "For 10 years, Dr. Susumu (Sus) Yamamoto, Fumie Yamamoto and Maggie Ikeda drove to the National Archives and Records Administration (NARA) and researched archived documents about the Nisei during WWII. They copied enough documents to fill a 10′ × 5′ × 8′ storage vault." These documents were later digitized and uploaded as an internet archive. See https://java.wildapricot.org/Research-Archive.

41. SEATIC, *Psychological Warfare Bulletin* 116 (March 1945). This document is included on page 169 of the last volume in the five-volume compilation of archival documents, which can be downloaded via the Digital Museum for The Comfort Women Issue and the Asian Women's Fund at http://www.awf.or.jp/e6/document.html. In part III the report provides this detailed account of the procedure that the interrogators were to follow: "The interrogator had a mimeographed questionnaire with space to check the various facts. He was instructed to engage the PWs in conversation, make the checks and comments as information came out naturally, or else wait into the interview to record the facts, in order to encourage free and frank testimony. Complete questionnaires and the subject of careful discussion and check between the interrogator and members of the OWI staff." The last sentence suggests that there could have been another layer of displacement and mediation of "free and frank testimony" by prisoners through a collective but also hierarchical "OWI staff" deliberation about the responses before they were written up and filed as the final interrogation report.

42. This is the outline of United States Office of War Information, Psychological Warfare Team attached to U.S. Army Forces C-B-I, *Japanese Prisoner of War Interrogation Report 23*, of Oyama, Iwao, which was conducted and composed by Karl Yoneda and Alex Yorichi on June 21, 1944.

43. United States Office of War Information (OWI), Psychological Warfare Team attached to U.S. Army Forces C-B-I, *Japanese Prisoner of War Interrogation Report No. 49*, October 1, 1944, 1.

44. OWI, *POW Interrogation Report No. 49*, 2.

45. OWI, 1. Yoshimi quotes this same passage as the remarks of "U.S. Army Sergeant Alex Yorichi" and then declares that "it is clear that, for many women who were sold and forced to become comfort women, the economic fetters of a sum advanced against their labor and deception about the nature of their work were intertwined" (Yoshimi, *Comfort Women*, 106). Here Yoshimi cites page 441 of *Shiryoshu*, the 1992 collection of archival documents that he edited.

46. OWI, *POW Interrogation Report No. 49*, 1, 3–4, 6.

47. "Lift Secrecy on Exploits of Nisei G.I.'s in I-B Theater," *India-Burma Theater Roundup* 4, no. 11 (November 22, 1945), www.cbi-theater.com/roundup/roundup112245.html.

48. Yoneda, *Ganbatte*, 156, 159.

49. Chan, *Burma: The Untold Story*, 93.

50. United States Office of War Information, *Psychological Warfare Team Attached to U.S. Army Forces C-B-I, Japanese Prisoner of War No. 48,* September 4, 1944, 1.
51. Chan, *Burma: The Untold Story,* 94.
52. Chan, *Burma: The Untold Story,* 94.
53. Chan, *Burma: The Untold Story,* xi.
54. Chan, *Burma: The Untold Story,* 94, 95. Chan's repeated devaluation of what the women could offer in the way of useful military intelligence is followed up with a fascinating and very detailed account of an exchange with a Japanese woman about a bundle of Japanese military scrip that she was hiding in her obi: "Something like our own scrip used in Europe and Asia, it was a paper promise by the Japanese government to pay by some unspecified date the amount of ten Burmese rupees. With the loss of northern Burma and what appeared to be the eventual total defeat of the Imperial forces, the scrip was undoubtedly worthless. Grant and I slowly placed the bundles back on the ground in front of Mama-san. Grant looked at me and I nodded my agreement to what I knew he was thinking. He looked at the girls, shrugged, and then as gently as he could explained to the old lady that what she had was money printed by the Japanese and now that the Japanese had been defeated, the money was worthless, had no value." Hirabayashi then offered a small compensation: "He explained we could probably exchange the scrip for cigarettes, candy, and food with American and Chinese souvenir hunters.... Mama-san explained the whole caper to her girls. Some laughed, some cried, and when I thought of what these girls had endured to earn this worthless scrip I was heartsick" (97). This account has been repeated several times by Hirabayashi in videotaped testimony.
55. OWI POW *Interrogation Report No. 49,* 2.
56. OWI POW *Interrogation Report No. 48,* 1.
57. OWI POW *Interrogation Report No. 48,* 1–2.
58. OWI POW *Interrogation Report No. 48,* 5.
59. SEATIC *Bulletin 2,* 13.
60. Walter Rundle, "Jap 'Comfort Girls,'" *CBI Roundup,* November 30, 1944.
61. Soh argues, "The four women in Plate 1.2 appear clearly to be in worse condition than the three Korean 'comfort girls' shown in Plate 1.1, supporting the point of the present study that underscores the wide range of situations concerning the comfort facilities and personal conditions of individual comfort women." Soh, *The Comfort Women,* 36.
62. "Siege of Sungshan Ends in Capture," *CBI Roundup,* September 14, 1944, www.cbi-theater.com/roundup/roundup091444.html.
63. Chan, *Burma: The Untold Story,* 97.
64. "First Filmed Evidence of 'Comfort Women' Found in U.S. Archives." *China Daily,* July 12, 2017, https://www.chinadailyhk.com/articles/64/52/70/1499832009091.html.
65. Sofia Lotto Persio, "World War II Mass Grave of 'Comfort Women' Documented in Graphic Video Was Discovered in the U.S.," *Newsweek,* February 28, 2018, https://www.newsweek.com/world-war-ii-mass-grave-comfort-women-documented-horrifying-video-discovered-823564.

CHAPTER 6: JUST COMPENSATION

1. Ministry of Foreign Affairs of Japan, "Statement by Prime Minister Tomiichi Murayama on the 'Peace, Friendship, and Exchange Initiative'" (August 15, 1994), https://www.mofa.go.jp/announce/press/pm/murayama/state9408.html, accessed July 1, 2007.
2. "The First Report on the So-Called Wartime Comfort Women Issue." The translated text of the report is online at the Digital Museum for the Comfort Women Issue and the Asian Women's Fund. http://awf.or.jp/e6/statement-05.html, accessed July 1, 2007.
3. According to Jennifer Chan-Tiberghien, "Interest in the subject quickly subsided after the government created the Asian Women's Fund in 1995 (96 news articles appeared between 1995 and 1999, compared to 332 between 1990 and 1994)." Chan-Tiberghien, *Gender and Human Rights Politics in Japan: Global Norms and Domestic Networks* (Palo Alto, CA: Stanford University Press, 2004), 76.
4. Heisoo Shin, "Seeking Justice, Honour and Dignity: Movement for the Victims of Japanese Military Sexual Slavery," in *Global Civil Society 2011, Globality and the Absence of Justice*, ed. Martin Albrow and Hakan Seckinelgin (Basingstoke, UK: Palgrave Macmillan, 2011), 15.
5. Norma Field, "War and Apology: Japan, Asia, the Fiftieth, and After," *positions: east asia cultures critique* 5, no. 1 (1997): 37.
6. Asian Women's Fund, "Memorandum of Understanding between the Asian Women's Fund and the Department of Social Welfare and Development of the Republic of the Philippines Regarding the Implementation to Lolas in Crisis Situation Project" (January 15, 1997), http://www.awf.or.jp/pdf/0191.pdf, accessed July 1, 2017.
7. Asian Women's Fund, "Memorandum of Understanding between the Department of Social Affairs of the Republic of Indonesia and the Asian Women's Fund Concerning Promotion of Social Welfare Services for Elderly People in Indonesia" (March 24, 1997), available at the Digital Museum for the The Comfort Women Issue and the Asian Women's Fund, http://www.awf.or.jp/pdf/0206.pdf, accessed July 7, 2007.
8. Chungmoo Choi, "The Politics of War Memories toward Healing," in *Perilous Memories: The Asia-Pacific War(s)*, ed. Takashi Fujitani, Geoffrey M. White, and Lisa Yoneyama (Durham, NC: Duke University Press, 2001), 396.
9. "Seoul Won't Seek Japan Funds for War's Brothel Women," *New York Times* (April 22, 1998). The article notes that "at least seven from South Korea" had received some money from the AWF at that point.
10. Lisa Yoneyama, *Cold War Ruins: Transpacific Critique of American Justice and Japanese War Crimes* (Durham, NC: Duke University Press, 2016), 125.
11. Chalmers Johnson, *MITI and the Japanese Economic Miracle: The Growth of Industrial Policy, 1925–1975* (Palo Alto, CA: Stanford University Press, 1982), 1.
12. Chalmers Johnson, *Blowback: The Costs and Consequences of American Empire* (New York: Henry Holt, 2000), 177.
13. David Arase, *Buying Power: The Political Economy of Japan's Foreign Aid* (Boulder, CO: Lynne Rienner, 1995), 17, 18.

14. Michael Schaller, "America's Favorite War Criminal: Kishi Nobusuke and the Transformation of US-Japan Relations," Japan Policy Research Institute Working Paper No.11 (July 1995), http://www.jpri.org/publications/workingpapers/wp11.html. In another fascinating and even more detailed account of Kishi's time in Manchuria, Richard J. Samuels writes: "Connections to the opium trade through radical nationalists and to industrialists, combined with his personal control of the movement of capital in and out of the puppet state, made Kishi singularly influential—and likely very rich. Indeed, while still in China Kishi became known for his consummate skill in laundering money. It was said that he could move as much money around as he wished 'with a single telephone call,' and that he did so both legally and illegally and for public and private purposes." "Kishi and Corruption: An Anatomy of the 1955 System," Japan Policy Research Institute Working Paper No. 83 (December 2001), http://www.jpri.org/publications/workingpapers/wp83.html. See also Lisa Yooneyama, *Cold War Ruins*, 31, 256n.
15. As Samuels later sums up this diplomatic exchange, "Dulles explained that the United States wanted a strong Japan to help it contain communism and clearly thought that a strong Japan required a unified center-right political organization." Samuels, "Kishi and Corruption."
16. Schaller, "America's Favorite War Criminal."
17. William R. Nester, *Japan and the Third World: Patterns, Power, Prospects* (New York: St. Martin's, 1992), 122.
18. Arase, *Buying Power*, 28. The OECD website defines ODA (official development assistance) as "government aid designed to promote the economic development and welfare of developing countries"; https://data.oecd.org/oda/net-oda.htm.
19. Schaller, "America's Favorite War Criminal."
20. Nester, *Japan and the Third World*, 121-22.
21. Jung-en Woo, *Race to the Swift: State and Finance in Korean Industrialization* (New York: Columbia University Press, 1991), 75.
22. Woo, *Race to the Swift*, 97.
23. Iain Pirie, *The Korean Developmental State: From Dirigisme to Neo-liberalism* (London: Routledge, 2008), 66.
24. Woo, *Race to the Swift*, 93.
25. Arase, *Buying Power*, 5. As Dennis Yasumoto put it even more starkly, "Japanese aid policy began as reparation arrangements, or as 'economic cooperation' agreements negotiated *in lieu of* reparations, with Asian nations Japan had occupied in World War II." "Why Aid? Japan as an 'Aid Great Power,'" *Pacific Affairs* 62, no. 4 (1989): 491, emphasis mine. Here I would point out that there is some degree of self-interest in all forms of reparations.
26. Dennis Trinidad, "Japan's ODA at the Crossroads: Disbursement Patterns of Japan's Development Assistance to Southeast Asia," *Asian Perspective* 31, no. 2 (2007): 111.
27. John White, *Japanese Aid* (London: Overseas Development Institute, 1964), 18.
28. Arase, *Buying Power*, 77.
29. Terutomo Ozawa, "Japan's New Resource Democracy: Government-Backed Group Investment," *Journal of World Trade Law* 3 (1980): 3.
30. Arase, *Buying Power*, 79.

31. Carol Lancaster, "Japan's *Oda: Naiatsu and Gaiatsu*," in *Japanese Aid and the Construction of Global Development: Inescapable Solutions*, ed. David Leheny et al. (New York: Routledge, 2010), 38–39.
32. Arase, *Buying Power*, 77.
33. Yasumoto, "Why Aid?," 494.
34. Lancaster, "Japan's *Oda*," 39–40.
35. Robert M. Orr Jr., "Collaboration or Conflict? Foreign Aid and US-Japan Relations," *Pacific Affairs* 62, no. 4 (1989): 476.
36. Edward J. Lincoln, *East Asian Economic Regionalism* (Washington, DC: Brookings Institution Press, 2004), 116.
37. Woo, *Race to the Swift*, 91, 92. A 2008 study of the Asian Development Bank posits that "Japan has sought to purchase influence through contribution," specifically by sponsoring two special funds within the ADB, the Japan Special Fund (JSF), and the Asian Development Bank Institute (ADBI) Special Fund. Joel Rathus, "China, Japan and Regional Organisations: The Case of the Asian Development Bank," *Japanese Studies* 28, no. 1 (2008): 92–93.
38. World Bank, *World Development Report 1989: Financial Systems and Development* (Washington, DC: World Bank, 1989), 1.
39. World Bank, *World Development Report 1989*, 132, emphasis mine. Although these conclusions clearly appear to recommend financial liberalization for developing countries, Robert Wade points out that the *World Development Report* "took a somewhat less extreme view" and that it was a different document, *Report of the Task Force on Financial Sector Operations*, issued a month later, in August 1989, which "took a strong view against government intervention in financial markets" and determined subsequent World Bank policy. Robert Wade, "Japan, the World Bank, and the Art of Paradigm Maintenance: The East Asian Miracle in Political Perspective," *New Left Review* 217 (1996): 6.
40. Wade, "Japan, the World Bank, and the Art of Paradigm Maintenance," 18.
41. Wade, "Japan, the World Bank, and the Art of Paradigm Maintenance," 13, 14, 15–16. A fascinating exception to this influence of U.S.-trained economists—but not to the pipeline of personnel from the elite U.S. research universities—at the World Bank is the figure of Jim Yong Kim, who served as the president of the World Bank from 2012 to his resignation, effective February 1, 2019. Kim was born in Seoul and immigrated to the U.S. as a young child. After completing medical school in 1991 at Harvard, where he studied with Christopher Murray (the co-inventor of the GBD/DALY metric), Kim received a PhD in anthropology, also from Harvard, in 1993. Kim was one of the cofounders of the nonprofit, community-based health care organization Partners in Health and later worked at the World Health Organization, where he served as the director of its HIV/AIDS Department (2004–2006). Between his appointments at the WHO and the World Bank, Kim was the seventeenth President of Dartmouth College.
42. Vincent Kelly Pollard, "Entering Global Civil Society: Japan's ODA Policy-Making Milieu from June 1992," *Japanese Studies* 16, nos. 2–3 (1996): 49.

43. Asian Women's Fund, "Statement by Chief Cabinet Secretary Kozo Igarashi on the Establishment of the Asian Fund for Women" (June 14, 1995), http://www.awf.or.jp/e6/statement-07.html, accessed July 1, 2017.
44. Radhika Coomaraswamy, *Report on the Mission to the Democratic People's Republic of Korea, the Republic of Korea and Japan on the Issue of Military Sexual Slavery in Wartime*. Report Submitted to the 52nd Session of the UN Commission on Human Rights (E/CN.4/1996/53/Add.1), 30. New York: UN Commission on Human Rights, Economic and Social Council, 1996.
45. Gabriel Palma, "Three and a Half Cycles of 'Mania, Panic, and [Asymmetric] Crash': East Asia and Latin America Compared," *Cambridge Journal of Economics* 22, no. 6 (1998): 792.
46. Robert Wade and Frank Veneroso, "The Asian Crisis: The High Debt Model versus the Wall Street–Treasury–IMF Complex," *New Left Review* 228 (1998): 10.
47. Chalmers Johnson, "Cold War Economics Melt Asia," *Nation*, February 23, 1998, 17.
48. Ha-Joon Chang, Gabriel Palma, and D. Hugh Whittaker, "The Asian Crisis: Introduction," *Cambridge Journal of Economics* 22 (1998): 649.
49. Johnson, "Cold War Economics Melt Asia," 16.
50. Robert Wade, "The Asian Debt-and-Development Crisis of 1997–?," *World Development* 26, no. 8 (1998): 1536.
51. Chalmers Johnson, "Economic Crisis in East Asia: The Clash of Capitalisms," *Cambridge Journal of Economics* 22 (1998): 653–61.
52. Palma, "Three and a Half Cycles," 790.
53. Diane Elson, "International Financial Architecture: A View from the Kitchen," International Development Economics Associates, January 2004, 1, www.networkideas.org/featart/jan2004/fa13_Diane_Elson.htm.
54. Palma, "Three and a Half Cycles," 797.
55. Wade, "The Asian Debt-and-Development Crisis of 1997–?," 1542.
56. I have seen many references to the so-called tequila effect. The reference to the so-called yellow fever appeared in a published lecture by Lawrence Summers, "International Financial Crises: Causes, Prevention, and Cures," *American Economic Review* (May 2000): 6.
57. Moisés Naím, "Latin America the Morning After," *Foreign Affairs* 74, no. 4 (1995): 50.
58. Johnson, *Blowback*, 208.
59. Joseph Stiglitz, "What I Learned at the World Economic Crisis," in *Globalization and the Poor: Exploitation or Equalizer?*, ed. William J. Driscoll et al. (New York: International Debate Education Association, 2003), 195–204.
60. Johnson, "Cold War Economics Melt Asia," 17.
61. Wade and Veneroso, "The Asian Crisis," 10.
62. Wade, "The Asian Debt-and-Development Crisis of 1997–?," 1544.
63. Elson, "International Financial Architecture," 10.
64. Walden Bello, "The Asian Financial Crisis: Causes, Dynamics, Prospects," *Journal of the Asia Pacific Economy* 4, no. 1 (1999): 41.

65. Bob Davis and David Wessel, "World Bank, IMF at Odds over Asian Austerity—Some Economists Contend That Harsh Measures Could Worsen the Crisis," *Wall Street Journal*, January 8, 1998.
66. Wade and Veneroso, "The Asian Crisis," 19.
67. Wade, "The Asian Debt-and-Development Crisis of 1997–?," 1547.
68. Ha-Joon Chang, "The 1997 Korean Crisis: Causes and Consequences," in *Brazil and South Korea: Economic Crisis and Restructuring*, ed. Edmund Amann and Ha-Joon Chang (London: Institute of Latin American Studies, 2004), 119.
69. Wade and Veneroso, "The Asian Crisis."
70. Kristen Nordhaug, "Asian Monetary Fund Revival?," *Focus on Trade* 51 (June 2000). Focus on the Global South, www.focusweb.org/publications/2000/Asian%20Monetary%20Fund%20revival.htm.
71. David Sanger, "Greenspan Sees Asian Crisis Moving World to Western Capitalism," *New York Times*, February 13, 1998. The article ends with this lengthy quotation from Greenspan's testimony: "In the last decade or so, Mr. Greenspan said, the nation has observed 'a consensus towards the, for want of a better term, the Western form of free-market capitalism as the model which should govern how each individual country should run its economy.' We saw the breakdown of the Berlin wall in 1989, he added, 'and the massive shift away from central planning towards free market capitalist types of structures. Concurrent to that was the really quite dramatic, very strong growth in what appeared to be a competing capitalist-type system in Asia. And as a consequence of that, you had developments of types of structures which I believe at the end of the day were faulty, but you could not demonstrate that so long as growth was going at 10 percent a year.'" Here I wish to point out how this triumvirate of Greenspan-Rubin-Summers quashed a serious and concerted effort within the U.S. government to monitor and regulate risky financial instruments like credit default swaps and over-the-counter derivatives. In early 1998, Brooksley Born, head of the Commodities Futures Trading Commission, proposed that these new over-the-counter derivatives be monitored and regulated, which was roundly rejected by Greenspan, Rubin, and Summers, along with Arthur Levitt, head of the Securities and Exchanges Commission. Their successful suppression of Born's initiative would set the unruly conditions for what would later become the Wall Street meltdown and later bailout of 2008. See Michael Hirsch, "The Reeducation of Larry Summers," *Newsweek*, February 20, 2009. See also the illuminating PBS *Frontline* documentary "The Warning" (2009) and the documentary feature film *The Inside Job* (2010).
72. Bruce Cumings, "The Korean Crisis and the End of 'Late' Development," *New Left Review* 231 (1998): 53.
73. Jan A. Kregel, "Derivatives and Global Capital Flows: Applications to Asia," *Cambridge Journal of Economics* 22, no. 6 (1998): 688.
74. Johnson, *Blowback*, 5–6.
75. Cumings, "The Korean Crisis," 51–52.
76. Johnson, "Economic Crisis in East Asia," 654.
77. Wade, "The Asian Debt-and-Development Crisis of 1997–?," 1544.

78. Quoted in Elaine Kim, "Sex Tourism in Asia," *Critical Perspectives of Third World America* 2, no. 1 (1984): 225.
79. Kim, "Sex Tourism in Asia," 224.
80. Cho Uhn, "Global Capital and Local Patriarchy: The Financial Crisis and Women Workers in South Korea," in *Women and Work in Globalising Asia*, ed. Dong-Sook S. Gils and Nicola Piper (London: Routledge, 2002), 57, 59.
81. Johan Lindquist, "Veils and Ecstasy: Negotiating Shame in the Indonesian Borderlands," *ethnos* 69, no. 4 (2004): 497.
82. Thanh-Dam Truong, "A Feminist Perspective on the Asian Miracle and Crisis: Enlarging the Conceptual Map of Human Development," *Journal of Human Development* 1, no. 1 (2000): 161.
83. Matsui Yayori, "Economic Development and Asian Women," in *Voices from the Japanese Women's Movement*, ed. AMPO-*Japan Asia Quarterly Review* (Armonk, NY: M. E. Sharpe, 1996), 63.
84. Amelita King Dejardin, "Economic Meltdown Has a Woman's Face," *Japan Times*, March 8, 2009, http://search.japantimes.co.jp/cgi-bin/e020090308al.html.
85. Jenina Joy Chavez and Rowena D. Cordero, *The Asian Financial Crisis and Filipino Households: Impact on Women and Children* (Bangkok: Focus on the Global South, 2001), 27–28.
86. Lori J. Pennay, "The Disproportionate Effect of the Asian Economic Crisis on Women: The Filipina Experience," *University of Pennsylvania Journal of International Economy* 21 (2000): 427–80.
87. Cho, "Global Capital and Local Patriarchy," 62.
88. June J. H. Lee, *A Review of Data on Trafficking in the Republic of Korea* (Geneva: International Organization for Migration, 2002), 24, 26, 21, 26.
89. Kimberley Chang and Julian McAllister Groves, "Neither 'Saints' nor 'Prostitutes': Sexual Discourse in the Filipina Domestic Worker Community in Hong Kong," *Women's Studies International Forum* 23, no. 1 (2000): 73.
90. Thanh-Dam Truong, "The Underbelly of the Tiger: Gender and the Demystification of the Asian Miracle," *Review of International Political Economy* 6, no. 2 (1999): 146.
91. Tani Barlow, "Asian Women in Reregionalization," *positions: east asia cultures critique* 15, no. 2 (2007): 295. Barlow provides these details: "The framers . . . noted that the most positive outcome of globalization for women was probably not marketization at all, which had a tendency to abrogate gains in female literacy in predominantly Muslim countries and gender equity in formerly communist countries. Rather, global restructuring had done most in the area of new social movements or women's organizations" (295–96).
92. Radhika Coomaraswamy, *Report of the Special Rapporteur on Violence against women, Its Causes and Consequences, Ms. Radhika Coomaraswamy, on Trafficking in Women, Women's Migration and Violence against Women, Submitted in Accordance with Commission on Human Rights Resolution 1997/44* (Geneva: United Nations, 2000), 21.
93. Hyunah Yang, "Revisiting the Issue of Korean 'Military Comfort Women': The Question of Truth and Positionality," *positions: east asia cultures critique* 5, no. 1 (1997): 54.

94. Pollard, "Entering Global Civil Society," 49.
95. "Seoul Won't Seek Japan Funds for War's Brothel Women," *New York Times*, April 22, 1998.

CHAPTER 7: ENDURING MEMORIALS

1. The full text of the two statements are at http://blogs.wsj.com/japanrealtime/2015/12/28/full-text-japan-south-korea-statement-on-comfort-women. See also "Japan and South Korea Reach Deal on 'Comfort Women'," *Fortune*, December 28, 2015; "The 'Comfort Women' Agreement," *Japan Times*, December 31, 2015; "The Comfort Women Agreement: A Win for Traditional Diplomacy," *Diplomat*, December 31, 2015; "The Japan-Korean Comfort Women Deal," *Forbes*, February 26, 2016; "Japan, South Korea Build Ties after 'Comfort Women' Deal," *Wall Street Journal*, July 28, 2016.
2. Associated Press, "Japan, South Korea Settle Wartime Sex Slave Dispute," December 25, 2015, https://apnews.com/3d9cec9f9b2e414a97a82c45b94ce2c1.
3. Yonhap News Agency, "Government Seeks Victims' Understanding over 'Comfort Women' Deal," December 29, 2015, http://english.yonhapnews.co.kr/national/2015/12/29/47/0301000000AEN20151229001951315F.html.
4. See "South Korea's 'Comfort Women' Reject Deal with Japan," *Diplomat*, December 30, 2015, http://thediplomat.com/2015/12/south-koreas-comfort-women-reject-deal-with-japan. The Amnesty International statement was released on December 28, 2015, and authored by Hiroka Shoji, its East Asia researcher. See https://www.amnestyusa.org/news/press-releases/comfort-women-deal-must-not-deny-survivors-justice.
5. Sol Han and James Griffiths, "Why This Statue of a Young Girl Caused a Diplomatic Incident," CNN.com, February 5, 2017, https://www.cnn.com/2017/02/05/asia/south-korea-comfort-women-statue/index.html.
6. The first memorial statue in Taiwan was unveiled in the city of Tainan on August 14, 2018, to commemorate the first "Memorial Day for Japanese Forces' Comfort Women Victims." August 14 was chosen because it was the day that Kim Hak-sun first gave public testimony in 1991.
7. The first volume of materials published by the Korean Council contains a reprint of a protest letter addressed to the Los Angeles public television station KQED about the depiction of Korean "comfort women" in the British documentary series *The World at War*, which was broadcast on May 5, 1988. Reprinted in *Chongsindae munje charyojip I [Resources on the Chongsindae Issue, I]*, ed. Korean Council (Seoul: Korean Council, 1991), 47. Tomiyama Taeko's artwork on "military comfort women" was exhibited in London as early as October 1988. See John Gittings, "Wednesday Women: Cold Comfort—Tomiyama Taeko's Art Exposes Japanese Guilt," *Guardian*, October 12, 1988. This article, which discusses both the history of the "comfort stations" as well as Taeko's criticism of its erasure, is one of the earliest reports on the issue in the European or U.S. press.

8. Jay David Bolter and David Grusin, *Remediation: Understanding New Media* (Cambridge, MA: MIT Press, 2000).
9. In September 1994, forty women, including some survivors and other activists, stormed the National Museum of Modern Art in Seoul and shattered more than a dozen cases displaying Japanese artworks in a show of protest. Zeno Park, "Protestors Vandalize Exhibition Hall of Japanese Art Works," *Agence France Presse—English*, September 2, 1994.
10. Asian Women's Fund, "The Statement by President of the Asian Women's Fund at the Final Press Conference," March 6, 2007, www.awf.or.jp/e3/dissolution.html.
11. Soh, *The Comfort Women*: 149.
12. Kim Tokchin, "I have much to say to the Korean government," *Index on Censorship* 24, no. 3 (1995): 153.
13. So-yang Park, "Silence, Subaltern Speech and the Intellectual in South Korea: The Politics of Emergent Speech in the Case of Former Sexual Slaves," *Journal for Cultural Research* 9, no. 2 (2005): 175.
14. Yoshimi, *Comfort Women*, 33. The oft-televised testimony of Yoshida Seiji, a Japanese veteran who had published two memoirs about his role in rounding up Korean women, was also crucial to supporting the survivors' claims. An August 8, 1992, article in the *New York Times* opens with "From his modest house in this distant Tokyo suburb, Seiji Yoshida, now 78 years old and bent by age, has become something of a nightmare for the Japanese Government: a self-described former war criminal eager to confess in front of the television cameras." "Japanese Veteran Presses Wartime-Brothel Issue," *New York Times*, August 8, 1992. In 1996 Yoshida admitted that he had made up details, and his account has been widely discredited. See "Seiji Yoshida's Lies about 'Comfort Women' Exploited by Japan's Right," *South China Morning Post*, October 12, 2014, https://www.scmp.com/news/asia/article/1614619/seiji-yoshidas-lies-about-comfort-women-exploited-japans-right.
15. Kim Yong-Sil, "How Can We Permit Their Sins?," in *War Victimization and Japan: International Public Hearing Report* (Osaka: Toho Shuppan, 1993), 58.
16. Quoted in So-yang Park, "Silence, Subaltern Speech and the Intellectual in South Korea: The Politics of Emergent Speech in the Case of Former Sexual Slaves," *Journal for Cultural Research* 9, no. 2 (2005): 196.
17. Ustinia Dolgopol, "Redressing Partial Justice a Possible Role for Civil Society," in *The Challenge of Conflict: International Law Responds*, ed. Ustinia Dolgopol and Judith Gail Gardam (London: Brill, 2006), 477.
18. Myrna Elizabeth P. Borromeo, "Media for Justice and Healing: The Case of Philippine Comfort Women Survivors," *Review of Women's Studies* 20, nos. 1–2 (2010): 98, 99.
19. Indai Lourdes Sajor, "Present Situation of 'Comfort Women' in the Philippines," in *War Victimization and Japan: International Public Hearing Report* (Osaka: Toho Shuppan, 1993), 27–37, 28.
20. http://www.jca.apc.org/video-juku/index-eng.html. It also "give[s] technical support to other women and human rights NGOs to create videos."

21. Choi, "The Politics of War Memories toward Healing," 406.
22. The sponsors of the tour included a diverse regional and international coalition of Japanese, Korean, and U.S.-based cultural, political, and educational organizations. Alongside the traveling artwork, some stops included a locally specific "community forum" that featured first-person testimony by a former "comfort woman." In the San Francisco Bay area, a community forum was sponsored by Korean Exposure and Education Program, Asians and Pacific Islanders for Community Empowerment (API Force), Arab Women's Solidarity Association (N. America), Asian Immigrant Women Advocates, Asian Women United, Center for Political Education, Center for Third World Organizing, Channing and Popai Liem Education Foundation, Committee for Human Rights in the Philippines, GABRIELA Network, Jamaesori, Kearney Street Workshop, Korean Community Center of the East Bay, Korean Youth Cultural Center, Shimtuh: A Korean American Domestic Violence Program, and Women of Color Resource Center. The Los Angeles part of the tour was organized by Young Koreans United of Los Angeles and sponsored by the House of Sharing and the Historical Museum on Sexual Slavery by the Japanese Military, both based in South Korea. The exhibition was also endorsed by the Korean Resource Center (KRC), National Korean American Service & Education Consortium (NAKASEC), UCLA Asian American Studies Center, Committee in Solidarity with the People of El Salvador, Asian Pacific American Labor Alliance, AFL-CIO, Okinawan Peace Network, Asian Pacific Islanders for Reproductive Health (APIRH), Korean Students Association of UCLA, Asian Pacific Coalition of UCLA, Korean Immigrant Worker Advocates, Coalition for Humane Immigrant Rights of Los Angeles, Gabriela, NIKKEI for Civil Rights and Redress, State Senator Tom Hayden, and Korea Exposure and Education Program (KEEP). This lengthy list attests to how the issue has served to bring together diverse local and transnational organizations and political subjects in the United States.
23. *Comfort Women: A Web Reference*, online.sfsu.edu/~soh/cw-links.htm. Given that its links were last updated on June 13, 2002, this page presents an interesting snapshot of the publications, websites, and resources available at that moment.
24. At one point this site included a "Chronology and Map" page that listed significant events beginning with the Sino-Japanese War of 1894–95 and ending with an exhibit organized by the group in Washington, D.C., titled "Comfort Women of WWII: An Indisputable Tragedy." The featured map, which detailed the location of "Major Military Brothels," was published in the August 5, 1992, edition of *Japan Times*. In addition, a "Photo Gallery" section featured twenty-one black-and-white archival photographs of mostly "comfort women," Japanese soldiers, and one recent photo of a demonstration. The WCCW site has recently been transformed to focus solely on one specific media project of the WCCW, which was billed as the Inaugural International Film Festival on Comfort Women (November 9–11, 2018).
25. Tessa Morris-Suzuki and Peter Rimmer, "Virtual Memories: Japanese History Debates in Manga and Cyberspace," *Asian Studies Review* 26, no. 2 (2000): 154.

26. Korean Council, www.womenandwar.net/english/support.php, accessed May 1, 2011. This page lists three different bank accounts to which visitors could route their donations in support of the proposed museum, the "Activities and Publications of the Korean Council," and the "Care and Welfare for the Survivors and Operation of the Shelter."
27. Korean Council, www.womenandwar.net/english, accessed May 27, 2011.
28. Korean Council, www.womenandwar.net/english, accessed April 28, 2011.
29. Korean Council, www.womenandwar.net/english.
30. Korean Council, www.womenandwar.net/english.
31. Regarding the third point in particular, the War and Women's Human Rights Museum could be connected to a transnational network of other museums such as the International Museum of Women (www.imow.org), which was founded in 1997 and is connected to the now closed Women's Heritage Museum. It touts itself as "an online social change *museum* that amplifies the voices of *women* worldwide through global online exhibitions, the arts and cultural programs" and an "innovative twenty-first century museum," which has put on both on-the-ground exhibitions in San Francisco and "global online exhibitions." There is also The Women's Museum™: An Institute for the Future, which is affiliated with the Smithsonian but located in Dallas, Texas. It opened on September 29, 2000 (http://www.thewomensmuseum.org). More pertinent still is a modestly scaled Women's Active Museum (WAM) on War and Peace, which opened in Tokyo in August 2005 (see https://wam-peace.org/en/). In addition to memorializing the historical atrocity, one of the main aims of WAM is to preserve the memory of the 2000 Women's Tribunal as part of a continued project for raising awareness about militarized sexual violence and sustaining international network of solidarity.
32. www.womenandwarmuseum.net/contents/main/main.asp.
33. Korean Council, http://www.womenandwar.net, accessed April 1, 2019.
34. See Yonhap News Agency, "Victims of Japanese Sexual Slavery Launch Independent Foundation," June 9, 2016, and "South Korean Activists Formally Launch Rival 'Comfort Women' Foundation," *Japan Times*, June 9, 2016.
35. www.hermuseum.go.kr/eng/mainPage.do, accessed January 2, 2019. This e-museum features a good number of archival photographs under the title of "The Picture of 'Comfort Women.'" The US Signal Corps photograph of Park Young-sim and three other women alongside the Chinese soldier (see chapter 5, figure 5.6) is prominently featured here as well. The e-museum also features an interesting time line of what are identified as "Major Events around the Time of the Atrocities (1907–1948)," which begins with three relevant international agreements, which Japan had ratified and thus was, in principle, bound by the 1907 Convention Respecting the Laws and Customs of War on Land, the 1910 International Convention for the Suppression of the White Slave Traffic, and the 1921 International Convention for the Suppression of the Traffic in Women and Children. A subpage of the website of the Ministry of Gender Equality and Family lists the e-museum under its policy objectives with respect to "Protection of Human Rights": "Open and manage website,

e-museum of the Victims of Japanese Military Sexual Slavery, in three different languages, Korean, Japanese and English including various informative and educational materials." See www.mogef.go.kr/eng/pc/eng_pc_f013.do, accessed April 2, 2019.

36. Wada Haruki, "The Comfort Women, the Asian Women's Fund and the Digital Museum," *Asia-Pacific Journal* 6, no. 2 (2008): 1. This identification was included in the introduction, written by Gavan McCormack, who was also the translator.
37. Wada, "The Comfort Women," 3.
38. Although it is beyond the scope of this avowedly broad and peripatetic book, especially so near to its conclusion, it is worth considering the Digital Museum in relation to the sizable body of scholarship on virtualization and museums across information studies, museum studies, and science and technology studies. One interesting problem that the Digital Museum poses is the relationship and tension between the two very different museum functions of *collecting*, which involves not just exclusive ownership of an offline artifact but also its cataloguing and exclusive, specialized study by a small group of museum "experts," versus *exhibiting*, which involves translating and framing the artifact for a "general" public.
39. Arjun Appadurai and Carol Breckenridge, "Museums Are Good to Think: Heritage on View in India," in *Museums and Communities: The Politics of Public Culture*, ed. Ivan Karp, Christine Mullen Kreamer, and Steven D. Lavine (Washington, DC: Smithsonian Institution Press, 1992), 44.
40. Elisa Giaccardi, "Memory and Territory: New Forms of Virtuality for the Museum," 2004, www.archimuse.com/mw2004/papers/giaccardi/giaccardi.html.
41. Asian Women's Fund, "To Our Visitors," accessed April 20, 2011, www.awf.or.jp/e-preface.htm.
42. Asian Women's Fund, "Historical Materials Regarding the Comfort Women Issue," accessed April 20, 2011, http://awf.or.jp/e6/document.html. This page refers to what it describes as the "facsimile edition" of the government documents with a differently translated title, *Collection of Materials Relating to the Wartime Comfort Women Issue: Government of Japan Survey*. A perplexing disclaimer appears at the bottom: "As the Copyright of this publication belongs to Ryukei-shosha, it is not permitted to copy it without recognition of the publisher."
43. The ATIS/SWPA (South West Pacific Area) interrogation reports, which come first, offer several additional insights that supplement the three documents that I discussed in chapter 5. They are organized according to the date of publication, with the first ATIS "Interrogation Report No. 24" of a Hanaki Yoshida dated December 31, 1942, and stamped as received by the General Headquarters of SWPA on January 10, 1943, containing one sentence: "PW saw both Japanese and Korean women in brothels at Rabaul" (reproduced on page 18 of volume 5 of *Shiryoshusei*). Thus, the Allied interrogators and leaders knew of the "comfort system" as early as the beginning of 1943. More strikingly, the subsequent ATIS reports suggest that there were questions about the "comfort system," including whether they were operated by the Japanese military or by civilians, how the women were

recruited and transported, the ethnicities of the women, and finally whether any of the women had been prostitutes before. In "Interrogation Report No. 25," brief mention of two "brothels" in Rabaul with "100 Korean and Japanese girls" is included at the very end of the report under "Social Life" (reproduced on page 23 of volume 5 of *Shiryoshusei*). In "Interrogation Report No. 31," a Private Muto Yokichi's testimony, "Brothels are provided in the army, and, at DAVAO he had seen Korean, Formosan and native women in them," appears under a section titled "Psychological." However, by the time that "Interrogation Report No. 36" was filed on February 23, 1943, the ATIS reports began to follow a standard outline, like the U.S. OWI reports. From here on mention of the "brothels" appears under a section titled "Conditions in Fighting Services." The more detailed information from a Private Yazawa, who was captured in the coastal village of Gona in Papua New Guinea, which appears in "Interrogation Report No. 37," provides a good sense of the questions that were asked: "Whenever troops were stationed in a locality in numbers, brothels were immediately established by both the Army and Navy. Korean and Chinese women were usually employed but occasionally suitable native women would be enrolled. Profits go to the Services" (reproduced on page 52 of volume 5 of *Shiryoshusei*). The underlined emphasis on the final sentence and the capitalization of "Services" are both intriguing and perplexing. Later ATIS interrogation reports (no. 48, no. 57, and no. 60) also make note of the infection rates and medical treatment of venereal diseases as well as prices (no. 57) in the discussion of the "brothels."

44. Asian Women's Fund, "Who Were the Comfort Women?," accessed April 20, 2011, www.awf.or.jp/e1/facts-00.html.
45. Asian Women's Fund, "Women Were Collected," accessed on April 30, 2011, http://awf.or.jp/e1/facts-04.html.
46. Asian Women's Fund.
47. Asian Women's Fund, "Women Were Collected," accessed on April 30, 2011, http://awf.or.jp/e1/facts-05.html.
48. Asian Women's Fund, "The Pacific War and Spreading Comfort Stations," accessed on April 30, 2011, http://awf.or.jp/e1/facts-06.html. The rest of the page briefly describes how "native women" in the Philippines and Indonesia and "Dutch women internees" were "made to be comfort women." The page ends by pointing to the specific case in certain rural areas that did not have officially designated "comfort stations" and where "native women were raped and abducted to Japanese garrisons buildings and were raped continuously there for a certain period of time" and argues that this group of *victims* "can also be redeemed as anothr [sic] comfort women who were forced to provide sexual services to officers and men." Although there is no specific ethnicity or nationality specified, the authors immediately state here that "in the Philippines, especially, violence against women was frequent."
49. Asian Women's Fund, "The Pacific War and Spreading Comfort Stations." As the Digital Museum re-narrates the story of the Kitamuras as inscribed in the documents compiled by the U.S. military, "They agreed to take on the job of gathering

women and girls and recruited 20 Koreans. With the payment of 300–1000 yen in the currency of that time to their parents, the couple believed that they bought these girls and that they became the couple's own property. This could be considered as the advance payment by which these girls were bound." This account places greater culpability on fellow Koreans, including the parents of the girls and women. Given these more provocative implications, it seems all the more perplexing and even irresponsible that the authors do not explicate the reasons for their characterization of the Kitamuras as Koreans.

50. Asian Women's Fund, "The Life in Comfort Stations," accessed on April 30, 2011, http://www.awf.or.jp/e1/facts-12.html
51. Asian Women's Fund, "How Did the Comfort Women Issue Come to Light?," accessed on April 30, 2011, www.awf.or.jp/e2/survey.html.
52. Asian Women's Fund, "How Did the Comfort Women Issue Come to Light?" accessed April 21, 2011, www.awf.or.jp/e2/survey.html.
53. See Setsu Shigematsu, *Scream from the Shadows: The Women's Liberation Movement in Japan* (Minneapolis: University of Minnesota Press, 2012).
54. Asian Women's Fund, "How Did the Comfort Women Issue Come to Light?" accessed April 21, 2011, www.awf.or.jp/e2/survey.html.
55. The English translation can be found at www.awf.or.jp/e6/statement-05.html. The opening paragraphs of the report also bear several indicators of hesitation and qualification: "The study shows that comfort stations *were established* at the demands of the Japanese military authorities of *that time*, with the *then*-military being directly or indirectly involved in the establishing and managing of those stations and the transfer of comfort women. The recruitment of comfort women was conducted *mainly* by private recruiters who had been requested to do so by the military. In *many* of those cases, the women were recruited against their will, through coaxing, coercion and the like" (emphasis mine). Keeping in mind the inevitable awkwardness of translation into English, I have italicized certain words to attend to the passive constructions and tempering modifications of this admission of government knowledge and active involvement. The Digital Museum reprises this equivocation.
56. Marilyn Strathern, "Introduction: New Accountabilities," in *Audit Cultures: Anthropological Studies in Accountability, Ethics and the Academy*, ed. Marilyn Strathern (London: Routledge, 2000), 1, 1–2, 2.
57. Asian Women's Fund, "The Establishment of Comfort Stations," accessed August 1, 2011, www.awf.or.jp/e1/facts-01.html, emphases mine.
58. Asian Women's Fund, "The Establishment of Comfort Stations."
59. Asian Women's Fund, "The Number of Comfort Stations and Comfort Women," www.awf.or.jp/e1/facts-07.html, accessed August 1, 2011.
60. Asian Women's Fund, "Messages from Japanese Contributors," www.awf.or.jp/e3/donators.html, accessed July 8, 2011.
61. Asian Women's Fund, "Projects by country or region—Philippines," accessed July 7, 2011, http://www.awf.or.jp/e3/philippine-01.html.
62. Asian Women's Fund, "Projects by Country or Region—Netherlands," www.awf.or.jp/e3/netherlands-02.html, accessed July 8, 2011.

63. Asian Women's Fund, "Voices of the Victims-Recipients of the Project of the AWF," http://awf.or.jp/e3/oralhistory-05.html.
64. Korean Council, www.womenandwar.net/english, accessed May 27, 2011.
65. Keiji Hirano, "Web Site Documents Wartime Sex Slaves," *Japan Times*, September 28, 2007, www.japantimes.co.jp/news/2007/09/28/national/web-site-documents-wartime-sex-slaves.
66. "South Korean 'Comfort Women' Mark 1,000th Rally for Japan Apology," CNN.com, December 14, 2011, http://news.blogs.cnn.com/2011/12/14/south-korean-comfort-women-mark-1000th-rally-for-japan-apology.
67. "Abe Rejects Japan's Files on War Sex," *New York Times*, March 2, 2007.
68. Totsuka Etsuro, "Proposals for Japan and the ROK to Resolve the 'Comfort Women' Issue: Creating Trust and Peace in Light of International Law," *Asia-Pacific Journal* 11, no. 1 (January 2013), http://apjjf.org/2013/11/1/Totsuka-Etsuro/3885/article.html.
69. David McNeill and Justin McCurry, "Sink the *Asahi*! The 'Comfort Women' Controversy and the Neo-nationalist Attack," *Asia-Pacific Journal* 13 (2015).
70. Quoted in Nishino Rumiko and Nogawa Motokazu, "The Japanese State's New Assault on the Victims of Wartime Sexual Slavery," *Asia-Pacific Journal* 12, no. 2 (December 21, 2014). The article notes "italics by author"; the emphasis is placed by Nishino and Nogawa.
71. Nishino and Nogawa, "The Japanese State's New Assault."
72. McNeill and McCurry, "Sink the *Asahi*!"
73. Quoted in Odaka Chiba, "Former Asahi Reporter Files Suit against University Professor, Publisher," *Asahi Shimbun*, January 10, 2015.
74. "More Than 10,000 Sue *Asahi Shimbun* over Retracted 'Comfort Women' Articles," *Japan Times*, January 25, 2015.
75. "Japan Revisionists Demand 'Comfort Women' Newspaper Apology," *Straits Times*, February 19, 2015.
76. McNeill and McCurry, "Sink the *Asahi*!"
77. Martin Fackler, "Japan, Seeking Revision of Report on Wartime Brothels, Is Rebuffed," *New York Times*, October 16, 2014.
78. Reiji Yoshida, "Government Requests Revision of 1996 U.N. Sex Slave Report," *Japan Times*, October 16, 2014, https://www.japantimes.co.jp/news/2014/10/16/national/history/government-requests-revision-of-1996-u-n-sex-slave-report/#.XLd346Z7nOQ.
79. "Civic Groups Ask UNESCO to List Comfort Women Records," *Korea Times*, June 1, 2016, www.koreatimes.co.kr/www/news/nation/2016/06/116_206047.html#.
80. *Japan Times*, November 6, 2015.
81. In December 2017, another striking sculpture, titled "Memorial in Honor of the Japanese Military 'Comfort Women,'" was installed at the National Cemetery for Overseas Koreans in South Korea. This multipart sculpture is arranged in the shape of an eye, with four walls of graduated height, which seen from above look like eyelashes: "This monument symbolizes both the eyes of the victims watching over us and our eyes, consoling the comfort women and remembering them

and the tears they shed." Each of the four walls of this "Wall of Time" features a different cutout of a female figure. "The Wall of Agony" is the first, smallest wall, with a bowing figure that "represents the long years of agony and despair the comfort women were forced to endure as they lived their lives as victims of heinous crimes." The second "Wall of Despair," with the figure now kneeling on the ground with a bowed head, continues the same theme. "The Wall of Solidarity" features the cutout of an older female figure, now standing side by side with two other female figures etched into the wall and "represents the period when these women worked together as human rights activists after they ceased to live as silent victims." Finally, the fourth, tallest wall returns to the outline of a young female, who is now aloft with butterfly wings extending from her body, which are etched into the wall: "The Wall of Sublimation symbolizes our prayer for the eternal rest and peace of the victims who, despite decades of suffering, inspired the world with their generous love before leaving this world." In the middle there is a dark square-slab fountain that features concentric circles spreading out from a large teardrop sculpture in the center. There is a subpage dedicated to this memorial at the e-museum maintained by the South Korean government. Visitors to the site can navigate virtually around the image, which also offers pop-up windows that give the names and explains the meaning of a particular detail. See www.hermuseum.go.kr/mogef_vr_e/index.html.

82. For example, a January 1, 2016, *New York Times* op-ed letter by Margaret Stetz in the aftermath of the 2015 South Korea-Japan agreement was titled "Girls in Japan's War Brothels." Stetz writes that "as survivors have testified, many targets of this brutal system of sexual slavery were not 'women,' but girls of 13 or 14. Many had not even begun menstruating when they were shipped as human cargo to battlefronts across Asia and subjected to daily rape. These were not only war crimes, but crimes of child sex trafficking. Until they are represented as such in textbooks in Japan—and in news articles in the West—there is no true justice for these victims."

83. Brittany Levine and Jason Wells, "Glendale Unveils 'Comfort Women' Statue, Honors 'Innocent Victims,'" *Los Angeles Times*, July 30, 2103. These memorials also demand to be studied in terms of how they marshal distinctive local coalitions and transnational networks of support *and* antagonism. For example, a group of Korean Americans paid the $30,000 cost of the statue in Glendale, but their campaign was supported by Japanese American Representative Mike Honda and Japanese American groups, including Nikkei for Civil Rights and Redress and the San Fernando Valley and the Japanese American Citizens League. The erection of the statue also received support from the sizable Armenian American community and their elected leaders in Glendale, who have their own specific passionate investment in the memorialization of the Armenian genocide and a resulting sympathy toward Korean American historical grievances against Japanese colonial domination. Another group of Japanese immigrants and Japanese Americans actively opposed the erection of the statue as endorsing and encouraging anti-Japanese sentiments in the U.S. After the statue was erected, one critical

contingent held a press conference at the site with protesters holding Japanese and U.S. flags and hoisting a bilingual banner behind the statue that declared, "Children need heart-warming monuments." In December 2013 the *Los Angeles Times* reported that three members of Japan's House of Representatives formally requested that the City of Glendale remove the statue. These protests have, in turn, reinforced the Korean American investments in protecting and preserving the statue.

BIBLIOGRAPHY

Allain, Jean. "The Definition of Slavery in International Law." *Howard Law Journal* 52, no. 2 (winter 2009): 239–76.

Allain, Jean. "The Legal Definition of Slavery into the Twenty-First Century." In *The Legal Definition of Slavery into the Twenty-First Century*, edited by Jean Allain, 199–209. London: Oxford University Press, 2012.

Allain, Jean. *Slavery in International Law: Of Human Exploitation and Trafficking*. Leiden: Martinus Nijhoff, 2013.

Allied Translator and Interpreter Section, Supreme Commander for the Allied Powers. *Research Report: Amenities in the Japanese Armed Forces*, No. 120. Tokyo: 1945. National Archives, RG 165, Records of the War Department General and Special Staffs, entry 79, box 342.

AMPO-*Japan Asia Quarterly Review. Voices from the Japanese Women's Movement*. Armonk, NY: M. E. Sharpe, 1996.

Appadurai, Arjun, and Carol Breckenridge. "Museums Are Good to Think: Heritage on View in India." In *Museums and Communities: The Politics of Public Culture*, edited by Ivan Karp, Christine Mullen Kreamer, and Steven D. Lavine, 34–55. Washington, DC: Smithsonian Institution Press, 1992.

Arase, David. *Buying Power: The Political Economy of Japan's Foreign Aid*. Boulder, CO: Lynne Rienner, 1995.

Arase, David. "Japanese Policy toward Democracy and Human Rights in Asia." *Asian Survey* 33, no. 10 (1993): 935–52.

Asia Watch and the Women's Rights Project. *Double Jeopardy: Police Abuse of Women in Pakistan*. New York: Human Rights Watch, 1992.

Asian Cultural Forum on Development. *Our Voice: Bangkok NGOs' Declaration on Human Rights: Reports of the Asia Pacific NGO Conference on Human Rights and NGOs' Statements to the Asian Regional Meeting*. Bangkok: Asian Cultural Forum on Development, 1993.

Asian Women's Association. "Declaration of the Asian Women's Liberation Committee in Japan." *Asian Women's Liberation* 1 (1977): 2.

Asian Women's Association. "Who We Are." *Asian Women's Liberation* 1 (1977): 4.

Asian Women's Human Rights Council. *AWHRC Monograph Series*. Quezon City: Asian Women's Human Rights Council, 1991.

Asian Women's Human Rights Council. *In the Court of Women II: Asia Tribunal on Women's Human Rights in Tokyo: Proceedings of the International Public Hearing on Traffic in Women and War Crimes against Women*. Quezon City: Asian Women's Human Rights Council, 1994.

Asian Women's Human Rights Council. *Traffic in Women: Violation of Women's Dignity and Fundamental Rights: Asian Conference on Traffic in Women, December 11–13, 1991, Seoul, Korea*. Quezon City: Asian Women's Human Rights Council, 1993.

Asian Women's Human Rights Council. *War Crimes on Asian Women: Military Sexual Slavery by Japan during World War II: The Case of the Filipino Comfort Women*. Manila: Asian Women Human Rights Council, 1998.

Asian Women's Human Rights Council. *Weaving the Future for Asian Women: Declaration of AWHRC Conference on Traffic in Women*. Quezon City: Asian Women Human Rights Council, 1991.

Atal, Yogesh. "Editorial." In *Violence against Women: Reports from India and Korea*, edited by Meera Kosambi, i–iv. Bangkok: UNESCO Principal Regional Office for Asia and the Pacific, 1993.

Awad, Mohamed. *Question of Slavery and the Slave Trade in All Their Practices and Manifestations, Including the Slavery-Like Practices of Apartheid and Colonialism*. Geneva: United Nations, 1971.

Awad, Mohamed. *Report on Slavery*. New York: United Nations, 1966.

Barkan, Elazar. *The Guilt of Nations: Restitution and Negotiating Historical Injustices*. Baltimore: Johns Hopkins University Press, 2001.

Barlay, Stephen. *Sex Slavery*. London: Coronet, 1975.

Barlay, Stephen. *Sex Slavery: A Documentary Report on the International Scene Today*. London: William Heinemann, 1968, 1977.

Barlow, Tani. "Asian Women in Reregionalization." *positions: east asia cultures critique* 15, no. 2 (2007): 285–318.

Barry, Kathleen. *Annotated Bibliography on Social and Cultural Causes of Prostitution in the United States and the United Kingdom*. Paris: United Nations, Educational, Scientific and Cultural Organization, Division of Human Rights and Peace, 1985.

Barry, Kathleen. *Female Sexual Slavery*. New York: New York University Press, 1984. First published 1979 (Englewood Cliffs, NJ: Prentice-Hall).

Barry, Kathleen. "Female Sexual Slavery: Understanding the International Dimensions of Women's Oppression." *Human Rights Quarterly* 3, no. 2 (1981): 44–52.

Barry, Kathleen. "International Feminism: Sexual Politics and the World Conference of Women in Copenhagen." *Gender Issues* 1, no. 2 (1981): 37–50.

Barry, Kathleen. "Keynote Address: Women's Rights as Human Rights." In *Women Empowering Women: Proceedings of the Human Rights Conference on the Trafficking of Asian Women*, edited by Aurora Javate de Dios, 20–33. Manila: Coalition against Trafficking in Women–Asia, 1993.

Barry, Kathleen. "The Network Defines Its Issues: Theory, Evidence and Analysis of Female Sexual Slavery." In *International Feminism Networking against Female Sexual Slavery*, edited by Kathleen Barry, Charlotte Bunch, and Shirley Castley, 21-31. New York: International Women's Tribune Centre, 1984.

Barry, Kathleen. *The Prostitution of Sexuality*. New York: New York University Press, 1995.

Barry, Kathleen, Charlotte Bunch, and Shirley Castley. *International Feminism: Networking against Female Sexual Slavery*. New York: International Women's Tribune Centre, 1984.

Blaxland, John. "Intelligence and Special Operations in the Southwest Pacific, 1942-45." In *Australia 1944-45: Victory in the Pacific*, edited by Peter J. Dean, 145-68. Melbourne: Cambridge University Press, 2015.

Boeckel, Florence Brewer. "Women in International Affairs." *Annals of the American Academy of Political and Social Science* 143 (1929): 230-48.

Boven, Theo van. *Study Concerning the Right to Restitution, Compensation and Rehabilitation for Victims of Gross Violations of Human Rights and Fundamental Freedoms: Final Report Submitted by Theo van Boven, Special Rapporteur*. Geneva: United Nations, 1993.

Bradley, Christine. "Why Male Violence against Women Is a Development Issue: Reflections from Papua New Guinea." In *Violence against Women*, edited by Miranda Davies, 10-27. London: Zed, 1994.

Brandt, Alan M. *No Magic Bullet: A Social History of Venereal Disease in the United States since 1880*. London: Oxford University Press, 1987.

Bristow, Edward J. *Vice and Vigilance: Purity Movements in Britain since 1700*. Dublin: Gill and Macmillan, 1977.

Brown, Louise. *Sex Slaves: The Trafficking of Women in Asia*. London: Virago, 2000.

Brownmiller, Susan. *Against Our Will: Men, Women and Rape*. New York: Fawcett Columbine, 1975.

Bulbeck, Chilla. "Women's Movements in the Asia-Pacific." In *Culture and Society in the Asia-Pacific*, edited by Richard Maidment and Colin Mackerras, 163-84. London: Routledge, 1998.

Bunch, Charlotte. "The Global Campaign for Women's Human Rights: Where Next after Vienna?" *St. John's Law Review* 69, no. 1-2 (1995): 171-78.

Bunch, Charlotte. "Women's Rights as Human Rights: Toward a Re-vision of Human Rights." *Human Rights Quarterly* 12 (1990): 489-98.

Bunch, Charlotte, and Roxanna Carrillo. *Gender Violence: A Development and Human Rights Issue*. New Brunswick, NJ: Center for Women's Global Leadership, 1991.

Bunch, Charlotte, Roxanna Carrillo, and Rima Shore. "Violence against Women." In *Women in the Third World: An Encyclopedia of Contemporary Issues*, edited by Nelly P. Stromquist, 59-68. New York: Garland, 1998.

Bunch, Charlotte, and Shirley Castley. "Introduction." In *International Feminism: Networking against Female Sexual Slavery*, edited by Kathleen Barry, Charlotte Bunch, and Shirley Castley, 8-14. New York: International Women's Tribune Centre, 1984.

Bunch, Charlotte, Samantha Frost, and Niamh Reilly. "Making the Global Local: International Networking for Women's Human Rights." In *Women's International Human Rights: A Reference Guide*, edited by Kelly D. Askin and Dorean Koeing, 91-113. New York: Transnational, 1998.

Bunch, Charlotte, and Niamh Reilly. *Demanding Accountability: The Global Campaign and Vienna Tribunal for Women's Human Rights*. New York: Center for Women's Global Leadership and the United Nations Development Fund for Women, 1994.

Burton, Antoinette. *Burdens of History: British Feminists, Indian Women, and Imperial Culture, 1865-1915*. Chapel Hill: University of North Carolina Press, 1994.

Carrillo, Roxanna. *Battered Dreams: Violence against Women as an Obstacle to Development*. New York: United Nations Development Fund for Women, 1992.

Carrillo, Roxanna. "Violence against Women: An Obstacle to Development." In *Gender Violence: A Development and Human Rights Issue*, 17-37. New Brunswick, NJ: Center for Women's Global Leadership, 1991.

Center for Women's Global Leadership. *International Campaign for Women's Human Rights: 1992-1993 Report*. New Brunswick, NJ: Center for Women's Global Leadership, 1993.

Center for Women's Global Leadership. *1991 Women's Leadership Institute Report: Women, Violence and Human Rights*. New Brunswick, NJ: Center for Women's Global Leadership, 1992.

Chai, Alice Yun. "Asian-Pacific Feminist Coalition Politics: The *Chŏngshindae/Jŭgunianfu* ('Comfort Women') Movement." *Korean Studies* 17, no. 1 (1993): 67-91.

Chan, Won-loy. *Burma: The Untold Story*. Novato, CA: Presidio, 1986.

Chang, Ha-Joon. "The 1997 Korean Crisis: Causes and Consequences." In *Brazil and South Korea: Economic Crisis and Restructuring*, edited by Edmund Amann and Ha-Joon Chang, 105-22. London: Institute of Latin American Studies, 2004.

Chang, Ha-Joon, Gabriel Palma, and D. Hugh Whittaker. "The Asian Crisis: Introduction." *Cambridge Journal of Economics* 22 (1998): 649-52.

Chang, Kimberley, and Julian McAllister Groves. "Neither 'Saints' nor 'Prostitutes': Sexual Discourse in the Filipina Domestic Worker Community in Hong Kong." *Women's Studies International Forum* 23, no. 1 (2000): 73-87.

Chan-Tiberghien, Jennifer. *Gender and Human Rights Politics in Japan: Global Norms and Domestic Networks*. Palo Alto, CA: Stanford University Press, 2004.

Chavez, Jenina Joy, and Rowena D. Cordero. *The Asian Financial Crisis and Filipino Households: Impact on Women and Children*. Bangkok: Focus on the Global South and Save the Children UK, 2001.

Chavez, Linda. *Contemporary Forms of Slavery: Preliminary Report of the Special Rapporteur on the Situation of Systematic Rape, Sexual Slavery and Slavery-Like Practices during Periods of Armed Conflict*. New York: United Nations, 1996.

Chavez, Linda. *Contemporary Forms of Slavery, Preparatory Document Submitted by Mrs. Linda Chavez on the Question of Systematic Rape, Sexual Slavery and Slavery-Like Practices during Wartime*. New York: United Nations, 1993.

Chen, Kuan-Hsing. *Asia as Method: Toward Deimperialization*. Durham, NC: Duke University Press, 2010.

Chen, Kuan-Hsing, and Chua Beng Huat. "Introduction: The *Inter-Asia Cultural Studies: Movements* Project." In *The Inter-Asia Cultural Studies Reader*, edited by Kuan-Hsing Chen and Chua Beng Huat, 1-5. London: Routledge, 2007.

Cheung, Fanny M., Malavika Karlekar, Aurora De Dios, Juree Vicht-Vadakan, and Lourdes R. Quisimbing, eds. *Breaking the Silence: Violence against Women in Asia*. Hong

Kong: Equal Opportunities Commission in collaboration with Women in Asian Development and UNESCO National Commission of the Philippines, 1999.

Chew, Lin. "Reflections by an Anti-trafficking Activist." In *Trafficking and Prostitution Reconsidered: New Perspectives on Migration, Sex Work, and Human Rights*, edited by Kamala Kempadoo, 65–82. Boulder, CO: Paradigm, 2005.

Chiang, Lois. "Trafficking in Women." In *Women and International Human Rights Law*. Vol. 1, edited by Kelly D. Askin and D. M. Koening, 321–64. Ardsley, NY: Transnational, 1999.

Cho, Uhn. "Global Capital and Local Patriarchy: The Financial Crisis and Women Workers in South Korea." In *Women and Work in Globalising Asia*, edited by Dong-Sook S. Gils and Nicola Piper, 52–69. London: Routledge, 2002.

Choi, Chungmoo. "The Discourse of Decolonization and Popular Memory: South Korea." *positions* 1, no. 1 (1993): 77–102.

Choi, Chungmoo. "Guest Editor's Introduction." *positions: east asia cultures critique* 5, no. 1 (1997): v–xiv.

Choi, Chungmoo. "The Politics of War Memories toward Healing." In *Perilous Memories: The Asia-Pacific War(s)*, edited by Takashi Fujitani, Geoffrey M. White, and Lisa Yoneyama, 395–409. Durham, NC: Duke University Press, 2001.

Chou, Chih-Chieh. "An Emerging Transnational Movement in Women's Human Rights: Campaign of Nongovernmental Organizations on 'Comfort Women' Issue in East Asia." *Journal of Economic and Social Research* 5, no. 1 (2003): 153–81.

Chuh, Kandice. "Discomforting Knowledge: Or, Korean 'Comfort Women' and Asian Americanist Critical Practice." *Journal of Asian American Studies* 6, no. 1 (2003): 5–23.

Chung, Chin Sung. "The Issue of Military Sexual Slavery and the International Labour Organization." *Korea Journal* 42, no. 1 (2002): 263–86.

Chung, Chin Sung. "The Origin and Development of the Military Sexual Slavery Problem in Imperial Japan." *positions: east asia cultures critique* 5, no. 1 (1997): 219–55.

Coalition against Trafficking in Women-Asia Pacific (CATW-AP). *Trafficking in Women and Prostitution in the Asia Pacific*. Manila: CATW-Asia Pacific, 1996.

Coalition against Trafficking in Women-Asia Pacific (CATW-AP). *Women Empowering Women: Proceedings of the Human Rights Conference on the Trafficking of Asian Women*. Quezon City: CATW-Asia Pacific, 1993.

Connors, Jane Frances, and Centre for Social Development and Humanitarian Affairs (United Nations). *Violence against Women in the Family*. New York: United Nations, 1989.

Coomaraswamy, Radhika. *Preliminary Report Submitted by the Special Rapporteur on Violence against Women, Its Causes and Consequences, Ms. Radhika Coomaraswamy, in Accordance with Commission on Human Rights Resolution 1994/5*. Geneva: United Nations, 1995.

Coomaraswamy, Radhika. *Report on the Mission to the Democratic People's Republic of Korea, the Republic of Korea and Japan on the Issue of Military Sexual Slavery in Wartime*. Report Submitted to the 52nd Session of the UN Commission on Human Rights (E/CN.4/1996/53/Add.1). New York: UN Commission on Human Rights, Economic and Social Council, 1996.

Coomaraswamy, Radhika. *Report of the Special Rapporteur on Violence against Women, Its Causes and Consequences in Accordance with Commission on Human Rights Resolution 1997/44*. Geneva: United Nations, 1999.

Coomaraswamy, Radhika. *Report of the Special Rapporteur on Violence against Women, Its Causes and Consequences, Ms. Radhika Coomaraswamy, on Trafficking in Women, Women's Migration and Violence against Women, Submitted in Accordance with Commission on Human Rights Resolution 1997/44*. Geneva: United Nations, 2000.

Coomaraswamy, Radhika, and Lisa M. Kois. "Violence against Women." In *Women and International Human Rights Law*, edited by Kelly D. Askin and Dorean Koenig, 177–218. Ardsley, NY: Transnational, 1999.

Crowdy, Dame Rachel. "The Humanitarian Activities of the League of Nations." *Journal of the Royal Institute of International Affairs* 6, no. 3 (1927): 153–69.

Crowdy, Dame Rachel. "The League of Nations: Its Social and Humanitarian Work." *American Journal of Nursing* 28 (1928): 350–52.

Cumings, Bruce. "The Korean Crisis and the End of 'Late' Development." *New Left Review* 231 (1998): 43–72.

De Dios, Aurora. "The Global Trafficking in Asian Women." In *Women Empowering Women: Proceedings of the Human Rights Conference on the Trafficking of Asian Women*, 185–87. Quezon City: Coalition against Trafficking in Women-Asia, 1993.

De Dios, Aurora. "Introduction." In *Women Empowering Women: Proceedings of the Human Rights Conference on the Trafficking of Asian Women*, 1–7. Quezon City: Coalition against Trafficking in Women-Asia, 1993.

De Dios, Aurora. "An Overview of the Trafficking Situation in Asian Women." Paper presented at the Asian Women's Human Rights Commission (AWHRC) Pre-conference and Workshop on Crimes against Gender-International Peace Festival in the Philippines, 1991. *AWHRC Monograph Series* 6, no. 1 (1991): 41–48. Quezon City: Asian Women's Human Rights Commission, 1991.

Demleitner, Nora. "Forced Prostitution: Naming an International Offense." *Fordham International Law Journal* 18 (1994): 163–97.

Derks, Annuska. *Trafficking of Cambodian Women and Children to Thailand*. Phnom Penh: International Organization of Migration and Center for Advanced Study, 1997.

Di, Lolita. "The Scars of War: Vietnam Comfort Women." *Nation of Change*, April 9, 2015. www.nationofchange.org/2015/04/09/the-scars-of-war-vietnam-comfort-women.

Dolgopol, Ustinia. "Knowledge and Responsibility: The Ongoing Consequences of Failing to Give Sufficient Attention to the Crimes against the Comfort Women in the Tokyo Trial." In *Beyond Victor's Justice? The Tokyo War Crimes Trial Revisited*, edited by Yuki Tanaka, Tim McCormack, and Gerry Simpson, 243–61. Leiden: Martinus Nijhoff, 2011.

Dolgopol, Ustinia. "Redressing Partial Justice: A Possible Role for Civil Society." In *The Challenge of Conflict: International Law Responds*, edited by Ustinia Dolgopol and Judith Gail Gardam, 475–98. London: Brill, 2006.

Dolgopol, Ustinia, and Snehal Paranjape. *Comfort Women: An Unfinished Ordeal. Report of a Mission*. Geneva: International Commission of Jurists, 1994.

Draper, William H., III. "Foreword." *Human Development Report 1990*, iii–iv. New York: Oxford University Press for the United Nations Development Program, 1990.

Drea, Edward. "Introduction." In *Researching Japanese War Crimes Records: Introductory Essays*, 3–20. Washington, DC: Nazi War Crimes and Japanese Imperial Government

Records Interagency Working Group and the National Archives and Records Administration, 2006.

Elson, Diane. "International Financial Architecture: A View from the Kitchen." January 2004. www.networkideas.org/featart/jan2004/fa13_Diane_Elson.htm.

Engen, Hans. *Slavery. Concise Summary of the Information Supplied with Resolutions 238 (IX), 276 (X), 388 (XIII), 475 (XV) and 525 A(XVII)*. (E/2673). New York: United Nations, 1955.

Enloe, Cynthia. *Does Khaki Become You? The Militarization of Women's Lives.* Boston: South End, 1983.

Fernand-Laurent, Jean. *Activities for the Advancement of Women: Equality, Development and Peace.* New York: United Nations, 1985.

Fernand-Laurent, Jean. *Report of the Special Rapporteur on the Suppression of the Traffic in Persons and the Exploitation of the Prostitution of Others.* Geneva: United Nations, 1983.

Field, Norma. "War and Apology: Japan, Asia, the Fiftieth, and After." *positions: east asia cultures critique* 5, no. 1 (1997): 1–50.

Flexner, Abraham. *Prostitution in Europe.* New York: Century, 1914.

Foo, Lora Jo. *Asian American Women: Issues, Concerns, and Responsive Human and Civil Rights Advocacy.* New York: Ford Foundation, 2002.

Friedman, Elisabeth Jay. "Gendering the Agenda: The Impact of Transnational Women's Rights Movement at the UN Conferences of the 1990s." *Women's Studies International Forum* 26, no. 4 (2003): 313–32.

Fukuda-Parr, Sakiko. *Feminist Economics* 9, no. 2–3 (2003): 301–17.

Giaccardi, Elisa. "Memory and Territory: New Forms of Virtuality for the Museum." 2004. www.archimuse.com/mw2004/papers/giaccardi/giaccardi.html.

Gilmore, Allison B. "The Allied Translator and Interpreter Section: The Critical Role of Allied Linguists in the Process of Propaganda Creation, 1943–1944." In *The Foundations of Victory: The Pacific War 1943–1944. Proceedings of the 2003 Chief of Army's Military History Conference*, edited by Peter Dennis and Jeffrey Grey, 149–67. Canberra: Army History Unit, 2004.

Goldman, Emma. *The Traffic in Women and Other Essays on Feminism.* New York: Times Change, 1970.

Goodman, Grant K. "My Own *Gaiatsu*: A Document from 1945 Provides Proof." In *Legacies of the Comfort Women of World War II*, edited by Margaret Stetz and Bonnie B. C. Oh, 171–92. Armonk, NY: M. E. Sharpe, 2001.

Halley, Janet, Prabha Kotiswaran, Hila Shamir, and Chantal Thomas. "From the International to the Local in Feminist Legal Responses to Rape, Prostitution/Sex Work, and Sex Trafficking: Four Studies in Contemporary Governance Feminism." *Harvard Journal of Law and Gender* 29 (2006): 335–423.

Harrington, Joseph Daniel. *Yankee Samurai: The Secret Role of Nisei in America's Pacific Victory.* Detroit: Pettigrew, 1979.

Hein, Laura. "Savage Irony: The Imaginative Power of the 'Military Comfort Women' in the 1990s." *Gender and History* 11 (1999): 336–72.

Hein, Laura, and Mark Selden. "The Lesson of War, Global Power, and Social Change." In *Censoring History: Citizenship and Memory in Japan, Germany, and the United States*, edited by Laura Hein and Mark Selden, 3–50. Armonk, NY: M. E. Sharpe, 2000.

Heise, Lori. "Gender-Based Abuse: The Global Epidemic." *Cadernos de Saúde Pública* 10 (1994): 135-45.

Heise, Lori. "Gender-Based Abuse: The Global Epidemic." In *Reframing Women's Health: Multidisciplinary Research and Practice*, edited by Alice Dan, 233-50. Thousand Oaks, CA: SAGE, 1994.

Heise, Lori. "Violence against Women: The Hidden Health Burden." *World Health Statistics Quarterly* 46, no. 1 (1993): 78-85.

Heise, Lori. "Violence against Women: An Integrated, Ecological Framework." *Violence against Women* 4 (1998): 262-90.

Heise, Lori. "Violence against Women: The Missing Agenda." In *The Health of Women: A Global Perspective*, edited by Marge Koblinsky, Judith Timyan, and Jill Gay, 171-95. Boulder, CO: Westview, 1993.

Heise, Lori. "Violence against Women: Translating International Advocacy into Concrete Change." *American University Law Review* 44 (1995): 1207-11.

Heise, Lori, with Jacqueline Pitanguy and Adrienne Germain. *Violence against Women: The Hidden Health Burden*. Washington, DC: World Bank, 1994.

Heise, Lori L., Alanagh Raikes, Charlotte H. Watts, and Anthony B. Zwi. "Violence against Women: A Neglected Public Health Issue in Less Developed Countries." *Social Science and Medicine* 39, no. 9 (1994): 1165-79.

Hershatter, Gail. *Dangerous Pleasures: Prostitution and Modernity in 20th-Century Shanghai*. Berkeley: University of California Press, 1997.

Hicks, George. *The Comfort Women: Japan's Brutal Regime of Enforced Prostitution in the Second World War*. New York: W. W. Norton, 1994.

Hoffman, Cecelia. "Foreword." In *Women Empowering Women: Proceedings of the Human Rights Conference on the Trafficking of Asian Women, April 2-4, 1993, ISO, Ateneo de Manila University, Quezon City, Philippines*. Manila: CATW-Asia Pacific, 1993.

Howard, Keith, ed. *True Stories of the Korean Comfort Women: Testimonies*. Compiled by the Korean Council for Women Drafted for Military Sexual Slavery by Japan (*Han'guk Chŏngsindae Munje Taech'aek Hyŏbŭihoe*) and the Research Association on the Women Drafted for Military Sexual Slavery by Japan (*Chŏngsindae Yŏn˘guhoe*), and translated by Young Joo Lee. London: Cassell, 1995.

Hua, Julietta. *Trafficking Women's Human Rights*. Minneapolis: University of Minnesota Press, 2011.

Human Rights Watch. *Owed Justice: Thai Women Trafficked into Debt Bondage in Japan*. New York: Human Rights Watch, 2000.

Human Rights Watch/Asia. *Rape for Profit: Trafficking of Nepali Girls and Women to India's Brothels*. New York: Human Rights Watch, 1995.

Humphrey, John P. "The United Nations Sub-commission on the Prevention of Discrimination and the Protection of Minorities." *American Journal of International Law* 62, no. 4 (1968): 869-88.

Ienaga, Saburo. *The Pacific War, 1931-1945*. New York: Random House, 1978.

Inoue, Reiko. "Introduction: Looking Toward Beijing." In *Voices from the Japanese Women's Movement*, edited by AMPO-*Japan Asia Quarterly Review*, xvii-xxi. Armonk, NY: M. E. Sharpe, 1996.

"International Conference of Traffic in Women and Children"—"Final Act." *League of Nations Journal* (July/August 1921).

Interpol. 1974. "Traffic in Women: Recent Trends." Report by the General Secretariat of Interpol. UN Division of Human Rights. Reprinted in Kathleen Barry, *Female Sexual Slavery*, 283–98. New York: New York University Press, 1979.

Joachim, Jutta. *Agenda Setting, the UN and NGOs: Gender Violence and Reproductive Politics*. Washington, DC: Georgetown University Press, 2007.

Joachim, Jutta. "Shaping the Human Rights Agenda: The Case of Violence against Women." In *Gender Politics and Global Governance*, edited by Elizabeth K. Meyer and Elisabeth Prügl, 142–60. Lanham, MD: Rowman and Littlefield, 1999.

Johnson, Bascom. "Eliminating Vice from Camp Cities." *Annals of the American Academy of Political and Social Science* 78 (1918): 60–64.

Johnson, Chalmers. *Blowback: The Costs and Consequences of American Empire*. New York: Henry Holt, 2000.

Johnson, Chalmers. "Cold War Economics Melt Asia." *Nation* 23 (1998): 16–19.

Johnson, Chalmers. "Economic Crisis in East Asia: The Clash of Capitalisms." *Cambridge Journal of Economics* 22 (1998): 653–61.

Johnson, Chalmers. *MITI and the Japanese Economic Miracle: The Growth of Industrial Policy, 1925–1975*. Palo Alto, CA: Stanford University Press, 1982.

Johnson, Roswell H. "Adequate Reproduction." *Journal of Social Hygiene* 5 (1919): 223–26.

Johnson, Simon, and John Kwak. *13 Bankers: The Wall Street Takeover and the Next Financial Meltdown*. New York: Pantheon, 2010.

Kang, Laura. "Conjuring 'Comfort Women': Mediated Affiliations and Disciplined Subjects in Korean/American Transnationality." *Journal of Asian American Studies* 6, no. 1 (2003): 25–55.

Kang, Laura. "Epistemologies." In *A Companion to Gender Studies*, edited by Philomena Essed, David Theo Goldberg, and Audrey Kobayashi, 73–86. Chichester, UK: Wiley, 2009.

Kang, Laura. "The Problem of Silence surrounding the Problem of Violence against Women in Asia." *Asian Journal of Women's Studies* 7, no. 4 (2001): 122–31.

Kang, Laura. "Surveillance and the Work of Anti-trafficking: From Compulsory Examination to International Coordination." In *Feminist Surveillance Studies*, edited by Rachel E. Dubrofsky and Shoshana Amielle Magnet, 39–55. Durham, NC: Duke University Press, 2015.

Kang, Laura. "The Uses of Asianization: Figuring Crises, 1997–8 and 2007–?" *American Quarterly* 64, no. 3 (2012): 411–36.

Keck, Margaret E., and Kathryn Sikkink. *Activists beyond Borders: Advocacy Networks in International Politics*. Ithaca, NY: Cornell University Press, 1998.

Kelly, Liz. "Inside Outsiders: Mainstreaming Violence against Women into Human Rights Discourse and Practice." *International Feminist Journal of Politics* 7, no. 4 (2005): 471–95.

Kennedy, Angie C. "Eugenics, 'Degenerate Girls,' and Social Workers during the Progressive Era." *Affilia* 27 (2008): 22–37.

Kenny, Katherine E. "The Biopolitics of Global Health: Life and Death in Neoliberal Time." *Journal of Sociology* 51, no. 1 (2015): 9–27.
Kern, Thomas, and Sang-hui Nam. "The Korean Comfort Women Movement and the Formation of a Public Sphere in East Asia." In *Korea Yearbook (2009): Politics, Economy and Society*, edited by Rüdiger Frank, Jim Hoare, Patrick Kölner, and Susan Pares, 227–56. Leiden: Brill, 2009.
Kim, Elaine. "Sex Tourism in Asia: A Reflection of Political and Economic Inequality." *Critical Perspectives of Third World America* 2, no. 1 (1984): 215–31.
Kim, Pu Ja. "Looking at Sexual Slavery from a *Zainichi* Perspective." In *Voices from the Japanese Women's Movement*, edited by AMPO-*Japan Asia Quarterly Review*, 157–60. Armonk, NY: M. E. Sharpe, 1996.
Kimura, Maki. *Unfolding the "Comfort Women" Debates: Modernity, Violence, Women's Voices*. New York: Palgrave Macmillan, 2016.
Kneeland, George J. *Commercialized Prostitution in New York City*. New York: Century, 1913.
Knepper, Paul. *International Crime in the 20th Century: The League of Nations Era, 1919–1939*. New York: Palgrave Macmillan, 2011.
Knepper, Paul. "Measuring the Threat of Global Crime: Insights from Research by the League of Nations into the Traffic in Women." *Criminology* 50, no. 3 (2012): 777–809.
Kosambi, Meera, ed. *Violence against Women: Reports from India and Korea*. Bangkok: UNESCO Principal Regional Office for Asia and the Pacific, 1993.
Kregel, Jan A. "Derivatives and Global Capital Flows: Applications to Asia." *Cambridge Journal of Economics* 22, no. 6 (1998): 677–92.
Lancaster, Carol. "Japan's ODA: *naiatsu* and *gaiatsu*." In *Japanese Aid and the Construction of Global Development: Inescapable Solutions*, edited by David Leheny and Kay Warren, 29–53. New York: Routledge, 2010.
Laughlin, Harry H. "Eugenical Sterilization in the United States." *Journal of Social Hygiene* 6 (1920): 499–531.
League of Nations. *Commission of Enquiry into Traffic in Women and Children in the East: Report to the Council*. Geneva: League of Nations, 1927.
League of Nations. *Report of the Special Body of Experts on Traffic in Women and Children*. Geneva: Imp. de la "Tribune de Genève," 1927.
Lee, June J. H. *A Review of Data on Trafficking in the Republic of Korea*. Geneva: International Organization for Migration, 2002.
Leppanen, Katarina. "Movement of Women: Trafficking in the Interwar Era." *Women's Studies International Forum* 30, no. 6 (2007): 523–33.
Levine, Philippa. *Prostitution, Race, and Politics: Policing Venereal Disease in the British Empire*. New York: Routledge, 2003.
Levine, Philippa. "'Walking the Streets in a Way No Decent Woman Should': Women Police in World War I." *Journal of Modern History* 66, no. 1 (1994): 34–78.
Limoncelli, Stephanie A. "International Voluntary Associations, Local Social Movements and State Paths to the Abolition of Regulated Prostitution in Europe, 1875–1950." *International Sociology* 21, no. 1 (2006): 31–59.
Limoncelli, Stephanie A. *The Politics of Trafficking: The First International Movement to Combat the Sexual Exploitation of Women*. Palo Alto, CA: Stanford University Press, 2010.

Lindquist, Johan. "Veils and Ecstasy: Negotiating Shame in the Indonesian Borderlands." *ethnos* 69, no. 4 (2004): 487–508.

Lowe, Lisa. *The Intimacies of Four Continents*. Durham, NC: Duke University Press, 2015.

Lubove, Roy. "The Progressives and the Prostitute." *Historian* 24 (1962): 308–30.

Manderson, Lenore, and Margaret Jolly. "Sites of Desire/Economies of Pleasure in Asia and the Pacific." In *Sites of Desire, Economies of Pleasure: Sexualities in Asia and the Pacific*, edited by Lenore Manderson and Margaret Jolly, 1–26. Chicago: University of Chicago Press, 1997.

Matsui, Yayori. "Economic Development and Asian Women." In *Voices from the Japanese Women's Movement*, edited by AMPO-*Japan Asia Quarterly Review*, 55–64. Armonk, NY: M. E. Sharpe, 1996.

Matsui, Yayori. "Overcoming the Culture of Impunity for Wartime Sexual Violence." In *Crossing Borders and Shifting Boundaries*, 237–50. Wiesbaden: VS Verlag für Sozialwissenschaften, 2002.

Matsui, Yayori. "Sexual Slavery in Korea." Translated by Lora Sharnoff. *Frontiers* 2, no. 1 (1977): 22–30.

Matsui, Yayori. "Trafficking in Women and Prostitution in Japan." In *Women Empowering Women: Proceedings of the Human Rights Conference on the Trafficking of Asian Women*, 2–4. Quezon City: CATW-Asia Pacific, 1993.

Matsui, Yayori. "Why I Oppose *Kisaeng* Tours." In *International Feminism: Networking against Female Sexual Slavery*, edited by Kathleen Barry, Charlotte Bunch, and Shirley Castley, 64–72. New York: International Women's Tribune Centre, 1984.

Matsui, Yayori. *Why I Oppose* Kisaeng *Tours: Exposing Economic and Sexual Aggression against South Korean Women*. Translated by Lora Sharnoff. Tokyo: Femintern, 1975. Originally published in Japanese as "Watashi wa naze Kiisen kanko no bantai surunoka," *Onna Eros* 2 (1974).

Matsui, Yayori. *Women in the New Asia: From Pain to Power*. New York: Zed, 1999.

Matsui, Yayori. "Women's Predicament: Why I Oppose *Kisaeng* Tours." In *Japanese Women Speak Out*, edited by "White Paper on Sexism-Japan" Task Force, 172–79. Tokyo: Pacific-Asia Resource Center, 1975.

McDougall, Gay J. *Contemporary Forms of Slavery: Systematic Rape, Sexual Slavery and Slavery-Like Practices during Armed Conflict. Final Report submitted by Ms. Gay J. McDougall, Special Rapporteur*. E/CN.4/Sub.2/1998/13. New York: United Nations, 1998.

McNeill, David, and Justin McCurry. "Sink the *Asahi*! The 'Comfort Women' Controversy and the Neo-nationalist Attack." *Asia-Pacific Journal* 13, no. 1 (2015).

Metzger, Barbara. "Towards an International Human Rights Regime during the Interwar Years: The League of Nations' Combat of the Traffic in Women and Children." In *Beyond Sovereignty: Britain, Empire and Transnationalism, c. 1880–1950*, edited by Kevin Grant, Philippa Levine, and Frank Trentmann, 54–79. New York: Palgrave Macmillan, 2007.

Miers, Suzanne. "Slavery and the Slave Trade as International Issues, 1890–1939." *Slavery and Abolition* 19, no. 2 (1998): 16–37.

Miers, Suzanne. *Slavery in the Twentieth Century: The Evolution of a Global Problem*. Walnut Creek, CA: AltaMira, 2003.

Miller, Alice M. "Sexuality, Violence against Women, and Human Rights: Women Make Demands and Ladies Get Protection." *Health and Human Rights* 7, no. 2 (2004): 16–47.

Moon, Katharine H. S. "South Korean Movements against Militarized Sexual Labor." *Asian Survey* 39 (1999): 310–27.

Morris-Suzuki, Tessa, and Peter Rimmer. "Virtual Memories: Japanese History Debates in Manga and Cyberspace." *Asian Studies Review* 26, no. 2 (2000): 147–64.

Naím, Moisés. "Latin America the Morning After." *Foreign Affairs* 74, no. 4 (1995): 45–61.

Nester, William R. *Japan and the Third World: Patterns, Power, Prospects.* New York: St. Martin's, 1992.

O'Callaghan, Sean. *The Yellow Slave Trade: A Survey of the Traffic in Women and Children in the East.* London: Blond, 1968.

Orr, Robert M., Jr. "Collaboration or Conflict? Foreign Aid and US-Japan Relations." *Pacific Affairs* 62, no. 4 (1989): 476–89.

Ozawa, Terutomo. "Japan's New Resource Democracy: Government-Backed Group Investment." *Journal of World Trade Law* 3 (1980): 3–13.

Palma, Gabriel. "Three and a Half Cycles of 'Mania, Panic, and [Asymmetric] Crash': East Asia and Latin American Compared." *Cambridge Journal of Economics* 22, no. 6 (1998): 789–808.

Park, Won Soon. "Japanese Reparations Policies and the 'Comfort Women' Question." *positions: east asia cultures critique* 5, no. 1 (1997): 107–34.

Parker, Karen. "Human Rights of Women during Armed Conflict." In *Women and International Human Rights Law 3*, edited by Kelly D. Askin and Dorean M. Koenig, 283–323. New York: Transnational, 2001.

Parker, Karen, and Jennifer F. Chew. "Compensation for Japan's World War II War-Rape Victims." *Hastings International and Comparative Law Review* 17 (1993): 497–549.

Pennay, Lori J. "The Disproportionate Effect of the Asian Economic Crisis on Women: The Filipina Experience." *University of Pennsylvania Journal of International Economy* 21 (2000): 427–80.

Perpiñan, Sister Mary Soledad. *Annotated Bibliography on Prostitution in East and Southeast Asia.* Paris: UNESCO Division of Human Rights and Peace, 1985.

Perpiñan, Sister Mary Soledad. "Confronting Prostitution Tourism: The Third World Movement against the Exploitation of Women." *Canadian Woman Studies/Les Cahiers de la Femme* 7, nos. 1–2 (1986): 125–29.

Pirie, Iain. *The Korean Developmental State: From Dirigisme to Neo-liberalism.* London: Routledge, 2008.

Pliley, Jessica R. "Claims to Protection: The Rise and Fall of Feminist Abolitionism in the League of Nations' Committee on the Traffic in Women and Children, 1919–1936." *Journal of Women's History* 22, no. 4 (2010): 90–113.

Pollard, Vincent Kelly. "Entering Global Civil Society: Japan's ODA Policy-Making Milieu from June 1992." *Japanese Studies* 16, nos. 2–3 (1996): 35–61.

Rathus, Joel. "China, Japan and Regional Organisations: The Case of the Asian Development Bank." *Japanese Studies* 28, no. 1 (2008): 87–99.

Raymond, Janice G. "Prostitution as Violence against Women: NGO Stonewalling in Beijing and Elsewhere." *Women's Studies International Forum* 21, no. 1 (1998): 1–9.

Reanda, Laura. 1991. "Prostitution as a Human Rights Question, Problems and Prospects of United Nations Action." *Human Rights Quarterly* 13, no. 2 (1991): 202–28.

Reilly, Niamh, ed. *Without Reservation: The Beijing Tribunal on Accountability for Women's Human Rights.* New Brunswick, NJ: Center for Women's Global Leadership, 1996.

Renzetti, Claire. "Editor's Introduction." *Violence against Women* 1, no. 1 (1995): 3–5.

"Review of League of Nations, *Report of the Special Body of Experts on Traffic in Women and Children.*" *Social Service Review* 2, no. 1 (1928): 166–68.

Roche, Susan E., Katy Biron, and Niamh Reilly. "Sixteen Days of Activism against Gender Violence." *Violence against Women* 1 (1995): 272–81.

Rockefeller, John D., Jr. "Introduction" to *Commercialized Prostitution in New York City*, by George J. Kneeland, vii–xii. New York: Century, 1913.

Rockefeller, John D., Jr. "The Origin, Work and Plans of the Bureau of Social Hygiene," January 27, 1913. Rockefeller Archive Center, Office of the Messrs. Rockefeller Records, Series O, Box 9, Folder 67.

Rubin, Gayle. "Thinking Sex: Notes for a Radical Theory of the Politics of Sexuality." In *Pleasure and Danger*, edited by Carole Vance, 267–319. Boston: Routledge and Kegan Paul, 1984.

Rubin, Gayle. "The Traffic in Women: Notes on the 'Political Economy' of Sex." In *Toward an Anthropology of Women*, edited by Rayna Reiter, 157–210. New York: Monthly Review Press, 1975.

Rubin, Gayle, and Judith Butler. "Sexual Traffic." *Differences* 6, no. 2 (1994): 62–99.

Russell, Diana E. H., and Nicole Van de Ven, eds. *The Proceedings of the International Tribunal on Crimes against Women.* Millbrae, CA: Les Femmes, 1976.

Sajor, Indai Lourdes. "Military Sexual Slavery: Crimes against Humanity." *World Bulletin* 14 (1998): 48–69.

Sajor, Indai Lourdes. "Military Sexual Slavery: Crimes against Humanity." In *Peace, Justice and Freedom: Human Rights Challenges for the New Millennium*, edited by Gurcharan Singh Bhatia, 163–79. Edmonton: University of Alberta Press, 2000.

Sajor, Indai Lourdes. "Present Situation of 'Comfort Women' in the Philippines." In *War Victimization and Japan: International Public Hearing Report*, International Public Hearing Concerning Post War Compensation of Japan, 27–37. Osaka: Toho Shuppan, 1993.

Samuels, Richard J. "Kishi and Corruption: An Anatomy of the 1955 System," Japan Policy Research Institute Working Paper No. 83, December 2001. http://www.jpri.org/publications/workingpapers/wp83.html.

Sancho-Liao, Nelia. "1992 Philippine Country Report on the Filipino Comfort Women." Paper presented at the Asian Conference on Comfort Women, August 10–11, 1992. In *War Crimes on Asian Women: Military Sexual Slavery by Japan during World War II: The Case of the Filipino Comfort Women, Part II*, edited by Dan P. Calica and Nelia Sancho, 7–14. Manila: Asian Women's Human Rights Council, 1993.

Schaller, Michael. "America's Favorite War Criminal: Kishi Nobusuke and the Transformation of US-Japan Relations." Japan Policy Research Institute Working Paper No. 11, July 1995. www.jpri.org/publications/workingpapers/wp11.html.

Schellstede, Sangmie Choi, ed. *Comfort Women Speak: Testimony by Sex Slaves of the Japanese Military*. New York: Holmes and Meier, 2000.

Schrover, Marlou. "History of Slavery, Human Smuggling and Trafficking 1860–2010." In *Histories of Transnational Crime*, edited by Gerben Bruinsma, 41–70. New York: Springer, 2015.

Schuler, Margaret, ed. *Freedom from Violence: Women's Strategies from around the World*. New York: UNIFEM, 1992.

Scully, Eileen. "Pre–Cold War Traffic in Sexual Labor and Its Foes: Some Contemporary Lessons." In *Global Human Smuggling: Comparative Perspectives*, edited by David Kyle and Rey Koslowski, 74–106. Baltimore: Johns Hopkins University Press, 2001.

Shigematsu, Setsu S. *Scream from the Shadows: The Women's Liberation Movement in Japan*. Minneapolis: University of Minnesota Press, 2012.

Shin, Heisoo. "Seeking Justice, Honour and Dignity: Movement for the Victims of Japanese Military Sexual Slavery." In *Global Civil Society 2011 Globality and the Absence of Justice*, edited by Martin Albrow and Hakan Seckinelgin, 14–28. Basingstoke, UK: Palgrave Macmillan, 2011.

Shin, Heisoo. "The Situation of the Comfort Women: An Update." In *Without Reservation: The Beijing Tribunal on Accountability for Women's Human Rights*, edited by Niamh Reilly, 43–44. New Brunswick, NJ: Center for Women's Global Leadership, 1996.

Skolnik, Laura, and Jan Boontinand. 1999. "The Traffic in Women in the Asia-Pacific." *Forum for Applied Research and Public Policy* 14, no. 1: 76–81.

Skrobanek, Siriporn. "Exotic, Subservient and Trapped: Confronting Prostitution and Traffic in Women in Southeast Asia." In *Freedom from Violence: Women's Strategies from around the World*, edited by Margaret Schuler, 127–37. New York: UNIFEM, 1992.

Skrobanek, Siriporn, Nattaya Boonpakdi, and Christina Janthakeero. *The Traffic in Women: Human Realities of the International Sex Trade*. London: Zed, 1997.

Smith, Jeremy N. *Epic Measures: One Doctor, Seven Billion Patients*. New York: Harper Wave, 2015.

Snow, William F. "The Program of the League of Nations Advisory Committee on the Traffic in Women and the Protection and Welfare of Children and Young People." *Proceedings of the Academy of Political Science in the City of New York* 12, no. 1 (1926): 411–17.

Soh, Chunghee Sarah. *The Comfort Women: Sexual Violence and Postcolonial Memory in Korea and Japan*. Chicago: University of Chicago Press, 2008.

Soh, Chunghee Sarah. "From Imperial Gifts to Sex Slaves: Theorizing Symbolic Representations of the 'Comfort Women.'" *Social Science Japan Journal* 3, no. 1 (2000): 59–76.

Soh, Chunghee Sarah. "Human Rights and the 'Comfort Women.'" *Peace Review* 12, no. 1 (2000): 123–29.

Soh, Chunghee Sarah. "Japan's National/Asian Women's Fund for 'Comfort Women.'" *Pacific Affairs* 76, no. 2 (2003): 209–33.

Soh, Chunghee Sarah. "Kim Hak-sun." In *The Historical Encyclopedia of World Slavery*, edited by Junius P. Rodriguez, 390–91. Santa Barbara, CA: ABC-CLIO, 1997.

Soh, Chunghee Sarah. "The Korean 'Comfort Women': Movement for Redress." *Asian Survey* 36, no. 12 (1996): 1226–40.

Soh, Chunghee Sarah. "Korean Council." In *The Historical Encyclopedia of World Slavery*, edited by Junius P. Rodriguez, 393–94. Santa Barbara, CA: ABC-CLIO, 1997.

Soh, Chunghee Sarah. "Military Prostitution and Women's Sexual Labour in Japan and Korea." In *Gender and Labour in Korea and Japan: Sexing Class*, edited by Ruth Barraclough and Elyssa Faison, 44–59. Abingdon, UK: Routledge, 2009.

Soh, Chunghee Sarah. "Prostitutes versus Sex Slaves: The Politics of Representing the 'Comfort Women.'" In *Legacies of the Comfort Women of World War II*, edited by Margaret Stetz and Bonnie B. C. Oh, 76–80. Armonk, NY: M. E. Sharpe, 2001.

Soh, Chunghee Sarah. "Sexual Slavery, Japanese Military." In *The Historical Encyclopedia of World Slavery*, edited by Junius P. Rodriguez, 579–80. Santa Barbara, CA: ABC-CLIO, 1997.

Soh, Chunghee Sarah. "Yun Chong-ok." In *The Historical Encyclopedia of World Slavery*, edited by Junius P. Rodriguez, 712. Santa Barbara, CA: ABC-CLIO, 1997.

Stetz, Margaret D. "Representing 'Comfort Women': Activism through Law and Art." *IRIS* 45 (fall 2002): 26–29, 83–84.

Stetz, Margaret D. "What the West Failed to Learn about War from the 'Comfort Women.'" In *Gender Violence: Interdisciplinary Perspectives*, edited by Laura L. O'Toole, Jessica R. Schiffman, and Margie L. Kiter Edwards, 223–29. New York: New York University Press, 2007.

Stetz, Margaret D., and Bonnie B. Oh. "Introduction." In *Legacies of the Comfort Women of World War II*, edited by Margaret D. Stetz and Bonnie B. Oh, xi–xvi. Armonk, NY: M. E. Sharpe, 2001.

Stiglitz, Joseph. "What I Learned at the World Economic Crisis." In *Globalization and the Poor: Exploitation or Equalizer?*, edited by William J. Driscoll and Julie Clark, 195–204. New York: International Debate Education Association, 2003.

Stone, James A. "Interrogation of Japanese POWs in World War II: U.S. Response to a Formidable Challenge." In *Interrogation: World War II, Vietnam, and Iraq*, edited by William C. Spracher, 17–75. Washington, DC: National Defense Intelligence College, 2008.

Strathern, Marilyn. "Introduction: New Accountabilities." In *Audit Cultures: Anthropological Studies in Accountability, Ethics and the Academy*, edited by Marilyn Strathern, 1–18. London: Routledge, 2000.

Sullivan, Barbara. "Trafficking in Women." *International Feminist Journal of Politics* 5, no. 1 (2003): 67–91.

Sullivan, Donna J. "Women's Human Rights and the 1993 World Conference on Human Rights." *American Journal of International Law* 88, no. 1 (1994): 152–67.

Summers, Lawrence H. "International Financial Crises: Causes, Prevention, and Cures." *American Economic Review* 90, no. 2 (2000): 1–16.

Takahashi, Kikue. "*Kisaeng* Tourism." *Isis International Bulletin* 13 (November 1979): 23–25.

Takeuchi, Yoshimi, and Richard Calichman. *What Is Modernity? Writings of Takeuchi Yoshimi*. New York: Columbia University Press, 2005.

Tanaka, Yuki. *Japan's Comfort Women: Sexual Slavery and Prostitution during World War II and the US Occupation*. New York: Routledge, 2002.

Terry, Jennifer. *Attachments to War: Biomedical Logics and Violence in Twenty-First Century America*. Durham, NC: Duke University Press, 2017.

Third World Conference on Women. *Nairobi Forward-Looking Strategies to the Year 2000: Report of the World Conference to Review and Appraise the Achievements of the United Nations Decade for Women: Equality, Development and Peace*. UN Doc., A/CONF.116/28/Rev.1, 1986.

Thoma, Pamela. "Cultural Autobiography, Testimonial, and Asian American Transnational Feminist Coalition in the 'Comfort Women of World War II' Conference." *Frontiers: A Journal of Women's Studies* 21, nos. 1/2 (2000): 29–54.

Toepfer, Susan Jeanne, and Bryan Stuart Wells. "The Worldwide Market for Sex: A Review of International and Regional Legal Prohibitions regarding Trafficking in Women." *Michigan Journal of Gender and Law* 2 (1994): 83.

Totsuka, Etsuro. "Proposals for Japan and the ROK to Resolve the 'Comfort Women' Issue: Creating Trust and Peace in Light of International Law." *Asia-Pacific Journal: Japan Focus* 11, issue 1, no. 7 (January 7, 2013). http://apjjf.org/2013/11/1/Totsuka-Etsuro/3885/article.html.

Trinidad, Dennis. "Japan's ODA at the Crossroads: Disbursement Patterns of Japan's Development Assistance to Southeast Asia." *Asian Perspective* 31, no. 2 (2007): 95–125.

Truong, Thanh-Dam. "A Feminist Perspective on the Asian Miracle and Crisis: Enlarging the Conceptual Map of Human Development." *Journal of Human Development* 1, no. 1 (2000): 159–64.

Truong, Thanh-Dam. "The Underbelly of the Tiger: Gender and the Demystification of the Asian Miracle." *Review of International Political Economy* 6, no. 2 (1999): 133–65.

United Nations. *Information Received from Non-governmental Organizations Pursuant to Commission on Human Rights Resolution 1989/35: Note*. Geneva: United Nations, 1989.

United Nations. *Report of the World Conference of the United Nations Decade for Women: Equality, Development and Peace: Copenhagen, 14 to 30 July 1980*. New York: United Nations, 1980.

United Nations. Department of Economic and Social Affairs. *Study on Traffic in Persons and Prostitution: Suppression of the Traffic in Persons and of the Exploitation of the Prostitution of Others*. New York: United Nations, 1959.

United Nations. Non-governmental Liaison Service. *Female Sexual Slavery and Economic Exploitation: Making Local and Global Connections: Report of a Consultation Organized by the Non-governmental Liaison Service (New York), San Francisco, California, October 25, 1984*. New York: United Nations Non-governmental Liaison Service, 1985.

United Nations. Sub-commission on Prevention of Discrimination and Protection of Minorities. Working Group on Contemporary Forms of Slavery. *Report of the Working Group on Contemporary Forms of Slavery at Its 17th Session*. Geneva: United Nations, 1992.

United Nations. Sub-commission on the Promotion and Protection of Human Rights. *Review of Further Developments in Fields with Which the Sub-commission Has Been Concerned. Written Statement Submitted by Liberation*. September 3, 1992. E/CN.4/Sub.2/1992/NGO/26.

United Nations Children's Fund. *Fire in the House: Determinants of Intrafamilial Violence and Strategies for Its Elimination*. Bangkok: UNICEF, East Asia and Pacific Regional Office, 1995.

United Nations Commission on Human Rights. *Contemporary Forms of Slavery: Report of the Working Group on Contemporary Forms of Slavery at Its Seventeenth Session.* June 23, 1992. E/CN.4/Sub.2/1992/34.

United Nations Development Programme. *Human Development Report 1990.* New York: Oxford University Press for the U.N.D.P., 1990.

United Nations Development Programme. *Human Development Report 1995.* New York: Oxford University Press for the U.N.D.P., 1995.

United Nations Economic and Social Commission for Asia and the Pacific. *Promoting Women's Rights as Human Rights.* New York: United Nations Publications, 1999.

United Nations Economic and Social Commission for Asia and the Pacific. *Violence against Women in South Asia.* New York: United Nations, 2000.

United Nations Economic and Social Commission for Asia and the Pacific-Population Division. "Advocacy for the Elimination of Violence against Women." *Asia-Pacific Population Journal* (2001): 49–59.

United Nations Economic and Social Council. *Report of the First Session of the Ad Hoc Committee on Slavery to the Economic and Social Council.* U.N. Doc. E/1660, E/AC.33/9, March 27, 1950.

United Nations Educational, Scientific and Cultural Organization. *International Meeting of Experts on the Social and Cultural Causes of Prostitution and Strategies for the Struggle against Procuring and Sexual Exploitation of Women—Final Report. Madrid, Spain, 18–21 March 1986.* SHS-85/Conf.608/14, 1–18.

United States General Accounting Office (GAO). *Economic Assistance: Integration of Japanese Aid and Trade Policies: Report to the Chairman, Subcommittee on Economic Resources and Competitiveness, Joint Economic Committee, U.S. Congress.* Washington, DC: GAO, 1990.

United States Office of War Information. Psychological Warfare Team Attached to US Army Forces India-Burma Theater. "Japanese Prisoners of War Interrogation Report No. 49." Ledo Stockade, October 1944.

Wada, Haruki. "The Comfort Women, the Asian Women's Fund and the Digital Museum." *Asia-Pacific Journal* 6, no. 2 (February 1, 2008).

Wade, Robert. "The Asian Debt-and-Development Crisis of 1997–?" *World Development* 26, no. 8 (1998): 1535–53.

Wade, Robert. "Japan, the World Bank, and the Art of Paradigm Maintenance: The East Asian Miracle in Political Perspective." *New Left Review* 217 (1996): 3–37.

Wade, Robert, and Frank Veneroso. "The Asian Crisis: The High Debt Model versus the Wall Street–Treasury–IMF Complex." *New Left Review* 228 (1998): 3–24.

Wan, Ming. "Japan and the Asian Development Bank." *Pacific Affairs* 68, no. 4 (1995): 509–29.

Warren, James Francis. *Ah Ku and Karayuki-san: Prostitution in Singapore, 1870–1940.* Singapore: Oxford University Press, 1993.

Warren, Kay B. "Trafficking in Persons: A Multi-sited View of International Norms and Local Responses." In *Japanese Aid and the Construction of Global Development: Inescapable Solutions,* edited by David Leheny and Kay Warren, 217–32. New York: Routledge, 2010.

Watanabe, Kazuko. "Militarism, Colonialism, and the Trafficking of Women: 'Comfort Women' Forced into Sexual Labor for Japanese Soldiers." *Bulletin of Concerned Asian Scholars* 26, no. 4 (1994): 3–17.

Watanabe, Kazuko. "Trafficking in Women's Bodies, Then and Now: The Issue of Military 'Comfort Women.'" *Women's Studies Quarterly* (1999): 19–31.

Watts, Charlotte, and Cathy Zimmerman. "Violence against Women: Global Scope and Magnitude." *Lancet* 359, no. 9313 (2002): 1232–37.

Welch, Claude E., Jr. "Defining Contemporary Forms of Slavery: Updating a Venerable NGO." *Human Rights Quarterly* 31, no. 1 (2009): 70–128.

Whitaker, Benjamin. *Slavery: Report [updating the report on slavery to the sub-commission in 1966]*. New York: United Nations, 1984.

White, John. 1964. *Japanese Aid*. London: Overseas Development Institute, 1964.

Wijers, Marjan, and Lin Lap-Chew. *Trafficking in Women, Forced Labour and Slavery-Like Practices in Marriage, Domestic Labour and Prostitution*. Utrecht: Global Alliance against Trafficking in Women, 1997.

Winkler, Allan. *The Politics of Propaganda: The Office of War Information, 1942–1945*. New Haven, CT: Yale University Press, 1978.

Woo, Jung-en. *Race to the Swift: State and Finance in Korean Industrialization*. New York: Columbia University Press, 1991.

Woolston, Howard B. *Prostitution in the United States*. New York: Century, 1921.

World Bank. *The East Asian Miracle: Economic Growth and Public Policy*. World Bank Policy Research Report. New York: Oxford University Press, 1993.

World Bank. *World Development Report 1989*. New York: Oxford University Press, 1989.

World Bank. *World Development Report 1993: Investing in Health*. New York: Oxford University Press, 1993.

World Health Organization. *DALYs and Reproductive Health: Report of an Informal Consultation, 27–28 April 1998*. Geneva: WHO, 1998. WHO/RHT/98.28.

World Health Organization. *Putting Women First: Ethical and Safety Recommendations for Research on Domestic Violence against Women*. Geneva: WHO, 2001. WHO/FCH/GWH/01.1.

Yamazaki, Hiromi. "Military Slavery and the Women's Movement." In *Voices from the Japanese Women's Movement*, edited by AMPO-*Japan-Asia Quarterly Review*, 91–100. Armonk, NY: M. E. Sharpe, 1996.

Yang, Daqing. "Documentary Evidence and the Studies of Japanese War Crimes: An Interim Assessment." In *Researching Japanese War Crimes Records: Introductory Essays*, by Edward Drea, Greg Bradsher, Robert Hanyok, James Lide, Michael Petersen, and Daqing Yang, 21–56. Washington, DC: Nazi War Crimes and Japanese Imperial Government Records Interagency Working Group and the National Archives and Records Administration, 2006.

Yang, Hyunah. "Revisiting the Issue of Korean 'Military Comfort Women': The Question of Truth and Positionality." *positions: east asia cultures critique* 5, no. 1 (1997): 51–72.

Yasumoto, Dennis T. "Why Aid? Japan as an 'Aid Great Power.'" *Pacific Affairs* 62, no. 4 (1989): 490–503.

Yoneda, Karl. *Ganbatte: Sixty-Year Struggle of a Kibei Worker.* Los Angeles: Asian American Studies Center, 1983.

Yoneyama, Lisa. *Cold War Ruins: Transpacific Critique of American Justice and Japanese War Crimes.* Durham, NC: Duke University Press, 2016.

Yoshimi, Yoshiaki. *Comfort Women: Sexual Slavery in the Japanese Military during World War II.* Translated by Suzanne O'Brien. New York: Columbia University Press, 2000.

Yu, Joyce. "Introduction." In *Female Sexual Slavery and Economic Exploitation: Making Local and Global Connections: Report of a Consultation Organized by the Non-governmental Liaison Service (New York), San Francisco, California, October 25, 1984.* New York: United Nations Non-governmental Liaison Service, 1985.

Yun, Chung-ok. "In Memory of Yayori Matsui." *Inter-Asia Cultural Studies* 4, no. 2 (2003): 190–92.

Zoglin, Kathryn. "United Nations Action against Slavery: A Critical Evaluation." *Human Rights Quarterly* 8, no. 2 (1986): 306–39.

INDEX

Abbott, Grace, 64–66, 68–70, 72, 79, 275–76n56
Abe Shinzo, 44, 196, 221, 253–54, 256
activism: Asian women as activists, 16; comfort women redress movement, 14; survivors as activists, 14
Akune, Kenjiro (Kenji), 170, 181, 182, 184
Allain, Jean, 101, 279n25
Allied Translator and Interpreter Section (ATIS), 166, 168, 171, 176–77, 240, 304–5n43
American Social Hygiene Association (ASHA): 67–69, 71, 72, 74, 76; *Journal of Social Hygiene*, 68
American studies, 35, 42
Anti-Slavery Society, 85, 91, 93, 101, 104, 278n7, 280n50
anti-trafficking, 5, 13, 42, 51–54, 60–64, 99–100, 262–63n18, 280n50; in the League of Nations, 56–59, 62–66, 73–80; in the United Nations, 80–82; 1933 International Convention for the Suppression of the Traffic in Women of the Full Age, 93
Appadurai, Arjun, 235, 247
Arase, David, 196–97, 199–200
archive: citational archive of traffic in women, 55; digital archive of comfort women problematic, 225; ethnographic archive, 36; of U.S. feminist scholarship, 35; photographic archive, 226; Rockefeller Archive Center, 67; United States military archive of the comfort system, 157–78, 188; United States National Archives, 156–57, 226

Asahi Shimbun, 255–56
Asian American: Asian American feminism, 43; Asian American studies, 42–43; induction as U.S. military linguists in World War II, 156–57; memories of the Asia-Pacific war, 157–61
Asian Development Bank (ADB), 202, 205
Asian Solidarity Conference on Japanese Military Sexual Slavery, 109, 230, 281n60; name change, 109, 114
Asian Tribunal on Japanese Military Sexual Slavery, 13, 109
Asian women: in international feminist organizing, 38; in global governance, 2, 4, 6, 9, 10, 14, 15, 56, 79; as human, 44; labor exploitation, 214–18
Asian Women's Association, 29–30, 39, 98
Asian Women's Fund, 191–94, 205, 218, 219, 224–25, 234–38, 246–47, 250–51
Asian Women's Human Rights Council (AWHRC), 11, 54, 109, 227, 282–83n3
Asian Women's Liberation, 34, 39, 214, 267nn25–26
Awad, Mohamed, 86; *Report on Slavery*, 86–89, 90–91, 278n11

Barlay, Stephen, 91–92, 97
Barlow, Tani, 217–18, 264–65n37, 299n91
Barry, Kathleen, 6–7, 33–34, 40, 93–95, 97–98, 122, 268n39, 272n6
Beijing Fourth World Conference on Women (1995), 13, 109, 190, 191, 218, 265n37
Boeckel, Florence Brewer, 273n16

Born, Brooksley, 298n71
Borromeo, Myrna Elizabeth P., 301n18
Bradley, Christine, 133–34
Breckenridge, Carol, 235, 247
British imperialism, regulation of prostitution in colonies, 59
Brown, Louise, 14
Brown Memorandum, 199
Brownmiller, Susan, 28, 32–33, 36, 267–68n35
Brussels International Tribunal on Crimes against Women (1976), 31, 123, 262n11, 283n5
Bunch, Charlotte, 6–7, 8, 39, 120, 122, 128, 132, 133
Bureau of Social Hygiene (BSH), 66–72
Burma/Myanmar: 23, 41, 156–62, 165, 177, 179, 185–86, 195, 243; Myitkyina, 158; 1954 reparations agreement with Japan, 197
Burton, Antoinette, 61
Butler, Josephine, 60–61

Cairo International Conference on Population and Development (1994), 4, 9, 126
Cambodian Women's Development Association, 55
Carrillo, Roxanne, 121, 132–33, 134, 137–41, 148–49
Castley, Shirley, 6–7, 122
Center for Women's Global Leadership (CWGL), 8–9, 120, 121, 126–28, 132–33, 134
Chai, Alice Yun, 30, 49, 267n27, 267nn29–30
Chan-Tiberghien, Jennifer, 294n3
Chan, Won-loy, 159–62, 165, 170, 172, 177–78, 180–83, 188, 289–90n16, 293n54
Chang, Ha-Joon, 212
Chavez, Linda, 12, 114
Chen, Kuan-Hsing, 19–21, 265n1
Chew, Jennifer F., 47
Chew, Lin Lap, 38
China, 19, 28–29, 32, 33, 53, 58–59, 75–77, 91, 118, 144, 145–46, 156, 157, 186, 188, 197, 198, 201, 206, 214, 226, 231, 244, 252, 256
Choi, Chungmoo, 21–22, 25, 228
Chongshindae, 3, 47, 109–10
Chou, Chih-Chieh, 14
Cho Uhn, 216
Chuh, Kandice, 50
Chung, Chin Sung, 11, 115–16

Coalition against Trafficking in Women (CATW), 54, 112, 263n21
Coalition against Trafficking in Women-Asia Pacific (CATW-AP)
Cold War, 2, 4, 8, 20, 21, 24, 31, 121, 193, 197, 213
comfort women: as international victims, 22; activism around, 31; problem of naming and translation, 46–48, 109–13; as a problem of knowledge, 21–23, 50; contending websites, 229–33, 302nn23–24; documentaries about, 228; 2015 agreement between South Korea and Japan, 221–23, 233, 252, 254
compensation: 1, 14, 111–16, 128–29, 190–93, 198, 202, 209, 222, 227, 234, 250–51, 255, 263n21, 270n64, 286n63; AWF, 250–51; for slavery and forced labor, 113; for sexual slavery, 114–15; International Public Hearing on Postwar Compensation by Japan, 113; unequal calculation of, 219
Connors, Jane Frances, 123, 283–84n10
Convention for the Suppression of the Traffic in Persons and of the Exploitation of the Prostitution of Others (1949 Trafficking Convention), 80–81, 84
Convention on the Elimination of All Forms of Discrimination against Women (CEDAW), 8, 83, 95, 120, 121, 123–25, 127, 128
Convention to Suppress the Slave Trade and Slavery (1926 Slavery Convention), 83
Coomaraswamy, Radhika, 9, 12–14, 114–15, 117–18, 256, 264n26
Copenhagen Second World Conference on Women (1980), 6, 97, 122; World Plan of Action, 95
crimes against humanity, 13, 115, 169
crimes against women, illegibility of, 13–14
Crowdy, Dame Rachel, 71, 79, 275n56
Cumings, Bruce, 212, 213
cyberspace, 229; cyber-activism, 229–31; cyber-memorial, 229, 232

debt, 25; debt bondage, 25, 34, 84, 102, 106, 118; debt crisis, 209; foreign debt, 25, 206–7, 210; sovereign debt, 213; U.S. debt, 212
Declaration on the Elimination of Violence against Women (DEVAW), 9, 83, 117, 120, 125–26, 128, 150

decolonization: by South Korea, 21, 25; feminist decolonial critique, 22–23; Korean women's protests, 26, 87
De Dios, Aurora Javate, 40, 52–54
deimperialization: Japanese deimperialization, 21, 49, 265n1; Japanese feminist deimperialization, 29, 49; South Korean deimperialization, 49
Demleitner, Nora, 62, 99
development, 9, 31, 120, 128; as structural violence, 215; Cairo Conference, 4, 9, 126; economic development of South Korea, 25; uneven capitalist development in Asia, 41, 59–60, 98, 194–205, 215; violence against women as barrier, 121, 138–39; women in development, 122, 133–34, 138–39, 141, 149. *See also* human development and World Bank
Digital Museum for The Comfort Women Issue and the Asian Women's Fund, 224–25, 233–52, 306n55
Dolgopol, Ustinia, 167, 290n24
Drea, Edward, 171–72
Dulles, John Foster, 197–98, 295n14

Elson, Diane, 208, 210–11
Engen, Hans, 84, 88
Enloe, Cynthia, 34–35, 268nn40–41
epistemology, 24, 150; Asia as method, 19–21; Asian women as method, 21–24, 46–50; authority of disciplinary knowledge, 45; claims to objectivity, 45; comparing knowledges, 20; epistemological challenge of comfort women, 21–22, 24, 50; epistemological enclosure of Asian women, 50; epistemological impasse in Asian studies, 19–20, 35; epistemological power of U.S., 20, 35; epistemological self-distinction, 45; hegemony of Western theory, 20, 36; nonknowing, 15, 21, 24, 59. *See also* Choi, Chungmoo; Chuh, Kandice; Lowe, Lisa; Truong, Thanh-Dam; Yang, Hyunah; Yoneyama, Lisa
Ewha University: October 1972 students statement, 25, 28; student protests against Japanese sex tourism, 25
expertise, 20, 50, 123, 212; area studies, 20; as citational archive, 55; Asian women as experts, 38–40, 55; disciplinary expertise, 45–46; expert investigations in the League of Nations, 76; feminist experts in the United Nations, 39–41, 150–51; as power/knowledge regimes, 35; U.S. social reformers, 65

Fernand-Laurent, Jean, 6, 95; 1983 *Report of the Special Rapporteur on the Suppression of the Traffic in Persons and the Exploitation of the Prostitution of Others*, 95–97, 99
financialization, 195, 203, 204–5; and financial crisis, 206, 208, 218; globalization of finance capitalism, 208, 214; U.S. advocacy of, 210
forced labor, 100, 113; Forced Labour Convention of 1930, 115–16
Fosdick, Raymond, 69–74
Fukuda-Parr, Sakiko, 136

GABRIELA, 11, 114, 227, 302
genocide, 4, 23, 27, 113
Germain, Adrienne, 141, 147–49
Giaccardi, Elisa, 236
Gil Won-ok, 232
Global Alliance against Traffic in Women (GAATW), 54, 55
global burden of disease (GBD), 121, 143–47, 151, 286n63, 287n67, 296n41
Global Campaign for Women's Human Rights, 9, 127–32, 191
global governance, 2, 4, 9, 10, 14, 16–17, 22, 56, 62–63, 79, 80, 86, 98, 100, 109–10, 115, 119–22, 126–31, 139–51, 194–97, 205, 217, 218, 254, 258, 264n37, 265n39, 276n66
Goldman, Emma, 37–38
Goodman, Grant, 165–66
governance feminism, 128
Greenspan, Alan, 207, 212, 217, 298n71
Grew, Joseph C., 196–97
Guam, 41

Haq, Mahbub ul, 134, 136
Hane, Michiko, 34
Harrington, Joseph Daniel, 158, 161, 289n8
Hein, Laura, 15
Heise, Lori, 121, 139–42, 146–50, 286n49, 288n71
Henson, Maria Rosa Luna, 113, 227, 250–52, 281n61
Hershatter, Gail, 64
Hicks, George, 167–68

Hirabayashi, Grant, 158, 159, 161, 165, 170, 172, 177–78, 182–83, 289n8, 291n32, 293n54
human development: 134–38; human development index (HDI), 134–35; *Human Development Report*, 134–38
humanity: crimes against humanity, 22; exclusion of Asian women from, 15, 22; exclusion of Koreans and Japanese, 23; inclusion of women as, 128
human rights, 4, 6–12, 14, 15–16, 40, 52, 85, 90, 112, 113, 128; gross violations of, 113; human rights approach to prostitution, 96; as U.S.-centric, 42; of women, 12, 14, 94–95, 119; post–Cold War shifts, 110; United Nations actions, 87–88; 117; U.S. violations of, 131; Universal Declaration of Human Rights, 83–84
Human Rights Watch (HRW), 42, 55, 262–63n18
Humphrey, John P., 85
Hwang Geum-joo, 227, 232

Ienaga Saburo, 154–55, 288nn4–5
imperialism: multiple imperialisms, 19–20; Japanese economic imperialism, 28; Japanese sexual imperialism, 28; League of Nations Permanent Mandates System, 100
Indonesia, 20, 22, 23, 41, 80, 141, 192–93, 194, 200–203, 206–7, 209, 211, 214, 215, 250, 305n48
inter-Asian, 20
inter-Asian feminism, 25–31; dissensus within, 49, 271n79; movement against sex tourism, 2–3, 38–39, 111, 266n16, 266n18, 267nn28–29; transpacific erasure of, 34–35, 41
International Agreement for the Suppression of the White Slave Traffic (1904), 62
International Commission of Jurists (ICJ), 107, 115, 167
International Convention for the Suppression of the Traffic in Women and Children (1921), 62, 242–43
International Convention for the Suppression of the Traffic in Women of Full Age (1933), 79, 80
International Convention for the Suppression of White Slave Traffic (1910), 62
International Feminist Network against Sexual Slavery, 39

international financial institutions (IFIs), 132, 208; and SAPs (structural adjustment programs), 215
International Labour Organization (ILO), 96, 115–16, 199, 207, 208
International Monetary Fund (IMF), 135, 195, 207–13, 217, 218
International Organization for Migration (IOM), 55
International Tribunal on Crimes against Women (1976), 283n5
Interpol, 97
inter-state agreements: 2015 South Korea-Japan agreement ("comfort women" deal), 233
intra-Asian: epistemological exchange, 20; exploitation, ???#; racism, 41, 49; reckoning, 20; violence, 21–22

Japan, 13–15, 48, 53, 55, 59, 63–64, 75–76, 115, 153–54, 165, 211, 244, 254–56; as colonial power, 101, 103; economic cooperation and competition with U.S., 203–4, 206–7, 218; economic dominance in Asia, 194, 199–202, 214; economic miracle, 28, 195, feminist activism, 25–31, 34–35, 266n16, 266n18, 267nn28–29; postwar economic recovery, 194, 197; role in global governance, 63–64, 202–4, 256; support by U.S., 196–98
Japanese Americans: internment in concentration camps, 169; Nisei linguists in World War II, 156, 157–59, 178–80; Japanese American Veterans Association (JAVA), 291–92n40; support of comfort women redress movement, 308n83
Japanese imperialism, 2, 19, 21, 276n66; categorization of Koreans as Japanese nationals, 276n66; categorization of inhabitants of Formosa as Japanese nationals, 276n66; colonization of Korea, 3, 266n18; economic dominance in Asia, 199–202, 214; foreign aid, 199–202, 295n25; military conscription of Korean and Taiwanese soldiers, 113; Western perception of, 23. *See also* deimperialization
Japanese military "comfort," system: 1, 4–5, 16, 23, 240–44; archival records of, 225–26, 240–44, 246–47, 256–57; as brothels, 91, 165–66, 171, 177, 240, 256, 278n17, 288n5, 290n19, 300n95,

304-5n43; as forced labor, 115; as forced prostitution, 12, 116, 167, 168; as genocide, 4, 23, 27, 113-14; as institutionalized camp brothels, 32; as Japanese Army brothel, 165; as licensed prostitution, 172; as military brothels, 12, 294n9, 302n24; as military sexual slavery, 109, 256; as rape centers, 248; as sexual slavery, 11-12, 45; as sexual slavery and a slavery-like practice, 13; as systematic rape, 12; as traffic in women, 5; as violation of the human rights of women in situations of armed conflict, 12; as violence against women, 12-13, 118; as war brothels, 290n22, 308n82; as war crime, 11, 13; as wartime military brothels, 254; documentaries about, 228; earlier references to, 26-29, 32, 153-55, 188, 278n17, 300n7; medical examinations of women, 243; photographs of, 125-26, 157-64, 170, 172, 177-78, 186-88, 244, 289nn15-16, 303n35; super-visibility of, 41-44; television coverage of, 226-27; survivors' artworks, 228-29; transpacific erasure of, 33, 39-41, 171-72; U.S. complicity in neglecting, 41-42; U.S. military documentation of, 161-62, 169, 181, 225-26, 289n8; war crimes tribunals, 22; websites about, 229-52
Japanese sex tourism, 2-3, 28-29; Korean women's critique of, 25; Japanese feminist analysis and protest, 26-28
Joachim, Jutta, 4, 121, 123, 132
Johnson, Bascom, 68, 70, 74, 275n49
Johnson, Chalmers, 196, 206, 207, 208, 210, 213

Keck, Margaret E., 9, 122-23, 140
Kenny, Katherine E., 144
Kim Bok-dong (Bok Dong), 11-12
Kim, Elaine, 38-39, 214, 267n28
Kim Hak-sun, 1, 3, 11, 226
Kim Hye-won, 2, 30
Kim Il-myon, 46, 110, 154
Kim Kun-ja, 222
Kim Puja (Pu Ja), 31, 49, 261n2, 267n31
Kim Sin-sil, 2, 30
Kim Tokchin, 226
Kim Yong-Sil, 227
Kimura, Maki, 270n59
Kinsie, Paul, 73

Kishi Nobusuke, 196-97, 295n14
Kitamura, Eibun, 176, 185-86
Kitamura, Tomiko, 176
Kneeland, George J., 72-73
Knepper, Paul, 58, 76
Kondo Uri, 38
Kono Statement (1993), 44, 234, 241, 246, 253, 256
Korea, Democratic Republic of (North Korea), 13, 19, 112, 205, 227
Korea, Republic of (South Korea), 2, 108, 126, 138, 140, 154, 175, 185, 228, 245, 250, 252; anti-Japanese movements, 185; as part of U.S. Cold War empire, 2, 20, 24; as sub-imperialist, 19-20; colonization by Japan, 1, 2, 19, 25-28, 47, 63, 242; decolonization, 2, 21; economic growth, 19-20, 194, 198, 199, 203, 214; feminist activism, 2-3, 11-12, 15, 25-26, 30-31, 38; financial liberalization, 210, 212-13; foreign debt, 206, 210; government actions on the Japanese military comfort system problem, 167, 192, 193, 218-19, 220-22; IMF interventions in, 212, 216; migrant workers in, 216-17; military rape of Vietnamese women, 192; participation in the war in Vietnam, 199; U.S. economic aid, 198; U.S. military occupation of, 110; women's labor, 110, 214, 216. See also *zainichi* (Koreans in Japan)
Korean Americans: investment in comfort women, 288-89n7; in Glendale, California, 308n83
Korean Church Women United (KCWU), 2, 30
Korean Council for Women Drafted for Military Sexual Slavery by Japan (*Hanguk Chongshindae Munje Taechaek Hyobuihoe*), 3, 50, 109, 112, 226, 233, 263n21, 264n26, 280-81n58; website, 302n24, 303n26
Korean military: participation in the U.S. war in Vietnam, 199; rape of Vietnamese women, 49
Korean War, 21, 28, 32-33, 194, 197, 199

labor exploitation, 38, 42; colonial and neocolonial forms, 59, 111; female labor exploitation, 16, 21; prostitution, 85; sexual exploitation, 25, 215
Laos, 24, 88-89, 93-94

Index 335

League of Nations: actions on traffic in women, 5, 56–60, 62–66, 69–81, 276n66; actions on slavery and forced labor, 83; Permanent Mandates System, 100; Temporary Slavery Commission (TSC), 102–3
Lee Hyo-chae, 111
Lee, June J. H., 217
Leppanen, Katarina, 79–80
Levine, Philippa, 59–60, 273n18
LILA-Pilipina, 250
Limoncelli, Stephanie A., 80
Lopez, Alan, 144–45
Lowe, Lisa, 24

Mainichi Shimbun, 226
Manderson, Lenore, 52, 119
Matsui Yayori, 26–31, 38, 40, 49, 266nn15–16, 266nn18–19, 267nn20–24, 268n39, 271n79
McDougall, Gay J., 48, 114, 248
memorials: of comfort women, 222–23, 307n81
Metzger, Barbara, 58
Mexico City United Nations Decade for Women Conference (1975), 31, 97
Miers, Suzanne, 85, 100, 102, 277–78n4
Military Intelligence Service Language School (MISLS), 156, 158, 291–92n40
Miller, Alice M., 42, 285n29
Mohanty, Chandra, 22
Moon, Katharine H. S., 14, 15
Morris-Suzuki, Tessa, 229–30
Murayama Tomiichi, 189–90, 194, 205, 218, 224, 236
Murray, Christopher, 144–47, 287nn67–68, 288n71, 296n41
museums: e-Museum of the Victims of Japanese Military Sexual Slavery, 233, 303n35; functions of, 234–25, 304n38; virtual museums, 235–36; War and Women's Human Rights Museum, 231–33, 303n31; Women's Active Museum on War and Peace (WAM), 235, 303n31

Nairobi Third World Conference on Women (1985), 8; Nairobi Forward-Looking Strategies, 8, 97; NGO Forum, 30
neoliberalization: 217, U.S.-led financial liberalization, 210; role of IMF, 211–12
Nester, William R., 198

O'Brien, Suzanne, 48
O'Callaghan, Sean, 91–92, 154, 278n17
official development assistance (ODA), 197, 200–202, 215
Oh, Bonnie B. C., 43
Orientalism: Asianization of female oppression, 41–42; Asianization of financial crisis, 208; Asianization of prostitution, 53; Asianization of traffic in women, 52; crony capitalism, 209; Lawrence Summers and "yellow fever," 297n56

Papua New Guinea, 23, 41, 133–34
Paranjape, Snehal, 167
Park Chung-hee, 25, 27
Parker, Karen, 47
Park Geun-hye, 222
Park Young-sim, 233, 303n35
Perpiñan, Sister Mary Soledad, 38, 40, 123
Philippines, Republic of the, 3, 20, 24, 34, 38, 40, 41, 52–53, 109, 160, 194, 202, 206–7, 214, 216, 219, 223, 227, 229, 250, 252, 256, 283n5, 305n48; Asian Women's Fund, 192–93
Pirie, Iain, 199
Pitanguy, Jaqueline, 141, 147–49
Pliley, Jessica R., 64
post–Cold War, 8, 110, 125, 134
postcolonial, 21, 52, 235, 267n9; postcolonial feminism, 36; postcolonial studies, 43
prisoners of war (POWs): Allied interrogations of, 156, 158, 164–65, 167–69, 171–72, 304–5n43; Asian American as interrogators and interpreters, 156–57; Japanese Americans as interrogators, 158; Korean women as U.S. and Allied POWs, 157, 161–64, 188
prostitution, 5, 6, 37, 66, 215, 216–17, 242–43; age of consent for women, 57; and trafficking, 53, 60–64; as female sexual slavery, 6–7, 93–95; as forced prostitution, 6–7, 85, 118, 139; as social problem in the U.S., 67; as slavery/enslavement, 7, 83–91, 94–99; as violence against women, 7, 123; as white slavery, 66–67, Asianization of, 53–54; exploited labor as economic prostitution, 37; feminist dissensus on, 123, 129; in the British Empire, 59–61; Japanese military comfort system as, 34; Japanese military comfort system as forced prostitution, 12–13, 28, 32; Japanese

336 Index

sex tourism, 33–34, 38; state regulation of, 60–62, 65, 70, 76; UN actions on, 6, 40, 80–82, 83–91, 94–99, 104, 106–9, 111–15; U.S. military-related, 3, 15, 24, 38, 68, 213–14; unknowability of, 64; vigilance against, 60–62

racism: anti-Asian racism, 41, 51–52, 209; anxiety over interracial sexual relations, 77–79; intra-Asian racism, 23; racialization of Koreans, 78, 276n66; racist double standards, 62; venereal disease as racial poison, 60
Reilly, Niamh, 133
reparations, 14, 193, 200; war reparations, 194, 197, 199–200, 295n25
Rimmer, Peter, 229–30
Rockefeller, John D., Jr., 66–70, 73–74, 275n46
Rockefeller Foundation, 287n67
Rotterdam Global Feminist Workshop to Organize Against Traffic in Women (1983), 6–7, 31, 38
Rubin, Gayle, 28, 268n43, 268–69nn43–45
Ruff-O'Herne, Jan, 110, 227

Sajor, Indai Lourdes, 4
Sancho-Liao, Nelia, 11, 227, 250
San Francisco Peace Treaty (Treaty of Peace with Japan), 27–28, 190, 197, 198, 222
Schaller, Michael, 196–97
Schrover, Marlou, 277n82
Scully, Eileen, 60, 62
Sen, Amartya, 135–36
Senda, Kako, 46, 154, 226
sex slavery in Japan Supreme Court ruling, 270n64
sex slaves: 111, inter-Asian feminism, 111; versus prostitute, 92
sex tourism, 25–28, 30, 33–34, 38
sexual slavery: 12, 13, 31, 42, 45, 87, 97–98, 268n39; sexual slaves, 25; female sexual slavery, 6–7, 8, 33–34, 39; Japanese military sexual slavery, 108–9; United Nations recognition of, 97–98, 114. *See also* Barry, Kathleen
Shin, Heisoo, 11, 13, 108–9, 112, 126, 256, 264n26, 280–81n58
Sikkink, Kathryn, 9, 122–23, 140
Skrobanek, Siriporn, 126, 184n17
slavery: colonialism and apartheid as slavery, 90; Convention to Suppress the Slave Trade and Slavery (1926 Slavery Convention), 87, 101, 103; Japanese military sexual slavery, 108–9; Supplementary Convention on the Abolition of Slavery, the Slave Trade, and Institutions and Practices Similar to Slavery (1956 Supplementary Convention), 84–85, 87; United Nations *Ad Hoc* Committee on Slavery, 83–84; United Nations Working Group on Slavery, 87, 104–8; white slavery, 91, 99–100; women, as victims of, 90–91; women's organizations against, 278n7; yellow slave trade, 91–92. *See also* compensation; forced labor; labor exploitation; sexual slavery and United Nations
Snow, William F., 68–71, 72, 74, 76, 275–76n56; *American Eugenics Society*, 68
Soh, Chunghee Sarah (C. Sarah), 45–47, 109–11, 188, 226, 229, 267n29, 293n61
Sonyeosang (Peace Monument aka "Comfort Women" Statue), 252–54, 258; in Glendale, California, 308n83
South East Asia Translation and Interrogation Center (SEATIC), 165, 171, 179, 240, 292n41
Stetz, Margaret, 43, 110, 308n82
Stiglitz, Joseph, 211
Strathern, Marilyn, 246–47
Sullivan, Donna J., 12
Summers, Lawrence, 287n67, 297n56, 298n71
Supplementary Convention on the Abolition of Slavery, the Slave Trade, and Institutions and Practices Similar to Slavery (1956), 84, 87, 104, 277n4

Taipei Women's Rescue Foundation, 11
Taiwan: 41, 242, 250; as sub-imperialist, 20; an Asian financial crisis, 209, 212; colonization by Japan, 19, 41, 66; Asian Women's Fund, 219, 250–52; comfort women memorials, 223, 300n6; economic growth, 2, 19–20, 192, 202, 203; feminist activism, 3, 11, 283n15; feminist organizing around Japanese military comfort system, 11, 109, 242–44, 256; government fund for Taiwanese victims, 192; Japanese sex tourism, 214; Taiwanese soldiers for the Japanese Imperial Army, 113
Takahashi Kikue, 266n18
Takazato Suzuyo, 38, 40
Takeuchi Yoshimi, 265n1

Index 337

Tanaka, Yuki, 168–70, 289n15
Task Force on Filipina Victims of Military Sexual Slavery by Japan, 114; formerly Task Force on Filipino "Comfort Women" (TFFCW), 11, 227
Terry, Jennifer, 290n17
Third World Movement against the Exploitation of Women (TWMAE), 38, 39, 98
Thoma, Pamela, 43
Totsuka Etsuro, 111–12, 115
traffic in women, 5, 35, 55; as field of expertise, 55; as metaphor for sex/gender binary, 35–36, as ruse, 35–37; as empirical phenomenon, 38; Asianization of, 5, 10, 38, 91. *See also* Golden, Emma; Rubin, Gayle
Treaty on Basic Relations between Japan and the Republic of Korea (1965 Treaty), 27–28, 112, 190, 198–99
Truong, Thanh-Dam, 214–15, 217

United Nations: 2, 3, 4, 13, 128; actions on traffic in women, 5–6, 81–82, 95–97, 99; *Ad Hoc* Committee on Slavery, 83–84; Children's Fund (UNICEF), 95, 283n3; Commission on Human Rights, 6, 11, 81, 85, 87, 89, 96, 99, 104, 108, 111, 128, 256; Commission on the Status of Women (CSW), 6, 81, 87, 90, 95, 97, 107, 125, 128; Committee on the Elimination of Discrimination against Women, 95, 123–24; Decade for Women (1975–85), 5, 7; Development Fund for Women (UNIFEM), 120, 128, 132–34, Development Programme (UNDP), 133, 134; Division for the Advancement of Women, 123; Economic and Social Commission for Asia and the Pacific (ESCAP), 217, 264–65n37; Economic and Social Council (ECOSOC), 83–84, 86, 96; Educational, Scientific and Cultural Organization (UNESCO), 40, 96, 256–57; Nongovernmental Liaison Service, 39; Security Council, 4; Sub-commission on Prevention of Discrimination and Protection of Minorities, 11, 85, 87, 89, 108–9; Working Group on Slavery, 87, 95–96, 98, 104–6; Working Group on Contemporary Forms of Slavery, 11, 106–8; 111–12, 116, 160
U.S. feminist theory, 30; as imperialist cosmology and epistemology, 36; as will to global authority, 35–36; construction of "Third World women," 23; Third World and postcolonial feminist interventions, 36; self-critical reckonings, 36; traffic in women as metaphor, 35–37
U.S. imperialism: Cold War military empire, 19, 28; epistemological hegemony, 20; U.S. feminist hegemony, 38–41
U.S. military intelligence, 156–57, 164–78; as part of Allied intelligence in World War II, 165, 171, 173, 176; Military Intelligence Service Language School (MISLS), 156, 169; of Japanese prisoners of war (POWs) 164–78, 181, 182, 240, 292n41, 304–5n43; of Korean comfort women, 161–62, 169, 181, 289n8; use of Nisei linguists in the Asia-Pacific War, 178–80. *See also* U.S. Office of War Information (OWI)
U.S. military prostitution, 2; as U.S. military R&R, 268n39
U.S. National Archives, 156–57, 161, 188, 226, 246, 252, 291–92n40
U.S. Office of War Information (OWI); 165, 172, 240; *Japanese Prisoner of War Interrogation Report No.48*, 184–85; *Japanese Prisoner of War Interrogation Report No. 49*, 164, 168, 173–78, 181, 182–85, 187, 240, 243, 289n8; Psychological Warfare Branch (OWI-PWB) 164, 165, 169–70, 172–73, 177, 180, 183–84, 292n41; template of POW reports, 172–73. *See also* Yoneda, Karl; Yorichi, Alex
U.S. philanthropic power, 66–74, 76, 128; and global governance, 66; and social sciences, 67–68, 73; as private surveillance and control, 61–68, 73. *See also* Bureau of Social Hygiene and John D. Rockefeller, Jr.
U.S. Signal Corps: photographs of Korean comfort women, 157–64, 170, 172, 177–78, 186–88, 244, 303n35; 164th Signal Photo Company, 289n14
U.S. universities, 42–43; and the World Bank, 204, 296n41

Van Boven, Theo, 111; Special Rapporteur on the Rights to Restitution, Compensation and Rehabilitation for Victims of Gross Violations of Human Rights and Fundamental Freedoms, 111, 113–14

Veneroso, Frank, 212
Video Juku, 228
Vienna World Conference on Human Rights (1993), 4, 9, 11, 131, 218; Declaration and Program of Action, 9; Global Tribunal on Violations of Women's Human Rights, 11, 131–32
Vietnam, Democratic Republic of, 20, 28, 33–34, 55, 94, 214, 283
Vietnam War, 24, 28, 32, 33, 267n35; South Korean industrial growth, 199; South Korean soldiers' rape of Vietnamese women, 49, 268n35; U.S. military expenditures and logistics, 194, 199, 208
visibility, 14; super-visibility of comfort women issue, 15–16, 41–44
violence against women (VAW): 7–10, 117–50; analogy to slavery, 130–31; as development problem, 126, 132–39; as public health problem, 126, 139–50; Declaration on Elimination of Violence against Women (DEVAW), 9, 117; expertise on, 125; state responsibility, 128–29; states as perpetrators of, 125–26, 128; Special Rapporteur on Violence against Women, 9, 117–18. *See also* Coomaraswamy, Radhika

Wada Haruki, 243
Wade, Robert, 204, 207–8, 212, 296n39
Wall Street-Treasury-IMF Complex, 218
war crimes tribunals, 27
Washington Consensus, 203–5, 208, 287n67. *See also* neoliberalization
Watanabe, Kazuko, 48
Welch, Claude E., Jr., 100
Western humanism, 22
Whitaker, Benjamin, 97, 105, 280n50
white slavery, 5, 51, 57, 58, 80, 91, 99–100; white slave traffic, 37, 56–57, 61, 62, 66, 67

Winkler, Allan, 291n39
Women's International War Crimes Tribunal on Japan's Military Sexual Slavery (2000), 265n37
Women's International League of Peace and Freedom (WILPF), 85
Women's League of the South Korean Christian Church, 25
women's rights as human rights, 8, 14, 42, 52, 110, 117, 132; Global Campaign for Women's Human Rights, 9; Global Tribunal on Violations of Women's Human Rights, 9, 11
Woo, Jung-en, 198, 199, 202
World Bank: 2, 41, 134–36; and Lawrence Summers, 287n67; and U.S. universities, 296n41; and violence against women, 9, 120–21, 126, 141–50; *World Development Report 1989*, 134, 296n39; *World Development Report 1993: Investing in Health*, 142–47, 287n67

Yang, Daqing, 291n34
Yang, Hyunah, 22–23, 266nn9–10
Yasumoto, Dennis T., 295n25
Yoneda, Karl, 161, 163, 170–72, 177, 180, 181, 183, 292n42
Yoneyama, Lisa, 24, 31, 193, 271n79
Yorichi, Alex, 165, 166, 170, 172–85, 292n42, 292n45
Yoshimi Yoshiaki, 48, 153, 165, 226, 290nn23–24, 292n45
Yu, Joyce, 133
Yun, Chung-ok, 2, 30–31, 47, 154, 159, 231, 245, 262n2, 271n79

zainichi (Koreans in Japan), 3, 30, 31, 46, 49, 154, 231–32, 245
Zoglin, Kathryn, 106, 108